THE TEACHING OF PAUL IN TERMS
OF THE PRESENT DAY

THE TEACHING OF PAUL

IN TERMS OF

THE PRESENT DAY

THE DEEMS LECTURES
IN NEW YORK UNIVERSITY

BY

SIR W. M. RAMSAY

SECOND EDITION

BAKER BOOK HOUSE
Grand Rapids, Michigan

Reprinted 1979 by
Baker Book House Company
from the 1913 edition published by
Hodder and Stoughton, London

Originally given as
The Deems Lectures
New York University

ISBN: 0-8010-7693-5

This volume is part of the ten-volume
William M. Ramsay Library
ISBN: 0-8010-7685-4

PHOTOLITHOPRINTED BY CUSHING - MALLOY, INC.
ANN ARBOR, MICHIGAN, UNITED STATES OF AMERICA
1 9 7 9

PREFACE

No apology is offered for adding to the vast sum of books about Paul. Much of what is in modern times written and preached regarding Paul is expressed in terms of an old system of education and thought. The expression is usually quite right in its own way ; but it requires an effort for the modern-trained mind to think after that fashion, and many have not made, and are not likely to make, the effort.

Growing up amid the life of the modern Universities in familiar relations with scientific and literary men, most of whom had no opinions about Paul or his philosophy, the present writer gradually formed his own conception of the teaching of Paul in terms of the education that surrounded him. These ideas have forced themselves into words, for which often the writer hardly feels himself responsible : they seemed rather to be a free translation from the Greek of the Epistles than the outcome of his own thoughts. These thoughts formed the subject of the Deems Lectures in New York University, November, 1910 ; but illness, which led to resignation from active University duty, protracted the labour of preparing them for publication.

In the interval Professor Deissmann's book, *St. Paul: a Study in Social and Religious History*, has appeared. He takes a sharply opposed view. To him

v

Paul was an uneducated man, possessing no literary excellence and no learning, a mere writer of letters in the vulgar speech, having a certain quickness in picking up scraps of philosophy and poetry that circulated among the people, unknown to and unmarked by the world, sometimes presenting in his letters difficulties which Deissmann compares to the difficulties felt by us in reading the illiterate epistles of uneducated Egyptian peasants. To the distinguished Berlin Professor, Paul was a man unknown to and unmarked by the world, profoundly conscious of and humbly confessing his lack of skill in words and in thought, a great religious genius by nature, but a mere obscure Jew, except for that religious enthusiasm. The historian Luke regarded Paul as the centre of interest wherever he went, dominating all by his personality, heralded before he came, alike in Thessalonica and in Rome, the man that has "turned the world upside down," the storm-centre of society, from whom originates revolution wherever he goes, educated in his thoughts and polished in his tone of courtesy, yet fiery and vehement in his temper, versatile and adaptable so that he moves at his ease in every class of society, the Socratic dialectician in the Athenian market-place, the philosophic rhetorician in the Court of Areopagus, the lecturer in the Ephesian School of Tyrannus, conversing in a tone of courteous respect with Kings and great Roman officials, "standing" before an Emperor, giving wise advice at a hasty council on a ship in the season of danger, cheering a dejected crew to make one more effort for life, reminding

Roman soldiers of their duty and Roman colonial magistrates of their error in trampling on Roman law, making a great trade corporation anxious about the future of its business and a small firm of slave-owners despondent about its income, the friend of the leading men in the province of Asia, to whom a wealthy Roman procurator with a queen as his mistress looked expecting to receive bribes : where Paul is all eyes and many hearts are attracted, while the vulgar and the mob and the Jews, the magians and the soothsayers, hate and fear him. I follow Luke, and I find in Paul's letters the work of a great master of language and of thought, who trampled on all artificiality and spoke freely in the voice of nature during an age when conventions and formality reigned supreme. The reader must judge for himself.

The first part of this book, entitled *Preparatory Questions*, discusses topics which were intentionally taken in hand before Part II. was sent to the printer. The third part, labelled *Subsidiary Questions*, takes up subjects which arose during the printing of Part II., and seemed to call for a more detailed treatment than suited the scale of that part. There are, however, several Sections in Part III. which might equally well be placed in Part I. One of the Sections (LII.) treats an important point in the order of Paul's letters, Section LI. an equally important legal point bearing on the case of Paul : the results of both are assumed in Part II.

I have intentionally avoided using the honorific prefix "St.," which places Paul on a conventional pedestal, and obscures the man, the missionary, and the teacher. It has in English lost entirely its original force in Greek usage. In Greek we use ὁ ἅγιος with the names of angels and archangels and the Spirit of God, and so in Latin *Sanctus;* but in English the convention would not allow St. Raphael, St. Michael, or St. Spirit.

I have to thank the Editors of the *Contemporary Review* and the *Expositor* for permission to work up as chapters of this book articles that have appeared in the pages of those magazines. I regret that in several cases references to other books are either stated vaguely without exact page, or omitted entirely. Much of this volume was written far from books (except two or three specially selected for travel). I had hoped to introduce specific references in the proof-sheets, but, as it turned out, the proofs had to be revised in equally difficult situations, and some chapters are printed without revision by the writer. The exigencies of a wandering life enforced this; but there is not a paragraph that has not been pondered over for years, and composed word by word in hard labour, before it was put on paper.

Also I thank the Aberdeen University Press and its press-reader for the care with which they have produced the book amid the difficulties of the situation.

W. M. RAMSAY

GROVE CITY, PENNSYLVANIA
August, 1913

PREFACE TO SECOND EDITION

ON the relation of Paul to Jesus, as the most creative, yet the truest, interpreter of the spirit of His teaching, what is stated on p. 18 should be enough : also see Index I. In reading over the sheets for this new edition, I have been struck with the fact that the view of Pauline Teaching given here is the natural development of the statement regarding the nature of Christ set forth in my book on the " Education of Christ ".

There has been the opportunity in this edition of correcting freely, as the type was standing. Owing to circumstances a great part of the first edition was printed without my seeing a proof. In the first sixty-four pages the corrected proof reached the printers : in 65-328 some corrections are stated in a list of Errata and Addenda : in 329-450 even these failed to arrive. The truly Christian spirit of the American people is shown by the patience with which they submit to the affliction of their postal service in the smaller towns, and the cheerfulness with which they even acclaim it as reasonably good. Often packets were not delivered : I went to ask, and was denied them : two days later they were delivered, as having been found on a different shelf, being too large for the ordinary receptacle. In one case a large packet of proofs which I confidently expected failed to arrive before I left a town. Some days later in another town I received notice that the packet was waiting me, and would be forwarded if I would send eight cent stamps in a prepaid envelope and would fill up a form enclosed. I received the packet at last in a third town, and found by the postmark that it must have been lying in the first post office when I called asking in despair for letters and tendering a new address. In the case of that post office popular judgment admitted that the service was careless, but cherished the hope that there would be a change of postmaster at the close of the year; therefore it was needless to do anything.

It may be added that, in view of Paul's use of the term *dynamis*, I have preferred the old-fashioned "dynamic," rather than "kinetic," as the antithesis of static.

I have omitted the last chapter, holding it for a later occasion, because new evidence regarding the family of Sergius Paullus has been found, and the chapter requires to be rewritten.

W. M. RAMSAY

EDINBURGH
26 *January*, 1914.

CONTENTS

PART I. PREPARATORY QUESTIONS

PART II. THE THOUGHT OF PAUL

xi

PART I. PREPARATORY QUESTIONS

I. Had Paul a Philosophy?

It is a difficult, perhaps an impossible, task to describe in the stages of its growth the way in which Paul had learned to contemplate the world around him and above him. Yet we must attempt to do so. Every one who thinks about a great philosopher must attempt to understand the steps by which his philosophy gradually assumed its mature form. To understand the thought of another is to understand the way of its growth. Accordingly the different influences which helped to mould Paul's mind will most readily become clear, if we try to conceive his thought in its origin and development.

My aim is to state an unprofessional opinion in the common terms of the present day, neither philosophical nor theological, but such terms as one who is neither a philosopher nor a theologian can use. I try to express the thoughts which gradually took shape in my mind as I traversed year after year the paths which Paul trod in Asia Minor. The scenery exercises a strong influence on those who become familiar with it; and one who is always thinking about Paul has (or thinks that he has) his mind insensibly tuned into harmony with Paul's, as he goes along the same road.

The modern traveller in a railway train has no such experience, and never learns what the influence of scenery is. He has no time to see it, while he is hurried past it to gaze for a moment on a new scene, which in its turn rapidly

fades away to the rear.[1]   He can hear no voice, for nature
cannot speak amid the noise of the train.

Very different is it when one travels after the old slow
fashion for two or even three successive days straight
towards one of those lofty peaks, which watch like beacons
and guides over the great plain of South Galatia, and at
last sees the details of the beautiful mountain grow distinct
and take separate form, as one comes within a few miles
of the city over which it keeps guard.   One thinks of the
feelings in Paul's mind, as he was travelling from Cilicia,
and first descried far ahead the great mountain which stands
high above Derbe.   To the Christian teacher that lofty peak
marked the place where lay the nearest of his Churches; to
the Roman it indicated the bounds of Galatic Lycaonia
and of the Roman Empire in which his work lay.   It is not
of picturesqueness or æsthetic charm · that one thinks in
such a scene.   There is a vague consciousness of this; but
the thought that fills one's mind is the memory of history
and human life.   The mountain now stands sentinel over
two or three tiny and dying Turkish villages, and one very
small village of refugees from Roumelia.   The present surroundings speak only of decay; yet it is life, not death, that
is suggested to the traveller's mind; but the life and the

---

[1] This section was written before Dr. Adolf Deissmann had performed the
two train journeys, which helped him to write his new work on St. Paul, and
was printed more than a year before that work had been published.   As
example of the distorting influence of knowledge acquired by a railway
journey I quote from p. 18: "At the present day it would be possible, on
horseback and then with the railway, to get from Colossae to Ephesus in
case of need.   At any rate in 1909 I did the journey from Ephesus to
Laodicea, which is near Colossae, and back again in two days (13 and 15
March)."   Such geographical remarks only darken the subject: one can do
much better at home with a map.   I find with sorrow that I am in such
marked disagreement with Dr. Deissmann's views about Paul's whole attitude and intellectual endowment: see Preface and Section LIV.

thought thus suggested lie in the past and the futur, not in the present.   One then understands, as one heas the voice of nature, why the mountain is still called the Pigrim Father (Hadji Baba); it is the divinely appointed lanmark to guide the traveller and the pilgrim; it was the lirect gift of God, and is in every age regarded as one d the seats of the divine and gracious power that guars the land.

Paul did not talk sentimentally about the beauty d the mountain or the scenery.   No one would dare to peak after such patronising fashion in a scene like that ; to lo so would be felt as sacrilegious.   One is thankful and gnteful for the awe and the guidance.   But just as it happned, when Paul, travelling by the Way of the Sea,[1] reachd the slight ridge of Kaukab, and saw for the first tim the prospect of Damascus open before his eyes, and contem-plated the scene of his self-chosen work, an emcional storm affected him in which his mind was raised abve its ordinary level to contemplate the Divine truth, so in some minor degree was it when the same man, hurrying towards the Galatian cities after his letter to reclaim the lost came within sight of the mountains that showed where Derle lay, and watched them hour after hour and day after day as he went onwards to his work among them.

[1] According to the early and the only good tradition Kaukab was the scene of his Conversion.   Modern dragomans, guiding their tourists along the usual modern route from Damascus to the source of the Jordan, point out the scene on that road, along which Paul did not go and where n tradition places it.   The Catholic pilgrims are taken to a place close to Damascus on the east: this scene was chosen when Kaukab was unsafe fr pilgrims owing to the terror of the Druses.   There can be no doubt that Paul would travel along by the Way of the Sea (i.e. the Sea of Tiberias), nd that the scene must be sought on that road.   Kaukab is the point on tha road where the traveller from the south reaches the crest of a slight ridg and comes into view of Damascus.

We are all asking the same great questions, and have been doing so through the centuries. Paul is one of those who, in trying to answer those questions, have gripped the heart of mankind. He has been hated by many, but always has been believed in by countless thousands, and his influence grows with the progress of time. No apology, therefore, is needed for the attempt to state what Paul means to one who has been nurtured amid the European Universities of the nineteenth century, and then has wandered for many years along the Pauline roads with Paul in his hands. Every great poet and prophet and religious teacher, while he speaks first of all to the men of his own age, has a message for all time His message is never antiquated, because he has penetrated beneath the surface to the deep-lying principles and the great forces that sweep through history and make the world's life. This message, however, has to be reinterpreted by each age for itself in terms of its own life ; and, as I might almost say, it has to be reinterpreted by every man or his own self in terms of his own life.

Paul has left to us no formal statement of his religious-philosophical position, such as would satisfy the modern undergraduate, who seeks for a degree with highest honours in the University. We have nothing from his hand even remotely approaching the character of a " Student's Manual of the Religion of Paul ". The Apostle was far too much immersed in affairs, even had the requirements and curiosity of moderns been within his range of vision. The urgent calls of the moment were always pressing upon him, and he could never satisfy himself that he was sufficiently responding to the calls : " we were afflicted on every side : without were fightings, within were fears " : and again, " beside those things that are without, there is that which presseth upon me daily, anxiety for all the churches : who is weak, and I am not weak ? who is made to stumble, and I burn not ? " [1]

Hence he wrote only occasional letters regarding special difficulties that occurred among his friends and converts. All his Epistles were real letters from a man to his friends, discussing the affairs of the moment and giving advice. The letter to the Romans comes nearest to the character of a formal exposition : among the Roman Church he had only a few personal friends ; [2] and little or no special knowledge of the conditions in that varied congregation appears in the Epistle.

Even that letter, however, is not a complete or formal treatise explaining his own opinions. It is rather a generalisation of his experience among his other Gentile Churches, the expression in a more systematic fashion of the advice and teaching which he had found most urgently required among them—rather homiletic than philosophic.

Yet every statement which he makes in any of his letters expresses the judgment of a man who had thought out for himself a certain system of philosophy and religion—who had not merely accepted a doctrine taught him by others, but had, while accepting this doctrine, brought it into relation with his own mind and experience and made it part of his independent and original thought. In this doctrine Paul had found what was needed in order to perfect his own

[1] 2 Cor. vii. 5 and xi. 28.

[2] That the last chapter of Romans is a misplaced fragment of a letter to the Ephesians (as a common modern theory maintains) is an idea which tends to distort one's view of the situation in the Imperial world and in the Church generally at that time. The importance of that chapter lies in the picture that it conveys of the constant motion which was going on in the early Pauline Churches. The facilities for travelling and for trading were fully used by the Christians, and it was largely among the travelling classes that Paulinism struck its roots. In itself the chapter, however, has no bearing on the teaching of Paul. Yet see on it pp. 433, 435.

life; and he had meditated on it until his whole past history and the whole history of his own race and of the world became to him a unity, as the gradual unfolding and manifestation of the will of God. Hence he judged every question that was submitted to him by his followers, and solved every difficulty which they had to meet, on the general principles into which he had thought himself and by which he lived.

In attempting to understand the way in which this system of thought and these principles of judgment had gradually developed themselves within Paul's mind so as entirely to recreate and mould his personality—as he says, "it is no longer I, but Christ liveth in me"[1]—we cannot hope for aid by discovering any stages of development within the range of Paul's own letters. His position was settled, and his system was already complete, before he was finally ordered to go forth unto the Gentiles. This call took place on his second visit to Jerusalem, which is briefly described in Acts xi. 30, xii. 25. The call is not mentioned at that point by Luke, but is implied in xiii. 2, Gal. ii. 9; the manner is described in xxii. 17-21. Paul then recognised the call; it was accepted as the Divine will by Peter, James and John (Gal. ii. 9); and it was acted on by the congregation in Antioch, which sent forth Paul and Barnabas to the work (xiii. 3). See p. 220.

There had indeed been earlier intimations given to him of his future work, but not such clear intimations that he understood them and obeyed them.[2] He was not ready for

---

[1] Gal. ii. 20.

[2] The final intimation, which led to immediate action, took place on his second visit to Jerusalem (Gal. ii. 1 f.), and is described by himself in Acts xxii. 17-21. This seems to be the right and necessary placing of that vision; but in this place I must simply presume the view which is required in order to understand properly the work and life of Paul.

them, and therefore failed to understand and to obey them. Later, when he looked back over his life, he saw that there had been such earlier intimations of his destiny, which he had failed to comprehend, because his system of thought and the basis of his religious position had not been fully systematised in his mind. He had been groping towards the light, but had not yet reached it. The first intimation was, certainly, obscure: it was conveyed indirectly, not directly (Acts ix. 15, xxii. 10), and the terms were not very definite (xxii. 15); but Paul, after he had at last heard and understood the clearer command, perceived that the same duty had been intimated to him from the first.

The very fact that now at last he understood the true nature of the call showed that he was fully prepared to answer it. The recognition of the right way to put the question of career leads one on to answer the question. The answer is already implicit in rightly formulating the question. That is the truth of science, as well as of life. To know how to put the right question marks the creative man in science as in life. The beginner can neither put the right question, nor rightly set about the solution of the complicated general problem.

No development, therefore, in the religious position of Paul can be traced in the letters. His religious thought is as complete in the first as in the last.[1] The apparent differences between them in regard to the expression of his teaching are due to two causes.

(1) He had to adapt his teaching both to the special needs and to the varying power of comprehension among

---

[1] In Section LII. it is pointed out that the earliest of his letters is Galatians not 1 Thessalonians. Galatians is quite mature in its teaching, but Thessalonians was written to very immature correspondents, who could not have comprehended a letter like Galatians.

his pupils. He had to solve the pressing difficulties of the moment, and he had to speak to them in language that they could understand. It was necessary to raise those pagans to a higher moral platform before they could even comprehend many of the requirements of morality as Paul understood it. Their judgment had been distorted, and needed to be straightened. The Jews around him started on a far higher moral standard, and could feel needs and be conscious of sin as the pagans could not. You must talk of mathematical principles in very different ways to an untaught and to a moderately well-trained learner ; and so it is with moral principles, as any intelligent missionary among a rude or a savage race can bear witness.

Paul had to create the consciousness of the sin and the need, before he could guide rightly the ignorant gropings after " Salvation," [1] which were everywhere manifest in the pagan world. Hence he came among the ignorant Corinthians " not with verbal or philosophic skill, setting forth the mystery [i.e. the deeper and more complicated explanation of the nature] of God ". He used no " persuasive words of wisdom ". He blazoned before them in simple description " the [Divine] Spirit and the power" thereof. It was only " among the mature that he used philosophico-religious language ".[2] He would not, in modern parlance, have talked to an ordinary audience of "the teleology of the finite consciousness ". A deep truth underlies those words, but that way of expressing the truth must be reserved for an audience in a University, highly trained in philosophic terminology : it conveys no meaning to the uneducated

---

[1] All men in the Aegean lands were seeking for " Salvation," and making prayers and vows for it, but wherein it lay they knew not: stelae recording such vows ὑπὲρ σωτηρίας are remarkably common.

[2] 1 Cor. ii. 1-6.

man. Hence the letters to the Ephesians or Colossians, who had already been trained and practised in Christian thought, are more philosophic and mystic in language than the Corinthian letter. Yet in all his letters the same philosophy, the same religion, and the same mysticism lie below the surface.

Again to Timothy, a Christian of long standing and experience, yet himself a simple nature without higher philosophic training or innate power, a special mode of presenting the advanced and practical teaching was appropriate.

(2) Paul learned much about the best way of approaching the pagan world. In method of presentation of his message, and in the line of attack on the Roman world (as a stage in the attack on the entire world of man), there is a distinct development, which is however already almost fully completed in the Corinthian letters.

Still, with all the difficulties of the task clearly in mind we essay it simply because we must. Paul insistently presses on the minds of men, and we cannot get clear of him.

II. METHOD AND PLAN

We take it, then, for granted that Paul started his mission to the Roman world (Acts xiii. 3) having already in mind a philosophic and carefully meditated view of human life in its relation to the Divine power that moves and guides the universe. We are to try to express his view as it would present itself to one trained in the schools of the present day. There are, however, certain preliminary questions which present themselves, each demanding some notice.

One question which has been much discussed deserves and rewards some attention. It is generally admitted that Paul's Tarsian origin and experiences formed an influence in his life. He was a Jew, but a Jew of Tarsus, and a Roman Jew. He was a burgher of a very aristocratically constituted city, where citizenship was narrowly restricted : he was a member of the supreme aristocracy of the world, as born a Roman citizen.[1] I have always held and expressed the opinion that, except for these formative influences, Paul could never have been what he was. Yet he is fundamentally the Jew. The force, the fire, the depths of his nature, are Hebrew ; but his Jewish power is tempered and ordered and in a measure guided by his Greek training and his Roman position in the world.

I have often used a homely and simple illustration to explain what seems to me to be the right measure of these two influences on Paul's mind. If you take a glass half-filled with wine and add water to it, then the water mingles in and affects every drop of the liquid that fills the glass, but the power and the spirit come from the wine

[1] This is outlined in *St. Paul the Traveller and the Roman Citizen*, and more fully described in *Cities of St. Paul.*

alone. The Greek influence is to temper and to order, but it added no fire to the nature of the great Apostle.

As Paul himself says,[1] he owed much to the Greeks; but he was not indebted to them for any religious stimulus, nor did he learn from them any religious thought or method. A recent fashionable theory is that he was profoundly influenced by the pagan mysteries, and even that he was initiated into the mysteries and borrowed from them much with which he transformed and adulterated the simple teaching of Jesus. This theory rests (as I think) on a complete misunderstanding of the thought of Paul, and is therefore valueless for our present purpose; but, as will be pointed out in Section XLVIII. of Part III., recent discovery regarding the Mysteries shows that Paul knew and condemned their spirit and their method.

In one respect, however, Paul's situation amid the Graeco-Asiatic world and its religious life exercised an immense effect on him. Therefrom springs his intense hatred for idolatry.[2] It was not his Hebrew experiences that produced his passionate detestation of idolatry. Idolatry as a present danger in Israel could implant this detestation in the old Hebrew prophets; Israel was then always on the point of slipping back into pagan rites and superstition; but in Paul's time it was no longer a pressing danger among his people. They had learned their lesson slowly; but at least they had learned it long before Paul was born, and they had learned it completely and for ever.[3]

In Tarsus, however, and the cities of the Graeco-Roman world, idolatry presented itself as the great enemy, impeding the victory of Hebraism and the coming of the Messiah, who was the dream and the vision of Paul's early life. It was the embodiment of Satan's power, contradicting and preventing the purpose of God.

[1] Rom. i. 14. [2] On this subject see also Section XXIII.
[3] See also Section IX.

Luke, as usual, has caught this trait in Paul's character. "His spirit was provoked within him as he beheld the city full of idols," is Luke's description of what Paul felt at Athens. The chosen home and centre of Greek education was the nursing-ground of idolatry. Paul found that Greek philosophy was hostile to him; but he never entertained the same hatred for it as for the popular form of paganism.[1]

However, as I have been criticised for assigning too much influence to the Hellenic element in the mind of Paul, I shall attempt to justify my view; and it will tend to keep the discussion on more profitable lines if I put what I have to say in the form of a criticism and a reply to criticism. I take the criticism from Principal A. E. Garvie, an excellent and highly esteemed authority: see Sections V. and VI., also XIX. and XXVIII.

While we must regard Paul's thought as developing in an ordered fashion from the childhood of a Jewish boy in a Greek city and in the position of a Roman born, we must also bear in mind the great crisis of his life, *viz.*, his Conversion. He was not one of those natures which develop in a smooth and uniform course from first to last. He was a nature of fire and passion, a volcanic nature, subject to great and sudden changes. His experience of Jesus, whom as he says he had seen, and to whose victory over death he could testify from eye-witness, had remade his life. From this great event he reckoned his course anew. From it he counted the years of his life.[2] Henceforth, he was a new man, a different man with different thoughts and aims; and yet he was the same Paul throughout.

Here we are struck with the same fact which will fre-

[1] Compare Section XIX. and p. 303.
[2] In Galatians i. and ii.

quently meet us in the sequel : in all that concerns Paul we can usually express him and his thought and his intentions in a pair of contradictory statements : he is, and he is not : he was a different Paul, and he was the same Paul.

It is not proposed to discuss here the phenomena of his Conversion. We are to content ourselves with his own statements and his own view of that event. It was a sudden, unprepared, completely revolutionising change. Nothing had been in his mind consciously that seemed to prepare the way for it. He was sailing on a diametrically opposite course. Suddenly he was seized by a higher power, and set on a new course. Yet it was the most real, as well as the most powerful, issue in his life. He never could doubt about its meaning or its character. The Divine Power had taken hold of him, and swayed him as God chose. This is what Paul says; this is what he thought; and we are studying him as he was.

Further, it is not part of our task to speak of the position of Paul in the development of early Christian thought, or of his relation to his contemporaries. I content myself with a few words in Section VII. f. about the relation of St. Paul to St. John. The New Testament as a book, or set of books, begins with Paul and ends with John. From one point of view the New Testament is a single work; from another point of view it is a collection of separate writings. It is the same thought throughout, and yet it differs according to the personalities through whom it finds expression. The few pages which I give to this topic are also thrown into the form of a criticism or a reply to criticism.

Paul deals with life, not with speculation. He does not seek to discuss problems, but to help men. He had no patience with subtle questions and speculations : all such discussion was in his esteem mere verbal trifling. He thought of, and spoke to, men and women. "Avoid silly talking," he says, "it will eat like a canker: it grows towards ungodliness."[1] Avoid people that talk about such empty questions, "whom I have handed over to Satan, that they may learn not to blaspheme".[2] You should learn to work and live and teach, not to talk.

We must take Paul with his limitations. We do not go to him for an intellectually plausible system of abstract philosophy. Yet his teaching makes very high intellectual demands: see Section III.

Another question emerges, not because it appears to me to reward discussion, but simply because it has been raised and has caught the attention of the world, and has even been incautiously answered in the affirmative by scholars who did not realise what was implied in the affirmation. This is the medical question, whether Paul was afflicted with epilepsy. To the medical mind that presents itself in this harsh form: are the visions of which he speaks the symptoms of epileptic madness? Medical friends of my own have declared unhesitatingly that Paul's visions can be paralleled in any asylum for epileptic lunacy.

Such a statement could never be made by a scientifically trained man, unless there were a certain resemblance between the two cases. In one respect, however, the resemblance fails completely, Paul's visions have moved the world, and changed the current of history, and profoundly affected in one way or other the thought of all educated men. On no rational system of thought can it be admitted that the dreams of an epileptic lunatic could become a force to transform all educated human life. That answer seems in itself sufficient;[3] but I add to it a brief discussion from the medical side in Section XLIX.

[1] 2 Tim. ii. 17.   [2] 1 Tim. i. 20.
[3] It is stated in my *Historical Commentary on Galatians*, p. 423 ff.

III. Is Paul's Philosophy Convincing?

Is the system of the Pauline thought of such a nature as to convince the reader, to overpower and lead captive his judgment? That question might be asked. In reply we ask: has there ever been a system of philosophy that convinced the world, and dominated the intellect of men? The aim of philosophy is not to convince and to lead captive, but to make men think; it ought to stimulate independent thought, and not to rule or dominate the mind.

In the modern schools there is no philosopher of the past or the present who is not constantly a subject of criticism. Many modern lecturers on philosophy give to all their prelections on any great thinker the form of an exposition of his errors and an indication of what he ought to have said and written.

Paul is not convincing in the sense of the above question. He requires much from the reader or the hearer. His subject is always, from first to last, the nature and the life and the death of Christ: the life of Christ is much, the death of Christ is everything. This is, after all, a thing that cannot be explained or expressed in words. The nature, the position of Jesus Christ in the world, His relation to man and to God, remains and must always remain beyond the power of man to conceive or to describe. He remains unintelligible to the human mind, above it on a different plane; and yet He is the most powerful, the most tremendous, the most creative and epoch-making fact in the life of mankind. Human history culminates with Him, and takes a new start from Him.

The being of Jesus must be appreciated, not merely as an intellectual fact, but as related to the entire nature of man. It is a force, a power, an impulse, that must sway the mind of the reader or hearer; otherwise he cannot follow or understand Paul.

The demand that Paul makes on his readers is enormous. They have to bring half of the whole; otherwise the whole is almost naught to them. They may appreciate the beauty of the thought, sometimes even the rhythm of the language and the extraordinary ability of the exposition; but, after all, that is next to nothing, unless they supply the power to live and the will to believe.

A word of explanation, to prevent misunderstanding of my purpose. When I speak of the Christianity of Paul I assume that what he taught was the teaching of Jesus expressed in a form that should be intelligible to the pagan world, and that his doctrine was not a sophisticated development out of it. This religion, as Jesus and as Paul taught it, is the religion of an educated people—educated in moral as well as intellectual power to understand and comprehend. It presupposes a high standard of mind, and requires the capacity of thinking and moving on a lofty plane, not merely morally, but also intellectually.

To say that this religion is pitched on a high moral plane is of course admitted by all as obviously and necessarily true. The only question is whether it does not pitch its moral demand too high. Is it not asking too much when it requires that we live the right and the Divine life? Who shall live the Divine life? There have been, and there are, men and women who can die the Divine death, either as the martyr true to principle, or as the devotee who cuts himself off from the world and lives the life of death to the world. But Christianity demands that we live the Divine life in the world and amid its activities. Who shall succeed in doing this? Who can do this? Who can purify his heart and his thought?

Others say, " You shall not do evil ". Christ says, " You shall not think evil ".

Who dare hope that such a doctrine of life can be successful in its appeal to men, and especially to savage races and degraded people? The rapidity with which Mohammedanism often succeeds in raising savage tribes to a higher moral level is contrasted with the much slower influence exercised by Christian missionaries in similar cases. Should we not be contented with the lower level and the rapid elevation to that lower level?

History has returned the answer.

The extension of Mohammedanism over a savage people is usually marked by a sudden great moral elevation followed by a long gradual deterioration. An ideal which can be realised cannot satisfy human need. The ideal must ever remain in front tempting the eagerness of man to strive onwards towards it. If it can be attained, it is imperfect. The ideal which is above man is Divine: when it is attained in this world it is no longer Divine.[1]

Man cannot acquiesce in anything short of the Divine and the perfect. The lesson of history is that Christianity is right, because its ideal cannot be attained by man ; and Islam is wrong because its ideal can be and has been attained. The teaching of life is : Strive after the difficult, for the easy is valueless. The Divine alone is real and lasting : all else is illusion and transitory : the true life of man is a never-ending struggle towards the unattainable.

Christianity makes an equally great demand on the in-

[1] This is practically the same reply that Pascal in his *Lettres Provinciales* made to the Jesuits.

tellect. It calls for the highest and the deepest insight: it imperiously demands at the outset the ability to distinguish between the true and the false, and the readiness to sacrifice the false and to cleave to the true. What are the fundamental propositions of Paulinism, the axioms on which Paul builds up his philosophy? These are two; and of these two axioms the second is merely the complete statement of what is involved in the first. The first axiom is this: "God is"; the second axiom is, "God is good". The first is valueless except through the second. When you say that "God is," your axiom is useless, if the God whose existence you assert is not the true and real God. As Moses declared to the people, so says Paul: "I set before you life and death: choose life".

In that alternative is contained the grand choice in this world. Every man must choose. If you choose a God, whose issue is death, you are not choosing God: you are choosing the unreal: you are following after an illusion. Paul makes, and Christianity makes, this enormous and supreme demand that you must be able to distinguish truth from falsehood and reality from illusion. He does not try to prove these axioms, he does not attempt to demonstrate the necessity of this initial step. He boldly assumes that "God is the living and real God," and that his hearers recognise and admit this, and that only the foolish and the blind are ignorant of the truth.

IV. Did Paul See Jesus?

One of the most fundamental questions in regard to the point of view from which Paul regarded the Saviour is whether Jesus in life had been a complete stranger to him or had been personally known to him. The article by Professor J. H. Moulton in the *Expositor* for July, 1911, p. 16, therefore, profoundly interested me; and still more Professor Johannes Weiss's *Paul and Jesus*, which I immediately procured on Professor Moulton's recommendation. In the *Expositor*, May, 1901, p. 362, I published an article stating reasons for the same view, that Paul knew Jesus in the vision on the road near Damascus, because he had seen Jesus in life and recognised the man whom he had known.[1] When Professor Weiss on p. 40 expresses his " wonder how the whole school of modern theology has been able so readily to reject the best and most natural explanation of these difficulties, namely, the assumption that Paul had seen Jesus personally, and that the sight had made an indelible impression on him," he may perhaps be interested to learn that one who looks at this subject solely as an historian, and who has no pretension to be a theologian, took the same view.

It must have been about the year 1901 that I ventured to express the same opinion in an address at Sion College;

[1] It was § li. of a Historical Commentary on First Corinthians. The short article being in a foreign tongue was not likely to attract the attention of the distinguished Professor of Heidelberg, any more than it has caught the attention of Professor Moulton.

and, in the discussion which followed, the Rev. Mr. Relton (as I think) expressed the opinion that I must inevitably regard the words of Second Corinthians v. 16 in very much the same way as Professor Weiss does in his book, pp. 42-53. I had not myself observed the bearing of this passage from Second Corinthians; nor should I have been able to argue so subtly and skilfully as Professor Weiss has done for his interpretation ; but, since Mr. Relton drew my attention to the passage, I have regarded it as a possible, but far from the most convincing, argument on this side.

More than ten years have passed since that article was printed ; and the more I have thought over the subject, the more has its importance been impressed on me. Often I have had to speak on the subject ; and as time passed the clearer grew in my thought a certain picture and vision of the Apostle. With much that appears in Weiss, I gladly find myself in perfect agreement. As he says (p. 29) that near Damascus " the figure of the Messiah, whose coming from Heaven was the object of such deep desires and prayers, might appear to the Apostle ; he was profoundly moved by these longings. . . . But . . . by what signs did Paul recognise the figure as Jesus ? " Peter and others recognised Jesus (I Cor. xv. 5 ff.) : Paul also recognised Him. In both cases they recognised Him because they had seen Him. I can only quote the words of Weiss (p. 31) : " Paul's vision and conversion are psychologically inconceivable except upon the supposition that he had been actually and vividly impressed by the human personality of Jesus ".

Paul describes himself as a witness that Jesus was living quite in the same way in which he describes Peter and the rest as witnesses. They were witnesses, because they knew the man whom they had seen. Paul would not offer his evidence as in the same category with theirs, if he merely believed what he was told. He believed, because he recognised the man whom he had seen in life.

For this recognition it is necessary that the event should have occurred not too long after the death of Jesus. Recognition would be most effectual and would weigh most with others, in the case of a person who had not been very long dead. When Paul classes himself as a witness with Peter and the rest, he does not mean that they recognised Jesus within a few days or weeks of His death, while he recognised Jesus after eight years (as would be the case according to the chronological theory—hopelessly wrong, in my opinion, on other grounds—that the Vision of Saul occurred after A.D. 37, many years later than the Crucifixion). This consideration furnishes a subsidiary, though not in itself an absolutely conclusive argument, against that chronological theory.

The point of view which has been taken in the preceding paragraphs is after all external, though, as put by Professor Weiss, it is very strong. To my own mind the most conclusive reason lies in its bearing on the development of Saul's mind and thought. In this respect I find myself in diametrical opposition to the Heidelberg theologian. To him Paul's Conversion was the outward and final culmination of a long and slow inward process. He says on p. 35 (referring to the view which he quotes from Kölbing), that Paul "possessed a very close and clear knowledge of the person and work of Jesus; it would almost appear that Paul before his conversion had read that Gospel of Mark from which Kölbing takes the essential features of his picture of Jesus". Weiss then proceeds: "At any rate, the main idea is undoubtedly correct . . . he must already have been half-persuaded, and have plunged into the task of persecution with forced

zeal and an uneasy conscience ".   On p. 36 he proceeds :
" It is certainly correct to assume that the faith of the first
disciples also influenced Paul"; and on p. 37, "we may
therefore adhere to the opinion that the 'Spirit of Jesus,'
working through His disciples, eventually conquered Paul :
the figure of Jesus was so convincingly apparent through
the lives and characters of His adherents that Paul's powers
of resistance eventually grew wearied, and mentally he was
prepared for the ultimate change that he himself realised ".

With this picture of the process in Paul's mind, I regret
to find myself in absolute disagreement.   One may pass
over what is, in my opinion, the hopeless incongruity that a
man like Paul, in order to still an uneasy conscience and to
force himself to resist the conviction which was gradually
growing in his mind, " plunged into the task of persecution "
and of murder.   Had Saul felt a moment's doubt he must
have stopped to think.   He could not have continued to
outrun all his contemporaries in cruelty and desire to im-
prison, and even to kill, those about whom a suspicion was
growing in his mind that they might after all be right.
This psychological impossibility might be insisted on at more
length, but we pass over it, and we rest our case on the statement of Paul himself, corroborated by Luke, but quite independent of Luke's evidence.

In the first place, Paul lays the strongest emphasis on the
fact that his change of mind and life was wholly independent
of the older Apostles.   He came to his new career through
a sudden and direct relation between Christ and himself.
He stood over-against God, and he was struck down by God
and grasped by Jesus.   If we give up that, what are we to
accept from Paul about his own past life?   We are plunged
in a sea of uncertainties ; some things we accept and some
we reject in his testimony.   We accept or reject in virtue of

some prepossession or psychological theory, and not in virtue of Paul's own statements.

In the second place, Paul states in the strongest way that he was in the full course of unhesitating and fanatical persecution. He had no doubt. He hated that impostor, and he was resolved to exterminate all that were deluded by Him, and to trample out the embers of the dying fire. There was in the mind of Paul, according to his own emphatic words, no preparation for the great change in his life, no process of gradually assimilating this teaching. He had, once for all, been convinced by that shameful death on the cross, that the man Jesus was an impostor who had degraded and brought into contempt the most sacred belief of the Jews, the belief in a coming Messiah and in an elevation of the whole race once more to its rightful position in the world.

Now take into account Paul's nature and his acquired character. He was fully possessed by all the Jewish obstinate and fervent belief in what he considered right. He hated the Man that had parodied the Messianic idea and shamed the chosen people. What process of reasoning would have convinced such a man? What argument would have weighed with him? He was blind and deaf to all human evidence. One witness, or fifty, or five thousand, would have weighed equally with him; and their weight would have been nought. Their evidence was all delusion, all untrustworthy. They had some virtues, for they were, after all, Jews; but they were destroying the hope of Israel by their perverted delusion. That Israel might live, they must die, so far as the Roman law allowed; in Damascus, governed by a foreign king, there was more hope of massacre than there was under Roman law in Judæa, and there for some reason the Christians had taken refuge in considerable numbers. To Damascus, therefore, Paul went.

Human reasoning and testimony could have had no effect on Paul, as he describes his own condition. He was suddenly convinced: Christ seized him: the power of God irradiated him. He recognised as living in the Divine glory the man whom he had believed to be a dead impostor. He knew the man by sight. He heard His voice and His words.

I assume here, because this is not the place to discuss it more fully, that there are occasions when one man can hear what another cannot hear, and when one man can see what another cannot see. That Paul knew to be true. He had felt it; he had seen and he had heard. On this the rest of his life was built. You cannot get away from this. So he says; and on this belief he founded his career, and conquered the world.

I believe, and know from experience, that the thought of one mind may, in certain circumstances, be heard by another. No one can take from me what I know to be true; although, as a whole, the circumstances and comforts of modern life alike in Britain and in Germany are unfavourable to the development of that sensibility. Yet the power exists potentially in most people, though often weakened and deadened by the fortunes of life; and it can and does become active in a few.

The view that seems to emerge from the long discussion of the subject is the same view that Paul himself states, and Luke and others believed. Saul, with his perfect confidence in the truth and righteousness of his own opinions—a kind of belief such as may be found among young men, trained by great masters and leaders, venerating their teachers, intensely desirous of knowing the truth, enthusiastic to the highest degree, zealous for the right as they conceive it, and strenuously bent on living the Divine life and spending themselves in their career of duty—was wholly impervious

to reason and to evidence.   He knew far better than these
followers of Jesus.

Some other way than mere word was needed to move
him.   He had to be convinced that Jesus, whom he had
thought a dead impostor, was a living God.   He saw the
man, and recognised Him.   He would believe no other
person ; he believed his own senses and his own knowledge.
Nothing except himself would convince him.   He was a
witness that Jesus was living.   As he says : " Have I not
seen [1] Jesus Christ our Lord ? "   He ranked himself as a
personal witness to the truth on which his future career
rested ; and this change of mind and life came on him
suddenly like a flash of lightning.   There was no preparation for the change.   Paul was one of those who learn the
greatest things by intuition, as in a flash of inspiration.

There was a motive cause, sudden and overwhelming.
This cause was that he saw alive and recognised the man
whom he had believed to be dead.

The permanent effect on Paul was most striking in respect
of one detail.   The cross, which had hitherto been the
" stumbling-block " in his way, which he regarded as typical
of the triumph of Rome over his own race, the Chosen
People, and as the visible expression of the disgrace and
shame inflicted on Israel by its conquerors, that cross he
henceforth regarded as typical of the triumph of Jesus over
Rome, and as symbolical of the powerlessness of the mighty
Roman Empire to touch the man whom it had condemned
and tried to kill, but tried in vain.   In His Crucifixion,
Jesus celebrated a triumph over all His enemies : He nailed
to the cross the condemnatory document : He leads in the
long train of His triumph (as the Roman general led through

---

[1] The word ἑόρακα is as strong a word as could be chosen.   Paul claimed
to have seen Jesus face to face, as he says in Acts xxvi. 16.

the Roman streets) His conquering soldiers who trust in
Him (Col. ii. 15; 2 Cor. ii. 14). Paul henceforth gloried
in this symbol of victory and Divine power more than in
anything else. He learned by eyesight, as well as in other
ways, what the cross really meant.

In 1 Corinthians ix. 1 and xv. 8 Paul emphasises specially
that he had seen Jesus. This is the point on which he lays
great stress. He is comparing himself with the Apostles.
He saw Jesus as they saw Him. He is an eye-witness as
they were.

The evidence of the Acts seems at first sight somewhat
different. To those who are ready to accept the evidence
of the Acts when it suits them, and to throw it overboard
whenever they dislike it, the statements on this subject contained in that book will matter little; they take just what
they want, and leave the rest. But to those who treat the
Acts seriously and rationally as a historical work from which
the modern critic is not free to pick what he likes and throw
aside what he likes, but which he has to judge as a whole,
the case is different. Why does Luke in his three accounts
mention only once (Acts xxvi. 13-20) that Jesus appeared
to the eyes of Saul?[1] Here Paul relates that as he rose
and stood on his feet before Jesus, detailed instructions were
given him as to what he should do: part of his work was
to bear witness of what he saw.

Yet, although this detail is not explicitly stated in the
other two accounts which Luke gives of the scene, yet in
both it is implied that Paul saw Jesus at that time, Luke's
space was narrow and his accounts are brief; but he implies much that he does not expressly record.

In the first account given in the Acts ix. 4-8 Luke men-

---

[1] Similar terms are used in 1 Corinthians ix. 1, xv. 8, and in this passage
of the Acts, ὤφθην and εἶδες or ἑόρακα.

tions that the men who were with him "stood speechless, hearing the voice but beholding no man". We are to gather that they were half aware of something which was happening, and the statement that they beheld no man naturally implies that Paul did see some man. There was much to tell about that scene ; some of the details are omitted in this, as in every account, because in Luke's brief narrative it was not possible to mention everything.

In the second account, which Luke in Acts xxii. quotes from Paul's own mouth, there is no direct mention by Paul himself that he saw Jesus. But as to this we notice two facts. In the first place, Paul's object is not to compare himself with the older Apostles, as it is in 1 Corinthians. His purpose in this hurried, almost breathless, address to the Jews, who had been on the point of tearing him in pieces, was simply to touch their hearts. This was not the most suitable detail to select at the moment. In the second place, he quotes from Ananias, a Jew of high character and standing among the people, some details of this incident : the evidence of Ananias was likely to weigh with this audience. Ananias, as Paul says, visited him after some days, and recited to him as proof of his authority the whole incident ; he reminded Paul of what had happened, and among other things, that he had been chosen "to see the Righteous One, and to hear a voice from His mouth". The point which seemed afterwards so important to Paul, when he was writing to the Corinthians, is here put first in the words of Ananias.

Accordingly, in every one of Luke's three narratives, we find that the detail on which Paul lays such stress in writing to the Corinthians appears as a feature of the incident, sometimes more emphasised, sometimes less, but always either implied or formally expressed. In every case the details which were selected stood in some relation to the urgent pressure of the moment. Neither Paul nor Luke ever gives an absolutely complete account, such as we should like to possess, of all the things that happened on this wonderful occasion: to do so would have required a book on a much larger scale than the Acts.

V. The Hellenism of Paul

A preliminary question about the thought of Paul imperatively demands some notice. How much did he learn from
his surroundings and early life as a Roman citizen, a member
of the privileged aristocracy of the Roman world, born and
educated in a half-Greek city, " the one city which was
suited by its equipoise between the Asiatic and the Western
spirit to mould the character of the great Hellenist Jew "?[1]

My friend Principal Garvie—if he will permit me to call
him so, though we only once met, and I know him better
from his written than his spoken words—challenges my position that " Gentile influences were far more potent factors
in Paul's development than has hitherto been generally
recognised ".[2]   I have maintained this, and still maintain
it. These Tarsian influences were what marked out Paul,
already before his birth, as the man who was destined to be
the Apostle to the Gentiles.[3]   The expression fades into
insignificance if it is not taken in this way ; it becomes
a mere general statement of the vague truth that, wherever
he lived and whatever he was by birth, the purpose of God
had chosen him out to be the Apostle of the Roman and
Greek world.   But can we add that it made no difference to
that purpose whether he was born in Jerusalem or in Meso-
potamia, in Ethiopia or in Tarsus ?   This is not, as I believe,
the way in which the New Testament should be read.

---

[1] This is quoted by Dr. Garvie from, I think, the *Cities of St. Paul*.
[2] In the *Expositor*, May, 1911, p. 346 ff.   [3] Gal. i. 15-16.

The view which I have repeatedly maintained is that the Jewish nature and character was the strongest and the most fundamental part of Paul's endowment.[1]　This has been so much emphasised by others that I was absolved from any need to discuss it ; and I professedly left this side of his nature apart, both because it had been so vigorously insisted on, that there was nothing to gain by repeating what had been already better said, and because I was not competent to treat that side of Paul's character.　I do maintain, however, that the thought and plans of Paul are " wholly inexplicable in a mere narrow Hebrew, and wholly inexplicable without an education in Greek philosophy ".　A Palestinian Jew could never have grown into the Apostle of the Graeco-Roman world.　He was an outsider in that world.　He could not touch its heart or even feel its pulse, as Paul could do.　Paul had a certain power of comprehending it that no Jew of Palestine could attain.　He began in the Roman world on the level which our greatest missionaries have been able to attain only by many years of study and thought and growing familiarity, and which others of our missionaries have regretted their failure to attain throughout a long and useful life.

The real question is whether or not I have laid too much stress on the Hellenic side of Paul's thought.　It is a question of degree.　Principal Garvie admits that there was a Hellenic side, but thinks that I have assigned too much importance to this aspect of Paul's thought.　I have frequently said that the Jewish side of Paul's nature was the foundation on which his whole character was built up and the strongest and most determining part of his mind ; but I have left it to better qualified scholars to analyse and

---

[1] It is my habit to begin every lecture I give on this subject by this statement.　See also p. 12.

describe it. Principal Garvie does not, and could hardly exaggerate its importance; but he seems to me to minimise unnecessarily the other side. We are, however, agreed that both sides exist; and it is largely a matter of words to assign the proper emphasis to each.

I mentioned two respects in which Paul had taken up into his thought the ideals of Hellenism: "Hellenism had showed how the freedom of the individual could be consistent with an ordered and articulated government, and it organised a system of State education";[1] and Paul insists on freedom and on education as essential to the Christian life. To my statement Principal Garvie objects that I have myself admitted that, as regards the freedom of the individual, "we can trace this Pauline idea back to its origin in the teaching of Jesus"; and he goes on to say that "surely the phrase of James, 'the law of liberty,' shows that the idea of freedom is involved in the distinctive Christian conception of salvation". And "again the second idea, the necessity of education in the Christian life, is surely not so peculiar as to need so special an application. The Jews, too, cared for education; Jesus had given much pains to the training of His disciples," etc.

I think I have emphasised as strongly as any one both the importance of the idea of freedom in the teaching of Jesus,[2] and the "truth which will soon be discovered and emphasised by the Germans, and will then be brought over and emphasised among us, that the Hebrew nation was at that time the most highly educated people in the world—in the true meaning of the word education".[3]

[1] It failed to keep true to its ideal, and Hellenism gradually sank to be the heritage of a few.

[2] *Luke the Physician and other Studies in the History of Religion*, p. 92 ff., following in the footsteps of Harnack.

[3] *The Education of Christ*, p. 67.

What I can do I have tried to do in the way of making these truths the basis of all my studies ; but you cannot exhaust the idea " freedom " or the word " education " in a sentence or in a paragraph or in a book. You have to feel them and live in them in order to know what they mean. In the first place, if Jesus had " freedom " and " education " in His heart, it does not follow that His disciples caught those ideas and worked them out. The disciples, as we know from the Gospels, used often to lament that the meaning of Jesus's words was hidden from them, and that they had failed to comprehend Him. Is it so unusual a thing for the pupils of a great teacher to miss his meaning? Does not every teacher in a university learn by experience that, except in so far as he dictates his lectures and has them reproduced to him (which trains the power of memory, but not of thinking), the examinations which he sets to his pupils are a constant humiliation to him, because he finds that the things on which he has lavished all his efforts at explanation and clear statement are reproduced to him more or less wrongly, by 90 per cent. of his classes? Yet he will find years later that he had not failed so completely as he fancied, and that pupils had caught far more than they could express in an examination, because the ideas which they had caught, but could not formulate on paper, were more useful and educative than the part which alone appeared in their examination work.

Who would compare the Socrates depicted to us by Xenophon, with the Socrates set before us in Plato's Dialogues? There is little inner resemblance between them ; it is only in externals that the likeness can be traced. Xenophon understood only in the narrower style of his own mind anything that Socrates said ; Plato understood Socrates in his own way, and was roused by his master's teaching to reach conclusions which Socrates did not contemplate, or contemplated only dimly. If you ask whether Xenophon or Plato best understood Socrates, I cannot understand any one voting for Xenophon. Plato set before us one of the greatest figures in human history. Xenophon sets before us a striking and even heroic personality: his practical mind could recognise and show to us a man who could powerfully influence other men: he was incapable of seeing or appreciating the great philosopher. The impulse which Socrates gave to Greek thought proves that he was one of the great master-thinkers of the world, such as Plato, but not Xenophon, shows us.

It is therefore not sufficient to say, as both Principal Garvie and I have said each in our own way and each with equal emphasis, that the idea of freedom was fundamentally involved in the teaching of Jesus. How was it, and in virtue of what education and character was it, that Paul caught this feature in the teaching of Jesus? There had to be something in the mind of Paul to respond to the teaching of Jesus, otherwise he would have remained as deaf to it as the mind of Xenophon was to all (or almost all) the higher teaching of Plato.

If there is any quality which beyond all others distinguishes the teaching of Jesus, it is that He "rose high above such a narrow idea" as that of Jewish exclusiveness. I trace to Paul's mixing in the Roman world and his early training in the Stoic school his familiarity with "this wider and nobler idea of a unity and brotherhood that transcended the limits of a city or a tribe; but the conception of universal brotherhood remained as yet an abstract and ineffective thought, devoid of driving power to move the world". So long as Paul knew this idea only in the abstract and ineffective way of the Stoic thought, or in the half-hearted fashion of the Roman Empire (where the distinction, first between slaves and free, second between the Roman aristocracy, the provincials, and the subject races such as those of Egypt, obscured the general principle), the thought remained only external to him. It was when he had to recreate the whole religious and philosophic foundation of his life, during the two years of quiet meditation which followed on the epoch-making experience of his conversion, that he began to comprehend what lay in the idea of Universal Brotherhood as taught by Jesus: "there can be neither Jew nor Greek, there can be neither bond nor free, there can be no male and female: for ye are all one in Christ Jesus".[1] What was it that enabled Paul to comprehend, and to express to others, the full meaning of that "freedom" which Jesus taught? What, but his wider experience, his better realisation of the inchoate facts of the Roman world, his familiarity with the abstract and unapplied teaching of the Stoics? He was prepared to grasp the truth, and he comprehended it in the form and fashion that made it suitable to the educated middle class of the Roman world.

Moreover, although Principal Garvie quotes from James the phrase "the law of liberty," one need not hesitate to maintain that the phrase is post-Pauline. The writer of the Epistle attributed to James (whom I am quite ready to regard as James the "president" of the Apostolic Council) had certainly been strongly influenced by Paul, and had not confined his studies to the narrower type of Jewish literature. When the three leading Apostles recognised Paul as divinely appointed to be the Apostle of the Gentiles, it implies a very great step on their part. It does not merely mean that they accepted Paul as permitted to do something

[1] Gal. iii. 28.

which they did not wish to do themselves. It means that they accepted Paul as commissioned directly to take the leading part in one branch of their duty; but it did not absolve them from taking an interest in this duty and a general oversight of it. The Council of the Apostles, several times called in the Acts simply "The Apostles,"[1] still retained a general superintendence of the entire work throughout the Church over the whole world; and this authority was fully acknowledged by Paul (Acts xv. 2; Gal. ii. 2).[2]

In men like Peter and James and John the recognition of this duty implies a corresponding growth and broadening out of their ideas and plans. It is pointed out elsewhere[3] that the original Council of the Apostles, especially the leaders of the Council, were never prevented by any scruples or prepossessions or prejudices from learning, even though their teachers were younger and less experienced than themselves. Stephen carried the Apostles with him wholeheartedly in his resolute breaking of the old ties and opening up of the Church to the world. So did Paul, when his time came. It was after these lessons had been learned that James spoke of "the law of liberty". He then recognised that, though his eyes had formerly been holden that he could not see, still the law of liberty was embodied

---

[1] In the Acts, sometimes, "the Apostles" simply means the governing body of the Church in Jerusalem, without implying whether many or few were present. So, e.g., in Acts ix. 27 Paul was brought into the presence of "the Apostles," but from himself (Gal. i. 19) we learn that only James and Peter were present: whether many or few, "the Apostles" were the supreme administrative body. The idea is Roman: one member of the board has the power of all. There was no need for a quorum to exercise the powers of the board.

[2] The misconception which identifies the visit to Jerusalem of Galatians ii. 1-10 with that described in Acts xv. 2-30 destroys the perspective of Church history in the first century. The visit described in Galatians ii. 1 ff. is briefly noticed by Luke in Acts xi. 30, xii. 25.

[3] *Pictures of the Apostolic Church* repeatedly.

in the teaching of Jesus.   For the Apostles the test always
was that the new teaching should simply be an explanation
and a declaration of the truth as it had been originally
taught them.

But the influence of Hellenic surroundings on Paul's
early life and the growth of his mind should not be restricted
to the higher ideas of his education: it is equally applicable
to the cast of his language.   I need not do more than refer
here to the paper on this subject which forms part of my
*Luke the Physician and other Studies in the History of Re-
ligion*, pp. 285 ff., on "St. Paul's use of Metaphors from
Greek and Roman Life," and to the argument there stated
that these metaphors (to a much greater degree than the
similes of Philo) show how deeply the early familiarity with
the surroundings of Hellenic life had affected the fabric of
his mind and his style of expressing his thought.

Finally, I may quote the opinion of a distinguished
German scholar, Professor Johannes Weiss, on this subject.
There are many people in this country to whom nothing can
commend itself unless it appears in the German tongue; and
I may therefore quote from his *Paul and Jesus*, 1909, p.
59 ff., §§ 11-13, "Previous comparisons have not sufficiently
appreciated that which may be stated in one word as Paul's
Hellenism".   Much of what Weiss has said in that work
is exactly in accordance with my views.   He carries his
statement even further than I have gone; but his arguments and reasons are in the same spirit as those from
which I started.   There are, however, some expressions
from which I should dissent, e.g., "For Paul, the unit is the
country or nation, not the individual" (p. 66).   According
to my view the unit for Paul is the individual human soul;[1]
but he marches in his victorious course from Province to

---

[1] This needs to be amplified from what is said in Section XLV about the
family.

Province, and counts his steps by their capitals. He did not think of countries or nations, but of Provinces, as the constituents of the empire; and he accepted these political entities as passing phenomena, powerful for the moment. The real and permanent element in the world was the soul of man and the soul of God.

VI. The Childhood and Youth of Paul

Just a few words more with regard to the Hellenism of Paul in response to Principal Garvie's courteous and friendly paper![1] The character of the great Apostle was far too complex to be conceived and expressed in exactly the same way by two students who approach him on different and independent lines. Principal Garvie and I will doubtless continue to study, and to differ in certain matters, and, as I believe, each to respect the other's opinion.

There are just two points on which we might perhaps approximate without much difficulty to a common view through clearer conception of the meaning of Paul's own words.

(1) Principal Garvie quotes the Apostle's account, as given in Acts xxii. 3, of his training, "brought up in Jerusalem at the feet of Gamaliel"; and says that, while "the exact age at which Paul came to Jerusalem" is uncertain, "yet surely it must have been as a boy of twelve or thirteen at the very latest, if the words are not to be emptied of all meaning".

As to this I am compelled to differ.[3] This estimate of age would suit Acts xxii. 3 quite well; but would it suit Acts xxvi. 4, where Paul defines "my manner of life from my youth up, . . . among mine own nation and at Jerusalem"?[2] What meaning are we to gather out of the words

[1] *Expositor*, November, 1911, p. 470 f.

[2] I need not here go into the question of reading. The true text, which certainly has "and at Jerusalem" (τε), only makes clearer the fact that Paul did not come to Jerusalem and Gamaliel until he could be called a *νέος*.

[3] I am glad to be in agreement with De Deissmann, *St. Paul*, p. 92.

40

"from my youth up"? I see nothing in xxii. 3 to prove that Paul came to Jerusalem at thirteen years of age or earlier. I see everything in xxvi. 4 to prove that he came later than thirteen. One who had come to Jerusalem as a young boy under thirteen would not have said "from my youth up," but rather "from my childhood up". Paul was a young man, *Neos*, when he came to Jerusalem to study, or even before he came. A *Neos* was a grown man, not a child of thirteen.[1]

So far as concerns his studying in the rhetorical schools at Tarsus (which may for want of a more exact term be called the "University" of Tarsus), we have no reason to think that an able boy might not attend these schools at an early age. We have no exact statistics on the subject, and no knowledge. In such matters the age of entering on higher study varies widely. My wife's father was fully ready for the University of Glasgow at eleven years of age, and was kept at home for a year until he was more mature physically. Two of the best classical scholars I have come in contact with entered the University of Aberdeen at fourteen; and I have known several who would have done much better to come a year or two earlier than they did. Yet seventeen has been the most common age in my experience, although the average is raised by a certain number of much older students. In such matters averages are quite valueless as a standard to apply to an individual case.

Moreover, it always remains an open question how much Paul learned from the educated atmosphere in which he was brought up as a boy, how much from formal instruction

[1] Even though, as I think, *neos* (strictly, a fully-grown man of military age) encroached on and displaced *ephebos* (Latin *adulescens*, a youth approaching full growth, about seventeen or eighteen) in Anatolian usage, still a boy of thirteen would hardly be even an *ephebos*.

in public classes, and how much from training by individual teachers in his own home.   There is a general tendency, of which I find numberless examples in my own circle of acquaintance, to set down to the credit of schooling much which is due simply to the natural growth of the intellectual and physical powers of the boy or girl.   One attributes to the influence of the school a good deal which would have been learned apart from school.   I do not intend or wish to depreciate school training: unless the school is very poorly managed, its influence is powerful and beneficent.   Especially in cases where custom or carelessness entrusts the education of a child mainly to schoolteachers and frees the parents largely from the onerous duty of training the child, the importance of the school and the school-teachers is incalculable.   Yet, even taking all this into account, I have nothing to retract from the above sentences.

This extra-scholastic training Paul received in abundance and in impressive and judicious form, as I should be inclined to gather from Philippians iii. 5.   Such training has always been characteristic of Jewish home life, and its central point and main force lay in the family festival of the Passover with its religious and historical lessons.

Probably Principal Garvie has built more than I should be ready to accept upon the single word " brought up " in Acts xxii. 3,[1] as if it necessarily implied the rearing of a child.   This, however, is too much to infer.   The simple and the compound verb are not used solely of children, a point on which we need not here enter.   The two passages, Acts xxvi. 4 and xxii. 3, taken together, seem to me to be perfectly satisfied by the interpretation that Paul, when he became old enough to choose for himself—an age which

----

[1] ἀνατεθραμμένος.

varies greatly in different persons—deliberately selected and devoted himself to the Divine service in his own land among his own people at the Holy City, and went up to Jerusalem to learn at the feet of Gamaliel. Other passages in his letters, especially Philippians iii. 15 and the *Apologia pro vita sua* in 1 Corinthians vii. 25 f.,[1] seem to me to require the interpretation that Paul was brought up to a certain stage at Tarsus in the fashion needed for a Jewish boy who was born in the local aristocracy as a Roman citizen and a burgess of Tarsus, and that with full knowledge and conscious choice he selected, like Moses, the life of serving God and his people through training in the Law at Jerusalem.

That Paul spoke the " Hebrew" language fluently seems in no way inconsistent with the upbringing in a Pharisaic household of Jews who were Roman citizens. In modern times I have known Jews who learned Hebrew early in life, though living in western European lands, far removed from many of the influences which were acting on a strict Jewish household in Tarsus, such as the visits to Jerusalem for the feasts and the easy free connexion with the Holy City. That a household of Graeco-Roman citizens should at once remain strictly Jewish and yet be learned in all the wisdom and the subtlety of the Roman Imperial world of the East, seems to me quite natural and in perfect accordance with previous and subsequent Hebrew history.

(2) Principal Garvie says that "Paul's familiarity with Greek and Roman life as shown in his metaphors, the last argument which Sir William Ramsay offers, seems to me adequately accounted for by what I have freely conceded of Gentile influence on Paul in his early years, in his travels, in his visits to his native city ". As to Paul's "early years," that is the point in discussion ; and the Principal seems

---

[1] *Expositor*, October, 1900, p. 288 f.

to concede at one time what he refuses at another. According to his own expression on p. 472, "Jewish exclusiveness would have prevented what" he here concedes. If it was allowed by his parents and the national Jewish feeling in Tarsus that Paul should mix so freely in childhood with the Greeks, that he learned to speak with wonderfully sympathetic insight[1] regarding the intensity of effort in sports (which were abhorred by the strict Palestinian Jews), and to compare this intensity of effort needed in athletic sports with the spirit needed for living the truly religious life, why should he be debarred from coming into any relation with the Greek education, which was absolutely necessary to enable his father to play his part as a Roman citizen and a Greek burgess?   As a boy under fourteen he was, on that theory, allowed to come during his most impressionable age into a position of complete familiarity with the spirit of Greek athletic and municipal life, so that words and ideas taken from it suggest themselves to him in the mood and at the moment when he is most inspired with the beauty and character of the true life.   When he rises to the most sublime utterance regarding the magnificence and perfection and glory of the Saviour's victory on the cross, he expresses his glowing thought in metaphor from a Roman triumph, which of course he could never have seen and about which he could have learned only in the course of a Roman education in the duties and dignity of Roman citizenship.

All this implies, so far as I can judge, a deep and hearty comprehension of Graeco-Roman life, and remains wholly inexplicable without that comprehension.   Who can comprehend without sympathy?   The idea is unthinkable.

---

[1] The sympathetic feeling which breathes through the words of Paul in several cases can be appreciated only by those who have competed with the enjoyment of childhood in such athletic games.

Nor does later Gentile influence on Paul " in his travels and in his visits to his native city," seem to me to furnish any adequate explanation. Either the visits took place during the years when he was still young and impressionable —the very point under discussion—or they were too late to meet the facts of the case. I do not think that he went to Jerusalem to study there during some months of each year, and returned to Tarsus to spend his holidays at home, like a modern University undergraduate. He went to Jerusalem to devote his life to his people and his God and the Law of God. Experiences such as he had in his travels as a Christian, when he was over thirty, or perhaps over forty, do not mould the inmost spirit in such a way that metaphors from those experiences rise to the mind in moments of deep feeling, as is the case with a number of the athletic metaphors used by Paul to express the ideas that he thought most holy and Divine. Principal Garvie, as I think, is in some places thinking of the Tarsian-Roman Paul, while in other places he attributes to him the feelings of a narrow Palestinian Jew.

There is not the shadow of a trace of evidence that either Paul or the Hellenistic Jews considered Greek philosophy to be in itself " a corrupting influence ". Nor does Principal Garvie adduce any evidence to that effect : he only speaks on p. 472 of Greek philosophy as a thing which Paul " must have regarded as a corrupting influence ". Certainly Paul was in the last degree unlikely to spend any time after he became a Christian in studying philosophy. So far every one will agree. Paul had already gone through it and come out on the other side (as the Oxford undergraduate said about Jowett and Hegelianism). It was not necessary for a mind like Paul's to spend long years in studying Greek philosophy, as the ordinary modern College pupil

does.   He caught up its ideas and traversed the philosophy
of his time as a great mathematician sweeps over a new
treatise in his subject, making himself master of it all in the
time that an ordinary person would spend in failing to
comprehend the first few pages: the mathematical genius
recognises much that is already half consciously outlined in
his own mind.

Let us take an analogous case from the character of the
legislation of Moses (if, for the sake of illustration, and
without any disrespect to some great modern scholars who
deny that an individual corresponding to the name Moses
ever existed, we may assume for the moment the reality of
his life and work): one might argue that he was a highly
educated man, familiar with all the wisdom of his time.   It
is probable that this inference would be controverted on
the ground that Moses was too characteristic and patriotic
and enthusiastic a Jew to have studied extraneous literature
deeply, were it not for the recorded fact that Moses was
educated mainly in that non-Jewish wisdom.

So it was and must be with Paul.   We know about Moses
from the record.   We know about Paul only from his writings ;
and they show him to be not only a typical " Hebrew sprung
from Hebrews," but also a man capable of mixing on equal
terms with the educated men of the Graeco-Roman world.
Similarly, Luke describes him as discussing philosophy with
the Athenian Stoics and Epicureans, and giving a specimen
of his philosophic teaching before the Court of Areopagus,
as a friend of the educated Asiarchs in Ephesus, and aston-
ishing the Roman governor in Cyprus by his exposition of
moral principles.

It was the wideness of Paul's early experiences and training
that made him the one Apostle able to appreciate fully, to
lay special emphasis on, and to make clear to the world the

spirit of freedom and the universalism in the teaching and life and death of Jesus.[1] See pp. 33-36.

It is sometimes asserted that it was not Paul's previous education, but his present experience of Christ as Saviour and Lord, which so vitalised for him those features of the teaching of Jesus that others had failed to appreciate.[2] But this "present experience of Christ as Saviour" was as vividly and vitally present to the other Apostles as to Paul; and the question is, why at first they "failed to appreciate" the side which Paul appreciated. It was the individuality, the nature, the character of Paul which, after he had been laid hold of by Jesus, "vitalised for him features . . . which others had failed to appreciate"; and Paul, in his whole nature, had been made by his entire education and previous experience.

The rest did not catch this feature as Paul did; but as soon as Paul caught it and stated it clearly, the other Apostles as a body appreciated it, and accepted Paul's position. The only Christian who seemed to be on the point of catching the Pauline view before Paul was Stephen, the great Hellenist Jew.

The experience of a higher teacher is always the same. Let him state his view as clearly as he can to a class, and he is fortunate if even one catches immediately the spirit, and what the teacher deems the fundamental truth of the teaching. The rest, however devoted and in a sense appreciative, are Wagners to this Faustus.

Principal Garvie and I are so far in agreement that we regard the Jewish inheritance and nature and home training

---

[1] It is in my view necessary to hold closely together in thought the three : the teaching was of small value without the life and the death. So Paul held, and such is the fact. That is the one answer to those who maintain that the historical truth of the life and the death of Jesus is unimportant, and that what is really important for the world is His teaching.

[2] Quoted from Principal Garvie.

as the fundamental and dominant factor in the thought and life of Paul.   First of all, at all times, in all situations, we feel in him the Jew.   But I incline to lay more emphasis on the fact that in Paul we feel always the educated Jew, trained to life as a Roman citizen in the most aristocratic position among the population of the great Hellenised, yet more than half Asiatic, city of Tarsus.   Principal Garvie would lay less stress on this side of Paul's complex individuality.   I can understand the philosophic position of Paul only on the theory that the expression of his views was influenced by Greek philosophy, whereas the Principal (if I rightly apprehend him) thinks that it was not so influenced.   The difference is, in a sense, slight ; yet it implies considerable difference in our estimate of Paul's cast of thought and his early training.   In the following sections I shall attempt to put my own conception from my own point of view.

Only in regard to one sentence of Principal Garvie's last article [1] must I wholly and absolutely disagree.   He says on p. 471, "to me it seems more probable that Paul was more affected by the Tarsian environment on his visit after his conversion than during his early years".   On the contrary the influence which I seem to see in Paul is one that lies too deep to belong to his mature life, and one that depends on circumstances too inharmonious with his mental attitude after he became a Christian to be assigned to that period.   Only in childhood and the earliest youth is such an influence possible.   That Paul during his long residence in Cilicia and Syria, after he fled from Jerusalem, was still engaged in thinking out the philosophic basis of his religious position I would fully concede, though probably the most important part of that work had already been done

[1] In the *Expositor*, November, 1911.

in the Arabian solitude ; but nothing seems to be more unlikely than that during even the final stage of this process he should be studying Greek philosophy or Hellenic manners and customs.   In recasting his religious and philosophical position, his whole previous education served to mould the definition of his new thought, as it gradually took clear form in his mind, and his entire past life was an infinitely more important influence in determining that form than the circumstances of the present moment in Cilician society.

VII. St. Paul and St. John [1]

The relation between Paul and John is important for the comprehension of the New Testament as a whole. What is adumbrated in Paul, is wrought out finally in John's Gospel and his First Epistle to its absolute perfection. Paul inaugurates, and John completes, the New Testament.

Yet to us in the West it is sometimes necessary to read Paul in order to understand John : often Paul comes nearer to our way of thought than John. Always, however, each must be read in the light of the other. We are conscious of a definite evolution of the religious consciousness as we pass from Paul to John ; but it is an evolution towards full comprehension of the original teaching of Jesus ; and it is by no means the case that, as some scholars have maintained in recent times, the " Church's consciousness " constructed for itself a new religious thought. From first to last both Paul and John were moving within the drift of Christ's thought : they were both interpreting, according to their nature and experience, the true content of His teaching.

We cannot regard John's Gospel as specially comprehensible to the Gentiles, though it was written in Asia for Asiatic Hellenes. It is deeply Palestinian in its cast of thought and expression ; and the religious atmosphere in which it moves is non-Hellenic to a greater degree than the writings of Paul, which are more strongly tinged with Hellenism. Inasmuch

---

[1] This Section is nearly the same as Chapters XVII. and XVIII. of *The First Christian Century*, as the writer discovered only on August 17, 1913. Another example would have been chosen, if he had remembered that this was the case. Yet the mistake was useful, as it led to a discovery stated on p. 55.

as John wrote in Asia Minor, perhaps at Ephesus, a sort of prepossession has grown up that his Gospel was most easily understood by Greeks. Yet early quotations do not justify the belief that his Gospel was most popular, or most frequently read by the early Gentile Christians. On the contrary, as Principal Iverach has pointed out, John is much less frequently quoted by the early Gentile Christian writers than the other Gospels.

I take here one slight example of what seems to me a wrong way of contemplating the writings of John and their relation to the older Christian books. This is an example which is more of manner and style than of thought, and yet one that is of considerable interest. It occurs in Dr. Moffatt's *Introduction to the Literature of the New Testament*, where on p. 562 we find it stated " as a feature of the later age" that, in the Fourth Gospel, "the dialogues beginning with the introduction of some figure pass over into a disquisition or monologue in which the author voices, through Jesus, his own or rather the Church's consciousness, usually upon some aspect of the Christology which is the dominant theme of the whole book. The original figure is forgotten, . . . and presently the so-called conversation drifts over into a doctrinal meditation upon some aspect of Christ's person."

One marvels, first of all, at the phrase " so-called conversation". Where is any of the given instances called "conversation"? Certainly not by John, who thought of them in a very different way. Who calls them conversation? Solely and simply the modern writer, who has never apprehended the manner, or imagined to himself the purpose and intention, that rule the Fourth Gospel. To him what he calls a " conversation" must be and remain a conversation.

Take just one of all these examples—in chapter iv. of this Gospel the disciples, when they came back to the well, found Jesus, "and they marvelled that He was talking

with a woman: yet no man said. 'What seekest thou?' or
'Why speakest thou with her?'" The verbs that are used,
ζητεῖν and λαλεῖν, are perfectly suitable to the investigation
of problems and to formal exposition. The woman herself
went to the city and told the men, "Come and see a man
which told me all things that ever I did: can this be the
Christ?" There is here no word about a conversation. The
woman recognised instantly that, in continuation of the re-
quest by a traveller for water at a well's mouth (the commonest incident of travel in the East), what might have turned
into a conversation in the usual tone between a man and a
woman alone at a well became at once a serious discussion
about the greatest and gravest things in life; and she drew
the inference, "Can this be the Christ?"

The scholar in his study, however, can see here only a
"so-called conversation," and marvels that this conversation
ever became anything else.

We see, then, that John does not use the term "conversation," or anything corresponding to it: he was interested in these "so-called conversations" on account of the
doctrinal meditation into which they pass. They begin as
personal scenes, often marvellously individualised; and they
gradually or instantaneously pass into an exposition. But
why not? Why should the author be debarred from following out his own bent? He has produced the greatest book
in all literature by doing so; but the modern scholar cannot
see the greatness and forbids the method.

In the second place, why is this method peculiar to and
characteristic of the second century? Why was it impossible in the first century? The assumption is that it is a
"feature of a later age": no evidence is offered for the
assumption; there is none. The modern writer starts with
the fixed idea that the book is late, and anything and everything in the book becomes to him forthwith a proof of

lateness. He never asks why the detail is late, or what marks it as of the second century. He simply assumes.

In the third place, there is stated in a footnote one single analogy to the method which we find in John; and this analogy is taken from one of the few parts of the New Testament which admittedly has been composed in the first century, and at the very beginning of Christian literature, *viz.*, the Epistle to the Galatians ii. 15 f. This analogy stands in a footnote, and is perhaps an afterthought; but how can a critic, by a quotation from a first century book, prove his assumption that this method of John's could only be originated in the second century? Because John uses the method, it is late; and his Gospel is late because it uses the method.

The argument then proceeds that "this method [in the Fourth Gospel] precludes the idea that the author could have been an eye-witness of these scenes, or that he is reproducing such debates from memory". Why so? What proof is given of this? None, except some German opinion and the passage from the Epistle to the Galatians. Now, that passage is autobiographical : Paul relates his own debate with Peter, and gradually "drifts over into a doctrinal disquisition," while "the original figure is forgotten," and we hear no more about Peter and have no "record of his final attitude or the effect which he produced".

It would not be easy to produce a more perfect parallel. The critic knows it, and quotes it, and argues that, inasmuch as this method was used by Paul in the first century, therefore it could not be used by John, but that its occurrence in a work bearing John's name proves that the work was written in a later age. Is this historical reasoning, or literary criticism, or sheer prepossession with a fixed idea that anything and everything observed in the Fourth Gospel is, and must be, a proof of lateness and "pseudonymous origin"?

In the fourth place, with regard to this method, which the critic unhesitatingly takes as indicating second century origin without any proof that it is usual in the second century —simply assuming that such a way of writing belongs to the second century, of which we know extremely little— I would venture to maintain that the method is peculiarly characteristic of the first century. It belongs to the period when the facts were still close at hand, and not afar off: it belongs to the period when the lesson and the moral and the principle were still felt to be the most important—not that I believe the facts ever were regarded as in themselves unimportant, but they were at first more familiar and were assumed as familiar.

Finally, this method is very characteristic of Paul, who slips so unconsciously from narrative of events to his own inferences from them, that it is hard to tell where narrative ends and hortatory inference takes its place.

So it is in the passage quoted, as above, from Galatians ii. 13 ff. So again it is in the passage 1 Corinthians xi. 25-34, where I defy any one to detect at what point the narrative passes from a direct simple recital of the words of Jesus, first into what may be a drawing out of the truth involved in the words, then into what must be such an exposition, and finally into a pure hortatory lesson deduced by Paul from what he began as a narrative. There is in the passage no desire and no intention to paint a picture or describe a scene. There is only the intense and overmastering passion to bring out the bearing of the acts and words on the present situation.

To put the case in a word, the method of John in this respect is the method of Paul. If one belongs to the first century, there is no reason why the other also should not belong to the same century.

We may add that the story of the Samaritan woman was

known to Luke. In a noteworthy passage, Acts xvi. 13 ff., the historian tells how Paul and his companions came to a new country, where the Gospel was strange. They went to a stream, and sat, and talked with the women, especially one, who was influential, possessed of capital to deal in expensive foreign cloth, head of a household, which did as she directed. Her influence "opened a door" for Paul. Jesus came to a new country, where His message was strange. He sat by a spring and talked to a woman. She was influential, and brought the men to see and hear one who was perhaps Christ. Like Jesus, Paul was entreated to stay. The analogy proves that the story was familiar in Christian circles in the first century, and was not an invention of the fourth Gospel.

The small point which we have been considering is an example of method, and we find that even in method the same unstudied and unconscious way of allowing narrative gradually to change into reflection and lesson is common to both Paul and John.

It would lead far beyond the plan of this book to compare the two apostles, and to show how the same teaching is in each coloured by the individual character of the writer. Only on one point does it aid our purpose to dwell for a moment in the following section.

VIII. The Confident Faith of Paul and John

The spirit of absolute and unhesitating confidence in the truth and certainty of their message is common to both Paul and John. They know that the facts have occurred, and they know that the victory is assured. Not a trace of wavering or hesitation can be found in their writings. Where in rare cases an expression of doubt occurs in Paul's letters, it is regarding his own strength and endurance; yet even about his own power he rarely speaks doubtfully, because the strength is given him sufficient for the duty; his weakness gives the better opportunity for the Divine power to act through him.[1]

Two words and two ideas are particularly characteristic of John: these are "love" and "victory". Paul conjoins them in a typical sentence, "we are more than conquerors through Him that loved us and gave Himself for us".[2] The sentence is almost as typical of John as it is of Paul. There is almost an echo of it in Revelation i. 5, "Unto Him that loved us, and loosed us from our sins by His blood, and made us to be a kingdom, . . . to Him be the glory and the dominion".

The idea of victor or conqueror is specially characteristic of the Revelation. The victor is he that is "faithful unto death,"[3] he "that keepeth my works unto the end".[4] It is a characteristic trait that this is the book, and this the time, when victory was most dominant in the writer's mind. He was a prisoner condemned to hard labour on a rocky islet of the Aegean Sea. Against him was arrayed all the power

[1] 2 Cor. xi.   [2] Rom. viii. 37.
[3] Rev. ii. 10.   [4] Ibid. ii. 26.

56

and majesty of the mighty Empire. The Emperor's policy was to exterminate this little sect. Yet every Christian martyr's death was a victory. Every conflict was a new opportunity for showing how powerless the great Roman Empire was against this little band of men. If in any case the Emperor gained an apparent victory and coerced some individual into obedience to his command, this was only because that individual was unfit to be a member of the conquering band, which won victory after victory by unfaltering faith and quiet endurance.

In a sense, however, the victory lies in the future: the Empire shall continue a long time. There shall be ten Emperors ;[1] in the Eastern imagery of prophecy and revelation "ten" means a large number, but still a number that is finite and comes to an end. This future series of sovereigns "receive authority as Emperors *for one hour*".[2] I know of nothing more strikingly, more completely triumphant than this expression. All this long and stately succession of sovereigns over the mighty Empire of Rome hold authority *for one hour*. An hour was the smallest division of time known to the ancients: they speak of "the movement of an hour," *viz.*, the time that the shadow on the dial requires to move from one line to the next, where we should use the expression "in a minute," or more hyperbolically, "in one second".

The same thought occurs in Paul :[3] "our momentary light affliction worketh for us more and more exceedingly an eternal weight of glory". It is a thought natural to such men at such a time. In their estimation time sinks into insignificance when compared with eternity: duration in time is nothing: whether long or short, that which is measured by time, and which reaches an end, is of no consequence. Patient endurance for the moment is the law

---

[1] Rev. xvii. 12. [2] *Ibid.* [3] 2 Cor. iv. 17.

that both John and Paul inculcate in regard to the evils of the present political system in the world.   In every one of the seven letters to the Churches, John emphasises the same moral: he that is faithful unto death, he that endureth, is the victor.   Paul discourages all political agitation. Such action puts the ephemeral in place of the eternal, and labours for the evanescent and the valueless instead of the enduring and real things of life.   Seek for the real and permanent, seek after the kingdom of Heaven: all other things will come about of themselves.

In modern phraseology something of the same truth would be expressed by saying that true political progress is better attained by the growth of higher moral spirit throughout the community, by the spread of education, by the gradual emergence of the people generally on a higher plane of thought and judgment and ideals.   True progress has to be bought by work and by suffering; and the work is the work of God, not the work of the devil.   Nothing can be permanently attained by war or by fire or by sword or by modern engines of destruction.   These are the works of the devil.   As Paul says,[1] "the works of the flesh are manifest which are . . . enmities, strife, jealousies, wraths, factions, divisions, parties, envyings . . . they which practise such things shall not inherit the Kingdom of God.   But the fruit of the Spirit is love, joy, peace, long-suffering, kindness, goodness, faithfulness, meekness, self-control.   Against such there is no law."

If apparently any progress seems ever to be achieved in that way of violence, the price is not yet paid and has to be paid in double assessment, in the only coin that the law of God accepts, in work and in suffering.   We are now in Great Britain paying the price for the "reforms" that were apparently gained by violence in the middle of the nine-

[1] Gal. v. 19-23.

teenth century; the price lies in the false methods, the resistance to law, whether passive or active, the industrial war and the general unrest, and all the other myriad disorders of the present social system. The "reforms" are not real or beneficial until the people as a whole has earned them by deserving them and by ability to use them wisely.

Through the Revelation there runs a tone of exultation over the fall of Rome, the desolation of the great capital of the world. This is spoken of in Chap. xviii. as if it had already taken place; but that is a prophetic figure. What is absolutely certain is stated by the prophet as now happening or already completed. The prophet stands outside of time; he speaks on the plane of eternity; there is to him no future and no past; all is present before his vision.

In the Revelation the strain of exultation is almost too highly wrought, and has in it something of the old Hebrew fierceness. In the middle of the conflict John saw only the evil of the great Empire. The Empire was the enemy of God, bent on exterminating the congregation of Christ, and thereby merely bringing about its own annihilation. He did not see, or does not remember, that the great Empire formed part of the Divine plan: he has no thought of what it achieved in its own imperfect fashion, the comparative peace which it introduced in place of general war, the order and the degree of freedom which it maintained through the whole Mediterranean world, the security of life and the freedom of speech which it substituted for the constant dread of spoliation and oppression, and which had given the Church the opportunity to teach, and to spread through the provinces of the Empire, and to establish itself even in the great city, the Roman Babylon. All this Paul, on the other hand, recognised and emphasised; but he also recognised quite as thoroughly as John that the Roman government must pass away, that it was false in its methods, that it could not permanently tolerate the Church of God, that its deep-seated antagonism and opposition to the Church must become manifest. The Emperor pretended to sit in the sanctuary of God, and flaunted himself as the incarnate God in human form; and no lasting peace could exist between the Imperial rule and the Divine order of the world. In the due season this must be revealed, and the Lord shall then come and shall annihilate the Empire and its system and its power. This however, as Paul says, is not in the present; it lies in the future; and it cannot be until the real character of the Empire and the false God-Emperor has been made clear and unmistakable, i.e. until the Empire has outlived its time and become an evil and a hindrance instead of a partial protection to the Church as the restrainer of the worst evils of disorder, anarchy, bloodshed and war.[1]

In the Revelation the tone of exultation over the fall of Babylon-Rome is so unmixed with any consciousness of the mission of the Empire as to be painful and almost repellent to the student of history. This tone belongs to the moment of battle; it is the tone of the horrified spectator, who from his island-prison marked the course of the struggle, and the martyrdom of one after another of the patiently resisting saints, beginning with " Antipas, my witness, my faithful one, who was killed" at Pergamon, where is the temple and throne of the Emperor-Satan.[2]

Amid all the wonderful imagery and the splendid confidence in and insight into the Divine purpose, which characterise the Revelation, this one-sidedness prevents it from reaching the highest plane of Divine Truth. It does not stand on the level of the fourth Gospel: it falls below the level of Paul's insight and sympathy. Yet it marks a stage in the development of John: it explains the one great

[1] 2 Thess. ii. 2 ff. See p. 253 and *The Cities of St. Paul*, Part VII.
[2] Rev. ii. 13.

pyschological difficulty of the fourth Gospel: it shows the
training by which the disciple who is mirrored to us in
the Synoptic Gospels could grow into the writer of the
fourth Gospel.[1]

After war comes peace.   After the stress and storm of
conflict comes the quiet spirit of restful victory.   Then—

> The worst turns the best to the brave;
>   The black minute's at end;
> And the element's rage, the fiend voices that rave,
>   Shall dwindle, shall blend,
> Shall change, shall become first a peace out of pain,
>   Then a light.

This is the spirit of the fourth Gospel; this is the spirit
of " love " that characterises it.   It rests quietly in victory;
but it does not speak or boast of victory like the Revelation.   It is pitched entirely on the key of quietness, of
perfect assurance, of absolute sympathy with the Divine
nature, the Divine purpose, and the love of God.   This
makes it the one greatest book in the world: it rests
steadily on the level to which Paul is struggling, and to
which he attains with difficulty.   We mark in Paul the
striving towards this level, and the attainment of it in
moments of highest insight and revelation.   We mark in
the fourth Gospel the calm peace of him who has attained
this level, who attained it through the living death of the
convict in Patmos,[2] from which he emerged into a second
life for the Church after having gazed on the mysteries of
life and death.

This is the reason why it has been said[3] that the New
Testament begins with Paul and ends with John.   It begins

---

[1] On this see the exposition in the writer's *Letters to the Seven Churches.*

[2] The condemnation to hard labour on an island-prison was regarded as
one of the severest forms of punishment, worse than simple death, and on a
level with exposure to wild beasts.

[3] Section II.

with the man always straining onwards towards the higher life. It ends in the man who has attained and has passed through the gate of a living death into life. The fourth Gospel is the climax of the New Testament; and there the Testament must end, for there is nothing to add.

The force which moved in Paul and John is an idea that will constantly come up in the rest of this book. This force is Faith, " an intense and burning enthusiasm inspired through over-mastering belief in, and realisation of, the nature of Jesus—an enthusiasm which drives on the man in whose soul it reigns to live the life of Jesus". This force we cannot define more clearly: we see it, but we cannot analyse it, or tell its constituents: it is the ultimate and simple Divine fire. Yet we must constantly speak of it and assume it as known. To know it rightly you must come in contact with it, and be possessed by it. Accordingly, much of what is said in these chapters will depend for its understanding on the vividness with which one appreciates the meaning and force of Faith.

According to Paul, Faith leads on to freedom. Error or sin is an enslavement of the mind:[1] the Divine nature is freedom. Freedom is the consciously chosen identification of one's own will with the Will of God and the order of nature through which that Will expresses itself: when that is achieved, all the evolution of the Will of God around us is the free expression and realisation of our own will and choice. Freedom is the end and goal of self-realisation: we have not reached, but we are striving towards it.[2] " Ye were called with a view to freedom," and " with freedom Christ set us free ".[3]

---

[1] Rom. vi. 17 : "ye were the slaves of sin "; cp. 22 f.

[2] This is quoted from the writer's statement in *Pictures of the Apostolic Church*.

[3] Gal. v. 13 and 1.

PART II. THE THOUGHT OF PAUL

IX. THE BASIS OF PAUL'S THOUGHT—(I) GOD IS

Probably no one will hesitate as to what was the fundamental principle in the thought of Paul. His whole mind was built on the foundation : *God is.*

It was impossible for a true and patriotic Jew in his time to doubt about this fundamental truth. The glory of the Jewish race lay in its firm grasp of this principle. Many generations and many centuries had been needed to weld the belief into the fabric of the Jewish mind. Only after many errors, many lapses, many a slipping back into polytheism, did this fundamental principle at last establish itself. The books of Moses, the reiteration of the Ten Commandments, the family teaching and the Passover, could only by slow degrees eradicate any possibility of an alternative from the mind of the Jews. The age of the great Prophets and the teaching of history at last fixed it deep in the Jewish heart.

To the Jew the whole glory of Hebrew history was concentrated in this belief. This it was that distinguished his people from every other nation. One people alone held firmly the truth, to which here and there amid other races a great philosopher or a great poet attained by a rather halting and uncertain course. So Aeschylus had attained it : " Zeus, whatever He is and by whatever title it is right to call Him, I address Him by this name ".[1] How great a statement this is ! How much it contains of Greek history

[1] *Agamemnon*, 152.

and of Greek thought. Yet how poor it seems in comparison with the simple and majestic principle of the Jews : *God
is—the living and real God.*

Every great man in the Jewish race had been great in
virtue of his firm hold on this truth ; and his greatness had
been proportionate to the firmness of his grasp. To doubt
the existence of the One Living God was to destroy the
basis on which the nation's greatness rested.

Paul never attempts to demonstrate the existence of God :
he assumes His existence. The fool might say in his heart
"there is no God"; but Paul does not speak to the fools
and cannot be understood by them. He starts from this
principle always. He addresses only those who believe it,
however wavering and insufficient may be their hold on it,
whether they do so by nature or through the compelling
and convincing power of experience in life. Paul presumes
a certain element of wisdom and insight among those whom
he addresses. The absence of this elementary power of
rightly judging he regarded as a proof of moral degeneration,
i.e. of sin.

He does not attempt to prove to his hearers that *God is.*
They must see it for themselves. God has not left Himself
without witness, in that He did good and gave them from
heaven rain and fruitful seasons.[1] These are the free
gifts of God. Men recognise this, and know that it is He
who is filling their hearts with food and gladness. To the
present day in Paul's own Asia Minor a bounteous spring
flowing from the rock or the earth and transforming the
ground through which it flows from a dry desert into a
fruitful garden, is called by those who enjoy its benefits,
Hudaverdi, "God-has-given".

To such men, who had understood this elementary fact

[1] Paul and Barnabas in Acts xiv. 17.

of the world, Paul addressed himself.[1] To the rest, a few
so-called philosophers, he did not speak. This address
opened the pagan world of Greece and Rome to him, for
almost all accepted this principle after some fashion. The
Divine power, which they worshipped without recognising
its real nature, he set forth to them. He pointed out all
that followed from this initial and fundamental truth.

To Paul and to every Jew the living God was a real
power, external to man : He was not the creation of human
thought, but independent thereof, not a phantom of the
mind, but an absolute and self-existent reality. Further, as
man has been made in the image of God, this self-existent
primal reality is a person. He lives.

From this axiom that there is one personal God, the single
self-existent and all-powerful reality, Paul's thought began.
To him it was the starting-point of all thinking and the
guarantee of man's power to think rightly : it was driven
home into his nature by the generations that lay behind him,
self-evident and final, an ultimate and direct perception
not demonstrable by reasoning or argument, but recognised
intuitively. In the perception of one's own existence there
is involved the recognition or the assumption of the existence of God. You cannot get behind that. Thought moves
onward from that.

Such, then, is Paul's position. You must have that or
nothing. In God alone is confidence. With Him the
world becomes intelligible and real, as the envisagement or
the work of God. Without Him the attempt to think and
to live is a rudderless drifting on a troubled sea.

This direct perception Paul would call the first expression
of Faith. By Faith we know this primal truth. " Faith is
the giving substance to things hoped for, the test of things

[1] Acts xvii. 23.

not seen. . . .[1] By Faith we understand that the universe has been framed by the word of God."   Faith is the guide and the moving force in every right act of human life. Without this power of Faith we cannot make even one sure step.

To the loose and vague thinker this seems a big assumption—but that is only because he thinks loosely and vaguely.

[1] Hebrews xi. 1 may be quoted as indirectly attesting the ideas of Paul. That Epistle was composed in communication with him, by an intimate friend who expresses from an independent point of view and in non-Pauline words the fundamental idea of Paulinism (see a paper on this subject in the writer's *Pauline and other Studies in the History of Religion*).

X. The Basis of Paul's Thought—(2) God is Good

The religion of Paul was definitely and absolutely inconsistent with the characteristic Oriental doctrine of a pantheistic type. Yet all such forms of thought start, as Paul
did, from the perception that man by the very fact of his
existence is separated from God and ought to aim at reunion with Him.

Why then did not Paul take the step which so many
Asiatic forms of religious thought have taken? How did
he avoid the pantheistic view and the inference from it,
which was so tempting to an intensely emotional and de-
votional nature like his, that man should seek re-absorption
in the Divine through liberation from the human nature,
that man should strive to lose his individuality and to be
merged in the one God? So far as we have yet gone, we
do not see where and why Paul, starting from the same
initial principle, diverged so widely from the general trend
of Oriental religious thought.

He was saved from this step by the whole force of
Hebrew tradition and the promise given to his fathers.
The Promise had been made and must be fulfilled; and
fulfilment of the Promise led in the diametrically opposite
direction from that dream of absorption in the Divine
nature, which was the goal of the highest Asiatic religious
thought outside of the Hebrew people. The fulfilment of
the Promise lay in the perfecting of the race through the
perfecting of the individual, not through the annihilation of
his individuality.

The Promise is just a more simple expression, such as an early people could most readily understand, of the philosophic principle that God is good. In the act of creation God has bound Himself; He has given a pledge or a Promise. He will never violate the Promise, which He has repeated often to His chosen people. What God has done must be good and perfect; it cannot fail or become worse; it must grow towards perfection. Man, who was made in the image of God, must attain to the true end of his nature in some way and by some process, planned from the beginning by God. This process was to be realised through the coming of the Messiah. That is the Promise, or the Covenant or Testament (διαθήκη).

Promise, Covenant, Testament, are terms that describe only in a crude and imperfect way the act which they designate. Being English terms, their meaning is not exactly the same as that of the ancient Greek or Hebrew words which they translate. Moreover, even the ancient terms denote human actions, whereas this action of God is unique and unlike any ordinary event: it is alone in its class, and names that describe other acts do not exactly suit this one. Yet each of these terms describes quite correctly some side or aspect of it. Like a promise this action of God's is purely voluntary: it comes entirely from one side and is received by the other: the giver is all-powerful, the receiver has no influence over it (except the influence of prayer). Like a covenant this action is legally binding and cannot be broken: it makes and is the law, and has all the force and inviolability of law. Like a testament[1] this action is a legal document, in which one party

---

[1] The term is not much used in the text of the English Version; but it is the ordinary rendering of the Greek term διαθήκη, and it is the name given to each part of the Bible.

alone confers by his free disposition complete validity and legal force, and in which the person benefited simply accepts without having any authority to influence the act. On the other hand, the term covenant is unsuitable in so far as it suggests the idea of two parties entering into a voluntary agreement: the term testament is free from the suggestion that there are two parties, but it has serious defects as implying that it is revocable at any time by change of mind in the testator, and that it comes into force only at his death [1]: the term promise loses all the solemnity and the terror (so to speak) of the law.

The Promise of God is the necessary expression of His goodness. It is His free gift to man, yet it arises inevitably from His character and His relation to man. It is the outcome of His nature, for His nature is love. The early Hebrews did not lay much stress on the love which is the nature of God. They dwelt far more on His power, as was inevitable in the earlier stages of their history, because wisdom began (as the Preacher says) with the fear of the Lord; and thus they were taught by the law as their pedagogue to obey and to be in a certain degree wise. Yet they had a firm hold on this expression of the love of God in the Promise, which implies that ultimately His love will be triumphantly and unmistakably manifested.

---

[1] Even in that early stage of the development of a testament, when it was instantaneous in its effect and irrevocable (according to Maine, *Ancient Law*), the testament denuded the giver to enrich the heir; but such a stage need not be considered.

XI. THIS PRINCIPLE IS SEEN, BUT CANNOT BE PROVED

That God is good, that He has made the Promise to the Hebrews and through them to the whole of mankind, was not a principle that Paul sought to prove by any ratiocination. He seems always to say to his audience, "You know it for yourselves". In the perception that God is, there is also involved according to Paul's view the perception that God is good. Only through a perversion of view can we imagine that God really exists without being good, for it is only through His gifts and goodness that we perceive His existence. From His works we know Him.

This principle was burned into Paul's nature by generations of experience. He was the heir to many centuries of Jewish history. None but a Jew could have had that perfectly firm and unhesitating grasp of this truth. The fabric of his thought is purely and simply Hebrew. Already before his birth he was marked out, first as Apostle, and secondly as Apostle to the nations, because the whole of Hebraism and all the results of Jewish wisdom and religious experience were interwoven in the constitution of his thought. He could not hesitate himself. He could not understand, nor sympathise with, nor pardon and make allowance for, any hesitation on the part of others. They must see. They must know. His own intense and unhesitating belief, the very fact that he could not allow any doubt, or seek to demonstrate to his hearers the axioms of the Faith, made him a power among men. Had he been capable of feeling and of pardoning doubt, he might have been greater as a lecturer on abstract philosophic theory, but he could never have become such a power in the world as he was and is.

Here again Faith is the initial force which makes men recognise this truth. Faith is really a force that moves the minds of men. It is not a mere fact : it is a driving power. The failure to recognise this truth is already a mark of de-generation and degradation, i.e. of sin, which deteriorates and distorts the will. Paul estimates the sanity and the working power of men according to their ability to discern and believe the unseen. The Divine truth is not to be handled and weighed with common scales. It is appre-ciable through the natural power, granted to all men, to recognise the truth, and the natural tendency to follow it. This power is Faith, and by their possession of the power we must estimate men.

These may seem to be two very big assumptions. What right has Paul to take as the obvious and necessary prin-ciples of right thinking, these two axioms, that God is, and that God is good? Is that philosophically justifiable, or must we admit that after all Paul had not thought out a philosophic basis for his religion, and that the Greek form of thinking was in the last resort alien to him and lay out-side of his circle of thought?

The refusal to doubt the truth of one's thought, however, is not necessarily a proof of an unphilosophic mind. The tendency to divest oneself of one's thought, to hold it apart from oneself and contemplate and reason about it, and frame arguments to justify it, was discordant with Paul's emotional and active nature. He found that this tendency became strong in his Hellenic Churches, as they were established. The purely philosophic mind was in danger of losing itself in abstract contemplation ; and all the while there were the Greek cities, the Roman Provinces, the barbarian tribes, the whole world, to conquer, to convince and to save.   Such abstract speculation was hateful to Paul. He saw in it the enemy taking a new form in his young Churches ; and as this enemy grew more clearly defined he denounced it with the vehemence of his nature.

Those who regard the thoroughgoing denunciation of this kind in the Pastoral Epistles as un-Pauline miss a certain side of Paul's nature.   In those letters he does not refute, but simply sets aside as wrong and hateful and fatal all the heresies and false teaching to which he refers.

In the case of a Church like Colossae, founded a few years ago by his coadjutors, or of the Galatian Churches, founded not long before by himself, he could in his letters regard their errors as due to a mistaken zeal for right.   Especially was that the case with the Galatian converts : they were full of eagerness to do well : they were unsparing in exertion and in the observing of useless yet burdensome ceremonies.   Their zeal had to be guided ; and the way to guide them was to proclaim and explain more fully the Gospel with its knowledge now revealed, i.e. its mysteries and their meaning.

Later, however, in the letters to Timothy at Ephesus, another method was needed.   It was vain to explain mysteries and revelation to those who were deliberately wasting the golden opportunities for making the resurrection known to the heathen and for saving the world, while they indulged in curious speculations about the nature of the resurrection and its time, and the meaning of time, and so on.   Such people had already too much knowledge, or rather too much conceit of their knowledge.   They did not need more knowledge, they wanted the whip and the rod.

There is a fit time for all things, a time for the refutation of errors by the imparting of further knowledge, and a time for denunciation and flat condemnation.   Just as Paul would have denounced the pagan hearer who declared that there was no God, and would have refused to argue where argument was vain and unprofitable, so in A.D. 66 he denounced the Ephesian Christians who theorised and allegorised and reasoned instead of acting.   The Christian life, to him, lay not in contemplation but in work.

Such was Paul's character.   Is it inconsistent with a consciously thought out basis for his action?   Is it unworthy of the mind that has passed through the philosophic stage, and gone on to the religious stage, and resolved to carry its religion to the world?   This impulse to move the world was to Paul the essential nature of God and of the man who is made in the image of God.   God exists to make and to perfect the world.   The world is His creature, and He is the Creator : but a creator who creates nothing is a contradiction in terms.   Equally self-contradictory and absurd is the creature that disregards its Creator and tries to ignore Him and to live without Him.   Every breath that we draw is through the Divine power.   Every thought that we think is through the Divine mind.   Nothing is rightly understood except in its relation to that First Power : the world becomes real only as the envisagement of Him.   If we refuse to recognise this, and if we turn away from God, we are reducing our own life to a negation ; and we are turning from life towards death.   There is no truth without this recognition of God : there is no real truth except this, that God is.   Every other truth arises out of this in orderly evolution.

That then is Paul's position, and it is a perfectly sound philosophic position.   As he says in Romans xi. 36, " from

Him and through Him and to Him are all things ".[1] Outside of Him there is nothing, for anything that existed apart from Him would be an independent existence over against Him, and therefore a negation of the truth that *God is*. So again in Ephesians iv. 6, " one God and Father of all, who is over all and through all and in all," [2] or in 1 Corinthians viii. 6, " to us there is one God the Father, from whom are all things and we unto Him,[3] and one Lord Jesus Christ through whom are all things, and we through Him ". Everything originates from God and returns to Him ; the Divine power through whom the world is maintained and carried on in its process or evolution is the Son and Saviour. God is the goal and final stage of salvation ; the process of salvation moves on " with a view to God," i.e. it is a process of returning through Jesus to its origin.

It is of course implied in this that God is not real and existent apart from the world which He has created. It is His nature to concern Himself with His creation, to regulate it, to make it good. It is the true nature of man to have faith in the justice and goodness of God, and never to regard Him as malevolent or as careless of man. The pagan doctrine that God is cruel and must be soothed and propitiated, the philosophic doctrine that the gods live a life apart from and heedless of the world, are both equally abhorrent to the Hebrew belief and to Paul as a Hebrew sprung from Hebrews.

In the nature of the real and true God it is also involved that He must be always in communication with the men whom He has created. They are not merely " from Him " : they are also " through Him ". In every act and thought and

---

[1] εἰς, i.e. with a view to Him, to attain to Him again.
[2] Compare Col. i. 19 f.
[3] εἰς, the same preposition as in Romans xi. 36, used with the same force.

word of theirs pulses the Divine power, for they are made after His fashion. He must rule and guide His creatures. They have to attain the goal and return "to Him". In doing so they realise His will and purpose. It is in accordance with the nature and consciousness of man that they must recognise that will in the process of realising it. To know it and to become conscious of it are equivalent to the working out of it in life. To know God's purpose and will you must make that purpose your life: nothing merely abstract and inactive is real knowledge. You must live it before you can know it.

This way of consciously living their knowledge comes only "through Him": therefore the knowledge is communicated by Him to man. Once more the motive power lies in Faith. The intense belief, this mighty driving power, brings man into relation with God. Man knows with all his heart and might that God cares for His creatures, and that He cannot stand apart and leave them unaided to their own devices; He is constantly guiding men, and revealing Himself to them if they will only listen to His voice. Everything that takes place in the world around us, when rightly understood, is the expression of His will and the declaration of His character. All the powers of nature are His messengers, and "if He thunder by law, the thunder is still His voice"; but most true it is that (as the prophet of old found) the Lord was not in the wind, nor in the earthquake, nor in the fire, but in "a sound of gentle stillness".[1] To each and every man, according to his nature, the will of God is manifested in the most suitable way, if he is ready to hear; and one must will intensely with all the power of one's nature, if the attaining unto God is to be possible.

[1] The literal translation, as given in the margin of the Revised Version (1 Kings xix. 12).

In the case of Paul the critical and epoch-making manifestation of the Divine will and nature took a form that
appealed primarily to the senses, and only subsequently to
the intellect. The reason why that fashion of revelation to
the man of most acute and powerful intellect among all
who were then living was suitable and necessary has been
discussed in Section IV.

Paul was well aware that revelation of the Divine purpose
may take place in many ways. In Acts xvi. 6-10 it is
described as having been made to him three times in three
different fashions: he himself must be the authority here.

The characteristic of all such revelation is absolute certainty. When a man has heard the Divine voice, there is left
no room for doubt. What he has heard or seen becomes a
lasting possession and a power in his life. He sees the
nature of the world and the permanent values of things in
a new way, and he cannot acquiesce in his former valuation
of them. In every case where a man, in what we might
call a moment of inspiration or exaltation, seems to himself
to appreciate more truly the nature of the world, his own
relation to God and to other men, and the worthlessness of
the things [1] that men chiefly strive after, Paul (as I doubt
not) would recognise a Divine revelation. There are such
moments, few or many, in every man's life, when conventional values are recognised as shams, and one stands face
to face with truth, or as Paul would say, with God.

Faith is the force that raises man above all hesitation
regarding the goodness of God. If the experience of life
instils a doubt, as the losses increase, as apparently purposeless and unmerited suffering obtrudes itself all around, as
friends depart—the one penalty of growing old—and life

---

[1] Philippians iii. 8, " I suffered the loss of all things, and do count them
but refuse ".

grows grey in their absence, or if history appals us with its crimes and massacres and the ruin of great civilisations, what is Paul's answer? Suffering is training and preparation : we must suffer that we may attain the glory of God : through Faith we have this assurance about the future : we must "suffer with Him, that we may be also glorified with Him : I reckon that the sufferings of this present time are not worthy to be compared with the glory that shall be revealed to us-ward ".[1] The assurance of this is the guarantee that it will be. Paul's feeling was expressed in the words of the old Hebrew prophet, " though He slay me, yet will I trust in Him ". The suffering, the evil, the disappointment, are a stage in the purpose of God.[2]

This reliance on the goodness of God we attain through the power of Faith, and do not learn through any process of ratiocination. We must feel that there is this Divine purpose and promise, that the world is the unfolding of the will of God, that the will of God is the soul of history, that "to suffer is to learn " (in the literal phrase of the Greek poet). But this you must assume—through Faith : you must accept —through Faith. To be able to do this you must strip off all your wisdom, you must get down to the simple first principle that God is good : you must be born again : otherwise you cannot hear the voice of God, and you cannot enter the Kingdom of Heaven. No merely intellectual acceptance can ever exercise any power over the deeper feelings of man.

---

[1] Romans viii. 17 f.

[2] τὸν ὑποτάξαντα, him who subjected it (Rom. viii. 20), is certainly God and not some power counteracting God.

XII. The Contact with Greek Thought

At this point [1] we begin to come in contact with Greek influence and Greek expression in Paul's conception of religion. Yet it would be a profound blunder to lay too much stress on this, or to infer from such a passage as Romans viii. 20 ff. that Paul regarded evil as undeveloped good, and as a necessary stage in the upward progress of man towards God. Gloss it over as you may, wrap it up in such form of words as you please, the Greek idea of sin or error is always involved in that opinion, which is radically opposed to the Hebraic and Pauline idea. To the Greek [2] what he might call sin (ἁμαρτία) was only a failure to hit the true aim, an overplus or a falling-short which keeps him from hitting the right mean: it was a mistake ultimately intellectual, a stage in the process towards true knowledge and wisdom and Sophia. However some Greek thinkers might attempt to introduce into their idea of "error" or "sin" an element of volition, they could not get free from this thoroughly Greek way of contemplating the problem of evil except by de-Hellenising their thought (as some were trying to do, though imperfectly and in theory); but of this, owing to the loss of most of their writings, we are imperfectly informed.

[1] That suffering is learning was the lesson on which Aeschylus insists, e.g. *Agamemnon*, 170.

[2] Aeschylus has a deeper and truer conception of sin than any other Greek of the Classical period: to him sin is typically the issue of ὕβρις, the arrogant trampling on the right order of nature.

To the Hebrew Paul, on the contrary, sin is not merely an error of the intellect : it is a deterioration and degradation of the will, progressive and illimitable, ending in death, as " righteousness " leads towards life. To the Greeks sin was a failure; to Paul it was a crime. The Greek blamed the Gods, or Fortune, or Necessity, or Ate, or some such superhuman conception, for his error. Paul laid the fault on man himself. To the Greeks, error was an episode, happily and usually only temporary, in the natural life, a failure to balance accurately the various powers of nature which unite to form the man's being, producing as a consequence the temporary ascendancy of one among these powers. In the estimate of Paul sin was a deliberate declination from nature, carrying man away from the Divine life, weakening his will and leading him inevitably onward in progressive deterioration, out of which the only hope of salvation lay in a reinvigoration of the power of Faith, so that the sinner might be strengthened in will towards salvation. To take a rough illustration, the career of a drunkard exhibits in a simple form the Pauline conception of sin ; the first indulgence weakens the moral power, which continuously deteriorates with fresh indulgence, so that there is no limit to the depths of infamy and degradation yawning to engulf the sufferer; no cure is of any value, no drug has any real influence, unless the will of the drunkard can be strengthened ; and (so far as experience shows) no salvation is possible for him except through reawakening his faith in the goodness and kindness of God.

In this simple case the contrast between the Greek and the Pauline view is clear. To the Greek the drunkard is a worshipper of the divine power Akrateia. To Paul he is a slave of the devil, turning his back on God and good and on faith in the goodness of God. To recreate Faith in the criminal is the only way of Salvation: no other force or power is of any avail.

Thus Faith is the force which makes a man capable of hearing the Divine will. The perfect belief that God does enter into communication with man and the strained eager longing to be so favoured are both necessary. Faith is not merely an intellectual belief: it is a moral and an emotional force. At every stage and in every act of the higher life, Faith is the one supreme requirement. Without it nothing can be achieved. With it everything becomes possible.

Although our examples and quotations must necessarily be taken from Paul's writings, and therefore belong to his Christian period, yet I cannot doubt that, when he was persecuting the Church, or still earlier, when he chose the Divine life and came to Jerusalem, he was eagerly bent on hearing and obeying the Divine voice. As he said to the High Priest and the Council, "I have lived before God in all good conscience unto this day"; and undoubtedly he included in this claim his early pre-Christian life. He had from infancy believed in the Promise, and was ready always to stake his life on the assurance that the Promise must be fulfilled and the Messiah must come. It was through a new revelation, made possible because of his unhesitating Faith in the Promise, that he learned that the Messiah had already come; and the conviction that his mind and life must be remade was the necessary result of this revelation.

As yet we have found no Greek element in Paul's thought except the way in which he explains the suffering and the apparent evil in the world. This is not necessarily or exclusively Greek; but, as we shall see, it is expressed by Paul in a form that is characteristic of Hellenic philosophy.

XIII. COMPARISON WITH THE CONFESSION OF ISLAM

Something can be gathered from a comparison between the Pauline basis of thought, as stated in these two principles, and the Confession of Islam. Mohammedanism is essentially a revival of the Hebrew religion in a form suited to appeal to the Arab tribes. Although (as I believe) it must have arisen in the soul of Mohammed after intercourse with Christians—and especially with Christians who had rejected the orthodox doctrine through disapproval of the stress which that doctrine laid on the person and the sacredness of the Mother of God—and although it accepts the Divine character of Jesus, yet it loses almost all the Christian development of Judaism and emphasises specially the older and simpler elements in the common Faith.

The Confession of Islam is expressed in two propositions. The first is practically identical with the first of the two Pauline axioms: it shows merely verbal variation, though there is much history and psychology and poetry (on which we need not dwell) underlying the difference: "there is no God but God". The second proposition exhibits very marked variation from the second Pauline axiom, yet the difference is less than appears superficially. "Mohammed is the Messenger of God": the stress is here laid on the personality of Mohammed, a historical fact explaining the development of Islam from the original Jewish Faith as expressed in the first proposition of the Islamic confession: Mohammed was the prophet and apostle to whom the further truth of Islam was revealed. In other words, revelation by God has been continuous and progressive through Judaism to Islam; the old Hebrew prophets had shared in this revelation of truth (as was fully admitted by Mohammed); but their knowledge required to be completed by Mohammed's revelation. The fact that Mohammed was a man to whom the truth was revealed by God is the guarantee offered by Islam that revelation of the Divine nature and will to man is always possible.

Thus, apart from the historical fact, the second proposition involves several fundamental truths about the nature of God. God reveals His truth to man in a progressive series of acts: He cares for man, and guides man's course in the world: He is good. Still, Islam lays little emphasis on the kindness or the love of God, even less emphasis than Judaism did. It has fallen back from the great progress which Christianity made in that respect. It lays almost all stress on the greatness, the power, the justice, the awfulness, of God: the Promise of God fades away into an extension of Islam by force, by massacre and slavery, by the Holy War, so that it shall become the universal religion by the extermination of unbelievers.

The comparison shows how thoroughly Hebraic was the texture of Paul's religious thought: the development of Hebraism in his mind was not an addition of any foreign or discordant element, but merely the explanation and emphasis of an element already existing. Even in Islam, that revival of Judaism, the same element is not wholly lost, but is left unemphasised and partly distorted.

XIV. The Promise the Free Gift of God, yet Earned by Man

The Promise is the free, gracious act of God, proceeding out of His own nature and purpose, and not earned by man as a reward or resulting from any joint agreement or bargain between the two parties. For example, some such bargain between God and man is supposed according to certain common pagan conceptions of sacrifice.

Prometheus offered a victim in sacrifice, and divided the carcase into two parts, offering the gods their choice; they chose the larger heap, which included all the bones and worthless parts of the victim, leaving to the offerer the finest portions of the flesh.

So, again, the Hindus acquired merit (*dharma*) proportionate to the number and splendour of the victims offered; and each acquisition of *dharma* was stored up as invested power in the bank of faith, until in one case a king acquired such an accumulation of strength as to be dangerous to the gods themselves. So in the common conception of Greek and Roman suppliants the act of prayer was a regular bargain between the worshipper and God; the suppliant entreated for such and such reward, stipulating by vow that he would pay so much in offering and gifts: if the deity thought the offering sufficient, he fulfilled the prayer, and the suppliant paid his vow: it was, however, always possible that the suppliant might cheat the god after the prayer was granted, though by such dishonesty he incurred the wrath of the god and was sure to suffer ultimately through some act of the divine power, for he had made his god his enemy.

So again the blood of the victim was in some cases regarded as a means of giving strength to the god and thus enabling him to fulfil the prayer of the suppliant.[1]

All such theories of the Divine nature were to Paul degrading to man and sure to work a deterioration in his character and conduct ; and this deterioration is progressive, increasing from stage to stage. The Promise and the gift of salvation are the free act of the goodness of God, unbought by man.

Yet while this act is perfectly free and not prompted by the conduct of man, it must be earned by man before it becomes operative. There is no contradiction between the two statements : the Promise is the free gift of God, and yet it must be earned by man. The two assertions seem to Paul to be quite harmonious.

As Paul said to the simple Lycaonian pagans of Lystra, rain and fruitful seasons are the free gift of God to men, "filling their hearts with food and gladness". The rain and the climate and the soil are always there ; but the food and gladness are gained by work. Before soil and rain can be made to produce harvest, there is much labour needed on the part of man. He has to earn the gifts before they become anything to him. He has to go out of himself, to expend energy, to sacrifice the present for the future, and to give a part of himself, before the free gifts of God materialise in real benefit to him.

There is always needed this double action, on the part

---

[1] This was specially characteristic of the cults in which the dead man, weak and bloodless in death, was yet an embodiment of superhuman power, that could be strengthened to help living men.

of God and on the part of man. The latter must respond to God. He must seek for Him. Such is the rule of the universe. The Divine in man answers to the Divine above man, and makes a step in the long course upwards toward reunion. This principle is evident in the humbler and more material sphere ; otherwise human life would fail. Judaism and Christianity universalised this principle over the moral universe. In other words, the Hebrew Faith, as Paul learned it from his birth and inherited it from his forefathers, forced into his nature the truth that we attain to God, not by sacrificing and shaking off our individuality, but by perfecting it.

From the statement of this truth we started in Section X., and to it we now return.

This apparent contradiction, that the Promise is a free gift of God and yet must be earned by man, is stated most emphatically in the letter to the Philippians iii. 7-15. His righteousness is not his own: it is the gift of God through Faith: there is nothing else of the smallest value in the whole world except this knowledge, through which he has obtained fellowship with the sufferings of Jesus and has come to be in conformity with the life which was consummated by the death of Jesus. He had no part in attaining this condition: he had simply been seized upon by Christ without conscious action on his own part. Yet, as he also says, he has not yet actually succeeded, on his own side, in seizing Christ : he has not yet attained : he has not yet been made righteous: in other words, his part has not yet been completely performed. He is only struggling onwards through the hard trials of life, forgetting everything except the prize of righteousness that lies before him, hurrying towards the goal like a runner straining every nerve and staking all his energy in reaching the mark and gaining the prize. He has not attained salvation, and yet he has attained it. He has not been made perfect, and yet he is made perfect: "let us therefore, as many as are perfect, be thus minded" (verse 15).

The perfect union with God, then, is the complete development and perfection of the individual nature. Not even Mohammedanism, much as it has sacrificed of this truth, has forgotten it wholly. Islam is a religion of energy and of work (though history shows that it has not remained true to its start).

XV. The Purpose of God

Some years ago the present writer attempted to summarise in three propositions the Pauline philosophy of history.[1] It will help to clarify our ideas on the subject, if we compare those propositions with the fundamental Pauline principles or axioms as they are stated in the present work.

The first proposition was "*The Divine alone is real: all else is error*". This is merely a statement of the effect in history and society of the first and most fundamental principle in Pauline and Hebrew thought, "*God is*". Start from that principle: think as Paul thought, view life as he viewed it: the result of your contemplation expresses itself in that proposition: "*There is nothing real except God*". This proposition is simply the converse of that fundamental principle.

The second proposition was "*A Society, or a Nation, is progressive in so far as it hears the Divine voice: all else is degeneration*". Here a new idea is introduced, *viz.* progress. The writer's object in stating those three propositions was simply to express broadly the observed facts of history. Human history is a history of progress: but progress depends absolutely and wholly on one condition, and cannot be achieved without it.

It may here be added, not because I wish now to reply to criticism, but simply to make clearer the present explanation of the subject, that objection was taken by some critics at the time to this second proposition, on the ground that it

[1] In *The Cities of St. Paul*, Part I. "Paulinism in the Graeco-Roman World," p. 12.

ignores and denies the development which runs through the history of mankind. The criticism is false, and misapprehends my words.

In this second proposition it is stated as the normal fact that human history is progressive, if a certain condition is observed. Progress is the law of nature; it is to be expected; it ought to take place; but it is not inevitable and invariable; on the contrary it is comparatively rare in history; most men and most nations degenerate except in so far as they are urged and forced on by the few who are active and progressive.

There is no necessary contradiction between the two assertions, that progress is normal, and that progress has been rare and unusual. As Paul would put it, God's intention was that progress should be the course of man's life, but His intention has been impeded and prevented by the evil and the fault of man. What, then, is evil? Is it stronger than God? Is it able to thwart the will of God? It has been in the past able to do so; but it cannot always do so; for the will of God must in the end triumph. Here we are brought face to face with the problem of sin; and to put in our current language Paul's solution of this problem so that it shall not be misunderstood by us is no easy matter, and will need some time and careful preparation.

The general principle, however, is certain; and has been laid down in Section X. as the second Pauline axiom, "God is good". He cannot be God, if His will does not triumph. He cannot be good, if His creation is to be a wreck. This second axiom finds its historical solution in development: there is a progressive, though slow, triumph over evil. Thus the law of development stated in the second proposition is implied in the second axiom: the presence of evil, suffering, sin, and degeneration in the world which God has created are reconciled with the truth of that axiom through the law that these exist to be overcome in the upward progress of mankind.

The will of God is the soul of history. Such is the philosophic theory of Paul. To him the process of human affairs was the gradual evolution of the Divine Will within those conditions of time and space that hedge man in. Paul presents to us the appearance of the Christ in the world as the culmination of the older period of history and the beginning of the new period : the past leads up to it and finds its explanation in it : the later time starts afresh from it. The purpose of God unfolds itself throughout. That in some cases evil seems to us successful is due to our taking too narrow a view : take a wider view, fetch a wider compass, and you perceive that the Divine will is triumphant in its own way and at its own proper time.

Hence Paul's thought must always be interpreted as dominated by his conception of the Divine purpose working itself out step by step : "When the fulness of the time came, God sent forth His Son, born of a woman, born under the Law," or " When it was the good pleasure of God, who had marked me out for that end even before my birth, to reveal His Son in me, that I might preach Him among the Gentiles ".[1] In these and other places, historical events occurring in the succession and process of time, day by day, or year by year, are pictured as steps in the working out of a foreordained purpose.

This is a thoroughly Hellenic way of expressing the truth. Greek poetry and Greek philosophy, in their highest and most characteristic manifestations, always picture history after this fashion, beginning from the opening paragraph of the *Iliad*, where the confused and tangled web of the Trojan

[1] Gal. iv. 4 and i. 15 f.

War is described as a series of steps by which "the will of the supreme God worked itself out to its consummation," Διὸς δ' ἐτελείετο βουλή. The pure Hebrew might content himself with unshakable faith in the principle that *God is good*, and that He will give good at His own time; but the Greek mind seeks to understand the means and to imagine the process.

In the second proposition, then, we meet the Greek-trained Paul: it may be doubted whether a Jew wholly ignorant of Greek thought would ever have framed his thought in this exact way. The Jewish way is not out of keeping with this (for both are good attempts to describe the same great truth in more or less figurative terms); but it starts from a different point of view, picturing God as the potter who deals at his will with his vessels and his clay, and advancing from this side towards the same ultimate truth.

Yet, although my purpose was to show Paul as the Apostle who most clearly regards human nature and history as progressive, various critics described me as denying that there has been development and progress in the world. I maintain that there must be progress, and that there has been progress; but human history is very far from being a continuous record of progress. And further, I venture to assert that a scientific investigation which starts from the assumption that all history is a history of progress must lead far astray. What of China, or India, or the Mohammedan lands, or the savage degenerates—in short, the greater part of the world? Have they been progressive? How often in history are we struck with the same phenomenon, a brief period of progress followed by a long time of retrogression and degeneration. Take the religion of Apollo, and the subsequent history of Greek religion. Take the teaching of Aeschylus and the subsequent history of the Attic drama. Take the Mohammedan countries, whose history as a whole has been usually a sudden outburst of moral fervour and enthusiasm, followed by a long period of deterioration and decay.

How frequently one observes in history a clearer and stronger perception of the nature of God acting on a people, and causing a marked improvement, but not able to clarify itself in a continual progress towards truth. Progress ceases because the nation no longer hears the Divine voice.

Or take even European civilisation : it prides itself on its progress, but it is transforming the world into a series of vast armed camps, and inculcating in practice the standard of judgment that a nation ranks as great, not because of its excellence in literature or art or learning or moral rectitude, but because it has trained itself to be able at need to kill the largest number of its neighbours in the shortest possible time. That is not the way in which the few judge ; but that is the standard of the many and of the diplomatists and ambassadors. Is that progress? Either it is a temporary madness, or it is degradation.

A friend of the present writer, a great Oxford scholar, used to display some beautiful old book, a fine edition of a classical author, and say "They talk of progress". There is much in Europe that is not progress. Yet still progress is the law of nature and the will of God.

The third proposition was, "*All men and every human society can hear the Divine voice ; but they must co-operate ere the communication can take place*". That is the condition on which progress rests. The Divine element in man must strive towards God.

XVI. The New Birth

Paul stands out in his letters and in history as a man filled with an intense, flaming, consuming passion for "righteousness". To attain this "righteousness" is the true end of man. Righteousness is the nature and character of God; and to be made one with God, to be in fellowship or communion with God, must necessarily be the true goal of human life. Since *God is*, the single and perfect existence, the truth and reality of the world, man who, by his existence as man, is separated from God, sees before him the one straight path whose goal is God; and to that goal he must either move onwards, or degenerate and "die".

Accordingly these and many other various expressions describing the end and purpose of man are practically equivalent: they are rough attempts to express in imperfect human terms, through imperfect imagery and figurative expression, the same thing. To attain unto righteousness, to be in communion with God, to gain everlasting life, is the true career of man; and this is Salvation. The pagans around were, as has been already said, praying for Salvation, seeking it by vows and dedications. That is the striking fact of the Graeco-Roman world. Paul preached to those who already were ignorantly seeking what he offered; or to put the matter from a different point of view, he caught up the term Salvation ($\Sigma \omega \tau \eta \rho \iota a$) from them, put his own meaning (i.e. Jesus's meaning) into it, and then gave it back to them. They offered to purchase Salvation by vows, or tried to extort it by prayers and entreaties from the

94

gods; but what they meant by it was largely material and ephemeral good; in the dedications and vows the word sometimes appears to mean little more than health, or prosperity or good fortune, or a union of all three. Yet the word never wholly excludes a meaning that comes nearer to reality and permanence: there lies latent in it some undefined and hardly conscious thought of the spiritual and the moral, which made it suit Paul's purpose admirably. The pagans could rarely have expressed in definite words this vague "something more," which they begged from the gods; and yet probably almost all the dedicants whose records we decipher had a certain dim consciousness of this indefinable good thing which they desired over and above mere safety and health and worldly prosperity.

As Professor H. A. A. Kennedy [1] says excellently: "All these statements [specimens of which have just been given] are certainly justifiable, as expressing each a side of the truth in which the mind of Paul can rest with perfect satisfaction. They are all, moreover, consistent with one another, for they are all closely linked with his personal Christian experience." These last few words are especially excellent; it is in the final resort always Paul's own life that determines his knowledge, and so it must be with every Christian. You know nothing really until you have lived it, worked it into your nature and life, and made it a part of yourself. All the various expressions of this thought which are found in Paul's writings arise out of his own experience; they are not arrived at by abstract philosophic thought, but forged on the anvil of life and work.

As the aim of life Paul looked for permanence. The Divine nature always *is:* there is for God only the present tense, " I am ". The certainty, the permanence, the reality

---

[1] *St. Paul's Conceptions of the Last Things,* p. 6 f.

of God are contrasted with the variability, the transitoriness, the uncertainty of all else. As Professor Kennedy translates the words of Steffen, Paul "sighed, as scarcely any other has done, beneath the curse of the transiency of all that is earthly".[1] He longed for the assurance which lies in union with God.

Here Semitic thought closely approximates to Hellenic philosophical expression. It is one of the central ideas in Greek philosophy that the whole universe and every object in it exist through constant motion and change. Nothing remains the same. Some things change more quickly, some more slowly; but all things are involved in this ceaseless movement. You cannot step twice into the same river, for its water flows by, and new water takes its place. You cannot twice climb the same hill, for it is disintegrating and wearing away by a never-ceasing though slow process of change. There is nothing fixed, nothing trustworthy, and therefore nothing real in these things. Existence which is merely a constant process of change is not in a real sense existence.

Thus Paul's thought comes back always to the first principle that God is, while nothing else is. All other things seem to be, but they only mock the mind with the illusion of being. The philosophic mind is compelled by its own nature to get back behind them to the permanent and the real. It can acquiesce in God, and in nothing else, for there is nothing but illusion except in Him; and only the superficial and unphilosophic mind can be content with outward appearance without underlying reality.

Of all these expressions for the one truth, however, probably the most suggestive and the one which best seizes the

---

[1] *St. Paul's Conceptions of the Last Things*, p. 6: Steffen in *Zft. f. N.T. Wissenschaft*, 1901, ii. p. 124, to which I have not access at present.

reality is that you must be born again, you must enter on a new life; "if any man be in Christ, he is a new creature ";[1] "it is no longer I that live, but Christ liveth in me".[2] Already, in this life on earth, the new life has begun, and one's old self has died. The Divine life has begun; the goal is attained; the man is merged in God and united with God, because his former self has died, and "Christ liveth in me" (as every true Christian can say in so far as he is a true Christian). There is nothing in Paul's words and experience that arrogates anything peculiar to himself, or anything that differentiates him from "all the saints". There is but one experience, and one true life free and open to all.

This new life begins through the death of the old nature: the death takes place through suffering, and (as Paul figuratively puts it) you must crucify the old self, for "they that are Christ's have crucified the flesh with the passions thereof".[3] This is the law of the universe: the birth of the new is the death of the old: through death we enter on life: in science it is expressed as the transformation of force.

These are figurative expressions, some of which are used by Paul and others by John. They denote the same idea, from practically the same point of view. Nicodemus wholly failed to understand what it meant to be born again; and it is not recorded that the further explanation in John iii. conveyed a clearer meaning to him at the time. The thought was so totally new to him that at first it seemed to him meaningless and impossible. What does it mean to us? How shall we express it in modern everyday language, seeking for other figures and other forms which come more into harmony with the cast of current thought?

May we not say that in this series of figures taken from

---

[1] 2 Cor. v. 17.   [2] Gal. ii. 20.   [3] Gal. v. 24.

birth and new life, we have the same idea that we call development or rather evolution?

In this connexion we must again quote and scrutinise more minutely that most typical and illuminating passage in Paul's letters, Philippians iii. 10 ff.

> Having . . . the righteousness which is through faith in Christ, the righteousness which is from God by faith : that I may know Him and the power of His resurrection and the fellowship of His sufferings, becoming conformed unto His death : if by any means I may attain unto the resurrection from the dead. Not that I have already obtained or am already made perfect : but I press on, if so be that I may lay hold on that for which also I was laid hold on by Christ Jesus. Brethren, I count not myself to have laid hold : but one thing I do . . . I press on toward the goal unto the prize of the upward calling of God in Christ Jesus. Let us therefore, as many as are perfect, be thus minded. . . . Brethren, be ye imitators together of me.

Two apparently contradictory assertions are here brought together, and Paul passes from the one to the other, and back again. On the one hand he has gained the righteousness of God ; he is made perfect : he is worthy of imitation ; that he should be so, was the purpose of God, which worked itself out in its own way through the developing events of his life. Paul is the Christian ; and what he says every true Christian, every ἄγιος, every saint, can equally say. His experiences are the experiences of all the saints. "Christ . . . was made unto us wisdom from God, and righteousness, and sanctification, and redemption."[1] The man who calls on others to imitate him is claiming to be the model for them : men are made in the image of God, and only one who has the righteousness of God can be a model to other men : yet every saint can claim to be so.

On the other hand, in the same passage, Paul is also

---

[1] Cor. i. 30. "Gentiles . . . have attained to righteousness, even the righteousness which is of faith " (Rom. ix. 30).

saying that he is not perfect: he has not yet attained righteousness:[1] life is the goal towards which he is struggling, and the prize which he is striving to win. "Be thou faithful unto death, and I will give thee the crown of life." But the crown lies in front: there is still a way to traverse, hard and trying, before the prize is won. Death must be faced and traversed as the gate of life.

Thus almost in the same breath Paul is saying "I have attained" and "I have not yet attained". How shall we reconcile the two apparently contradictory expressions? There is no real contradiction: the two unite in one complete idea, and the idea is growth.

[1] The word "yet" is omitted by many good authorities (including B and all Latin); it is needed for the thought, but is naturally supplied from the preceding sentence; and the emphasis and variety are heightened if it is left to the reader to supply. The temptation was to insert it from the influence of the preceding.

XVII. LIFE IS GROWTH

If we try to put this idea in the simplest and barest form, man, as he is placed in this world, must either move onward towards the better, or degenerate towards the worse. He cannot stand still. He cannot remain the same, as if he were fixed and unchanging. In the flux of the world, nothing can continue fixed and permanent. Movement towards the better is movement towards God and towards life : in fact, it is in itself really and actually life. Movement towards the worse is degeneration and is already death. In Paul's thought degeneration and death are equivalents.

Now without some power to move him, man degenerates, and thus comes death. A motive power is needed to start him and keep him on the upward path to the better ; and this motive power Paul found in faith, the belief in an ideal, the belief in the existence of something higher, and in the possibility of reaching it (which implies the wish to reach it). There is no other force sufficient. Everything else has failed, as the history of man shows.

Thus faith is the power that sets man moving in the right direction ; but this is not an external power ; it is a power that works in and through the mind of the man. It is the Divine power, and yet it resides in the human mind, because it is the Divine fire in the nature of man.

This is a difficult idea, for it seems to involve the contradiction that without external aid man must fail, and yet that he succeeds through a power within himself. Each

statement can be made with perfect truth, contradictory
as they appear. At every point in the life of man, you find
yourself involved in a similar apparent contradiction :
you can at every point say, as Paul says here, this is and
this is not: he has attained and he has not yet attained.
This lies in the nature of growth: at every moment that
which is growing ceases to be what it has been; it does
not remain the same for two consecutive moments; but
the change is not merely purposeless or vague or shifting,
it is change controlled by a law and a purpose; and this
law of development is the Divine element amid the ceaseless
variation.

Thus I find myself driven to assert that Paul is the
preacher of development and growth, and that only from
this point of view can we at the present day put a meaning
on his teaching which is thinkable by people in the special
stage of thought on which we now stand, advanced beyond
the past, but still very far from perfect. The teaching of
Paul, i.e. the mind of Christ, seems to assume, in every age
and to every person, a form peculiarly adapted and sufficient
for the occasion. It has to be rethought (as was said in
the outset) by every one for his own purpose to suit his
own need. It is infinite in its suitability; but always
each man must see it for himself, and each thinks that he
sees something special to himself. The variety, however,
lies, not in the teaching of Paul, but in the nature of men,
who contemplate it through the colouring medium of their
own various character.

Whether I have succeeded in making clear my reasons,
I know not ; but I find myself compelled to begin afresh
and to approach the whole problem from another point of
view. To Paul human conduct is a problem of growth: it
is dynamic, not static. In this view everything is seen in

a new light.   Righteousness is not a state, but a process of growing or approaching towards the nature of God.   Sin is not simply a fact or a characteristic, definite and stationary; sin is a process of degeneration and deterioration, continuously accelerated, and gathering increased momentum. The sinner is a person driven down a hill; his velocity is constantly accelerated; and it becomes more and more difficult for him to stop his course or to turn back.   Yet to turn back is necessary if he is to begin to move towards righteousness.   Some tremendous power must be brought into play to arrest the impetus of the degeneration towards evil, and cause a movement in the opposite direction towards good and God.

Life means the fulfilment of the purpose of one's existence : to fail and to frustrate that purpose is death.   " Sin entered into the world, and death through sin." [1]   The double statement is put most emphatically in the form : " The wages of sin is death ; but the free gift of God is eternal life ".[2]   Such is the order of God : " whether (servants) of sin unto death or of obedience (to His will) unto righteousness ".[3]   Righteousness and life are here practically convertible terms; and these sentences would be equally true and equally intelligible, if the words were interchanged.

The question has been asked and seriously discussed whether Paul would have gone so far as to maintain that, if there had been no sin, there would never have been in the world such a thing as death.   This is one of those academic questions with which Paul would have had little patience. If the world, and the Divinely ordained course of the world, had been different from what they are, then many things else would have been different.   It is profitless, and worse than profitless, to discuss such questions.   They approxi-

---

[1] Rom. v. 12.   [2] Rom. vi. 23.   [3] *Ibid.*, 16.

mate perilously to the logomachies against which Paul ful-
minates in writing to Timothy and Titus.

When death is conceived as the transition of force from
one form to another, it has a different meaning from the
other sense, in which it is spoken of as the equivalent of
sin. In the latter case it is really degeneration, in which
every right feeling, right judgment, and right impulse,
gradually become atrophied and cease to exist. The man
who fails to carry into effect the Divine purpose of his
being is ceasing to live ; and when all hope is lost he is dead.
The common metaphor by which we speak of such a man
as dead originates from a true instinct. After all, even in
the physical sense, how difficult it is to predicate death as
final and absolute. In the case of drowning, a person may
be practically dead ; and yet sometimes, after hours of
therapeutic work, the breath may be recalled ; and all that
can be said is that he would have been pronounced dead
hours before, if it had not afterwards been proved that he
could still live. I know the circumstances of a case in
which a man was pronounced dead by two of the best
physicians in France after typhoid fever ; and yet was
brought back to life after many hours of effort by non-medical
belief and activity. Still more difficult is it to predicate
moral death. There are admittedly many cases in which a
person who had seemed utterly dead to all moral feelings
and hopelessly lost, has been restored to life. He was really
dead ; and yet, after all, there is no moral death so absolute
and complete as to be beyond the redeeming power of
faith and of Christ.

All the issues of life and death are under the power of
God and subject to His control.

XVIII. CHRIST A POWER IN MAN?

Now comes the question, whether this way of looking at life is justifiable in philosophy or in common practical sense. It is of course admitted by the questioner that the power of a true and noble idea in history has been extraordinarily great. The influence of such ideas can hardly be exaggerated. The history of mankind is made by them and transformed by them through all the stages of its progress. Without such ideas there is no progress, for they are the Divine element in the world, and the Divine within the collective thought of nations responds to the impulse of a noble idea, where the nation is fitted to receive and comprehend it. The memory of every educated person will supply to him countless examples from past history; and it is needless to linger over this subject, except to say that often a historical process has been in reality originated and impelled by an idea rather than by the more apparent reasons of material advantage or political strength which also may seem to be involved. This topic may, however, be left to a historical survey.

It will also be admitted that the transforming and impelling and regenerative power of an idea over the individual man is extraordinarily great. In one's own experience every one knows how even the reading of a noble thought can rouse the emotions and quicken the pulse, and how sometimes the contact of one's mind with such an idea has affected the whole of one's thought, and even given a new direction to one's subsequent life.

This is not merely an analogy: it is a slighter example of the same nature and the same force. In all such cases the Divine nature within us recognises and responds to the Divine without, and grows stronger by taking into itself a new yet kindred element. I believe it is allowable to say that the mind of Jesus embraces the sum and perfection of all great ideas, and His influence on the world operates in the same fashion but to an immeasurably stronger degree, through infinite love, perfect truth, and absolute power, all combined to influence the human mind that it has laid hold upon.

How far it may be right to say that the intensification of that kind of influence to an infinite degree raises it into a higher category I do not presume to decide. Who can gauge the difference between the finite and the infinite power? But that this is the right way of attempting to understand the process of faith, and that this places a true philosophic interpretation on it, and that this power is vouched for by common and universal experience, I believe. In every case where a great idea impels the mind of one man or of a nation, it works through the belief which it rouses; and this belief and confidence strengthen the human nature to the daring and achieving of what otherwise would lie far above and beyond human powers.

Those who have studied the remarkable book of Nevius on "Demoniac Possession" will be inclined to say that this is far from exhausting the phenomena under consideration, and will be inclined to claim for the name of Jesus an immeasurable and limitless power over man. Nevius, who at the beginning of his missionary experience in China had no belief in the reality of demoniac possession, but regarded all cases so classed as examples of obscure phenomena of a nervous or hysterical character, found himself obliged by the facts that came within the range of his own observation, and were corroborated by the observations of many trustworthy colleagues, to change his opinion. He came to believe that there was such a thing as real obsession or possession by diabolic power; and he recognised that in numerous cases—almost every case where it was tried—the appeal to the name of Jesus exercised a soothing and more or less curative influence even on obstinately or ignorantly pagan minds.

Here we trench on the sphere of the miraculous, that is, on what has not yet been properly understood. The book is worthy of study, and the subject deserves more careful and systematic observation. Do such cases occur especially or only in China? Are not many of them readily explicable through the power of a latent idea which is revivified by the mention of the name?

XIX. The Alternative: Impersonal Power or Personal God

According to the teaching of Paul, there is nothing really and in the highest sense true except (1) the axiom that God is, (2) what arises inexorably and necessarily out of this fundamental principle. The universe around us, then, becomes intelligible to us only through its relation to God, the original power which gives reality to all the rest of things.

There are some who prefer to regard this primal reality under the impersonal term "power" or "force" or "energy". It is to a certain extent immaterial for our present purpose whether you speak and think of "the power which constitutes the whole," or "God who constitutes the whole". After all, distinction of gender is here merely figurative; the nearer one comes to the Divine, the less important does such a distinction become. In common experience it may be observed that "it" and "which" are used nearly as much as the personal pronoun and relative "he," "she," "who," about the child in the first months or years of its life: now, as Wordsworth says, the young child is nearest to the Divine :—

Trailing clouds of glory do we come
From God, who is our home:
Heaven lies about us in our infancy!
Shades of the prison-house begin to close
Upon the growing Boy,
But he beholds the light . .
At length the Man perceives it die away
And fade into the light of common day.

The difference lies in the recognition of personality; but one need not, therefore, quarrel with those who prefer the impersonal form, "the force which constitutes the whole," to the personal form. That difference stands apart from our purpose; and we welcome the admission (which modern science has from its own side reached by its own methods) that a certain unifying principle does give intelligibility to the universe; and that this principle is not immobility, but force or energy.

We prefer to give a personal form to the fundamental proposition; and we believe that those who choose the impersonal form miss much of true philosophic thought. This impersonal statement of the first principle in the Universe leaves no place in its philosophy for man, and man then becomes an alien, so to say an impertinence or an anachronism, in the scheme of the universe. Such a principle, if it remains hard and does not develop towards a recognition of personality, must lead at last to the Oriental non-Hebrew systems of thought, which find the necessary goal and true end of human existence in shaking off human nature and becoming once more merged in the ultimate and primary energy.

Still we must welcome the recognition of this one constituting "force" as a stage in thought, which is likely sooner or later to produce the consciousness that this is a half-way position; and we therefore find in it an approximation to a better statement of the one ultimate nature. Here we have room and atmosphere wherein to work. On the contrary, we had neither room nor atmosphere in that dull and blind materialism out of which, during the last half of the nineteenth century, scientific theory was gradually and slowly struggling.

To Paul, however, the distinction between the personal

and the impersonal expression was, in a religious view, vital—certainly vital in his ordinary preaching. Only misapprehension and misdirection could result if he addressed the masses in terms that might seem to admit the distinction as indifferent; for it is not indifferent, but essential and vital.

There are, however, degrees of opposition. Some forms of religion or of philosophy were more hateful to him, and were regarded by him as more hostile, than others. The superstition and idolatry of the ordinary Anatolian cults he especially detested.

Paul knew well that there is a time for everything, and that only among them that are full grown should he speak philosophy.[1] Most dangerous was it to talk philosophically among the Corinthians, a middle-class audience, who possessed that half-education or quarter-education which is worse than a lesser degree of education combined with greater rustic sympathy with external nature. Among them he must insist in the most emphatic terms on the simple and absolute personality of the Divine power and message; he must " preach the Gospel not in philosophic terms," lest by the use of such terms the truth about the redeeming death of Jesus might lose meaning to them.[2] In speaking to this kind of audience he perceived that he must have in his mind nothing save Jesus Christ and Him crucified.[3] To a simpler almost rustic audience he could speak in terms that were wider and less precise, and bid them " turn from these vain things unto a living God ".[4]

---

[1] I Cor. ii. 6.

[2] " To preach the Gospel: not in wisdom of words, lest the cross of Christ should be made void " (I Cor. i. 17).

[3] I Cor. ii. 2: so in Acts xviii. 5.

[4] So the American Revisers rightly. The English Revisers wrongly retain from the Authorised Version " the living God ". I shall generally cite the

Paul had experimented in the more philosophic style
of address, when he engaged in discussion with the philosophic teachers of Athens and was required to explain his
doctrine before the Court of Areopagus and the audience
of interested and curious persons who always thronged the
courts in that period, and whose keen partisanship and applause or disapproval were more powerful influences even
with professional lawyers (as Pliny says) than the opinion
and verdict of judge and jury.   On that occasion and in
those circumstances Paul used a non-personal form of expression: "What therefore ye worship in ignorance, this I
set forth unto you"; and perhaps also a sentence or two
later "that they might seek the Divine, if haply they might
feel after it and find it";[1] and certainly afterwards "we
ought not to think that what is Divine [or 'the Godhead']
is like unto gold or silver or stone, graven by art".   Paul's
purpose in his address is to start from the admission of
this universal principle, that the Divine nature is immanent
in the whole universe including man, who is its progeny,
and to argue that his audience must logically take the
needed further steps, first to regard the Divine as a personal
God, then to understand the purpose of God in regard to
man through the mission of "the man whom He hath
ordained," and finally to comprehend the ideas of final
judgment and the resurrection of Jesus.

Incidentally I may take this opportunity of acknowledg-

American Revision, which appears to me superior to the English Revision.
Many years ago I was struck with the fact that, when I tested a number of
the cases in which the American preference is indicated at the end of the
English Revised Version, the American reading proved better than the
English.

Acts xvii. 27.   Western authorities read the neuter gender in 27, as all
good MSS. have in 29.

ing that I went too far in my book called *St. Paul the Traveller and the Roman Citizen*, p. 252, when I declared that the Apostle "was disappointed and perhaps disillusionised by his experience in Athens. He felt that he had gone at least as far as was right in the way of presenting his doctrine in a form suited to the current philosophy ; and apparently the result had been little more than naught." I did not allow sufficiently for adaptation to different classes of hearers, in one case the tradesmen and middle-classes of Corinth, in the other the more strictly university and philosophic class in Athens. It is true (as is there shown) that Luke recognised and recorded the change in style of preaching at Corinth ; but on the other hand it is improbable that Luke would have preserved a careful report of the address at Athens, if he had not considered it typical of Paul's method when speaking to an educated Hellenic audience.

It now seems to me quite inadequate to say that Paul, feeling disappointed with the results of this Athenian address resolved to change his style finally and permanently to the purely personal evangel. The fact is certain, that (as both Luke and himself mention) he did adopt the latter method definitely and emphatically at Corinth ; yet the inference is also equally certain that both Luke and Paul must have regarded the other method as justifiable in suitable circumstances— the method, *viz.*, of taking the impersonal philosophic position as his basis and upon this foundation building up his doctrine of the personality of this primal force, the purpose and plan of the personal (as Paul would say, the living) God in regard to man, and the rest of his evangelical teaching. If he used the latter method less, his choice implied no disapproval of it as in itself wrong, but only a preference for the other method as more effective, because far more suitable to the world of the Roman Empire generally.

The speech which Paul delivered before the Court of Areopagus presents many points of interest, and raises many important questions. Hence the best course will be to relegate it to a separate place in Part III., as it would require too much space and too detailed attention in view of the arrangement here. In a special section it can be treated more conveniently and more fully.

In Paul's attitude towards the philosophic statement of the nature of God, we perceive the Hellenic and philosophic side of his mind. The doctrine of an impersonal Divine nature or Divine power may be taken as the beginning of a recognition of the higher truth. Knowledge or truth in religion is not to Paul a hard, definite fact presented in the unchangeable terms of a creed or confession : it is a living idea, capable of infinite growth towards the higher truth, or of perversion and degeneration through being misunderstood and overgrown by error. The idea, though in a sense imperfect, is true so long as it is growing towards truth. The force through which it grows is Divine.

XX. The Righteousness of God

The true end of life is to attain, or in more accurate language to realise, the righteousness of God in the personality of the individual man. This term, "the righteousness of God," is an exquisite and wonderful expression, concentrating in itself the whole of Paul's aspirations and theory and teaching. His aspirations are his teaching. He is what he teaches, and he teaches what he is. To him "to live is Christ," and the goal is a higher life attained through the term of death, for it is "rich to die, to cease upon the midnight with no pain," and thus to enter by the gates of death into the new and higher life. That process is always going on, moment after moment: the old perishes, and the new begins, because the new is only a transformation of the old, as the fundamental or constitutive force of life passes out of one state or one form into another; and this constitutive force is God.

Of this force (which is God) in man, the life, the reality, the essence, lies in progress towards the goal. Attainment is the reaching of the goal; and the goal is in a sense attained at every moment and in every effort by which the man strives onwards towards it. Yet the goal is not attained if the effort is relaxed and the process of continuous attainment stops. So long as the effort is maintained, the goal is being always attained, and yet it is not attained: it is reached, and yet it still lies in front. Here you are once more placed in presence of the same apparent contradiction which is expressed in that typical passage from Philippians iii.

10 ff. (quoted in Section XVI.); and the solution lies in
the idea of growth, evolution, development, the continuous
reaching forward towards the higher life, the forgetting of
what has already been attained, the strengthening in man
of the Divine possibility which is innate in him, and thereby the growth into conformity with Jesus, in whom that
Divine element wholly overmastered the human element
and reigned supreme.

The " righteousness of God" is not to be thought of as a
quality or characteristic which is possessed by God, or of
which God could divest Himself.   The nature and being of
God is righteousness : that is involved in the axiom that
God is good.   The same righteousness belongs also to man
in the sense that it is the goal and end which man has to
attain.   This righteousness is God, and it may come into
the possession of man.   Just as God is love, so God is righteousness ; and just as man may become possessed of love,
so he may come to possess righteousness.

Paul, then, as we saw in Section XVI., could declare
that he (i.e. every saint, every true Christian) possessed
that "righteousness of God" which was the goal and ultimate end of his whole life and work, that he had attained
already that salvation which he was to gain as the prize
of the race of life.   Is this a permissible and justifiable
mode of expression?   Is this the sound and true teaching?
Such is a question that may arise at this point ; and it must
be answered with an unhesitating affirmative.

The case may be illustrated by the analogy of another
question : Do we possess freedom of will or not?   Freedom
of the will is that to which we may attain as the crown of
growth and the prize of life ; but we do not possess it to
begin with, nor do we fully possess it in our life.   Our will
is largely enslaved by external conditions ; yet we have the

potentiality of freedom, and we can grow towards the realisation of it. Thus we possess freedom of will, because we can attain towards it if we live aright, and the process of attaining is the proof of our possession. We are free, because we can be free. We have freedom, because we are able to attain freedom.

So it is with righteousness, the righteousness of God. In the striving towards it, we have already grasped it. He who is growing towards it, has it reckoned to him as his own, according to Paul's expression. It is counted to him because it is his—through the grace of God working in him, and through his new life, for he is new born and new made.

This "accounting of a person as righteous" who has never previously done anything good or righteous[1] is, therefore, not retrospective, and does not merely imply that his sin is forgiven. Mere forgiveness of sin by God would be a purely negative idea; but here we are in presence of a positive power or force. That a man's sins are forgiven does not make him righteous. A parent may forgive his son, or a friend may forgive his neighbour; but thereby the son or the neighbour need not necessarily benefit so as to become better; very often he is no better, and the process may have to be repeated even to seventy times seven, and still be required again and yet again. We want something positive, some energy in the man who is forgiven, before the "righteousness of God" is reckoned to him. There is not here involved any fictitious imputing of righteousness (as it were by a "legal fiction"); still less is there any actual imparting of righteousness to a man who had none (as if so much money were placed to the credit of a bankrupt). The man himself is remade, and righteousness grows in him through

[1] So Paul says emphatically in Romans iv. 5.

his faith in a Divine idea, and the power that this exercises over his whole nature. This growing righteousness is, in the most real sense, the righteousness of God, the righteousness which is God. The growing tree is the tree, and yet it is only attaining to the perfect tree.

The process then is threefold : it originates from faith, it takes place by means of faith, and it results in faith (ἐκ πίστεως, διὰ πίστεως, εἰς πίστιν). The three expressions are not conjoined in any sentence of Paul's writing, although we have here brought them together. The first and third are conjoined in the splendid expression of Romans i. 17, " therein [in the Gospel] is revealed a righteousness of God from faith unto faith," and this follows after the words " the Gospel . . . is the power of God unto salvation to every one that believeth ". The two expressions " from faith " or " by faith " (ἐκ πίστεως) and " through faith " or " by faith " (διὰ πίστεως) approximate closely to one another. The former tends to be used where the ruling thought in Paul's mind is of the Divine power acting on or in the man's nature, and the latter when the thought is rather of faith working from within the man's nature outwards.

These two manifestations of faith are really, however, one. The power of God exists in and through man. As we saw in Section IX., a God who remains apart from and uninterested in man does not fulfil the first axiom that God is : He must show Himself in and through man. A God that is mere negative creative possibility is not the real and living God. God, in order to be really God, must be a positive creating power. Through man God shows Himself in His real and living power. Not merely is it true that there must be God. It is equally true that there must be man, in whom the power of God manifests itself. Hence the faith which works from without on the nature of man is identical with the faith that works from within the nature of man. The former finds its expression in the latter.

The result of the power of faith in action is to recreate or to reinvigorate itself. It grows of and from itself through expressing itself in deed. The condition of faith is that it must express itself: it must create, because it is essentially creative; it is of God, and like God it exists and lives through exerting itself. Faith is a force, not a mere dead fact; and a force that does not act, but remains passive, has ceased to be a force. The faith which exists in a man's nature, therefore, must either drive him on into action, or cease and die.

Further, the nature of this force is to grow stronger through exerting itself. Where faith has once entered, it becomes forthwith the driving power in the man's character: it absorbs into itself all the man's nature and mind: there remains nothing else alongside of it within the man: all else is subordinated to it and driven on by it. This power is capable of infinite expansion. Through its activity it grows; and, as the man's entire nature is now summed up in it, that nature grows stronger through action. In each step forward that the man takes under the impulse of this power of faith, he leaves behind him the old self and assumes a new self. He recreates himself in growing, i.e. in acting; or rather, "it is no longer I that live," as Paul says, "but Christ liveth in me" [1] and through me. The Divine power having once seized on the man must be complete master of him and progressively victorious, going on from strength to strength; otherwise it must die out in the degeneration of the man's nature.

There is, however, a certain tendency in man always to rest content with the present moment and the present con-

[1] Gal. ii. 20, a passage that must constantly be quoted.

dition.   Even when man has once attained, that tendency
towards contentment and acquiescence may come into operation.   But the feeling of contentment with the attained
degree of self-realisation (which is the realisation of the
Divine element in man) must not be permitted to last
beyond the moment, for the Divine, the righteousness of
God, lies always in front; and one has not yet, at any
moment in the course, attained.   To cease effort is to permit the beginning of degradation, i.e. "to die".   One
cannot remain as one was.   If progress and effort stop,
deterioration begins.

A driving power, therefore, is needed, not merely in the
first effort, by which one turns one's back on sin and
struggles towards righteousness, but in the sequel.   The
new effort is a new start, each new effort is again the first
step in a process that stretches onward towards God.   The
past effort, which gained one stage, is forthwith left behind,
and another effort is needed.   In each and every effort the
driving force is the same; it is faith, belief in the ideal, the
firm conviction that God is good.   One starts from faith,
one makes the succeeding steps by means of faith, and at
each step one attains to a higher power of faith.

The idea that God is working out by a process that extends
through the ages the issue of salvation for the individual
man, is expressed very clearly in Romans viii. 28-30.   First
of all, in verse 28, Paul puts in the strongest terms as a starting point his fundamental principle, that God is good : " We
know that to them that love God all things work together for
good, *viz.*, to them that are called according to His purpose".
Everything that happens, however painful or hard, contri-
butes to benefit those who love God.   Such apparent
trials and blows of fate must not be contemplated in too
narrow a view.   In the narrow view they seem calami-

ties ; but if you take a wider view, if you contemplate life as a whole, if you observe how all the circumstances and conditions of life " work together " in the order and purpose of the world, then you find that the total effect is purely for good. Hence the further definition is added : " they that love God " are explained as " they that are called according to His purpose ".

Here the will and " counsel of God " (as Homer, *Iliad,* i. 5, and the great Greeks would call it) is introduced. This Hellenic and philosophic view is always found moderating and informing Paul's thought. That " counsel " works itself out to its final end through the tangle and confusion of the mixed good and evil of human fortunes ; and the medley of good and evil becomes intelligible only through the Divine will which can be traced in it. Nothing can be understood except in its relation to God. His will is the principle of order which gives unity to the mass of contradictions and difficulties ; and this order expresses itself as growth or development or evolution.

This process or evolution is stated in the next two verses : " Whom He foreknew, He also foreordained to be conformed to the image of His Son, that He might be the firstborn among many brethren ; and whom He foreordained, them He also called ; and whom He called, them He also justified [i.e. enabled to become righteous] ; and whom He justified, them He also glorified ". God with perfect knowledge saw and knew the whole universe : in other words, the universe is the unfolding in time of His purpose. From the human point of view this knowledge is entitled foreknowledge ; but, in the nature of the Eternal " I am," this knowledge is only the outlook over the universe as a whole, outside of time, on the plane of eternity, i.e. as present, permanent, real. Towards this permanence Paul is always looking ; for it he longs (as we saw in Section X.), and he finds it only in God.

This knowledge or foreknowledge of the character and situation of each individual implies the marking out already before their birth of certain individuals to attain the end and consummation of human life, which is that they should grow into conformity with the image, i.e. the personality, of Jesus—for such is (as we have seen) the perfection and goal of man to Paul. It also leads to the calling at the proper moment, "in the fulness of the time," of these individuals; as for example Paul says about himself in Galatians i. 15: "when it was the good pleasure of God, who marked me out from before my birth, and called me through His grace, to reveal His Son in me, that I might preach Him," carrying into effect the long-preparing purpose of God. This calling is the act of God, originating from His good-will and choice; but at the same time the choice is not merely arbitrary or capricious; it is the carrying into effect of a plan in accordance with the nature of the universe and of the individual; and it presupposes that the individual on his part is able to hear the call and to respond to it.

In the calling, as in the foreknowledge, it is also implied as the certain and necessary sequence that the individual is justified, i.e. that his course turns towards the good and that the idea of the good and the aspiration after the good take possession of his whole nature and personality, so that he struggles with all his might towards the true end of human life and towards perfect conformity with Jesus. It also is implied that this course is ultimately successful, and that the consummation is attained and the individual is "glorified". The success, subsequent in time, explains and justifies the calling, for the success was before the mind of God from the first.

XXI. Is there a Limit to Salvation?

Now, why are some called and not others? Is this just or right? And what has Paul to say about those who are not foreordained and called? They are many. What is their fate? What is their place and part in the purpose of God?

The Apostle's purpose does not lead him to answer this question, although it is one which must justifiably and necessarily rise in the mind of every person. Paul was not writing philosophic treatises, but stimulating and hortatory letters. He knew the nature of a Graeco-Romano-Judaic audience. It was not the problem of the fate of the un-called that could interest their thoughts or touch their hearts. The melancholy tone that always becomes the permanent characteristic of a long-established paganism was already deeply fixed in the minds of his Graeco-Roman hearers. He had to rouse in them hope, love, and faith, all nearly dormant forces in their nature, so far as the higher forms and aims of those forces were concerned. He had to give them something worth living for and worth dying for.

It was quite useless to set before such minds and eyes a picture of the misfortune of those who were not called. No misfortune could be worse than what they already endured. No lot could be more wretched than that of a Roman noble as their poet Lucretius painted it: "sick of home he goes forth from his large house, and as suddenly comes back to it, finding that he is no better off abroad.

He races to his country house, driving his carriage-horses in headlong haste; he yawns the moment he has reached the door, or sinks heavily into sleep and seeks forgetfulness, or even hurries back again to town.   In this way each man flies from himself, and hates too himself, because he is sick and knows not the cause of the malady; for if he could rightly see into this, each man would relinquish all else and study to learn the nature of things, since the point at stake is the condition for eternity." [1]

Such was the frame of mind in which the mass of pagans dwelt, and in which they prayed and made vows for salvation.   To words of threatening or denunciation of future suffering the ears of such men would be deaf.   Lucretius in the passage immediately preceding has just been declaring that all threats of punishment in a future life were mere fable, and that the only reality lying behind such denunciation was the ceaseless misery that men suffered in their present life on earth.

Such people had no faith in the present, and no hope for the future: they were filled with a thorough disbelief in the world around them, and utter despair as to the future. Threats and terrors meant nothing more to them in the future than they were already suffering in the present: with these their whole horizon was clouded.

Paul had to recreate the better nature of these men ; and this he did in the only way possible, *viz.*, by recreating their belief in the goodness of God, and with this their hope, and as a result their power of loving and serving.   It was a matter of no interest to him to discuss speculative questions or even to set forth a complete and well-rounded system of philosophy.   Those to whom he addressed himself did not want a system of philosophy; they wanted life, hope,

---

[1] Lucretius, iii. 1059-1069, shortened from Munro's rendering.

salvation. Their vows and their prayers were all for " salvation ". See also Section XXXVII.

It must not, therefore, be concluded from Paul's almost total silence on this subject, the fate of those who were not called, not foreordained, not justified, that he had never thought about it. To a certain extent he recurred to his fundamental principle that God is good, and took refuge in the unfathomable depth of the Divine counsel ; " His decisions cannot be sought out in detail, nor His ways traced ;[1] for who hath known the mind of the Lord ? or who hath been His counsellor ? " The entire plan of the universe and the whole purpose of God cannot be comprehended by man. We have to reach, by faith and by direct insight and by the natural power of believing, the truth that God is good, without being able to prove it logically ; we have the assurance in our heart that this axiom is true, but we cannot demonstrate its truth to one who disbelieves it.

Further, we must accept the world as it is. We have to deal with the universe and its facts, and it is folly to think we could improve them if we had our way, or if we had been consulted. "Who art thou that repliest against God? Shall the thing formed say to him that formed it, Why didst thou make me thus?"[2] It is the idea of a child or a fool that, if he had had the making of the world, he could have made a much better one.

The Apostle, whether intentionally or not, has given very little indication of his views regarding the choice of those who are called and the fate of those who are not called. While many are not called, yet there stands always the axiom that God is good, and that therefore His purpose, however incomprehensible to us, must justify itself in the final and complete view ; but that fundamental principle

[1] Rom. xi. 33.   [2] Rom. ix. 20.

must not be pressed to the dangerous extreme that the grace of God will in the simple sense save every one.   Paul does not teach a universal salvation.   He does indeed speak of God's purpose "to reconcile all things unto Himself"[1]; but he does not explain this further, and leaves it in apparent contradiction with his general teaching (as contained, e.g., in Philippians iii. 18, i. 28; Romans ii. 4-8, etc.).

As passages like Romans iii. 7 f., vi. 1 f., 15 f. show, Paul had reason to fear lest, by insisting that the infinite grace of God must triumph in the long run, he might do harm to the raw pagan hearers, who would be inclined to ask, and who did sometimes ask, Why should we not continue to sin, and trust to the sure love and grace of God to save us from the consequences?   He replies that there is a judgment, that the choice must be made between sin and righteousness, and that there is punishment for sin: and he makes it clear that salvation can be attained only in one way, and that those who miss that way cannot be saved, but lose the lot of life and the grace of God.   He does not, however, dwell much on this aspect of the justice of God; but prefers, whether from his own natural bent or owing to experience of what was most efficacious, to lay emphasis on the free offer of salvation to all.   His teaching and his mind were filled with the thought of eternal life in Christ.   He spoke little about the doom of death, and that little was expressed chiefly in his earliest teaching to the Thessalonians (though it also appears a good deal in his second letter to Timothy).

There remains in Paul's public teaching, so far as his letters reveal it, a certain unsolved discrepancy between his fundamental axiom of the goodness of God and his *dicta*

[1] Col. i. 20; cp. Phil. ii. 9-11.

as to the death, or destruction, or wrath, that awaits the unrepentant.   This we must admit.   It is not our business to set forth a complete system of philosophic teaching, but simply to state what Paul taught.   He leaves us to accept through the power of faith this discrepancy between the fundamental axiom, which is true and necessary, and the other fact which we can neither deny nor explain.   There is, however, a possible opening to a reconciliation of the discrepancy, which will be alluded to in Section XXV.

If, however, we are to put in one sentence according to the spirit of Paul's teaching the reason why some are not called, the cause lies in themselves : the call is not given because it would be unsuccessful : they do not hear the voice.   The hearing of the call implies and brings and makes success. God never speaks in vain.

XXII. THE IDEA OF GROWTH AND DEVELOPMENT
IN THE TEACHING OF PAUL

A parallel to the triple expression "from and through and to faith," p. 116, is found in Romans xi. 36. There, immediately after the highly emotional sentence regarding the counsel of God, which is so immeasurably beyond the comprehension of man, Paul ends the brief paragraph with a measured and rhythmical phrase, "of Him, and through Him, and unto Him [1] are all things," which may be roughly paraphrased as an assertion that the entire universe originates from God, and its existence (i.e. its order and evolution) continues by means of God, and its development culminates in the attaining (i.e. the re-attaining) to God. Just as the whole universe comes from God, and exists through Him, and with a view to Him, so faith (which is the working of the spirit of God in man) is the originating and maintaining and consummating force in the reconciling of man to God.

This is a glorified form of the ancient Anatolian thought which was latent in the paganism of Western Asia. Paul raises to an infinitely higher level the beautiful old idea that all men—and especially the chiefs and heroes—come from the Great Mother, all are nourished and instructed and guided and advised by her, and all return to her kindly bosom at death—the Great Mother being the mother earth. A touch of the enthusiasm which characterised the pagan votaries of the goddess lingers in the almost lyrical character of Paul's loftier utterance. As we read a paragraph like this,

[1] With a view to Him: εἰς following after and balancing ἐξ and διὰ.

we feel that it is not necessary to regard the even more markedly rhythmical and lyrical phrases of 1 Timothy iii. 16, or Ephesians v. 13-14, as fragments of contemporary hymns quoted by Paul: they may with equal reason be looked upon as examples of the lyrical expression to which the Apostle rose in moments of emotional and mystic enthusiasm.

The righteousness, then, which man possesses is a process of growth towards the supreme righteousness of God. It is the young tree which will grow into the consummation and the perfect form: it is the seed which will produce that fruit. This thought of growth or development is always present in Paul's mind, when he speaks of the righteousness which is attributed to, or set to the account of,[1] man. Hence, in interpreting his thought to his audiences in the Greek and Graeco-Asiatic cities, he frequently has recourse to the metaphor of growth culminating in the production of fruit. So in Philippians i. 11, "being filled with the fruit of righteousness, which is through Jesus Christ". So again in Colossians i. 9-10, "that ye may be filled with the knowledge of his will . . . bearing fruit in every good work, and increasing in the knowledge of God". Here comes in the apparent self-contradiction which is involved in the idea of development, on the one hand "filled with the knowledge of God's will," and yet on the other hand still " increasing in the knowledge of God,"—for the knowledge of His will is the knowledge of Him and of His nature and work. So also in Ephesians v. 8-11, "the fruit of the light is in all goodness and righteousness and truth," whereas " the works of darkness" are unfruitful. By this

---

[1] λογίζομαι is a metaphor from the keeping of accounts, a metaphor which is more characteristic of the Roman than of the Greek thought and writers. It is also perhaps characteristic of the Jewish mind.

Paul means that there results from the " works of darkness " no good fruit, no progress towards God, but only degeneration and evil. Sin is not inactive. It is as real and vigorous, according to Paul's ideas, as righteousness. It is just as dangerous as righteousness is beneficent.

In accordance with this governing thought Paul twice speaks of those who gain salvation as " in process of being saved " (σωζόμενοι). Similarly the lost are often called ἀπολ-λύμενοι, who are in process of perishing. In the latter case the idea of a still incomplete process is more often marked by the tense than in the former. The lost may always turn towards salvation; there is always offered to them the opportunity of changing and returning to God; but Paul calls the saved just as frequently " those who have been saved " as " who are in process of being saved ".[1] There is in the double description of those who are saved the same apparent contradiction of completed and uncompleted process about which we have already spoken. Those who have entered on the process of salvation rarely turn back : those who have put their hand to the plough do not often withdraw it : to begin the process of salvation is itself salvation. On the contrary, those who are in the process of ruin may always return.

In 2 Corinthians iii. 18 the life of the saved is described as a continuous process of transformation from one stage of glory to another. Each step forward in the path towards righteousness attains a higher level and glory ; and this new stage in turns becomes a mere stepping-stone to attain the glory beyond and above.

That this idea of growing, or developing, or being perfected, is implicated in all the teaching of Paul, as it appeals

---

[1] σεσωσμένοι, Eph. ii. 5 and 8 ; σωζόμενοι, 1 Cor. i. 18, 2 Cor. ii. 15 (compare also Acts ii. 47).

to us at the present day, must be presumed. Men of the modern spirit, in whom this idea is the mould for all their thought, must find Paul incomprehensible, unless they recognise that all his thought bears the same form. The good life is a process of perfecting (τελείωσις). No word in Paul is more lucid or more typical of his teaching than this.

The meaning of the term τελείωσις is clearly explained in Romans viii. 29. It is a process of transformation into the likeness or image of Christ, so that men may be His brothers, and He may be the eldest of many brethren. They begin by being actually unlike Him, though having the potentiality of becoming like Him ; they end by being like Him. Such are the first and the final terms in this process. The process itself is defined in the words just quoted from 2 Corinthians iii. 18 ; it is a series of stages in the gradual growth of what Paul names "glory," i.e. the glory, the splendour, the nature of God.

In 1 John iii. 2 the two terms of the process are defined thus : " Now are we children of God, and it is not yet made manifest what we shall be. We know that, if He shall be manifested, we shall be like Him; for we shall see Him even as He is." The apparent inconsistency between Paul's statement in Romans viii. 29 (that the process ends in our becoming children of God, and brothers of Christ, with the likeness of brothers to one another), and John's statement that we are now children of God, is merely another example of what constantly appears when we contemplate the process of growth as Paul describes it. We are in a sense what we are growing to be : we have attained because we shall attain : we possess the righteousness of God because we are developing towards it : our nature is perfected because it is in the process of being perfected : we are the children of God in so far as we are making ourselves His children.

XXIII. Righteousness and Sin

As Paul was filled with an intense, flaming passion for righteousness, so he was filled with an equally intense hatred for sin. The life of man is to him quite as much a struggle to get free from sin, as it is a growing into the righteousness of God.

The form in which the power of sin most clearly manifested itself in the Pauline world was idolatry. This he hated with all the strength of his nature, not merely because idolatry was a philosophic error regarding the nature of God, but because through that error it started mankind on the wrong course towards bad and harmful ends, and became thus the cause of numberless errors and sins. A merely speculative and abstract error about the nature of God might conceivably remain an error in word, not in power, and, if this were so, it need not be very seriously considered; just as a philosophic truth, if it remains abstract and theoretical, a matter of word and not of power, may exert no practical influence and earn no commendation from Paul. But in idolatry the false conception of the Divine nature has become active and misleading, and makes itself a terrible power among men. On this account Paul hated it and fought against it all his life. He had lived amid idolatry. He knew its nature, its power, and its effect.[1]

Sin is a force acting on man's nature, which expresses itself in the deterioration of the individual, and which steadily

---

[1] See also Section II. on this subject.

becomes stronger and more dominant in him. At every step that man takes backwards towards degradation and death, he becomes weaker and less fitted to resist the power of sin that rules him. His nature grows more and more corrupt. His will loses tone, and becomes enslaved to the passions or caprices of the moment.

Moreover, the power of sin increases, not merely in the individual, but in the family and the race. The stern old Hebrew principle that the iniquity of the father is visited upon the children is only an aspect of this domination of sin. The race deteriorates: the family grows weaker and poorer, and dies out: society and the pressure which it exerts on the individual turn towards evil.

All these statements require to be more carefully scrutinised in detail.

Righteousness consists in, and is perfected through, the approach of man nearer and nearer to God. The word "approach" must not be misinterpreted or misapplied. It must be taken as an expression of spiritual truth, not of local character. God is not in one place more than in another. We do not go to any special point or place in order to find Him there. Place is a term of limitation, and can be applied to the illimitable and the infinite only because we have to use the limited ideas and terms of finite existence for want of more appropriate and correct words. Man approaches to God only in the approximation of his spirit and nature to the spirit and nature of God. He is transformed into the same image from glory to glory; and as Professor H. A. A. Kennedy says,[1] the likeness is not mere outward appearance, for to Paul the term "image" means appearance that "rests on identity of character, community of being".

Sin, as the contrary idea to righteousness, consists in the

---

[1] *St. Paul on the Last Things*, p. 294.

movement of man away from God, that is to say, in the
increasing divergence of his spirit from that of God, and the
increasing opposition between his nature and the nature of
God.   It is not simply a definite, unchanging fact; it is a
process; and its character is to become accelerated as it
continues.

Moreover, sin is not merely a process; it is also a force,
and it becomes in itself a power ever growing stronger and
stronger to draw man away from God.   That this is so is
evident from the situation of man in relation to God and
to the universe.   Man is placed in the difficulty of having
to re-attain to God.   The difficulty is there to be overcome;
and through overcoming it the Divine element in man is
strengthened, and he grows in likeness to God.   The difficulty constitutes the opportunity.   Only through the possibility of a choice does man learn to exercise his power
of choosing the right and rejecting the evil.   Thereby his
nature is strengthened, and he attains towards real freedom
of will.   In the strengthening of his will he is strengthening
the Divine nature within him.   The will of God is that man
should do good; and the will or the spirit of God acts in
man to make him choose the good.

Thus, on the one hand, it is true to say that the evil in
the world exists in order to give man the opportunity of
overcoming it and attaining to God.   The evil is in this
view the measure of man's separation from God; and
human life well lived is the traversing of this intervening
distance.   Without evil there cannot be the human part of
the universe, for unless the human is separated from the
Divine, there would be no humanity and no cognisable
universe.   From this point of view, then, evil is mere negation, formless and empty distance between man and God.
It is the condition of the act of creation; now the nature

of God is to create, and without interposing the distance that separates Himself from man He could not create this universe.

Yet, on the other hand, evil which is not overcome is thereby made active. If the will of the man fails and is not strengthened by achievement, it does not remain as before, but is weakened. The nature of the man thus becomes less like the nature of God; the distance by which he is separated from God is widened; and his energy for work in the future is diminished. The widening gap that intervenes between him and God, the loss of sympathy with and desire to attain to God, becomes a power to dominate and enslave his will and control his action. The opportunity which is missed, the possibility of right choice which is not used, leaves behind the omission an inheritance of increased inability to face and overcome the difficulties of the world.

Being now less like God, and being further separated from God, through the growth of weakness and idleness, sluggishness and inactivity, man loses some portion of his original endowment and power of comprehending God and good. Such an endowment man possessed in the beginning:[1] what can be known about God was clear at first in his mind and judgment, for this power was the original gift of God to man.[2] He loses it by not exercising it; it is clouded and distorted, and the intelligence is darkened.

From all this there result error and misconception of the nature of God; and thus comes idolatry. The form of idolatry which was most familiar to Paul and to his readers was the representation of the incorruptible God after the image and likeness of corruptible man (as especially among the Greeks), or of birds and quadrupeds (as especially among

---

[1] See also Sections IX. XI.   [2] Rom. i. 19.

the Egyptians), and serpents (as was common everywhere).[1] Instead of contemplating the Divine power as it is in its reality, men invented these foolish forms, trying by human skill to compensate for their gradual loss of ability to see God, who was now further removed from them.

It is involved in Paul's view, and this was his inheritance from the ancient and characteristic Hebrew conception, that man degenerates through error; and that man's earliest religious ideas are not so wrong and false as his later conceptions. Backsliding goes on steadily, when it has once set in. In other words, the savage of the present day is not primitive man, but man in an advanced stage of degradation; and idolatry in the Greek or the Egyptian or other pagan forms is the result also of degradation from an earlier simplicity, which had not been so far removed from the truth as the modern savage is.

This Pauline doctrine is not admitted by recent speculations regarding the history of religion and the growth of mythology. On the contrary, the postulate is assumed by almost all investigators, that the history of religion is a history of continuous progress. It is not part of my purpose to defend Paul's teaching (for it can defend itself), nor yet to compare it with modern speculative theories; but it is involved in my design to show that his teaching is reasonable and consistent with the highest modern thought. To do so fully would lead us too far afield at present, because it would require a complete study of comparative religion and comparative sociology from an unfashionable point of view.

There are, however, two or three points that can be stated briefly without fear of contradiction. There is, for example, no possibility of disputing the fact that extreme polytheism

[1] Rom. i. 23.

is a later development alike in Greece and in Egypt: so much is admitted universally. Behind that extreme polytheism, as it was current in the time of Paul, there lay in many cases the simpler and older religion of the common man—not the philosopher who sought and invented a highly philosophic explanation of polytheism, but the uneducated rustic. This common man was often content to reverence "the God," to be guided by some vague perception of the will of "the God," to make vows and prayers to "the God," and to record a confession of his failure to act according to the will and ritual of "the God". The ideas and actions of the common man were false and bad in many respects; his training and surroundings from childhood had been calculated to turn his conduct into wrong grooves; but at least his views continued to be in many respects the simple issue of his native intuition, of his intercourse with the phenomena of nature, and of his daily contemplation of those eternal witnesses, the sun and the sky. The deep things of God, the invisible things of God, His everlasting power and Divine nature,[1] were only to a small degree within the ken of the common man ; but he had the beginning of knowledge in his heart, and he had received too little education to lose hold of the simple beginnings, though he had been trained to misapply these initial conceptions.

In the second place, the modern savage is in some and even in many cases found dwelling amid the remains of a higher civilisation. His world and his society have degenerated around him, and his habits and thoughts in maturity are the product of a long degradation. This situation sets in strong relief the truth of Paul's other opinion, derived from his old Hebrew training, that the sins of the fathers are visited upon the children. This is a

[1] Rom. i. 20.

scientific fact of the highest importance. All educated men are now alive to it. All are seeking to find some way to elude it, or to minimise the evils that arise through it. Something, as we think and hope, could be done to give the children a fairer start, and a more even chance in life; but how ineffective have our efforts been as yet, and how powerless has European civilisation proved to save the children from the consequences of their fathers' guilt.

The stream of life does indeed purify itself as it runs; the punishment of the children in the old Hebrew doctrine lasts to the third and fourth generation; but there are certain causes and consequences that last longer and cause a permanent deterioration of society, or even (as physicians say) poison the springs of life at its source.

Sin cannot be localised or confined to one individual in the succession of the generations. We all suffer through the sins of our parents, and we all transmit the consequence of sin to following generations. Racial guilt is a real and powerful force. The Hebrew teaching is fully justified by experience and science; and Paul, who assumed its truth, was right.

In short, a good life consists in the overcoming of difficulties. Such is the law of nature, or, in other words, the will of God. A difficulty or trial which is not overcome gives an opening to sin: it is the triumph of inertia in the character of the man who fails to do well: his nature ceases to grow, and slips back to weakness and degeneration: the Divine element in him fails and is dulled, whereas by conquering difficulties it would grow stronger and brighter. The progressive development of man, the realisation of "the chief end of man," consists in that strengthening of the Divine within him, in the raising it through the stages of life from glory to glory, in the growing sympathy with the place and work of God in the world, and in the consequent identification of one's personal happiness with the life and triumph of the Divine will.

On the contrary, the force of inertia does not remain constant under failure, but is increased. From being a mere hindrance, it grows into a power actively working on the nature of the man, encouraging his self-conceit,[1] making him more and more selfish and self-centred. He expels from his mind all sense of the Divine around him and above him; and thus he loses the desire to attain to God, and makes his own pleasure or success the end and aim of his life. He substitutes for the true God his own conception of what God is. In ancient times and among uneducated races, he expressed his conception in some external and visible form or symbol; and thus arose the kind of paganism with which Paul was familiar in the Graeco-Roman world. In more educated races, the false conception of God is often an ideal of some kind, and is special to the individual mind. Such ideals may be and often are of a comparatively lofty order, and the life which aims at realising such great ideals partakes of the nobility of its object. The nobler the ideal, the nearer does it approach the nature of the true God, and the more does the life which strives towards this ideal approximate towards the life of the seeker after God. Yet there remains always a certain manifest difference, for the created ideal, lofty as it may be, partakes of the mind which has created it; and the man who seeks after it is not aiming at an object above himself, but is satisfied with the expression of himself.

The lower kind of paganism, such as St. Paul knew, externalised its own conception of God in a visible form, which appealed to others, and was almost always common to a

[1] Rom. i. 21.

whole race, or a tribe, or an association. Along with it there invariably grew up a formal cult and ritual (from which the individual ideal of the higher paganism generally remains free), because the veneration which is common to a number of persons must frame for its expression a series of actions which are incumbent on all as symbolical of the common purpose. With the ritual grows up a body of priests, who know the series of prescribed actions and guide the conduct of ignorant devotees.[1] The passions, the ignorance, the vices and the failings of the multitude, mould the customary ritual, and express themselves in it. The history of paganism, therefore, always becomes a racial degeneration ; because paganism is in its nature human and erroneous, and does not seek after the ideal of the true God.

[1] The stages of this growth are described more fully from the same point of view in the present writer's article on " The Religion of Asia Minor " in Dr. Hastings' *Dictionary of the Bible*, vol. v. p. 126 f.

XXIV. The Pagan World of the Roman Empire

The picture which Paul draws in Romans i. 24 f. of the results of idolatry in the deterioration of moral character in the society of the Graeco-Roman world is not exaggerated, provided one remembers that it was not true of every individual member of the race. There were noble characters in pagan, especially Roman society. There were philosophers, whose life in many respects corresponded to their philosophy. But the general standard of conduct and of judgment was extremely low, and (what was worse) had been deteriorating through recent centuries.

The force of sin in the form of idolatry was in a marked degree one which worked on a race through the generations, and caused a steadily progressive deterioration in the social standards of conduct for the individual and of moral judgment generally. Paul had seen this progressive deterioration in the Graeco-Roman world, and traced it to its cause. The pagans themselves were fully alive to it, and described it in almost equally strong terms; but they did not trace it to the same cause as Paul did, though they saw something of the truth. Lucretius ascribes this deterioration and unhappiness to religion: "Human life lay foully prostrate upon earth crushed down under the weight of religion": the "victory over religion brings man level with heaven": and therefore "we must well grasp the principle of things above" in order to see the world aright, and to realise how "great are the evils to which religion could prompt".[1]

[1] Lucretius, i. 65-126.

139

All this Paul could and might have said in almost the same words [1] as Lucretius; yet the meaning which he put in them would be totally different.　Lucretius would eliminate all religion, and relegate all gods to "the lucid interspace of world and world" where they live at ease and neither care nor think about men; and he would substitute for belief in a personal God the study of "the principle of things above, the force by which everything on earth proceeds".　Considering that, to a certain extent, Paul might have adopted the philosopher's most typical words, we must recognise that (as was stated in II. and XIX.) he was not so diametrically opposed to philosophy as he was to idolatry, and that in suitable circumstances he would have felt himself free (as at Athens) to rest his argument to certain minds on the philosophical basis, and show that this basis was only a stage on the way to the fuller truth.

[1] Naturally, Paul would use the term "superstition," where Lucretius speaks of "religion": but all religion was superstition to Lucretius, and he would not have objected to the use of the more opprobrious term.

XXV. The Wrath of God

Such is the order of the universe; and the universe is the embodiment and expression of the will of God. The progress of man towards God, i.e. salvation, according to the will and intention of God, is the consummation of the Divine love. Conversely, the retrogression of man away from God, his growing unlikeness to God and his increasing inability to comprehend the will and nature of God, is the consummation of the Divine wrath. Hence "the wrath of God is revealed from heaven against all ungodliness and unrighteousness of men, who hinder the truth in unrighteousness"; and this wrath is manifested against them, because they go wrong in spite of the knowledge of God which by nature they possess. (Rom. i. 18.)

This "wrath of God" can be defined more clearly when we compare the expression "day of wrath"; and it is rightly treated by Professor H. A. A. Kennedy[1] as an equivalent expression (though used from a different point of view) to the other terms, "destruction," "perdition," etc., which express the lot of the sinful. The inference from it is clear, that there is only one power in the universe, that all proceeds from God, that sin is permitted in the purpose of God and is a fact and condition of His created universe. "The creation" (i.e. the universe as created) "was subjected to vanity" (i.e. to failure in attaining the ultimate purpose

[1] *St. Paul on the Last Things*, p. 313: "the terms which he employs to denote the fate of the unbelieving are ὄλεθρος, θάνατος, φθορά, ἀπώλεια, ἀπόλλυσθαι, ὀργή".

141

intended by God), "not of its own will" (i.e. not because it deliberately and intentionally aims at and desires failure), "but by reason of Him who subjected it" (i.e. because this is a stage in the evolution of the purpose of God), "in hope that the creation itself also shall be delivered from the bondage of corruption into the liberty of the glory of the children of God." I should venture to gather from this that in Paul's conception the failure is temporary and the vanity is evanescent, "the evil is null, is nought, is silence implying sound,"—but that this is so only when we take a wider view of the universal purpose of the Creator. There shall be a new heaven and a new earth;[1] but these come only after a great lapse of time in the movement of the ages.

In the life of individuals the purpose of God has not the width of scene necessary for perfecting itself. That purpose works on a greater scale and through a wider sweep of time. The individual man, therefore, does not in Paul's view fill up a complete cycle of time; but is only a unit in a greater whole, or, so to say, a link in a long chain; and the Divine will works itself out through a cycle vastly longer than the life of the individual. Paul never wholly separated himself from the old Hebrew point of view, that the Promise of God is given to the race not to the individual, that the Divine purpose works itself out in the nation, and that the individual cannot be regarded as a complete and independent part of the scheme of the universe, but is merely a unit and part of the race.

May we not see in this a hint respecting the direction in which Paul would have proceeded, if he had been called upon to explain the fate of the sinful individual and to reconcile this with the good purpose of God and the necessary triumph

---

[1] 2 Pet. iii. 13 ; Rev. xxi. 1.

of that purpose ?[1]   I do not presume to put words into the mouth of Paul, or to suggest groundless hypotheses as to the way in which he would have explained what in his letters he has not found occasion to explain : I would avoid even the risk of seeming to do this.   Yet there is sufficient reason to assert that he had not wholly cut himself off from the Hebrew view (a view characteristically Oriental), that the individual must be judged in his family and his tribe and above all in his nation.   We of the West are in modern time, perhaps, too apt to think only of the individual isolated from others in his life and fate, and to interpret Paul as if he were wholly of our mind in this way of looking solely at the single being as a complete entity and never regarding him as a mere unit in the nation, whose destiny ultimately controls and overrides his fate.

[1] See above, Section XXI.

XXVI. Sin as a Force and Power over Man

As regards the relation between God and man we are always encountered by the difficulty—one might well say, the impossibility—of expressing and even of understanding its nature. This relation is, obviously and necessarily, a unique thing in the universe of our knowledge. There is not, and there cannot be, any other relation similar to it; we cannot aid understanding by comparing it with anything else: and all metaphors fail to fit the conditions fully, however useful they may often be.

Like everything else that concerns God, this relation of man to Him has to be perceived by direct intuition, or, as Paul would put it, through the power of faith, which is for us "a conviction of things not seen".[1] Just as we recognise and know through faith that God is and that God is good, without being able to demonstrate by logical argument that either axiom is true, so we recognise and know that, as was pointed out in the previous Sections, mere increase in the distance that separates man from God, or (to use our other form of expression) increasing unlikeness of man to God, does not remain a mere abstract proposition, but becomes a force or power acting on the will in such a way as to weaken the sympathy of the human for the Divine nature, to lessen in man the power of recognising the Divine character and purpose, and to enfeeble the desire of man for reunion with God.

If we are challenged to prove this assertion that increase

[1] Heb. xi. 1.

of distance from God becomes a power of evil, we cannot demonstrate it. It is involved in the nature of our relation to God. We feel it and we know it. It is an ultimate or primary fact from which we have to start. In Pauline language, we live by faith alone.

This truth, however, is simply another form of the axiom that God is good : He is good because He draws man to Him naturally. Like seeks to like through a sort of attractive power which the one exerts on the other; and the lesser, i.e. man, moves towards the greater, i.e. God. Such is the natural fact, or the purpose of God, which acts and is so long as man has not lost his simple and natural character. Yet even this metaphorical expression that "like draws to like" is utterly inadequate as a statement of the relation : it is only a figurative description which in some degree helps comprehension, but it is both incomplete and positively inaccurate in some important respects.

The term "attractive force," then, is merely another metaphor by which we attempt to express the relation between the Creator and the created. The righteous action is the actualising of this force ; and the performance of such an action makes the power stronger, so that we feel righteousness as a force in us, in which the force of faith is merged. The two become indistinguishable in fact, though distinguishable in language. Such is the nature of this force and the law of its action.

It is only another side of the same law and nature, which rules and constitutes righteousness, that the failure to perform the righteous act—which is tantamount to the performance of the unrighteous act in the supposed situation—not merely weakens the force attracting the individual to God, but actually brings into existence a counter-force, the power of evil, which tends to draw the individual away from God, to intensify his unlikeness to God, to increase continuously his distance from God.

These various ways in which we have attempted to state the nature of sin are merely metaphors drawn from human experience to aid comprehension, and not philosophical definitions. Sin, therefore, is a force and a power, not simply a fact. When we speak of sin widening the distance from God, that metaphor is insufficient to suggest that sin thereby strengthens itself and establishes its hold on the man's will. Such, however, is the law according to which this failure to act righteously works; it is not a mere negation, it is more than simple non-righteousness. It is, or it becomes, the power of evil ruling the will of man.

Yet for this we have no more proof than there was for the two previously stated axioms (or rather the two forms of the same axiom). Such we know: such we perceive: the experience of the world in past history and in contemporary life is inexplicable otherwise.

Hence arose the intensity of Paul's hatred for sin. This hatred is his heritage from his Hebrew ancestry, from the past history of his people, from the dealings of God with the forefathers. It was a flame burning more intensely in him than in other Jews, because his native power was stronger; but it was a purely Jewish force, and utterly unlike any feeling that was characteristic of pure Hellenism. His hatred of idolatry, one special class or form of sin, was natural to a typical Jew brought up in a pagan city.

The Jews in Paul's time began life on a higher moral platform than the Gentiles. The Law had been a stern and salutary master (*paidagogos*), forcing them onwards. But it was not able to carry them beyond a certain point: they could not obey it completely: it was a yoke imposed as an external thing: it was not able to produce real righteousness, but only the semblance of righteousness, because the acts which it enforced did not spring from the free will of the individual, i.e. from the Divine element in him striving of its own initiative towards the Divine end. Hence the act, which was outwardly right, did not result in sufficiently vitalising and strengthening within the man that force which is righteousness.

Yet this action according to the Law, although it could not make the individual man righteous, did produce an effect on the nation, and so ultimately on the individual through the nation. It produced a national righteousness, in other words, a national standard of judgment according to the knowledge of moral principle, which was embodied in the law. It developed conscience and the consciousness of sin through the fact that the prohibition of sin stood always placarded before the nation in the law.[1] It is a true fact of psychology that such a national standard of judgment about sin, and such a national conscience, may be developed by generations of contemplation of a moral law; and the modern phrase "the Nonconformist conscience" attests the result as a historical fact in a living instance.

This national conscience, making a national standard of judgment about righteousness, produces a powerful effect on the individual member of the nation. He commonly has the national righteousness, being pushed forward to it by the compulsion of social requirements. This national or racial righteousness in a person, for which social compulsion and not the will and character of that person is responsible,

[1] " I had not known sin except through the law," Rom. vii. 7. " Through the law cometh the knowledge of sin," Rom. iii. 20. Compare Rom. vii. 13.

may be described metaphorically as static, not dynamic righteousness. It does not remake the individual. It does not recreate and reinvigorate his nature. He is not born again. Commonly, its effect is to make him more self-satisfied, more complacent, less conscious of the Divine.[1] Only dynamic righteousness, which springs from the individual striving towards reunion with God, can make him a new man; and such righteousness cannot come except through the force of faith, which is a possession of the individual soul.

The national righteousness, of which we have been speaking, has many advantages. When the individual falls short of it, he is conscious that he is untrue to the national character. This consciousness that one is falling below the national standard continues so long as the law remains a living force in the race or in the individual. If the law comes to be felt only as a dead prescription of works, it ceases to be a master that forces the nation on towards its standard; and yet even then it has not lost all its power and usefulness.

Paul always felt that the Jews, even though they were not gaining true righteousness through the law, were starting on a higher standard of judgment and knowledge than the ordinary Gentiles. " I bear them witness that they have a zeal for God, but not according to a right intuition." [2] It is much to have this zeal for God; but the zeal requires to be guided by a right perception of His nature and of man's relation to Him through Christ. Without that

---

[1] Rom. x. 3, " Being ignorant of God's righteousness, and seeking to establish their own, they (i.e. the Jews living according to the law and the national righteousness) did not subject themselves to the righteousness of God ".

[2] Rom. x. 2.

perception the Jews, in the issue, set up their own instead of the righteousness of God.[1]

Accordingly, Paul, like other Jews of his time, started with the immense advantage of this strong hatred for sin and zeal for God. Sin kept him from God. He regarded the power of sin almost as a personal enemy : it was to him Satan.

Sin, even more than righteousness, can be national and racial. As we have just seen, national righteousness, though in itself a good thing, never attained to be the true dynamic righteousness in the highest sense of the term ; but sin that is national and inculcated through the national standard of judgment can be just as harmful, as dangerous, and as hostile to right, as when it proceeds from individual initiative. Satan, the power of evil, can rule in a nation and set up his throne in its capital, and be all the more powerful and terrible in consequence. Thus, in Paul's estimation, the political and social conditions, whether Imperial or municipal, which impeded his work of spreading the Gospel, were hindrances put in his way by Satan, the enemy.

Whether, or how far, Paul considered Satan as literally and strictly a personal being, must remain uncertain. He had not entirely freed himself from a lingering belief in "principalities and powers" intermediate between God and man ; and thus, on the one hand, it was easy for him to believe in such a purely evil power, subordinate to God, while on the other hand, through the stimulus of his intense hatred for sin, it was always easy for him to fall into the use of metaphorical or half metaphorical language, picturing the power of sin as a personal being whom he could abominate, and against whom he could more easily rouse in his pagan

---

[1] Rom. x. 3, quoted in the last note but one.

correspondents the same intense hatred that he himself cherished.

Strong emphasis is in Paul often due rather to emotion than to intellect, even in cases where the subject and the purpose seem to be properly intellectual. The emphasis is not so much intended to ensure attention on the part of his readers, as forced out of him by the intense passion of his own convictions, which were not matter of cool intellectual assent, but ruled his emotions and the depths of his nature. Thus, however much the language he uses about Satan in some cases may suggest that Paul regarded him as a personal enemy, I would not venture to assert that this implies full intellectual belief in the existence of such a personality. It is not easy to define with certainty the range and limits of metaphor and the effect of emotion on expression in Paul.

After all, Paul was before everything a preacher and a missionary. To him the first and supreme duty was to make his converts hate sin and love righteousness; and it was far more important to make them dread and detest a personal Satan than to lead them into philosophical speculation about the purpose of God in permitting sin and about the whole problem of evil. If they began to theorise about the purpose of God in a creation of which evil forms a part, and about the necessity which imposed itself on the Creator, as a condition of creative action, to leave open the possibility of evil, i.e. separation from God, such vague and profitless theorising, and the logomachies which would arise therefrom, could only distract them from the first business of their life, *viz.*, to be good; and that danger was already apparent to Paul, incipient in the Corinthians, more advanced in the Colossians, and fully developed in the Asian churches when he wrote to Timothy.

XXVII. The First Adam and the Second Adam

How largely the idea of racial sin bulked in the mind of Paul appears in his treatment of the man Adam, and the primal sin which Adam committed and whose effects "the second Adam" obliterates. "Through one man"—*viz.*, Adam, whose historical character as being the first-created man Paul unquestioningly assumes—"sin entered into the world, and death through sin ; and so death passed unto all men, for that all sinned."[1]   The way to salvation was closed by Adam, and reopened by Jesus as "the second Adam".

The first man was the first sinner ; and thus death, which is the wages or consequence of sin, began, and has ever since continued to reign in the world.   As Dr. Denney says,[2] " Paul uses ' death' to convey different shades of meaning in different places, but he does not explicitly distinguish different senses of the word ; and it is probably misleading rather than helpful to say that in one sentence (here, for example) 'physical' death is meant, and in another (vii. 24, e.g.) 'spiritual' death.   The analysis is foreign to his mode of thinking.   All that 'death' conveys to the mind entered into the world through sin."   Dr. Denney adds that, in the second part of this verse, v. 12, Paul explains "the universality of death " : it rests upon the universality of sin.

For us, however, who are attempting to rethink in modern

[1] Rom. v. 12.   [2] Commentary on Romans v. 12.

terms the thought of Paul, it is absolutely necessary to attempt to distinguish in the process of our thought what side of the idea "death" should be determining and dominant in our mind, when we re-form or re-express a Pauline principle. Paul, as Dr. Denney says, never consciously defined to himself, or thought of defining, the different senses in which he seems to use the word : he had the whole idea "death" in his mind when he used the word. Yet, when he speaks of "death" as the wages of sin and as the lot of the wicked, he must have been conscious that this death is something different from its appearance as a stage in the path of righteousness, or even as the earthly end of that path.[1]   "For me to live is Christ, and to die is gain " : such "death" is not the lot of the wicked : it is simply a process in the transformation of his body into the spiritual body like that of Christ.   So when he says, " I through the law died unto the law that I might live unto God," he regards the death through which he passed as the end of the older stage in his experience and the entrance on the new life : through death he enters on life.

In this same passage, Romans v. 12, he seems to regard " death " as the removal from God, the final exclusion from God, the definite separation from God, which is consummated at the physical death, but has been going on throughout the career of sin.   This is the "second death" of which John speaks.

His words in Romans v. 12, however, have been interpreted as an assertion that all men sinned in Adam and fell with Adam.   What does this mean ?   Why should we now be punished in respect of anything that Adam has done, or

---

[1] John's phrase "the second death " may perhaps indicate a certain consciousness, common in the early Church, that the word has more than one meaning (Rev. ii. 11, xx. 6, 14, xxi. 8).

rewarded in virtue of anything that Jesus has done? That is a question which rises first in many human minds; but it is wrongly put, and the point of view implied in it is false. Paul does not say that all men are punished because Adam sinned, or because they were made guilty in Adam's guilt, but that all men, in proportion as (or because) all have during their own life sinned,[1] are punished through the death which began with Adam.

The sin of Adam inflicted incalculable injury on the human race, not by implicating all men in itself, but by involving them in its consequences. Such is the fact of the world: such is the experience of· life: such is the law of nature. Every day it is exemplified. The innocent suffer from the sins in which they have no share. The nation as a whole may be ruined by the folly or the crime of one man. This is the fact to which we must accommodate our life, and from which we must start in our philosophy. Paul saw in it the opening for the grace and kindness of God to show itself. If we suffer through the sin of the first Adam, it is in order that the second Adam may have scope for the infinite power and mercy by which He rescues all men, and justifies the Divine plan.

In the first place, Adam is the typical man, i.e. a fair and typical specimen of the genus man : not less, but if anything more, favourably situated than the ordinary man. With every advantage, with no inherited taint, he failed, and with him all men fail, because it is impossible that they should succeed where he could not succeed. Subse-

---

[1] "On the ground that," or "in the proportion that," seems to be the strict sense of ἐφ' ᾧ πάντες ἥμαρτον. "On condition that" is the most typical sense of ἐφ' ᾧ, and the use here naturally arises out of that, and is nearly identical in force with it. Death got power over them on condition that (or in so far as) they sinned.

quent generations of men have in themselves less chance of success than he, because they are born and nurtured amid surroundings already corrupted.   Paul holds fast by the old Hebrew doctrine that the children suffer in the sin of their parents for generations.   Sin affects society, brings disease, physical and moral, into the nation, causes a racial deterioration through which the descendants of Adam have all suffered.   History is the record of the stages through which the initial disobedience to law has worked out its consequences.   Social and medical science trace the laws according to which those consequences are worked out. Adam is the test case, according to Paul's view.   If he failed, none of his descendants can succeed through their own effort and initiative.

In the second place, if it be objected that this was an insufficient test, and therefore unfair, that objection misses Paul's meaning.   Paul does not rest his argument simply on the one test case of Adam.   He appeals to all history and experience.   Throughout the whole passage, i. 18-iii. 20, he has laboured to prove that all have sinned, and failed to attain righteousness ; and in v. 12 he briefly sums up that proof in the phrase " for that all have sinned ".

His purpose in v. 12 is not to argue that all are guilty of sin in virtue of Adam's primal sin, but that, as death came over all men through Adam's sin, so life becomes the portion open to all men through Christ's triumph in death over death.   The death of Christ proved to be the life over death, and His triumph is the triumph of mankind.

Reference to Paul's words elsewhere makes this quite plain.   Compare 1 Corinthians i. 21 : " As in Adam all die, so in Christ shall all be made alive ".   In this chapter of Romans the same statement is repeated in the immediate sequel : v. 15, " By the trespass of the one the many died "; v. 17, "By the trespass of the one death reigned through the one ". Men all die with Adam, because all sin : i.e., men all fail to attain righteousness, and need a Saviour.

Since the typical and representative man failed, and human nature is thus shown to be in its own power incapable of resisting sin, the only cure lies in another representative man, who triumphs over sin. This second typical man is Jesus : He must be in the fullest sense man, otherwise His case will not prove anything for other men or help them in any way : He stripped Himself of His high dignity and became the representative man ; and He proved what men can attain to in virtue of the Divine nature which is in them. It is an essential part of Paul's teaching, that there is in man this Divine element, which can grow until it dominates his whole nature. What man needs is some force to start him out of the inertia of sin on the course of growth towards the Divine truth.

As we have already seen, Paul finds this force simply in Faith, in the belief that it can be done because Christ has shown that it is done. For that growth towards the truth it is necessary that the man should, as Paul expresses it, die to sin : i.e., he must cease to move on in the way towards sin, and begin to move in the opposite direction towards righteousness. The beginning to do this is already accepted as salvation : the seed that is planted contains in it already the mature tree. The man who has once believed in that possibility has got the driving force which will impel him on in the course, hard as it is ; and this force is the fact that Jesus died for each individual man, separate and single, and by dying to the world of transience and mutation resumed His Divine personality.

It is not strictly correct to say that the appearance of Jesus as a figure in human history brought the Divine nature nearer to man.   It only brought the Divine nature more within the cognisance of human faculties and perceptive powers.   Thus this event seemed to bring God closer to man, because it made the cognisance of God by man easier.

So far as I can understand the thought of Paul, he assumes this as fundamental truth.   Jesus becomes real to us, a real power for us, only in so far as the belief in the power of His death enters into us, and becomes part of our living self with the force that a great idea and an intense enthusiasm exert on the nature and action of the man who feels them.   Ultimately He becomes, through the progress of our spiritual life, the whole of our living self: "it is no longer I that live, but Christ that liveth in me". The human self and the human nature is identified with the Divine nature, and yet the human personality and self-identity remains.   This is eternal life in Paul's doctrine. This is salvation.

XXVIII. THE SAINT AS KING

In the view of Paul the world lay round man like a sea of storm and vicissitude, in which each human being lived his life staggering onward from danger to danger, no sooner free from one trouble than involved in another. Everything was fleeting, changeable, constantly varying. In the words which have already been quoted,[1] Paul "sighed as scarcely any other has done beneath the curse of the transiency of all that is earthly ".

It was perfectly true, but it was not the whole truth, to say that for the Christian and saint the world around was just as evanescent, as incalculable, and as unintelligible, as it was for the sinner. The salvation which he had already gained did not lie in this human life. Although he was re-made, re-created, re-constituted, in Johannine phrase born again, yet human life continued to be as much as ever for him a stormy sea; he was "afflicted on every side, fightings around, fears in the mind"; and apart from all external discomforts, there was the more wearing anxiety for his converts and the sympathy with and participation in the troubles of every individual and of every congregation.[2]

The Stoic ideal of the truly wise man, the true *philosopher*, who was wholly superior to fate and to his surroundings, calm and unruffled amid whatever tempests howled around

---

[1] Quoted in Section X. from Steffen, *Zft. f. d. N.T. Wissensch.* 1901, ii. p. 124, after Kennedy, *St. Paul's Conception of the Last Things*, p. 6.

[2] 2 Cor. vii.; compare xi. 28.

him, absolutely unmoved by the troubles which over-
whelmed others—an ideal which in different expressions was
characteristic of later Greek philosophy generally,—Paul did
not approve.   His heart became only more open to suffer
with others, and more intensely sympathetic with their trials,
as he progressed in life : " Who is weak, and I am not weak ?
who is caused to stumble, and I burn not ? "   The philosophic
ideal of passionlessness and *Ataraxia* was infinitely remote
from his mind.   The relief for which he sighed did not lie
in that direction.

There was, however, a peace attainable in another direction.
" The fruit of the spirit is love, joy, peace, long-suffering,
kindness, goodness, faithfulness, meekness, self-control." [1]
The peace which is thus gained lies at the opposite pole
from *Ataraxia*.   Through infinite sympathy with suffering
comes freedom from suffering.   One is thus brought face to
face with another of the Pauline apparent self-contradictions :
by going infinitely far in one direction you find yourself
at the opposite pole.   Yet this is a truth of nature and of
physical law.

A modern poet who believed himself to be absolutely
anti-Christian, although his attitude towards the world and
the emotions of his heart had been made possible only
through centuries of Christian teaching, expresses in a
striking antithetic form a truth that is similar and illuminative.   It is, as he says, the nature of the True and the
Good that, the more it is divided, the more it is multiplied,
so that each subdivision is larger than the original whole ;
but Wrong, the more it is divided and participated in by
others, becomes less, until it may thus be entirely eliminated
from the world.   That, says the poet, is the hope of the

[1] 1 Gal. v. 22.

future, which alone makes life endurable for those who comprehend the horror and the deterioration and ruin of the world around us.

> Mind from its object differs most in this :
> Evil from good ; misery from happiness ;
> The baser from the nobler ; the impure
> And frail from what is clear and must endure.
> If you divide suffering or dross, you may
> Diminish till it is consumed away ;
> If you divide pleasure and love and thought,
> Each part exceeds the whole ; and we know not
> How much, while any yet remains unshared,
> Of pleasure may be gained, of sorrow spared.
>
> SHELLEY, " Epipsychidion ".

The thought is not that of Paul ; but it is the expression from a wholly different standpoint of a similar moral principle and an " eternal law " [1]. Its antithetic expression aids in the understanding of Paul's principle, yet its carefully balanced antitheses are the very opposite of Paul's style. In Paul the antitheses are not balanced against one another : they are the outcome of different moods and frames of mind, stated at different times, and rarely brought intentionally into juxtaposition.

Thus, after all, the Stoic ideal of the wise man is realised through Paulinism, but in a different direction, by voyaging over the sea of life to the opposite shore. That the Stoic paradox, " the wise man is the king," was not very far distant from Paul's mind is probable. " If by the trespass of one *man* death was king through the one, much more shall they that receive the abundant gift of grace and of righteousness be kings in life through the one Jesus Christ." [2] We have preferred to translate " be king " rather than " reign," as this comes nearer the root idea of the Greek

---

[1] The phrase is Shelley's in the immediate context.
[2] Rom. v. 17.

verb, and also because it shows a certain lingering of the
Greek philosophic ideal in Paul's mind. Paul's thought
is Hebrew, essentially and fundamentally, right through
from beginning to end ; and yet it has risen through Judaism
to a higher level and a nobler stage, so that Hellenism was
capable of being ennobled to harmonise with it. Paul's
essentially Hebraic religion was expressed by him in forms
and language which might be comprehended by the Greek
mind ; and he was able to express it in such forms and
words, because he had been brought up amid the surroundings of a Hellenised Tarsus and had shared in the society
and the education of a Graeco-Roman life.

This is the perfection of missionary teaching, to make intelligible an alien religion to a foreign people, not by dilut-
ing it or by transforming it, not by watering it down or by
assimilating it to the thought habitual to the foreign mind,
but by stating it in the most complete and uncompromising
form, yet in such a way that it is possible for the foreign
hearer to rise towards it along his own line of thinking.

There is a plane to which all perfectly natural and honest
thought can be raised. On that plane Pauline teaching is
expressed. No truth is inconsistent with such teaching.
Paul emphatically states and maintains that in the Gentile
thought there was truth, even the highest, indeed the sole
kind of truth, *viz.*, truth about the character of God and
man's relation to Him : " Gentiles, having not law, are law
unto themselves, in that they show the work of the law
written in their hearts, their conscience bearing witness in
accordance, and their reasonings in inmost meditation
accusing or else defending," [1] as they weigh their own

[1] Rom. ii. 14 f. The above translation appears to give the true sense.
The American Revision properly disconnects this from ii. 16 (which Westcott and Hort closely connect). There is no reference to the judgment day

action in silent thinking about right and wrong. In such a passage as this Paul had in mind the teaching, and possibly the actual lectures, of Athenodorus of Tarsus and similar philosophic teachers. A philosophy which could teach what is quoted from Athenodorus rested on a good foundation: it was fundamentally true, and could be developed into hearty sympathy with Paulinism, if only it developed freely and naturally.

I should not hesitate to see in 2 Timothy ii. 12, "If we suffer with Him, we shall also be king along with Him," a later influence of the thought in Romans as it had remained always in Paul's heart. The expression in that passage is an echo of Romans vi. 8, "But if we died with Christ, we believe that we shall also live with Him"; but the thought is modified by the idea of kingship which was in Paul's mind a few verses earlier, v. 14 and 17. The form which he chooses was intelligible and suited to the Greeks, because they had always before them the philosophic principle that the truly good man "is a King": he raises this principle to a higher level, but keeps the phrase. The passage in Timothy is not a quotation made by some later Paulinist from a church hymn that had been taken phrase by phrase out of Paul: it is a fresh expression of Paul's own favourite thoughts in slightly varying phraseology.[1]

The influence of Greek thought on Paul, though real, is purely external. Hellenism never touches the life and essence of Paulinism, which is fundamentally and absolutely

(as the punctuation of the two great English editors would imply), but to meditation by thoughtful pagans over their conduct. ii. 13 is continued by ii. 16, while ii. 14 and 15 are parenthetic. The true connection is disguised both in the Authorised and in the Revised Version.

[1] Although neither the English nor the American Revision favours the view, yet in 11, "Faithful is the saying," is an emphatic adjunct to the impassioned statement of verse 10.

Hebrew; but it does strongly affect the expression of Paul's teaching. Further, it lends to Paulinism the grace and the moderation, the sense of where to stop and how to avoid overstating, which is natural to Paul. It gives to him also that strong sense of the joy of the Divine life, which he expresses most emphatically to the Philippians, "Rejoice always," and to the Galatians,[1] but which is characteristic of him everywhere, even amid his equally strong sense that the Divine life is an unceasing strain and a struggle against trial after trial, which taxed his powers daily to the utmost.

Paulinism is essentially Hebrew; but it is Hebraism exalted to a higher level and a richer content. Hence many learned Jews deny that the letters of Paul are the work of a Hebrew, and assert that no Hebrew could have spoken so. What Paul added to the old Hebrew thought is the element that specially fitted it to reach the European and especially the Greek world; but this addition was not Greek or derived in any way from Greek philosophy, though it answers the questions of that philosophy. It was the true and proper development of Hebrew religion to its highest standard, and not a syncretism of Hebraic and Greek elements. Yet it was attained in the process of answering the great questions which had been raised by the contact of Judaism with the Graeco-Roman world.

[1] See Gal. v. 12, Phil. iii. 1, iv. 4, ii. 18.

XXIX. FAITH AS A POWER

The consciousness of power, energy, strength is one of the most characteristic features of the Christian experience and life, as they are described by Paul. "According to the power that worketh in us" is the range of our achievement, "above all that we ask or think."[1] So he declares in Philippians iv. 13, "I can do all things in Him that strengtheneth me". The energy is the Divine element in the man, present in him from the beginning, making him originally in the image of God, but weakened, obscured, apparently almost extirpated by sin and misunderstanding of the nature of God (yet never wholly and finally killed), and needing to be reinvigorated by the process that begins with the apprehension of the work and meaning and power of Jesus.

The Gospel which Paul preaches is not in word but in power. Hence he hated mere empty talk and vain discussion about even the highest subjects: they distract the attention of men from the real work of life: they tend to degenerate into quibbles of words, and empty logomachy. What he urges and desires and prays for in his converts is that they may be "strengthened with all power, according to the might of His glory . . . bearing fruit unto every good work, and increasing in the knowledge of God".[2]

This power, therefore, is co-extensive with "the know. ledge of God". The power and the knowledge grow together

[1] Eph. iii. 20.　　　[2] Col. i. 10 and 11.

163

stage by stage : the one cannot increase without the other increasing.   What is from one side knowledge of God, is from another side action like that of God.   Such knowledge is not abstract theory or mere passive thought.   It is not gained by a process of acquisition, like the growing knowledge of mathematics or languages.   It is gained instantaneously through the power of God seizing and holding fast the nature of the man.   It is in a sense perfect and complete from the first, because the man instantaneously sees God once and for all time, because he grasps instantaneously the nature of God and of his relation to God.   Yet in another sense it can grow continuously and indefinitely, not by becoming more complete and rounded in whole than it was at the first, but by expanding on all sides, and filling up more effectively the activities of the man, and enabling him to carry his activity into a wider range of relations with the world around ; and thus, as it were, making him realise with growing completeness the relation of the Divine nature to the whole universe, and the way in which God fills and inter-penetrates and constitutes men and history and everything that is.

This knowledge begins from completeness and culminates in completeness : the growth lies in the increase of energy and mastery, because its nature is energy.   It begins in the re-creation of a human mind and character : "ye have put off the old man with his doings and have put on the new man, that is being renewed unto knowledge after the image of Him that created him ".[1]   New creation is everything. Nothing else, neither ritual nor want of ritual, is of the smallest consequence in this rebirth of the human energy, " but new creation ".[2]

This aspect of the knowledge of God is, of course, rightly

[1] Col. iii. 9-10.   [2] Gal. vi. 15.

stated and emphasised by many writers. We would, however, not regard it as a kind of corollary or additional chapter to an account of Paulinism. This constitutes and is Paulinism: this is the essence of the teaching and Gospel of Paul. If we speak of adoption, and justification, and the imputing to man of the righteousness of Christ, all these are merely attempts to explain the nature of the inexplicable and the Divine: they are metaphors, and some have become poor metaphors to us, though they were rich and instructive to a former age. They have in large degree lost their meaning for us ; and the study of Pauline teaching frequently degenerates into a study of past methods and of old attempts at an explanation of Paulinism. Paul had to drive home into his hearers some conception of what he was aiming at; and in the attempt he had to use their ways of looking at the world, and to work on their habits of thought. No one knew so well as he that this was unsatisfactory and imperfect. Hence he always turned from the theoretical side of teaching to the practical: he exhibited to them the knowledge of God in the process of exerting itself actively: "he placarded before them the crucifying of Jesus ";[1] "he preached Christ crucified ".[2]

There are two instructive variations of the fundamental truth in the letter to the Galatians :—

V. 6.	VI. 15.
For in Christ Jesus neither circumcision availeth anything, nor uncircumcision; but faith working through love.	For neither is circumcision anything, nor uncircumcision; but new creation.

The second explains the first definition, and the first explains the second. The whole Epistle was written in one

[1] Gal. iii. 1.   [2] 1 Cor. ii. 2-3.

mood of feeling, at one time, and in the same white and fervent heat of passionate enthusiasm ; and the two phrases which conclude the two definitions are reiterations of what Paul felt so deeply.   In vi. 15, writing with his own hand, he is briefly recapitulating the gist of the whole letter ; and just as was customary in placarding laws and ordinances and public documents,[1] he puts in large letters the most important points.   So with this.   "Faith working through love" is equivalent to "a new creation".

This energy of the Christian is the Spirit of God working in him.   What is sometimes called by Paul faith working in him is at other times expressed as the Spirit of God. These are equivalent terms and ways of making clear the one fundamental power.   I do not call it the one fundamental *fact ;* because it is urgently important to remember that there are no facts, no hard stationary situations : there are only acts, processes, force, energy.   There is the power of evil, "the flesh," "the devil," sweeping away the nature of man from God, and there is the power of faith, i.e. the Spirit, seizing him, renewing his mind,[2] reinvigorating the Divine element that had been almost killed within him, bringing him towards God, setting him free from the power of sin which ends in death and turning his attention to the things of the Spirit,[3] making him a temple of God in which dwells the Spirit of God.[4]

In that last metaphor of the temple, the idea of force and growth is lost : it is a very external figure, and has no grip of the inner nature of the process.   It was, however, suitable after a fashion to the Corinthians, who were new converts

---

[1] The very word προγράφειν, to set forth openly, to placard in public, refers (as Lightfoot rightly remarks) to the custom of publishing documents of this class by a public copy in a conspicuous place before the eyes of all citizens.

[2] Rom. xii. 2.   [3] Rom. viii. 2, 5.   [4] 1 Cor. iii. 16.

from paganism, and continued from old habit to regard the power of God as something that dwelt in a temple. Paul had to raise their old way of thinking to a higher level, so that they could see more clearly the true nature of the relation between God and man. Through this metaphor he leads up the mind of the Corinthians to the higher, in fact to the highest possible and supreme level : "since you are the temple of God, the Spirit of God dwelleth in you". Beyond that there is nothing greater: there is nothing more completely and finally true : "the kingdom of God is within you," for "the Spirit of God dwelleth in you".

The result of this indwelling Spirit of God is to quicken and strengthen the capacity of the man to love. In love the human nature approaches most closely to God, for the love that God entertains towards man is the initial and the final law of the world. "Faith working through love" (Galatians v. 6) is another expression for this result: "the Spirit working through love" is an equivalent statement of the law of Christian life.

The apparently supernatural powers which were seen occasionally in specially striking manifestations were the "spiritual gifts"[1] of which the early writers often speak, and which the Corinthians so eagerly desired and aimed at. They are great and impressive expressions of the one permanent power dwelling in the Christian man; but, being exceptional in their appearance and not absolutely continuous, they are really less true and lofty and lasting, though they appear more striking to the external observer. It is the permanent, and not the occasional, that is the really and fundamentally Divine. As Professor W. P. Paterson[2]

---

[1] χαρίσματα τὰ πνευματικά.

[2] *The Apostles' Teaching*, i. p. 82. To Dr. Paterson's conversations, when we were colleagues in Aberdeen, I owe more than can be adequately expressed.

expresses it, " The Christian life consists, not in occasional spiritual exaltation, but in a walk in the Spirit ".[1]   Hence Paul, while respecting such powers and occasional manifestations, warns the Corinthians that these are not the greatest things.   Even though miracles seem to fail, yet miracles are not the most important expressions of the Spirit and power of God.   The continuous expression of that Spirit and power in love is the greatest, the truest, the most lasting.[2]   See Section L.

This spirit of God co-operates with the innate sympathy of man for God, and strengthens the natural perception of man in the belief that he is the child of God : this is natural to all men, so long as they give free play to their own nature.[3]   " The Spirit Himself beareth witness with our spirit, that we are children of God (Rom. viii. 16)." [4]

Further, the Spirit of God produces in man the power of insight into the nature of God ; it is a continuous and growing revelation of God to him ; it advances and widens his knowledge of God : " a spirit of wisdom and revelation in the knowledge of Him, keeping the eyes of your heart enlightened that ye may know " : [5]   " we received the Spirit which is from God . . . the Spirit which searcheth all things, yea, the deep things of God . . . that we might know ". [6]

It also gives us the power of expressing these " deep things of God ".   On this power Paul's experience induced him to lay special stress in writing to these Corinthians [7] who rather prided themselves on their ability to conceive and express

---

[1] Galatians v. 25.   [2] 1 Corinthians xiii. 13.

[3] So Paul said to the Athenians, Acts xvii. 27-29, quoting the words of more than one among the Greek poets.

[4] To " bear witness " here means to confirm and strengthen the perception that is naturally existent in man.

[5] Eph. i. 17, 18.   [6] 1 Cor. ii. 12, 10, 12.   [7] 1 Cor. ii. 13.

philosophically the truth of God. Paul tells them that only through the power of the Spirit can they express the things of the Spirit. Poetic phraseology, the technical terms of philosophy, metaphors drawn by man from the experience of life, all were inadequate and ineffective. Doubtless Paul would have included in this list of inadequate expressions some of his own metaphors in so far as they were human and external : only in virtue of the enthusiasm and the passionate feeling that surged through them did they become true : in themselves, as mere philosophical terms, they were incomplete and lifeless. "Which things also we speak, not in words which man's wisdom teacheth, but which the Spirit teacheth ; marrying spiritual ideas to spiritual words." Philosophical terms are valueless, dead, uncreative. Paul wants spiritual terms to convey his meaning ; and the intensity of his emotion gives life to them.

In 1 Corinthians i. 24, Paul "preaches Christ crucified . . . the power and the wisdom of God" : the scandal of the crucifixion is called not a fact but a power, the expression of God's ruling providence. This power and wisdom of God is not merely a force outside of man : it is also in man, expressing itself through the right action of man.

Again, that the idea of force or power is dominant in Paul appears in 1 Timothy ii. 15, which has generally been misunderstood through failure to perceive that the writer is describing the motive power of an immensely strong instinct in the human mind : see the next Section.

XXX. A Motive Power to Salvation

In 1 Timothy ii. 9-12, after an argument of a very involved Judaic type, difficult for Western thought to comprehend, Paul is led on to a profound remark, very characteristic of his special view. The commentators differ widely about its meaning, but we need not linger over their arguments, as they all fail to convince one another or us.

In the primordial association with the power of evil, the typical woman, the representative of the race, Eve, was led into transgression, but the saving power remains in her own nature : " She shall be saved by means of motherhood " (τεκνογονία). What is the meaning of this saying ? Dissension reigns, and hardly any interpreter agrees with any other.

We must note in the outset that the preposition διὰ with the genitive means " by means of," and that interpretations which take it as " by reason of motherhood " must be rejected. Motherhood is the means through which woman " shall gain salvation if her action is guided by faith, love, thankfulness, and self-restraint ".

The whole question turns on what Paul meant when he used this term τεκνογονία. He is thinking philosophically, and not of a mere physical process. We have to take into consideration the whole manner of expression in Greek philosophic thought, and the whole history of Greek progress in language and in thought from the simple and concrete to the philosophic and abstract, from Homer to Aristotle and Paul.

In that progress the Greek language was engaged in the
creation of abstract nouns, just as Greek thought was teaching itself to generalise and to distinguish between ideas
which are bound up with one another in the concrete world.
If we had before us the works of Athenodorus the Tarsian,
we should be better able to appreciate the linguistic task
which Paul had to perform when he sought to express in
Greek a Christian philosophy, and better able to understand
the way in which he attempted to solve the problem before
him.[1]

We must remember how simple and concrete are often
the terms by which Greek tried to express the highest
thoughts of moral and metaphysical philosophy. Plato
hardly attempted to create a language of the higher philosophy. He argues in the concrete example ; he takes
refuge in metaphor and poetry and myth, when he must
attempt to give expression to the highest philosophical ideas.
Aristotle set himself to create a technical terminology in the
region of metaphysics ; and how simple are his means ! The
essential nature of a thing is "the what-is-it?" of the thing
(τὸ τί ἐστι), i.e. " the answer to the question, What is it? "
The goodness, in its most ideal and abstract conception, of a
thing is τὸ ἀγαθῷ εἶναι : the law of its development is
τὸ τί ἦν εἶναι.[2] How perfectly plain and common are the
words ! How close to ordinary life ! And yet what a lofty
philosophic sense does Aristotle read into them.

Or again, let us turn to the Attic tragedy, which sounded
the depths and estimated the heights of human feeling.

---

[1] *St. Paul the Traveller*, p. 354 ; *The Cities of St. Paul*, p. 216 ff.

[2] I give my own idea of this disputed metaphysical term in words which
perhaps nobody will accept as a translation ; but at least all recognise
that the idea in Aristotle's mind was highly abstract and metaphysical,
while the words are chosen from the commonest range of expression used
by every Greek peasant.

I take an example which leads up suitably to the thought in this passage of the Tarsian Apostle—a passage the discussion of which by a modern writer[1] first opened to me the realm of Greek thought, and showed me, when I was a student in Aberdeen, how different is interpretation from translation, and how easily one may learn to translate without having any conception of the real meaning of an ancient Greek poet.

Sophocles in the *Electra* pictures Clytemnestra as she realises the dread bond of emotion that unites a mother to her son.   She appreciates its power all the better that it is unwelcome to her.   It is too strong for her, and masters her will.   And how does she express this?   She uses no abstract terms, but four of the simplest and most commonplace words, δεινὸν τὸ τίκτειν ἐστίν.   Those who are content with translating according to the lexicon would render these words, "the giving birth to a child is a painful thing," and miss all the wealth of feeling and thought that lies in them. There cannot be a doubt that Sophocles was expressing the truth[2] (which every one must appreciate in the real experiences of life) that there is no power in human nature more tremendous, more overmastering, more dread to contemplate in some of its manifestations, than the tie of motherhood. Only when the human nature in her is deadened and

---

[1] I have tried in vain to recall the writer and the book.   My memory in a vague way connects the incident with George Eliot.

[2] The context removes all doubt: the following words are enough—

> δεινὸν τὸ τίκτειν ἐστίν · οὐδὲ γὰρ κακῶς
> πάσχοντι μῖσος ὧν τέκῃ προσγίγνεται,

which the late Professor Lewis Campbell renders—

> To be a mother hath a marvellous power,
> No injury can make one hate one's child.

Moreover, the translation which is condemned in the text above approaches perilously near the grammatical crime of taking the present infinitive in the sense of the aorist infinitive.

brutalised or buried, can the woman become stronger than that tie. It is the divine strength moving in her, and it can bend or break her, if she resists.

In this feeling of motherhood Paul found the power that he needed for his purpose. Here is the Divine strength in the nature of woman, which can drive her as it will, and which will be her salvation, " if she continue in faith and love and thanksgiving with sober-mindedness "; but which may drive her in the wrong direction if it be not guided by those qualities.

The idea of self-developing power, of growth, of striving towards an end outside of oneself, always underlies Paul's conception of the relation of a human being towards God. To his Greek hearers he compares the true Christian life to the straining effort of a runner competing for the prize, because he knew that there he touched a feeling which was extraordinarily strong in the mind of a Greek man. In the woman's nature the maternal instinct presented itself as a force that had more absolute power over her than any emotion in a man's nature had over him. Paul rarely touches on the love between the sexes, and had small respect for it as a divine emotion capable under proper guidance of working out the salvation of either man or woman.

In giving expression to this psychological observation, Paul was under the influence of his own time, when philosophical expression was more developed. Abstract nouns had been created in great numbers to express the higher ideas of thought; an abstract noun was needed to express this idea of the power of maternal instinct; and Paul found it in τεκνογονία, which is a simpler and certainly not a less reasonable or correct term than a manufactured word like " philoprogenitiveness " or a question-begging circumlocution like " maternal instinct ". This Greek term may justly be translated " motherhood ".

Thus, as so often elsewhere in the Pauline Epistles, the difficulty which has been felt in catching the meaning is caused by taking a wrong point of view and disappears as soon as one looks from the right point of view. The "maternal instinct" does not require actual physical mother-hood. It may be immensely powerful in a childless woman and may be her salvation, though it is, of course, quickened in a wonderful degree towards her own child, and is sometimes dormant until so quickened.

I do not remember that Paul touches this spring of life in any of his earlier letters. But what rational critic would find in that any proof that this letter is not his composition? Is there any of Paul's letters which does not throw its own distinct rays of light on his character? Is there any that can be cut away without narrowing and impoverishing in some degree our knowledge of his nature? Must we regard it as an essential condition in proving the genuineness of any of his Epistles that it should contain nothing which widens our knowledge of him or throws new light on his character? Rather, it would be a conclusive reason against the Pauline authorship of a letter, if its acceptance or rejection made no difference to our conception of the Apostle's personality. Paul could not write a letter without revealing something new about his own nature.

Now we observe that, in writing to Timothy, Paul addressed one who had gained from his early home life a strong sense of what maternal feeling is. Paul had a marvellous power of unconsciously sympathising with his correspondents. It is only in writing to Timothy that he gives a picture of home life (2 Tim. i. 5) under a mother's care. He uses the word "mother" twice in writing to Timothy: except in two quotations from the Old Testament (Eph. v. 31, vi. 2), he uses it only three times in all the rest of his letters put together (Rom. xvi. 13, as a metaphor to express his affection for a friend's mother;[1] Gal. i. 15, iv. 26, in a generic and unemotional sense). He does not indeed show the want of love for a mother which is conspicuous in Horace,[2] but except in sympathy with Timothy he nowhere shows a deep sense of what a mother is and feels and does to her child.

These considerations explain why two words otherwise unknown in Paul's writings[3] are forced on him in expressing his thought on this subject. The word for grandmother is "un-Pauline"; but where else could Paul use it except in 2 Timothy i. 5? where else does his interest in family life appear? The word for motherhood is used only in 1 Timothy ii. 15, but that is the only place in which he speaks of the idea that lies in the word. The wider terminology of certain Epistles, called through a too narrow outlook "un-Pauline," really corresponds to and is the inevitable result of the wider range of his thought.[4]

---

[1] With this compare 1 Tim. v. 2 : παρακάλει . . . πρεσβυτέρας ὡς μητέρας.

[2] The writer has studied this side of Horace's poetry in *Macmillan's Magazine*, Oct., 1897, pp. 450-457, on "The Childhood of Horace," and advanced a theory to account for it. Horace never alludes to a mother's care, but sometimes to a mother's carelessness; he alludes tenderly to a nurse's care; he never mentions his own mother; he mentions with fond memory his father and his nurse (when the right text is read in a familiar passage of the Third Book of the Odes, *Altricis Pulliae*).

[3] Unknown also elsewhere in the New Testament.

[4] The use of the verb τεκνογονεῖν in the physical sense in 1 Timothy v. 14 is no proof that the abstract noun derived from it must also have the physical sense in Paul. Sophocles uses τίκτειν often in the physical sense; but that does not prevent him from employing it in the philosophic or emotional sense in the passage quoted above.

XXXI. The Measure and Estimate of Faith

In the Pastoral Epistles, as has been commonly held, "faith loses its unique significance and is almost reduced to a place side by side with other virtues," so that "the gift of eternal life appears almost as a reward of good living". At the present moment we are not discussing the authenticity of those Epistles, but simply the question whether this is a doctrinal position different from that of Paul's earlier letters, and characteristic rather of Paulinism as conceived by a pupil of the Apostle.

That in the earlier letters salvation is said to come through faith and the gift of God, not through works, is of course admitted. From that we start. That is emphasised over and over again in the letters ; and no quotations are needed to prove that this is the true Pauline teaching. But is that inconsistent with the statement that salvation is the result of the work and intense effort of the individual ?

There is no inconsistency ; and he that finds inconsistency between the two statements has never apprehended in a right way the true nature of the relation between man and God. Paul, who says so emphatically that salvation is the free gift of God through faith, can with equal emphasis utter the advice, "Work out your own salvation with fear and trembling ".[1] Both are true : they contemplate the same operation, but from different points of view. Such is the

[1] Philippians ii. 12: on the apparent (but only apparent) inconsistency involved see Sections XIV. or XXXIII.

true relation of the Divine nature to the human nature. One statement does not exhaust the character of that relation.

Moreover, faith is the driving power that turns man back from his tendency to degradation, and starts him in the course of movement towards God. The way to measure or estimate a force is through the effect that it produces : no other way is recognised by science. Now it will be observed that, where Paul is attempting to rouse, to stimulate, and to move the minds and hearts of men, he speaks most about faith and lays all the stress of his teaching on faith, but where he has in his mind the thought of judgment regarding men, he speaks of works, i.e. of the effect that this force produces.

In the practical problems of Church management, therefore, Timothy and Titus have to look to works as the standard of measurement. Only thus can they estimate the driving power in the heart of man. They cannot measure the faith, or judge the character, of their congregations in any other way. Yet throughout those same letters the characteristic Pauline view of faith is suggested in various passages, e.g. 1 Timothy i. 2, 4, iii. 9, v. 8, 12, vi. 12 ; 2 Timothy iv. 7 ; Titus iii. 5.[1]

The same thing is equally characteristic of the earlier letters, if we make allowance for the far greater part that is there devoted to stimulating, and the much less attention that is given to estimating. When in those letters Paul speaks of estimating the conduct and character of men, he has in mind the estimating which is done by God : although He knows the thoughts of the heart, He does not estimate the deserts of men by their faith, but by their works and their conduct. The Final Judgment partakes of the nature

---

[1] See Dr. R. F. Horton's Introduction to the Pastorals, p. 7.

of a trial issuing in a formal sentence: and even in this trial, at which all " the counsels of the heart are made manifest and the hidden things of darkness are brought to light," [1] the test which is applied is conduct.

"It is indeed surprising," says Professor Paterson regarding the Final Judgment,[2] " that no mention is made of faith." From our point of view, however, that is quite natural and inevitable. There can be no other scientific measure of a force than the effect it produces; and on this the estimate is based. " We must all be made manifest before the judgment-seat of Christ, that each one may receive the things done through the body according to what he hath done, whether *it be* good or bad." [3] "Whatsoever good thing each one doeth, the same shall he receive again from the Lord." [4] So again, writing from a slightly different point of view, Paul speaks to the same effect: "Not the hearers of the law are righteous before God, but the doers of the law shall be treated as righteous, . . . in the day when God shall judge the secret things of men according to my gospel by Jesus Christ".[5] If in Romans, Ephesians and Corinthians the judgment of God is consistently based on works, the judgment of men must still more necessarily be based on the same external standard, and not on the impossible attempt to estimate a hidden force in the heart and nature of man.

Those who would restrict the social and philosophic out-

---

[1] See 1 Cor. iv. 5.

[2] *The Apostles' Teaching*, i. p. 116. Such is the usual remark made by theologians on this topic.

[3] 2 Cor. v. 10.   [4] Eph. vi. 8.

[5] Rom. ii. 13-16. That the American Revision is right in so connecting the structure of the sentence seems clear, and has been already stated: the intermediate words are parenthetic. It refers to meditation in secret, not to the final judgment (as Westcott and Hort punctuate).

look of Paul, as a thinker and teacher for all time, to the bare and narrowest form of the statements which are made most frequently and most emphatically in the earlier letters, miss much of his thought and character. He did not try to win men by setting before them a complete system of philosophy. He hammered on the potent and penetrating nail of faith. This was the all-important means of getting into their hearts, and this is the most characteristic idea of Paulinism as a power to convert: no emphasis can be too strong on that point. This, however, does not exhaust the mind, or the philosophic position, or even the teaching, of Paul.

Now, when we attempt to go further and comprehend Paulinism as a complete system of thought and of teaching, and to show how it can make itself intelligible to men of the twentieth century, we must remember that he did not always preach to the unconverted or the newly converted and immature; and we should not exclude the possibility that he could organise and govern as well as persuade and convert. It is the denial, sometimes overt and conscious, sometimes half-unconscious, of this possibility, that causes much of the difficulty experienced as to the truly Pauline character of the teaching in the Pastoral Epistles. The importance of faith in the teaching of Paul was immense; but there was much more than faith in his teaching. Regarding this wider teaching there are only obscure hints in the earlier Epistles. On the other hand, it is the substance of the latest Epistles, because it is there suitable to the position of those to whom Paul was writing; and to condemn these as non-Pauline, because their teaching is more advanced, and " sub-Pauline " rather than " Pauline " (according to the fashionable terminology), is purely unscientific.

The emphasis which Paul lays upon faith is wholly justified and necessary. Faith is the motive power of good life: through its force man can begin to move towards God, and its continued impulse is needed right on to the end. We can make no step except through it. Without faith man is helpless: it is the power of the Divine within him, believing, hoping, loving, and seeking after the Divine around him. Too much emphasis cannot be laid on the indispensableness of faith.

It is not always easy for the practical expounder of Paulinism to find words that will rightly and exactly express the situation. In such perplexity, if you lay the superior stress on faith, you will not go far wrong.

Yet in attempting to comprehend the nature of Pauline teaching, we must remember that even Paul himself does not say that it is the only thing, nor even that it is the greatest thing. "Now abideth faith, hope, love, these three; and the greatest of these is love" (1 Cor. xiii. 13). The singular "abideth," instead of the plural, is not merely a grammatical feature: it bears closely on the sense.[1] Paul does not mean simply that each one of the three separately and by itself remains permanent. He never would say so emphatically that you can trust in the permanence of any one by itself without the others. He means that the Divine unity of faith, hope, love, is the permanent thing amid the flux and change of the world. Faith, as he says in xiii. 2, is by itself insufficient; however great faith I have, however my faith fulfils the supreme test, it would be nothing without love. In xiii. 13, he implies that any one of the three is incomplete without the other two. And, if you

---

[1] This I would venture to add to Dr. Harnack's exquisite statement of the quality of this passage, as set forth in the *Expositor* for May and June, 1912 (translated).

are determined to weigh them against one another, love is greater than faith as a constituent element in the Divine whole; and love is in itself the most lasting and most Divine thing in the universe, for it, more completely than anything else, is the Divine nature.[1]

[1] I may be permitted to refer to the chapter in my *Pictures of the Apostolic Church*, on 1 Corinthians xiii.

XXXII. Faith unto Salvation

When the true nature and meaning of the Pauline term "faith" is understood, we see that the greatest difficulties which Paulinism presents to the modern mind rest on a misconception of the word.

"Why should I be condemned because another man sinned, or made righteous because another has paid the penalty for me?" That is the question which constantly rises in one form or another to the mind of the ordinary man in modern time, and to a somewhat less degree probably in ancient time: every age has its own special difficulties to meet and its questions to put.

As has been pointed out in Section XVII, we are, according to Paul, condemned not because another man sinned, but because we ourselves sin; and I do not hesitate to say that according to Paul we are made righteous, not simply because another man, even Jesus, has paid the penalty for us, but because we, through faith in Jesus and in His death on behalf of all men, attain to righteousness.

This appears too markedly contrary to some widely received conceptions of Pauline teaching: is it justifiable as an expression of his thought?

The usual conception of Pauline teaching may be very roughly stated thus. Salvation is procured, not by ceremonial observance and ritual acts of outward homage and external respect towards Divine power, nor even by obedience to the highest moral law which requires that man should

182

"do justly and love mercy and walk humbly with God,"[1] but by faith alone: "By grace have ye been saved through faith".[2] Salvation is not obtained through merit of our own, nor is it the reward of excellent character or good conduct, but is the free gift of God, independent of ourselves. With this statement we find no fault, except in so far as it leaves out any further teaching.

That salvation cannot be obtained by ritual is quite in accordance with the judgment of the ordinary reasonable man, who wants to understand plainly and to think simply about his rule and conduct of life. He finds, however, that the words of Micah as quoted above express his own judgment and his own intention: he would choose to do well, to be just and merciful, and to be finally judged by God accordingly.

Paul does not object to this desire and choice of the ordinary reasonable man. Such was apparently his own original aim. He came to Jerusalem zealous to live the higher life; he eagerly desired to do rightly; and in attempting with his whole heart and soul to carry into effect this desire, he found himself trampling on what was best in his nation, an accomplice in the murder or attempted murder of the noblest among his own people, and a hater and enemy of the Lord Himself.

The discovery that his enthusiasm to serve God aright had led him headlong into such perverse and shameful conduct produced the most profound effect on his judgment. He saw that the result of the eager desire to live one's own life well through one's own effort must be utter failure. We cannot do what we desire to do: we are inevitably led into sin and wrong-doing, partly by our own nature, partly by the perverting influence of the errors and sins of

[1] Micah vi. 8.   [2] Eph. ii. 8.

preceding generations, as the iniquity of the fathers is visited on the children and produces in them an ever-increasing liability to error, partly by the very law itself which stands above us and which we strive to obey.   Paul felt keenly that the law had in itself been an influence to lead him astray : it had drawn his attention away from the truth : he had set it in the place of God, and it had concealed from him the true nature of God and the purpose of Christ (Rom. vii. 7 ff.).

Paul himself, therefore, had natural sympathy with that judgment and intention of the comman man.   He began in the same way, and he knew both what was good in that intention, and what was mistaken.

In the natural condition of human character, when it is not yet too much perverted by wrong choice and wrong aspirations, and has not yet begun to aim deliberately at wrongdoing for its own sake or as a means to gain some ulterior object, the ordinary reasonable man desires to do rightly, to act according to a good standard of conduct, and to gain thereby the rewards in character and in external blessings which ought (as he thinks) to accompany and result from good action.   His natural sense of right accepts this as a just principle and a fair measure of treatment.

It is often argued that righteous action of this kind is of a lower class than the righteousness that is gained by faith, and therefore would not be sufficient to merit salvation.   Theologians labour to prove this by a variety of considerations and arguments, on which we need not enter. The natural sense of fairness in the ordinary man of our time is not convinced by them ; and the Gospel of Paul, in so far as it is recommended by such methods, fails to touch him.

Such theological arguments are, however, beside the point :

they never touch the real problem with which we are here concerned : they do not interpret rightly the mind of Paul. To the Apostle the *crux* of the whole situation lay, not in the fact that righteousness if so gained is in itself of a lower order, but in the fact that righteousness cannot be attained in this way. If the way were possible, if it led to success and to true righteousness, all might be well. But it cannot lead to success : it does not produce true righteousness. Sometimes it leads to appalling error and crime : sometimes it produces less terrible, but still quite unsatisfactory results. There is no possible way of permanently right action except through the driving power of faith in the one greatest ideal, when it has made itself a real thing to us and in us.

Examine the question in every way you please. Take it historically. The history of the past was, as Paul saw and as every pagan thinker and poet (except Virgil, sometimes) acknowledged, a process of deterioration and degeneration. Man was not growing better. Racial sin had vitiated the whole fabric of society, and lowered the national standard of judgment and conduct. Take it in the typical case of the first man, Adam. He had sinned where every circumstance was in his favour. Take it in the individual case : no man can feel that, as he grows older, he grows better, except through faith in that greatest ideal which is Christ, and the consequent self-sacrifice with the hope and the love that accompany it.

Another way was needed. Except by another path righteousness could not be attained. God had shown that way through Jesus. It is the way of dying that one may live, of suffering that one may triumph.

XXXIII. The Gift of Christ

Every line of thought and argument and personal experience—the last doubtless the most efficacious with him—led Paul to the same conclusion. Man cannot save himself: he cannot work out his own salvation through his own efforts: he always goes wrong. The force of circumstances and of his own nature are too strong: the flesh is more dominant than the spirit in his physical constitution.

The lifting power of some great enthusiasm, the driving force of some supreme idea, must come to aid his personal efforts, and to strengthen in him the spirit in its struggle against the flesh. This God has provided from the beginning as part of the plan of creation which was originally formed in His mind: He did not introduce this device to remedy a defect that subsequently manifested itself in His creation: He had in view from the first the whole order of human history.

There is some point in the life of most men, when the consciousness seems to have been reached that one can of oneself do nothing for oneself; that one has failed to save oneself: that one's efforts have all been misdirected: that either one has been deliberately turning one's back towards God, and seeking after what was absolutely evil, or one's efforts to "keep justice and to do righteousness," [1] and to show the goodness which God desires in man,[2] have gone

---

[1] Isa. lvi. 1.

[2] Hos. vi. 6. "I desire goodness, and not sacrifice; the knowledge of God more than burnt-offerings."

astray. Thus each individual man learns that only through Divine aid can he attain what he has longed for or ought to have longed for. The time is ripe: "the fulness of the time has come".[1]

Similarly, at a certain point in the history of the world as a whole, the collective consciousness of mankind seemed to Paul to have reached the same conclusion through the collective experience of all men.[2] The world had failed to save itself and to improve itself. It was on the way to destruction through a steady and ever-accelerated deterioration. There was no possible aid for it through any human power, or device, or effort. No hope remained except in Divine aid through the coming of a Divine helper. When this conclusion was reached, then it seemed to Paul that the fulness of the time had come, and that the moment for the Divine purpose to complete itself had arrived. The almost universal belief throughout the Mediterranean world in the time immediately preceding the life of Paul[3] and during the first half of his life despaired of the future and thought that man had failed and that "salvation" could only come through the manifestation of some god on earth. This pagan experience seemed to Paul to attest the correctness of his own belief.

[1] Gal. iv. 4.

[2] "Mankind" and "all men" and "the world" here must, of course, be understood as meaning practically the Graeco-Roman world, ἡ οἰκουμένη, the world of the Mediterranean civilisation, which alone was known to Paul. This sense is usual at that time. Paul did not exclude the rest of the world: he included in theory both barbarian and Scythian, i.e. those who were alien to the Graeco-Roman world, but in practice he addressed that civilised world and his plans and thoughts were confined to what he knew.

[3] Perhaps the solitary exception was Virgil, who was full of hope; but his hope was in a vague form connected with the birth of a Divine child. Some would see in the child an expected son of Augustus, which appears to me unjust to the poet, a petty idea such as Virgil could not and did not condescend to. See papers in the *Expositor*, June and August, 1907, on this subject.

This was the moment that the Divine will and purpose
had found suitable to send into the world the Divine nature
in human form, placed under the law that he might rise
above the law, made subject to human trials and weakness
in order to prove superior to them, exposed to the temptations of man so that there might be exhibited a complete
and glorious triumph of " man " over all temptations.   That
in Jesus the Divine nature was stronger than in simple man
was true : otherwise, being a simple man, He could not overcome the limitations of human nature.   Yet this does not,
in Paul's philosophy of history, invalidate the fundamental
fact that Jesus was man : He was man that He might be a
pattern : He was God in order that the pattern might be
effective and final, absolutely conclusive once and for ever,
sufficient for all men and for each individual man before
and after Him.

That was what Paul called the supreme mystery.   It had
to be apprehended by each man for himself.   It was a matter of faith.   The highest test of human nature and will was
the capacity to apprehend and believe this great mystery, to
know that it was true and to base one's whole life upon it.
This stage is reached by the individual man when—perhaps
after long trial to achieve his own salvation, and work righteousness for himself—he has realised his helplessness and
incapacity : when he has learned that he must trust to the
God who is around him and outside of him, because the
Divine element is too weak within him.

This supreme moment in the life of a man is regarded by
Paul as the occasion when the Divine power seizes him, grips
him, reveals itself to him and in him.[1]   The gift of salvation, therefore, is the free gift of God who has taken hold
of the man.   The man himself has not earned it, has not

[1] Gal. i. 14 f.

deserved it, has done nothing to attain it. He is, as it were, compelled to the new course by the purpose and plan of God : he cannot do otherwise ; it is impossible for him to strive against the Divine order, or to kick against the goad. This is part of the order of nature in the evolution of the Divine will. The man has been seized and carried away by it. As part of the inevitable and foreknown order, it is fixed and settled before the foundations of the world.

That is, however, in no way inconsistent with Paul's other point of view that, in the judgment of God and of man, eternal life is the reward of what the man does in life (as has been shown by clear quotations),[1] and that the man " works out his own salvation ". These are merely expressions from two different points of view. Both can be true. Both must be true. If one is true, the other goes with it. A force that is ineffective is not a force. The power of God inevitably works itself out in the action of the man whom God has seized.

The apparent inconsistency lay only in a narrow or false view of the nature of God and of man in their mutual relation. Man has in him the Divine spark : he is capable of movement towards God only through the fact that God is within him. The first stage in salvation is the quickening of the Divine element in the man. Thus the Divine in man recognises the Divine outside of him. The great revelation, the manifestation by God of Himself to man, takes place ; and the man is remade, reconstituted, reborn, once and for ever. The rest of life crumbles into ashes, and disappears as if it were naught. This alone remains. From this life begins again.

Yet this new life is a hard life, a long strain, a continuous work, taxing the whole powers of the man from day to day,

---

[1] See Section XXXI.

often seeming to be too hard, and yet always making itself possible to him through the grace of God.   Each day brings a sacrifice of oneself, a death to the old and a birth to the new and the higher.   Such was Paul's experience in his own life ; and he pictures to his converts the Divine life as being necessarily the same for them.

XXXIV. Metaphor and Truth

In attempting to gauge the depths of Paul's thought from the language of his letters, we must distinguish between forms of expression which are intended specially as educative and those through which the inner nature of his ideas looks forth on the world more simply and clearly.

Intellectually, it was necessary for him to make the deep things of God intelligible to pagan converts, and he must use metaphors and images, which would help them to understand; he must start from their own thought and train their minds to appreciate a higher way; he was always confronted with the difficult problem of expressing infinite and eternal truths in the utterly inadequate language of finite experience ; and with a view to his audience he must use the words of ordinary educated speech and could not take refuge in technical or artificial terms.[1] Morally, he had to raise his hearers' standard of judgment and of life, so that the higher morality should be appreciated by them and establish itself in their minds and life.

All the early Christian teachers were confronted with the same problem. They had to create a new language to express a new religion, and yet they must use the current words as moulds, filling them with a new content. Paul was one of the most creative and successful masters of language that have ever lived; but the other Apostles were not mere followers of Paul, and in the beginning they had to

[1] An example is given in Section XXX.

speak without him as a model to imitate.   A Christian language was in process of evolving itself before Paul became a Christian.   It was addressed only to Jews, because in the pre-Pauline time Christian teaching was practically confined to the Jews, and it was adapted to their thoughts and customs and beliefs.   This earliest Christian speech, strongly Judaic in type, was not without its effect on Paul.

Among the forms of expression that were specially suited to elevate the conceptions of the Hebrews to a higher level were those which picture the work and the being of Christ by starting from the ideas of priesthood and of sacrifice. Such forms also appealed more or less to almost all pagans. Among the ancient peoples generally the relation of man to God was conceived as in a very large degree conducted through the medium of sacrificial offerings by the instrumentality of a priest who intervened and mediated between the worshipper and the deity.

Already the greatest of the Hebrew prophets were gradually emerging from that conception.   Christianity as a system of thought and life rose free above it.[1]   But the popular views had not attained to freedom in this respect; and it was necessary that the popular views should be elevated to the higher plane.   To do this it was necessary to begin from them, to assume what was good in them, and to develop and strengthen this element of right.

It is therefore not strange, but merely what was to be expected, that the author of the Epistle to the Hebrews—not Paul himself, but a writer who was in close relations and in hearty sympathy with Paul; not a pupil, but one who took an independent and authoritative view—[2] lays far more stress

[1] I do not mean that all people thought or even yet think so.   I am only attempting to express what appears to be the mind of Paul.

[2] This author, sympathetic, yet independent of Paul and influential himself, was probably Philip the Evangelist, writing at Caesarea during Paul's im-

on this idea than any other writer in the New Testament. The task which this author felt to be imposed on him was to explain to the Jewish Christian congregation of Jerusalem —as distinguished from their leaders (ἡγούμενοι), who are not addressed and who did not need such instruction—that, and how, Christ's teaching was the perfect, true, and finally complete religion. "The writer to the Hebrews," as Professor Paterson says, "deals with the Old Testament dispensation as pre-eminently a priestly and sacrificial system"; that dispensation was indeed founded upon Divine revelation; but it was narrow in its aims and very imperfect in its results.

The method of this writer, then, is to take the hopes and wishes current among the Hebrews, and show how they are more perfectly fulfilled by the doctrine of Christianity than by the old dispensation. In doing this, the writer naturally lays very great stress on the sacrificial and priestly aspect. As the Hebrews wished for a priest, the only true priest in the highest sense is Christ. Since the Hebrews considered that sacrifice is needed or desired by God, then the one true and perfect sacrifice was Jesus; this sacrifice was offered once and for all time; and there should be no thought of any need for the imperfect and unworthy sacrifices of the Hebrew ritual, after that supreme and perfect offering has been made.

The fact that the ideas of the ordinary Jews of Palestine had to be carried upwards to a nobler level should not be taken as any proof that Paul, or even the writer to the Hebrews, regarded the office of Christ as a priest and the

prisonment, and in frequent communication with him (see a paper on the authorship of Hebrews in *Luke the Physician and Other Studies*). Acts xxiv. 23 alludes to this freedom of communication between Paul and his friends at Caesarea.

sacrificial character of His death as being in themselves of real and essential importance, or thought that this aspect of Christ's work indicated the deepest truth regarding the relation between man and God. The minds of the Jews had to be trained by working on their past experience and acquired habits of thought. This device of describing Christ as "the priest," and His death as the one great, true and perfect "sacrificial offering," is merely a way of explaining truth and making it more easily intelligible in its real character to minds habituated to that point of view.

A modern missionary to savages, if he be wise, would take hold of their ideas in his teaching and develop them, and he would refrain from destroying any germs of good that lay in their conceptions of deity and Divine demands.

Paul does not insist much on this sacrificial and priestly side of the relation of man to God, partly because he tends to regard the old Hebrew dispensation more as a system of law than as a system of sacrifice by priests, partly because he appealed to the Greeks rather on the side of their philosophic and educated thoughts than through their pagan religious practices and ideas. Yet the ordinary pagans also regarded the relation of man to God as a system of gifts and sacrifices performed with the aid of a priest, who knew the proper rites and accompaniments ; and Paul sometimes approaches the minds of his hearers on this side.[1]   Generally, however, the context and the character of such allusions in his letters makes it clear that they are only illustrative and not essential ; and it is

---

[1] Ignatius is far more addicted to appeals of this character. He pictures the life of the Christian as a religious procession in which the sacred symbols are borne through the streets of a city ; and his mind had been powerfully affected by the pagan Mysteries, as his language often shows. This subject has been briefly touched in Chapter XIII. of the writer's *Letters to the Seven Churches.*

unfortunate that so much stress has been laid on them by some modern preachers, as if they touched reality and were not largely symbolical. So for example Ephesians v. 2, " Christ gave Himself up for us an offering and a sacrifice to God for an odour of sweet smell ". One might have thought that here the allusion to sacrifice and ritual is plainly metaphorical; but prepossession and the analogy of the Epistle to the Hebrews weigh with many scholars who quote this passage to prove that Paul classed the death of Jesus as literally and in the deepest sense a sacrifice, similar in character and purpose to the sacrifices of animals in the old Hebrew ritual. The comparison of 2 Corinthians ii. 14, " the savour of his knowledge in every place," shows that the allusion to sweet smell is wholly figurative.

The expression of Paul that Christ "gave Himself up " for man does not (as is often maintained) necessarily, or even probably, involve the thought of a ritual sacrifice. The word παραδοῦναι does not in itself suggest that, and the idea of sacrifice is introduced into Ephesians v. 2, not by this verb, but by the quotation from the Old Testament which follows, "an offering and a sacrifice for an odour of sweet smell". In such a passage as Galatians ii. 20 the same verb is used; but the conception of sacrifice is evidently absent from the author's mind.

When the blood of Christ is referred to in such passages as Ephesians i. 7, 1 Corinthians x. 16, Romans v. 9, the guiding thought of the context is not necessarily the idea of sacrifice, and in some cases is probably of quite different character. In Romans viii. 3, the idea of sacrifice is introduced into the English version by interpolating the words "as an offering," which have nothing in the original Greek to correspond to or justify them:

the context there shows that Paul's thought is moving entirely in the sphere of law, and not in the sphere of ritual.

There are other places, however, such as Romans iii. 25, where an allusion to the Hebrew ritual is probable or certain: especially 1 Corinthians v. 7 is a case in point. But certainly metaphor, not philosophic insight, is the character of these allusions.

All such passages may therefore be set aside as giving no proof or indication of the deeper movement of Paul's thought. They are educative and illustrative; they are used in order to rouse the minds of his readers to think, and do not spring from the philosophic basis of Paul's religious ideas, or serve as more than a mere index pointing towards it.

The one great exception probably is that to Paul Christ was the Paschal Lamb sacrificed for the people. This idea lay deep in the thought of the first century. It strongly affected the mind of John, as of Paul. It had great effect in moulding religious symbolism and imagery. It originates, probably, from the fact that Jesus was on the cross at the time when the Paschal lamb was being slain in preparation for the Passover feast.[1] But it is characteristic rather of early Christian thought and symbolism in general than of Paul in particular.

The same remark is true of the whole Pauline doctrine and practice of the Eucharist. So far from being an invention of Paul's (as has sometimes been maintained), or from having been seriously modified by Paul, the Eucharist in its entirety was taken over by him from earlier ritual.

---

[1] Perhaps He was taken down from the cross a little before the exact time of the slaying of the lamb; but this is immaterial, and was certainly considered immaterial in the early Church. The preparations for the Festival, and the providing of the lamb, had occurred earlier.

He found it in the Church, and he transmitted it to the Church as he found it.[1] Its value and its efficacy lay in the unchanged and pure preservation of the rite in its simplicity as it had been created by the Founder in His life, practised often by Him, and finally consecrated in the Last Supper. As invented, or even modified, by Paul or by any other man, the rite was null and empty.

After weighing these considerations we must conclude that the conception of the death of Christ after the image of the sacrifice of the Paschal lamb was early Christian, not specifically Pauline. It was, therefore, imposed on Paul from without, and not originated by him.

The priestly and sacrificial form of expression was really alien to Paul's most characteristic line of approach to this subject. It involved the idea of a priest as intervening, occupying the position of a mediator between man and God. The intervention of a priest was prescribed in the priestly law: the law "was ordained through angels by the hand of a mediator". To Paul, however, and to early Christian thought generally, the relation of man to God is direct, and not through a mediator. There can be no mediator between God and man except God Himself or the man himself. "To us there is one God, the Father, of whom are all things and we unto Him; and one Lord, Jesus Christ, through whom are all things and we through Him." [2]

The essential contrast between the Pauline and the sacrificial idea is so strong that the fashion of speaking about Christ as the priest and mediator must be regarded as in its origin a concession to Jewish feeling. In this matter the

---

[1] A series of papers in the *Expository Times*, 1910, states the writer's view.

[2] Gal. iii. 19, 1 Corinthians viii. 6, also 1 Timothy ii. 5. This is perhaps the thought in the obscure words of Galatians iii. 20: we cannot speak of a mediator where only one party is concerned: now God is the only party in the case.

Christian doctrine does away wholly with the function of the Hebrew priest. It is merely a device of instruction, a way of illustrating the preparatory and pædagogic character of the Jewish dispensation, to say that the place of the priest in that system is filled by Christ Himself in the Christian system. To the Jews this form of expression meant much in that early age of Christianity: it gathered up their ideas of ritual, brought them to a focus, and thus made the new doctrine intelligible to them in the light of the old. But in modern time there are many minds to which the priestly function seems alien and irrelevant, a mere relic of primitive and undeveloped and wholly inadequate religion; and the idea that the Pauline teaching or the essential nature of Christianity attaches, as such, sacrificial value or priestly character to the work of Christ, takes figure and symbol for reality, and is a profound error, which, besides being erroneous in itself, alienates in many cases the modern mind because it is incomprehensible to that mind.

It is more in accordance with Pauline thought to say that the narrow official priesthood of the old Hebrew system was merged in the universal priesthood of the Christian system. The intervention of the priest was no longer required, when each Christian felt his own direct relation to God and "worked out his own salvation". This idea of universal priesthood was strongly held in the earliest Church: "ye are an elect race, a royal priesthood" . . . "to offer spiritual sacrifices, acceptable to God".[1] The union of the offices of king and priest in the person of every Christian appears also in John, Revelation i. 6, v. 10, xx. 6: "they shall be priests of God and of Christ, and shall reign with Him a thousand years".

In the latter quotation the conjunction of kingdom and

[1] I Pet. ii. 9 and 5.

priesthood shows that the idea is totally unlike Paul's conception of the saint as king.[1]   Paul's conception is caught
from the Greek philosophy: the saint is king, because he
has been placed above the storms of worldly life.   On the
other hand, the union of priesthood and kingship in one
person is oriental and theocratic.   It carries us back into
primitive oriental society, when the god ruled his people
through his priest and representative on earth.   In Peter
the idea is expressed in quotations from the Old Testament,
but it is moral and symbolical; while in Revelation it has
hardened into an external fact placed within the limits of
time.   That is characteristic of the latter book; in it moral
ideas are pictured as if they had become facts of the temporal
universe; and this relation shows that the ideas of early
Christianity have been dwelt on in meditation by John
until they have externalised themselves and are so thought
about by him.[2]

In Paul this priestly character of the saint is wholly unimportant.   As to Peter, so to Paul, all the elect are saints
and holy; but the latter is content to regard this as a fact
of purity and morality: the elect are in the image of Christ:
while to the former it conveys the implication that the
elect are consecrated as priests of God.

The contrast between the different points of view which
Ignatius and Paul respectively occupy in regard to this
matter is the contrast between a person who, having himself grown out of paganism into Christianity, takes the best
forms and thoughts he had known in his own paganism and

---

[1] See Section XXVIII.

[2] Incidentally we note that this stamps the book as later, and is not consistent with a date under Nero.   The Hebraic and adopted element in the
book is of course earlier: that element John had learned and thought over :
he did not (as some maintain) transfer it literally to his pages, but it guides
and often suggests his imagery.

gives them a Christian connotation and development, and another who, growing up a Jew, with a horror of paganism, yet in long contact with the education and philosophic thought of the pagan world, expounds Christian teaching to the pagan world by using the best forms and thoughts of pagan education and elevating these to the level of Christian life, while he tends rather to shrink from using any specially religious form or idea of paganism. In saying this we implicitly dissent from the theory (which has become fashionable recently, but which will soon pass away) that the evolution of Paul's thought was stimulated or guided in any degree by the pagan Mysteries. That theory appears fundamentally false. Any resemblance is due to the fact that the Mysteries in the time of Paul were developed in answer to the popular need for religious stimulation and guidance, and that Paul presents Christianity as the only complete fulfilment of the popular need. This theory is referred to at greater length in the second Section of Part III. of this book.

Between metaphor and philosophic truth one must always distinguish in studying Paul. The purely religious writer, indeed, may always safely adopt the metaphorical type of language, confident that it will rouse the emotion and stir the spirit and affect the life of the hearers ; but if he has to satisfy the intellectual judgment he must distinguish. Even the terms " Father " and " Son," as used of the Godhead, are metaphorical : in their literal sense they denote a human relationship, which has no place in the Divine nature. They help to suggest to the human mind a certain tender, close relationship which is analogous to, yet absolutely different from, the human. In the Divine nature the Father and the Son are one person : in human nature they are two. In the Divine nature they are co-existent from the be-

ginning, co-eternal, of the same substance : in the human
nature one originates from the other at a certain time. The
·very word " substance " is almost metaphorical, when applied
to the Divine nature, for God is spirit.

The expression of Divine things, " the deep things of
God," has always to struggle with the utter inadequacy of
human language addressed to the finite intelligence, and
drawn from finite and partial experience. Yet it has to
suggest a " knowledge " that shall be perfect and non-
finite, the real " wisdom " or " knowledge of God ". Man
has to grope and to force his way along the path of knowledge. He gathers to himself detail after detail, and part
after part, taking them into his mind, making them portions
of himself by realising for himself the spiritual reality and
law, eternal, constant, infinite, that lies in or under the
finite detail or metaphor. Such knowledge, according to
Paul's vivid expression, is only " piecemeal " or partial
knowledge. It has to be done away, and real knowledge
substituted for it. The mind of man at last sees the truth
stand open and bare and clear before it, and knows instantaneously : it leaps over the infinite chasm—infinite, yet one
that must be crossed—that divides the finite from the infinite, and reaches its inheritance of Divine knowledge. Then
the partial knowledge falls away, after the mind has seen.
In the human life " we see in a mirror, darkly ; but then
face to face : now I know in part ; but then shall I know
fully even as also I was fully known ". So says Paul to the
Corinthians (xiii. 12).[1]

There is no room for hesitation or doubt regarding this
perfect knowledge. When the mind of man sees, it knows
at once and for all time ; it recognises its true self, for it
recognises the Divine, and the end of man is to recognise

[1] On this see also a fuller discussion in Section XLII.

his true nature in the Divine nature. And so Paul says, " then I shall know fully even as also I was fully known ". This perfect knowledge is the knowledge which God possesses, and it will in the moment of insight be exercised as God exercises it—" as I also was fully known " by the mind and purpose of God.

To fall back from this knowledge is fatal : it amounts to the denial of God after having seen Him : it is " the sin against the Holy Spirit," irremediable and unpardonable. Yet to fall back from this knowledge is not possible. Because this sin is unpardonable, therefore this sin is impossible ; for the love of God is infinite, and there is nothing that it cannot conquer, and nothing that it cannot pardon. Here again we are face to face with one of those apparent, but only apparent and not real, self-contradictions. This sin is unpardonable ; yet there is nothing that God cannot wash away. The finite intelligence in face of the infinite, owing to the partial, piecemeal, finite character of its knowledge, is always exposed to such contradictions ; it states what seems a fact, and then it sees the other side of the fact, and in trying to express this other side it seems to contradict its first statement.

Yet, while this perfect knowledge is gained finally as the end and crown of life—in other words, is a possession towards which we move, and which we attain only in putting off the human nature and attaining unto God—and while it is gained instantaneously and absolutely and for ever as a permanent possession, yet with equal truth one may say that it is involved in every step which we make along the path of knowledge and of real life. In the growth of knowledge, there is more than the adding of detail to detail and of part to part. The resulting knowledge is far more than the sum of the parts. It is a new thing. The parts are, so to say, done away and annihilated. One reaches truth for the moment. One recognises the truth, the Divine truth, one's own nature, one's real self. There is felt for the moment the glow of the fire of reality and of the Divine. The past, the details, have perished: one's former self has died: a new self springs into life. This is true in the moral and spiritual life (as was pointed out in a former Section): it is true also in the intellectual life on its highest side, for on that highest side the intellectual and the religious life are merged in one another.

In studying Paul it is always necessary to penetrate beneath the metaphor to the reality. What is adoption, as we find the term in his letters? The word adoption in contemporary society described a legal and social process, whereby a family which came to an end so far as blood was concerned, was perpetuated by a species of legal fiction through the introduction of an alien as a member. The process was foreign to the Jews: the term adoption carried no meaning to them, except as an exotic idea which they learned among the Gentiles. They attained the same purpose in another way. To the Greeks and to the Romans, however, adoption was a familiar process, and it roused warm emotional ideas in the minds of many. The term was therefore highly suitable in addressing such people as the congregations of South Galatia, for they knew it in the Graeco-Asiatic law.[1] But it is only a metaphorical expression, and not literally true. It expressed the process

---

[1] That the legal processes referred to in the Galatian Epistle are Graeco-Asiatic as applied in practical administration by the Romans, and that they differ from the analogous, but not identical processes of Roman law, has been proved in my *Historical Commentary* to the satisfaction of the highest authority, Professor Mitteis. The Romans were not such poor administrators as to force purely Roman law on peoples who possessed already a highly developed legal system.

of bringing into the family an alien to inherit the religious duties and the property of the family, and this process presented a certain analogy to the process of bringing in the Gentiles to share or to possess the glories promised to the Jews.   Yet the analogy is only an incomplete one : there are many points of difference between the two processes.   Paul seizes the points of similarity, and slurs over the differences. His readers did the same thing ; and therefore they learned to see what Paul had in mind.   If, however, one should start from this idea of the inheritance of the Gentiles through "adoption," and argue that, because the sinner is adopted as a son of God, therefore everything that can be predicated about a legal process of adoption among men can be predicated about the bringing of sinners into the inheritance of God, one would be led into endless blunders.

Now many arguments against the Pauline teaching are founded on misapprehension of his language, which was necessarily figurative.   His expression, owing to the bent of his mind (the result of race and inherited character, and his social environment in early years), was largely legal and even commercial.   If the legal aspect is pressed, extreme inferences can be drawn, and have been drawn ; and these inferences, which by some have been drawn in good faith and with a profound belief that was able to blind itself to much of the erroneousness, have been by others condemned and misjudged as absurdities.   They become absurdities, when they are looked at from the wrong point of view. Looked at in their proper character, as mere aids to understanding, the metaphors are wholly free from the absurd consequences which have been imported into them.

So, to take another example, the Christian term "redemption" acquires a connotation very different from the act of redeeming a slave or a captive, and must not be judged as if it were identical.   The analogy may be seized, and the difference left out of mind.

The use of the metaphor from building is peculiarly characteristic of Paul, and specially suitable for the Greeks.[1] It meant much to them.   The figurative character is here so plain that this metaphor is rarely pressed to a wrong use.

One example may be added of false view and inference regarding the position of Paul: this will form our next Section.

[1] Of the use of metaphor in Paul a paper in the writer's *Luke the Physician and Other Studies* treats at more length.

XXXV. The Beginning of Sin in the World

In regard to the origin of sin in the world there is in Paul's teaching the same seeming, but only seeming, contradiction that has so often met us already. After man and the universe had come into existence, sin began in the world at a particular moment through an act of the man. "Through one man sin entered into the world, and death through sin." It has sometimes been rashly inferred by unphilosophic speculation that there must have existed a state of sinlessness and moral perfection before the first act of sin was committed. Paul did not hold or teach that opinion. His doctrine and philosophic position exclude it. Such an inference from what he did state is unjustifiable. On the contrary, he says that "the first man is of the earth, earthy,"[1] i.e. the potentiality of evil was involved from the beginning, and sinfulness was implicit in the nature of the first man. Sin begins when man begins. The existence of man as divided from God, and as requiring to seek reunion with God, involves in itself the tendency towards sin as a possibility. If there were no sin or possibility of sin, there would be nothing, in Paul's view, to gain from God. The end of man's life is to attain freedom from sin, i.e. Salvation.

It would be merely senseless to argue that, in a literal interpretation of the story of Adam (which Paul indubitably regarded as true both historically and spiritually), the first man was sinless until the first sin was committed. That

[1] 1 Cor. xv. 47.

206

is a literalism too painful and too gross. In the evolution of man's history under conditions of time and space, the man exists and then sin enters. But the sin is potentially present in man from the moment of his creation. There is a moment when the potential becomes actual; but those who argue that Paul thought of a state of human sinlessness as reigning until Adam committed his first sin are incapacitating themselves for comprehending Paul.

As has already been stated, the permanent possibility of sin, and the position of man as exposed to the temptation of sinning and as ultimately triumphing over this temptation and attaining to reunion with God, are the Divine order of creation and the law of the universe. This possibility of sinning is the measure of what we have figuratively termed the distance separating man from God. The distance is entailed in the act of making man and giving to him a distinct individuality, in which he may exercise his separate powers ; and his life ought to be the gradual overcoming of the temptation to sin, the traversing of the distance that divides him from God, and finally the attaining to God once more. It is not too strong—though it is a statement that is liable to be misinterpreted and requires to be read with sympathy to distinguish between the good and the bad in our imperfect expression—to say that man is an imperfect Jesus, and as it were a Christ who has failed to realise the end of his being and the purpose of his creation ; that Jesus is the expression of the Divine purpose in the creation of man ; and that the life of Jesus is the guarantee that this purpose can be realised, will be realised, and (as one might almost say) must ultimately be realised. The nature of Christ is the idea of Salvation, which takes possession of the man,[1] and works in him in the way of driving him on

[1] Gal. ii. 20, Phil. iii. 12, 1 Cor. xiii. 12.

to work out his own salvation. It is merely another one among the many imperfect ways of describing the relation of man to God to say that, unless man is capable of sinning, he is not divided from God, and there can therefore be no complete creative act, until the new creature stands apart from the original Creative Power, able and free to choose for himself and to act for himself, i.e. to sin or to avoid sinning.

It may be asked, Is not this too awkward, too roundabout, too complicated a process; and therefore is it not unfair to man and unworthy of God? Why not make man so that he will come right and be righteous of himself and through his own unaided activity?

We might reply that, if man is such that he can (and therefore must) rise free from sin through himself alone, he is not really man: he is not divided from God, and there would have been in that case no act of creation, and nothing but God would exist: there would be no man. Let us, however, look at it in another way. If man were so made, he would in that case be (in modern phrase) a "Superman". Ancient thought seems to have dallied with this idea, and worked it out to its consequences as a belief in the existence of superhuman beings, permitted by God to exist. If we assume that such beings exist, freed from the fetters and imperfections of humanity, able to know and to act, the result must be (and has actually been, according to that ancient belief) that these beings are not reminded through their own failure that they must lean on God and trust to Him: accordingly they are confident in themselves and fail to keep Him in regard, and thus they are merely led into sin in another form: they are the wicked angels, the lost spirits of popular superstition.

In every supposition that either ordinary man, or "super-man," or powers and beings intermediate between God and man (such as the "angels and principalities and powers" of Jewish belief), can through their own nature and power know the truth and attain it of themselves, there is involved the consequence that the conscious memory of the Divine nature outside of them and the Divine goal in front of them dies out, and that "knowing God, they glorified Him not as God, neither gave thanks," and therefore that "their heart was made senseless and darkened". Thus their wisdom becomes folly; and their conception of the Divine nature is distorted; and the career of evil sketched by Paul to the Romans[1] ensues. Sin thus comes in by another way and in another form even more serious.

Ancient religious thought in an almost unconscious way developed this line of speculation to the ultimate issue that these higher beings become powers of evil, separate permanently from God, hostile to God, foes to man as the work of God, and bent on preventing man from fulfilling the purpose of God (except in so far as they repent, master their pride, and seek humbly to return to Him). The fanciful theory of the "super-man" was worked out by ancient thought in this form, and was thus disproved by reducing it to an absurdity. You cannot have the "super-man" without finding that you have merely got the "devil" under another name.

If, therefore, the division from God involved in the act of creation is real, the possibility of sinning is inevitably involved in it. If that division is not real, then there is nothing except the Divine, and no creation of human nature has occurred.

The consciousness of God in the human mind, present there as continuously and completely as possible, is the

[1] Rom. i. 21 ff.

condition of the higher life and the true end of human nature. Man advances towards this end by living it and making it real in his character ; as he learns to swim by swimming, so he learns to realise God, to be conscious of God, to know God, by doing so and being so. If he attempts to do right and to be righteous through himself and his own power, he is thereby forgetting God ; his consciousness of God is interrupted through his own "senseless" exaltation of himself into the place of God ; and he has turned his back and moved in the contrary direction away from God. The element of deliberate action and perverse choosing is involved in his conduct. Now, whereas the aim of life is reunion with God, i.e. absolutely unbroken, continuous and unending thinking with God and like God, it is purely absurd if men should try to attain this end by forgetting Him and "giving themselves the glory".

If our interpretation of this passage of Romans i. 21 ff. is right, Paul is there just stating the converse of his own words to the Galatians defining the true life,[1] "It is no longer I that live, but Christ liveth in me" : i.e. he (as the representative true Christian) thinks continuously and always with God, sees God in everything, has no consciousness except of the Divine purpose and will that moves and rules in every act of nature and of history, and thus his own individual will has been merged in the will of God, not by losing its distinct personality, but by attaining to its full development : he has not been absorbed and annihilated in the Divine, but in the Divine consciousness has attained the perfection of his own true individuality. He is reunited with God, and yet remains his individual self in glorified form and in spiritual body. But yet—"not that I have already at-

---

[1] Gal. ii. 20: the same thought is re-expressed in emphasised form, i.e. "in large letters," in vi. 14.

tained or am already made perfect; but I press on . . . toward the goal unto the prize of the upward calling of God in Jesus *who is the* Messiah ".[1]

There is but one "Way". The way of this Salvation is, and must inevitably be, the passionate, enthusiastic, whole-hearted recognition of the real nature of Jesus as the message of God, the merging of one's own nature in the recognition of this message, the living of the Christ-life, i.e. being "crucified with Christ," the sacrifice of one's older false self in order to attain to one's true self, the seizing of Christ as one has been seized by Him. This is the law of growth: the process is defined by its ultimate and perfect stage.

The completion of the process is involved already in the first step onwards, because the first step marks the guiding law of the whole. The Christian is already perfect, because he will be perfect; and yet immediately and always comes the instantaneous recognition that in all this process he himself has done nothing, but Christ and the message and purpose of God are working in him: not for one instant may he forget to give God the glory and render to Him the thanks,[2] otherwise the whole process is vitiated and turned to self-glorification, arrogance and deterioration. In each moment of growth all the process and the law are involved: one attains and yet one has not attained, but only grown a stage; and God remains in front, outside, beyond oneself, and the Divine in the man has still to press onwards towards reunion with the Divine which stands before. The reunion is ever in the process of being consummated, and yet is not consummated. Such is the law of the universe and the nature of Christ.

What then is Christ, and what is the knowledge of Christ and of God? Sections XXXVII. ff.

---

[1] Phil. iii. 12-14.   [2] Rom. i. 21.

XXXVI. Influence of Contemporary Custom on Paul

There is another difficulty in understanding Paul's teaching besides the figurative nature of the language in which he was compelled to appeal to the understanding of pagans and Jews in the first century. Not merely was he obliged to suit his expression to their powers of comprehension. His own comprehension was perhaps in certain respects imperfect. It is perhaps true to say that he was to some extent bound in the fetters of his time and guided in its way of contemplating the world. He was not free from the beliefs and even the superstitions of his age. How far they influenced his mind and thought is far from certain: in the present writer's opinion they exercised far less influence on him than some modern writers think, and less even than would appear from the occasional expressions which occur in his letters.

One might quote from his letters a certain number of phrases or statements, which are a riddle to exercise the ingenuity of commentators, and which are probably the expression of some belief or superstition current in Jewish circles at that time; but these are of small importance in studying the teaching of Paul. They are commonly mere incidental phrases. They hardly ever touch the essentials of his doctrine. They might all be left on one side without taking away anything from his teaching. Yet they are quoted by some writers, and dwelt upon at considerable length, as if Paul could be best understood through them and could not be correctly understood except through them.

Regarding these as wholly unimportant in their bearing on his doctrine, we need not linger on them; and they are here mentioned only to guard against the error of over-valuing them. They are of interest only in estimating the character of Paul as a man. He was caught in the net of his own age: in the non-essentials he sometimes, or often, remains impeded and encumbered by the tone and ideas of his age; but his teaching is for every age, and in all important respects rises clear and free above his own time and above all limitations and imperfections due to his circumstances, and soars into the empyrean of eternal truth. It is essentially true to say of him, as Ben Jonson said of Shakespeare,

> He was not of an age, but for all time.

At this point we shall discuss only one example. Some, or perhaps many, of Paul's references to angels are influenced more or less by popular superstition. Again, the instructions of a practical kind which he sometimes gives regarding the conduct of women are peculiarly liable to be affected by current popular ideas: there is no department of life in which a man's views are so apt to be coloured by early circumstances and training and by current social ideas as his views about the proper conduct of women. Where both angels and women are found in any passage, Paul is doubly liable to be fettered by current ideas and superstitions, and obscurity results.

When Paul orders women to wear veils always[1] he says, "if a woman is not veiled, let her also be shorn": an unveiled woman is as bad as a woman with her head close-

---

[1] 1 Cor. xi. 4-10.

cut or shaved. Now, the disgrace of having the hair cut is a purely external matter : the loss or the cutting may be due to accident or to precaution against disease : it involves only the loss of a natural adornment, and may naturally be regretted and mourned on that ground. After all, however, this is only a matter of social estimation, not of moral quality ; yet Paul, in using this comparison, assumes that it has a moral and religious character. The wearing of long hair is not an ethical duty, but only expedient, socially and æsthetically. Accordingly the attempt of Paul to exalt the wearing of the veil into a religious duty is discredited by the comparison which he uses for the purpose of clinching his argument. The one and the other duty stand on the same level. Neither is morally binding.

It is probable that Paul's early associations with Tarsus are largely responsible in this matter. The veiling of women was practised more closely and completely in Tarsus than in any other Greek or Graeco-Asiatic city known to Dion Chrysostom ;[1] and Paul, who had grown up to regard veiling as a duty incumbent on all women, now presents it to the Corinthians as a moral and religious obligation. He declares that women, *qua* women, ought to veil, and that it is an outrage on the nature of women not to do so. One cannot plead that he is merely urging the Corinthians to have regard to current social conventions and customs. It is quite true that one should not lightly outrage such social customs, and always Paul teaches so ; but here he presents the obligation to veil in a far more emphatic fashion as an eternal unvarying duty imposed on woman by her own nature and by the relation in which she stands to the universe as a whole.

In this matter we must, I think, recognise an instance

---

[1] The Oriental and non-Hellenic strictness that was practised at Tarsus in regard to veiling is described on the authority of Dion in my *Cities of St. Paul*.

of the Apostle's occasional inability to rise above the ideas of his own time. Old prepossessions, dominant in his mind from infancy, made him see a moral duty, where in our modern estimation only a social custom was really in question. In the modern European judgment, Paul seems to prefer the lower and poorer view of human and womanly nature to the higher and nobler view. Here he shows himself of an age, and not for all time. How different a conception does he exhibit of women, where he writes with the insight of a prophet to the Galatians (iii. 28) that in the perfected church " there can be no different rank and standard of estimation for male and female, for ye are all one in Christ ".

To buttress his opinion Paul has recourse to the popular superstition : " for this cause ought the woman to have authority on her head because of the angels ". In her relation to the universe as a whole she may come under the power of, and even be exposed to outrage by, demons or angels, unless she has on her head the authority which protects her from them.[1] It was a popular superstition that women were liable to fall under the influence of such angelic beings,[2] who were more powerful in many ways than men ; but through obedience to the social conventions they gained authority and immunity from the power of demons or angels. The veil was their strength and their protection, and the social convention was made more binding on women by the sanction and penalty involved in this belief.

Here we have an example of the first century Tarsian Jewish education, and its strong influence on the man. Yet how small a part of Paul's teaching is this ! how far it is

[1] The meaning of "having authority on the head " (1 Cor. xi. 10) is explained in *The Cities of St. Paul.*

[2] An example of this belief appears in Genesis vi. 2-4.

from even touching the essential elements of his doctrine! how out of harmony it is with himself in another place and another vein of thought!

One must, however, always remember that, to our judgment, Paul's method in reasoning is frequently liable to seem unconvincing. He sometimes draws his arguments and his illustrations and analogies from quarters that carry no conviction to our minds, and he trusts to the predilections that lay deep in every Jewish mind at that time. His quotations from Scripture are often divorced from their context, and used in a sense which is quite out of harmony with their fair meaning in their original position. His analogies are sometimes forced and, in our view, unnatural. It would, however, be a serious blunder to estimate the quality and the insight either of Paul or of Plato by the superficial appearance of their argumentation. The Platonic Socrates is presented to us as discussing with his own contemporaries; and he overpowers them by arguments that often appear to us extremely unfair and weak. But in both Paul and Plato there lies beneath the surface of their ratiocination the direct insight into truth. To understand them, we must accept their intuition at its real value, and not at the rank of the argumentation which appeared convincing, doubtless, to contemporary taste, but which does not appear so to us.

How far Paul's opinions about women should be regarded as springing from his insight into the divine force that moves the world, we do not venture to judge; they are out of harmony with ours; but the fault may well lie with us, and we may be judging under the prepossession of modern custom, which will perhaps prove evanescent and discordant with the plan of the universe and the purpose of God. Nature and the history of the future will determine; but on the whole matter we appeal from Paul to Paul himself, and from 1 Corinthians xi. 8, 9, to Galatians iii. 28. The mere fact that we can appeal from Paul to Paul, and from one saying to another, is a warning against the hasty conclusion that the whole of Paul's doctrine on the subject is summed up in any one sentence.[1]   There can, however, be no question that his argument or analogy drawn from the length of the hair confuses between what is only customary or æsthetic and what is ethically binding and universal.

Other examples of the influence exercised on Paul by current popular ideas and opinions might be quoted and discussed at length;[2] but they are quaint and curious, rather than instructive. They do not touch the greatness of Paul, and it would only tend to distort our views about the real nature of his teaching if we devoted further attention to this subject. The biographer of Paul will do well to study them more carefully, for they throw light on his personal quality as a human being; but we are not writing a biography at present.

[1] See also a later Section, p. 264.

[2] A case in point may be the much-discussed and obscure passage of 1 Corinthians xv. 29, "what shall they do which are baptized for the dead?"

XXXVII. The Happy Lot of Man

In all ages of the world many people, not seeing the real truth, but judging only from superficial and vain fancies, have been filled with the thought that this world is all awry, that "the times are out of joint," that fate is hard and cruel, that the lot of man is nought but misery from the cradle to the grave. Such had been the experience and the general opinion of the pagan world, whose writers were almost all penetrated (as we have already mentioned) with the thought of human misery, deterioration and hopelessness. Paul writes and speaks always with the knowledge of their opinions and words in his mind; and his attitude is never rightly comprehended by us until we have this fixed firmly in our minds. To that pagan world, to its statesmen, its philosophers, its writers, its common people, all either plunged in hopelessness about the future or quietly resigned to the conclusion, "let us eat and drink, for to-morrow we die," Paul came with his message of hope, joy, love, peace—in short, "Salvation". In contrast to their ignorance and despair, he is always transported with the lively and true perception of the beauty, the love, the kindness—in one word, the grace of God in all His dealings with men.

What an abundantly happy lot is that of mankind! what perfect and indescribably bountiful grace is God's! This was the message that the pagan world needed.[1]

[1] See Section XXI.

The Apostle rises to the loftiest height of enthusiasm, and expresses himself in a kind of lyrical and poetic prose, when he contemplates the saving grace of God, as shown in the plan which He had conceived in the foundation of the world and worked out stage by stage and detail by detail to its completion and perfection in Jesus Christ. Words almost fail him to picture " the exceeding riches of God's grace in kindness towards us in Christ Jesus," and " the unsearchable riches of Christ ".[1] Not merely do we receive from Christ. We are the riches of Christ. To that great honour have we been exalted by the grace of God. The assembly of the saints, the whole body of Christians, the Universal and Catholic Church, constitutes the inheritance of Christ. The purpose of God from the creation has been to create and complete this structure as the kingdom of God, "the wealth of the glory of Christ's inheritance among the saints ".

Thus we are necessary to God and to Christ ! What an honour and happiness to mankind ! The glory of God and the splendour of Christ cannot be made real and established definitely except through the completion of the salvation of man in the congregation of the saints. Our bliss is His glory. Paul heaps up word upon word to blazon before the eyes of the Asian Christians the grandeur of their lot in being made the completion and perfection of the eternal purpose of God, " the riches of the glory of the patrimonial estate of Christ ".[2]

We have become so familiarised from infancy with these and similar Pauline words that it needs an effort to hold them

---

[1] Eph. ii. 7, iii. 8: the thought of the richness and splendour and magnificence of our inheritance in Christ is peculiarly characteristic of Ephesians i. 8, 18, 3, etc.

[2] Eph. i. 18.

in thought apart from ourselves and gaze upon their true meaning, so as to realise the glittering and dazzling beauty of that which they describe. In modern times, however, we are always thinking and reasoning about the idea which is pictured in these words, as it is being slowly worked out in the Church of God and the civilisation and progress of men. The thought is not strange to us; on the contrary, it is the sum and kernel, and it contains the germ, of all modern science and modern speculation. Put in modern terms, it is the idea of evolution in history and science. Paul prefers to give it a personal form : the Will of God works itself out in the gradual creation of His Church : every other process is subsidiary to that : the Church as it shall be is the sum and the embodiment of every line of development. The growth of the world and of man towards the higher stage is the working out of the glory of the Creator and of His creation. Paul would not have put it in those words, for he was of the first century, and did not dream of or understand the nature of Science ; but none the less that is the real import in modern terms of what he said in such enthusiastic and half-poetic language.

To Paul this idea was not new when he wrote to the " Ephesians ". It was not attained to by him for the first time, while he was composing that wonderful letter, in some respects the greatest and most glittering and dazzling of all his letters. It had been reached by him in meditation before he was ready to carry his message to the pagans, and therefore it was his possession before he was finally called upon to lay aside all other duties and plans, pressing as they seemed to be, and to " Depart, for I will send thee far hence to the nations of the world ". That was the command urgent and imperative and requiring instant obedience, completing and making clear at last to Paul those previous instructions (which had been less lucid to him, because he was not yet ready and able to comprehend them).[1]   Such was the vision and the glory which he had seen in the fourteenth year before the winter of A.D. 56-7, accompanied with words unspeakable, "which it is not lawful for a man to utter". To the Christian mind there can be only one such vision, and that is the vision of the glory of God and the marvellous and perfect purpose of God, which in its completion will make manifest His goodness, His unspeakable goodness, His complete and perfect Salvation, His way with man.   In that purpose there was much that Paul must not declare, much that he might only contemplate, so as to fill his mind with it, and have it as a precious and power-giving possession to himself; and this possession was his greatest glory and his supreme consolation.

He had seen, and he knew, the glory of God; and the glory of God is the completion of His purpose in the perfecting of His creation.   This idea lay in his heart.   It gave fire and point and life and power to his words, but it must not and could not be declared fully at any time to men.   It could be revealed partially to the saints (for example, in the Ephesian letter), as they learned to appreciate it for themselves.   It was the sort of knowledge which can never be comprehended except by those who have risen to that level and seen for themselves.   It cannot be set forth to the ignorant, because it is too sacred, too perfect, and far beyond their understanding: "the word is sharper than a two-edged sword," and a sword is always dangerous to the ignorant, the stupid or the foolish. This knowledge is "the mystery of the Will of God," [2] a thing still hidden, though in process of being revealed, a rich possession to those who are growing into the knowledge of it.

---

[1] As already mentioned in a previous section, p. 8.
[2] Eph. i. 9 f., "to sum up all things in Christ".

XXXVIII. The Mystery of God

At the present stage it will best serve the purpose which is set before the present writer to allude to the meaning of this term "mystery" in Paul's letters. The word has been by some scholars defined as "something once hidden, but now revealed"; and it is regarded as being "always used in the New Testament in the sense of an 'open secret'".[1] That definition and description is partially, but, as I think, not wholly accurate, and is therefore not quite satisfactory, though it is in practice useful. It has got hold of the truth, and it has got hold of the right end of the truth. But the deeper expression of the truth is that the mystery is "something once hidden, but now in process of being revealed".

In a sense, of course, the mystery is revealed once for all and finally in Christ. That thought is rightly in the mind of the writers who employ that definition. But who knows Christ? We are only in process of comprehending Him, and so comprehending the mystery of "the wealth of the glory of His inheritance among the saints". Life is the process of acquiring this knowledge, which is forced on us, and which, so to say, seizes us and takes possession of us. The experience of life drives wisdom in some degree into the minds of all men, except in so far as obstinate resistance

[1] I quote from Rev. G. Currie Martin (to whom I am much indebted: writing in Turkey in tents or in trains, one has in hand little except the text of Paul), in his edition of Ephesians, Philippians, etc., in the "Century Bible," a tiny volume convenient for the traveller.

and determined prepossession by selfish desire or by over-conceit of knowledge, keep out the knowledge. Now, in proportion as in the process of righteousness, which is true and real life, "the saints" acquired this knowledge, it became possible for Paul to declare to them more and more fully "the mystery".

This mystery of God's purpose, of course, is declared, in a sense, and to some degree, in the first words that Paul addresses to an audience new to him : it is declared in every speech and in every letter more and more perfectly, as the hearers live themselves into a sympathy with and comprehension of the purpose of God. Yet there always remained something, nay much, of the mystery, "words unspeakable, which it is not lawful for a man to utter," hidden in the heart of Paul.

That is always the case with the great teacher, and the great writer. Who has ever had any deep power over the minds and life of men, that declared all he knew? There must always remain in the speaker's or writer's mind a large store of reserved knowledge. It is the power of the unspoken knowledge that gives driving and penetrating force to his words.

In none of Paul's letters is this knowledge and mystery so fully declared as in Ephesians. In prison, as he says in iii. and iv. 1, he has no thought about his suffering, or his want of power, or his subjection to the will of gaolers and guards. All that the law and all that the authority of officials imposes on him he accepts and does. That is right and just : they are placed in authority by the will of God for the time : they form a stage in the evolution of the Divine will, and for him the duty is to act in such matters according to the constituted law of the Empire. But they have no influence over him. His inheritance, his happiness, his knowledge of God's purpose, his complete and unhesitating confidence that this purpose is fulfilling itself even in " these bonds," all remain far outside of the competence of guards and officials.   Whatever they may do, even to the infliction of flogging or death upon him, is his triumph and their failure.   He is ready to depart: he is equally ready to continue his work, obeying the Imperial law and obeying the law of God.   It may be regarded as quite certain that he would not have tried to escape from prison, except under direct Divine command.   The slave or the prisoner should accept the lot and will of God.   (See pp. 58, 247-57.)

To the Corinthian philosophers and clever people he sets forth similar truth in a far more veiled fashion,[1] but still he "speaks wisdom among the perfect. . . . God's wisdom in mystery, even the wisdom that hath been hidden, which God foreordained before the worlds unto our glory."[2] In that passage also he describes the glory, the power, the royal and imperial lot of the Christian; and he plays with the Stoic paradox of the philosopher-king, rising, however, through irony (as in iv. 8-10) to lofty and mystic expression almost perfectly on a level with the language of Ephesians: "let no one glory in men.   For all things are yours: whether Paul, or Apollos, or Cephas, or the world, or life, or death, or things present, or things to come; all are yours; and ye are Christ's; and Christ is God's."   Ephesians does not condescend even to play with and to give new meaning to "persuasive words of philosophy . . . the wisdom of men".   It stands entirely on the level of the pure Christ-thought, embodied in the new Christian language, which Paul had already constructed to express this new and loftier thought, a language of the people, using few if any words that were not familiar to the fairly educated Graeco-

[1] 1 Cor. i.-iv.   [2] *Ibid.* ii. 6 f.

Roman public, yet transforming them all by the wealth of the thought which was shadowed forth in them.

This thought as set forth in Ephesians was, as we have stated, Pauline from the beginning of his work among the Gentiles. It was this reserve of knowledge that gave force to his opening address to the people of Antioch, and penetrated the whole city before he had completed his second week there (Acts xiii. 12 ff.). The message that he then preached was not taught him by any Apostle or man, but was gained through revelation and meditation:[1] he placarded or blazoned it before them:[2] it gave them marvellous powers, and the inheritance of God: it called them to freedom, it clothed them with Christ.[3]

The language of Galatians is simpler, i.e. expressed more in popular metaphor and familiar or common terms than that of Ephesians, but it is informed with the same knowledge and the same power: the knowledge is the power. The language of Ephesians is more poetic and ideal: it treats a philosophic subject, but one too transcendent and mystic to be susceptible of properly and strictly philosophic expression—especially to such a class of correspondents.

---

[1] Gal. i. 12, 17, iii. 7.   [2] Gal. iii. 1.
[3] Gal. iii. 5, 29, iv. 7, v. 13, iii. 27.

XXXIX. The Suffering of God

We now approach a point on which one hardly dares to speak, and in treating which the utmost reverence and humility and reticence is needed. It is not improbable that the great revelation to Paul—"unspeakable words which it is not lawful for man to utter" . . . so splendid that "by reason of the exceeding greatness of the revelations, there was given to me a thorn in the flesh, a messenger of Satan to buffet me, that I should not be exalted overmuch"—had reference to some such matter as this. If that be so, it is in his letter to the Ephesians that he comes nearest to making a statement on the subject. We must try to understand what he means in that letter, yet we must not rush in where it is unlawful to tread.

In Section XXXVII. I have almost unconsciously set foot on this subject[1] when using the words, "we are necessary to God and to Christ," and "we are the riches of Christ," and "our bliss is His glory". These words arose naturally out of the attempt to re-express the teaching of Paul about "the happy lot of man," for, as he declares, the assembly of the saints, the body of the Church, constitutes the inheritance of Christ.

Although the strong words were written almost inevitably and unconsciously, yet we cannot, on subsequent reflection, draw back from them. The happiness of man constitutes the glory of God and the inheritance of Christ; but, obversely,

---

[1] ἐνεβατεύσαμεν, to adopt the technical term, on which see the second Section of Part III.

the misery and the failure of man make the suffering of God. The one cannot be true without the other. Sin, which is misery and failure for man, makes suffering for God : it is the impeding of His will and the frustration of His purpose.

Either all that has been said in this book is wrong, and the point of view which has been taken in it is mistaken, or the last and fullest truth lies in the assertion that a sinful creation makes a suffering Creator, and sinning man makes a suffering God.

May not this offer a way towards understanding in some small degree that greatest of all mysteries, the most fundamental and yet the most incomprehensible truth in the world, the nature and work of Christ? It is incomprehensible because it is fundamental. All things rest on it. It rests on nothing deeper or simpler. It is the beginning, and it is the end. From this truth all knowledge begins, and in this truth all knowledge culminates.

Since it is the law of the universe and the Will of God that the sin of man makes the suffering of God, this is as much as to say that the penalty of man's sin is paid by God. That is the Divine purpose and plan, existent from the beginning, deliberately intended and contemplated in the creation of the world. It is part of the nature of God. The death of Christ was looked forward to by Him " before the foundation of the world," as the completion of His gradually unfolding purpose—" to sum up all things in Christ, the things in the heavens and the things upon the earth . . . according to the purpose of Him who worketh all things after the counsel of His will ".[1]

The supreme blessing which Paul in his prayer invokes for the Ephesians is that insight into the purpose and " the knowledge of God" may be granted them, so that they may

[1] Eph. i. 4, 10, 11.

understand how and why He has called them, and may appreciate what His inheritance is, and how it is achieved. It is achieved through the triumphant death and resurrection of Christ, and the absolute supremacy which Christ thereby attains in the completion of the Divine purpose.[1]   In Christ God made Himself subject to evident suffering.

The body of this triumphant and glorious Christ is the Church, of which He is the head.[2]   The Creator without the created is nothing : man is necessary to the glory and the purpose of God : Christ without His Church, so to say, would be like a head without a body.

The death of Christ pays in full the penalty of suffering which results from the sin of the creation ; and man, who through the sin had died, gains life through the payment of the penalty, and is inheritor along with Christ of all that He has gained.   This is not to be understood through the bare statement that one sins and another pays the forfeit on his behalf.   The Divine nature is in man—only in germ indeed, but still it is there.   The Divine nature suffers, and dies ; but in dying it rises superior to death.   It is re-created, or re-invigorated, or made triumphant in the man ; and he is thus identified with the body and the life and the glory of Christ.   By death he has entered into life. This is the knowledge of God.

Paul himself has through revelation become possessed of this knowledge :[3] he has "understanding in the mystery of Christ—the mystery which from all ages hath been hid in God who created all things".   This knowledge gains strength through love.   Love is the basis on which "the knowledge of God" is built up.   The end of the development is that the man who has the love and gains the

---

[1] Eph. ii. 18-21.   [2] *Ibid.* 23.
[3] Eph. iii. 3, 4, 9 ; 2 Cor. xii. 3 ff.

knowledge is "filled unto all the fulness of God," i.e. the Divine germ in him grows to fill up his entire nature, and "it is no longer he that lives, but Christ liveth in him ".[1]

Each individual man must gain Christ and the knowledge of Christ for himself; and Christ lives and dies for each. Yet mankind is a society. There is the great household of the world. Christ lived and died, not merely for the individual man who can know Him and lay hold of Him, but also for mankind. He is the ideal for the individual; He is the historical Jesus for the world into which He came.

In the gradual unfolding of the Will of God there are successive steps and various stages. (1) There is the individual man, the prophet and seer of the Divine purpose; (2) there is the one chosen people; (3) then finally there is the Universal Church of the entire world.

(1) The Divine Will chooses and seizes on certain individuals, the Apostles and Prophets. These keep alive the Divine spark of fire in the world. They vivify the nation among which they live, according as their nation hears them. Progress depends on the energy of those great and powerful minds, and on their influence on other men around them. They are the foundation on which a developing social system is built up.[2] They recognise and declare the purpose of God in the vicissitudes of history. They are the teachers and guides of their race.

(2) The nation which is to be great and progressive is the nation which produces a succession of such master-spirits. That was pre-eminently the case with the Hebrew race. It was the nation of the Promise, and it was the one race that gave birth to a continuous series of great spirits, which kept alive the consciousness and the reality of the Promise. The Promise presumes deserving; and it was through the spiri-

---

[1] Gal. ii. 20.   [2] Eph. ii. 20.

tual life which the Prophets nourished that this one nation deserved the Promise.

(3) The Jesus of history accomplished the unity of the whole world. He was for all, not for one race. The Promise, which was prospectively and potentially universal —through the seed of Abraham shall all nations be blessed— was made actively universal, because He was before the eyes of the whole world for the whole world. The whole world is to be the universal Church, "the household of God".[1] In this household all are united, not as being all the same or all equal. Each individual has his special character, and each has his appropriate function, suited to his powers in the Church, "the temple in the Lord . . . the habitation of God in the spirit".[2] This temple is the body of Christ; and the true social life is "the building up of this body, till we all attain unto the unity of the faith, unto the measure of the stature of the fulness of Christ".[3]

Now what authority has Paul for this? What assurance have we of it? How do we know it? In the last resort it must force itself on our judgment as inevitable and certain.

Paul, as he says, has revelation to rest on. For him this was sufficient and final. What have we to rest on? It is involved in the primal axiom that God is good. We have the direct intuition into the nature of the universe and of God. We cannot demonstrate, or prove it by argument. There is nothing deeper or more fundamental from which it can be deduced. We can see through the vivifying force of faith, which is a form of revelation, or we can by sympathy with Paul—a sympathy founded on the recognition of his power and the truth that shines through him—see in some degree what he sees and know what he knows. We can feel dimly the relation in which we stand to God. We

---

[1] Eph. ii. 19.   [2] *Ibid.* 21, 22.   [3] Eph. iv. 13; cp. iii. 19.

can know in a fashion the meaning of those metaphorical
expressions, such as that man is made in the image of God,
that man has in him a spark of the Divine fire and nature,
that man can can grow into likeness to God. The most
illuminative, however, and yet the most difficult form in
which this relation between man and God can be expressed
is the teaching of the Ephesian letter, that the fulfilment of
the Divine will and the completion of the Divine purpose
in man is the glory of God, and the thwarting of that will
and purpose through the sin of man is the suffering of God.

XL. The Knowledge of God

In Ephesians it is remarkable how completely the glory and the inheritance of "the saints" is identified with knowledge. "Ye can perceive my understanding in the mystery of Christ."[1] As Mr. Currie Martin says, "It seems natural and fitting that he should remind his readers how great an authority by the grace of God" he possesses; this authority is due to his comprehension of the mystery, i.e. to his knowledge. The verses that follow make the understanding of the mystery practically equivalent to the comprehension of the eternal purpose of God, and suggest that Paul regards it as the reason justifying his bold and confident access to Christ. Knowledge is power. The saying is trite, as applied to practical life, to business, or to science. The same saying, hackneyed in the modern application, is equally and perfectly suitable in regard to the doctrine of Paul: the knowledge of God is the power of God. That is the meaning of Colossians i. 9 f.: "that ye may be filled with the knowledge of His will in all spiritual wisdom and understanding, to walk worthily . . . bearing fruit unto every good work, and increasing by the knowledge of God;[2] strengthened with all power . . . unto all patience and long-suffering with joy".

The perception that this point of view is characteristic of the Ephesian Epistle is the chief basis for the opinion

[1] Eph. iii. 4.
[2] "By" not "*in* the knowledge of God". The rendering "by" is given in the margin of the Revised Version (English).

(widely spread among modern scholars for a time, but now gradually disappearing) that this Epistle is not the work of Paul, but of a successor. Our contention is that this "Ephesian" point of view is essentially and characteristically Pauline, but is more definitely and prominently expressed here than in any other letter. There is hardly any letter of his which does not give special and peculiar emphasis to some point in his teaching; but this gives no reason to deny the Pauline origin of the letter, if the doctrine is found to be expressed less prominently, or even merely suggested and implied, in his other letters.

It is urgently necessary for our purpose of clearly comprehending the nature of Paulinism, as always and in all matters the expression of the idea of growth towards God, as dynamic and not static, to study his conception of knowledge, the wisdom of God. We shall start best from an earlier Epistle, *viz.*, from 1 Corinthians xiii., and from Professor Harnack's exposition of it, in which he takes a view differing in some respects from ours.

XLI. Knowledge and Love

Paul in the "Hymn of Heavenly Love" (1 Cor. xiii.) draws a pointed contrast between partial or present knowledge and perfect (absolute) or future knowledge. As the mind and character of the Christian develops, his partial knowledge is put aside, and done away : that partial knowledge sees only obscurely, for it sees only the reflection of the reality (as in a mirror), and cannot gaze directly on the reality. I cannot but feel, however, that His Excellency Dr. A. Harnack, in his striking article in the *Expositor*, June, 1912, p. 493 f., over-emphasises the irreconcilability of the one kind of knowledge with the other, just as he also seems to over-emphasise the separation between knowledge and love.[1] These two topics—what is partial knowledge as compared with complete knowledge, and what connexion exists between knowledge and love—are in reality closely correlated, and must be considered together.

As I should venture to put the relation between love and knowledge, love acts as the force which leads man on from knowledge to knowledge. A driving power is needed. Not merely the intellect, but also the will, has to come into play in the process of knowledge. As experience with college students for many years showed, and as I often impressed on class after class, the moral quality is at least as important

[1] His words are, " in this hymn love and knowledge have nothing to do with one another. Neither does love lead to knowledge, nor knowledge to love." There is a sense in which this is true; but it needs to be guarded against too wide application.

as the intellectual in the making of the true scholar. He must struggle from stage to stage : the old knowledge gives place to the new, which is in its turn taken up into a higher stage. The power to go on continually, to stop never, to rest never, comes from the moral quality of the man; this gives the impulse and maintains it. Similarly, in Section XXX. it is pointed out that "the maternal instinct" is the great force that moves through the nature of woman, and that through this force she shall gain salvation, "if she continue in faith and love and sanctification with sobriety".

According to the exposition of Dr. Harnack (p. 494), the perfect knowledge, the absolutely best, for which Paul's soul longs, has nothing to do with love, though love is the best thing in the world and the best in this temporal life. But if the perfect knowledge has nothing to do with love, why is so much stress laid on it in this "Hymn of Love," whose object is to emphasise the power and value of love? Dr. Harnack acknowledges that "it is a point of some importance that Paul is led to this knowledge when he is thinking of love ; and in another passage of the same letter (viii. 3) he goes yet a step further : 'If any man love God, he is known of Him'. Here, also, he does not indeed say 'he knoweth God,' but still it is the preparatory step to that combination."

According to our view, "to be known of God" is in Paul's thought a correlative expression to the other, "to know God". He that is known of God knows God: the two acts are different sides of one process: the Divine within man reaches forth to the Divine outside of man, striving to be united to it, in proportion as the Divine outside of and above man lays hold of him and takes possession. God knows man by taking man for His own. And so the Apostle says in the same passage, "I shall know even as I am known". Dr. Harnack himself interprets this to mean, "as God knows me, so I shall know Him (and His ways)"; and he goes on to say, "How much Paul lives in the problem that is presented by the relation of our knowledge of God to God's knowledge of us is shown by several places in his letters". In illustration he quotes Galatians iv. 8: "Now knowing God, or rather being known by Him". To know God is here practically synonymous with being known by Him.

Now compare this verse with 1 Corinthians viii. 1-2: "We know that we all have knowledge.[1] Knowledge puffeth up, but love edifieth. If any man thinketh that he knoweth anything, he knoweth not yet as he ought to know; but, if any man loveth God, the same is known of Him." The line of progress is here through love: as a man grows in love of God, he becomes better known of God. The natural inference towards which viii. 1-2a points is that this progress is towards increase in knowledge of God; but forthwith in viii. 2b Paul turns the statement to the other side, and says that the issue of this progress is that the man is known of God. Then we may compare this Corinthian statement with Galatians iv. 8 (as just quoted) and Ephesians iii. 17 f., " that ye, being rooted and grounded in love, may be strong to apprehend with all the saints what is the breadth and length and height 'and depth, and to know the love of Christ . . . that ye may be filled unto all the fulness of God". It has been doubted what it is that the Ephesians are to be strong to apprehend, whether "the mystery" (iii. 4) or the love of Christ (iii. 18). For our purpose this is immaterial. He who knows the love of God, or the love of Christ, knows God, for goodness is the essence of God and His love is the expression of

---

[1] Probably the words " we know that we all have knowledge " are a quotation from the letter sent to Paul by the Corinthian Church.

His goodness. The passage implies beyond all doubt that through increase in love comes increase in the knowledge of God. Therefore in the " Hymn of Love " which glorifies the power and Divine character of love, the stress in the latter part is laid on knowledge, because through growth in love comes growth also in knowledge, the best thing in the world. Such is the teaching of Paul : love is the quality through which man most nearly approaches the nature of God, and to grow in love is to grow towards God. " I shall see face to face" shows that the perception will be mutual, i.e. that to be known will imply to know.

XLII. Partial and Complete Knowledge

Now, as to perfect knowledge and partial knowledge, how are they related to one another in the mind of Paul? It is true that he expressed a very low opinion of partial knowledge: it has to be eliminated and done away with: it must be replaced by another quite different kind of knowledge. This partial knowledge feeds the vanity of man (1 Corinthians viii. 2): it tends to make him proud and conceited, and is therefore an extremely dangerous quality. There is nothing Paul dreads more in the nature of man than his tendency to think too much of himself and to put himself in the place of God instead of giving God the glory,[1] in other words, to make himself the centre of his universe instead of regarding God as at once the centre of his being and the goal of his development. The result of this is that he loses his perception of the nature of God and his love of God, whom he misrepresents more and more completely in his own imagination.[2]

[1] Romans i. 21 f.

[2] Modern experience confirms the judgment of Paul that great danger lies in over-estimation of oneself. It is well known that an exaggerated estimate of one's skill and power proves in many cases to be a sign of incipient insanity. In an asylum for lunatics there is no symptom so widespread as the preoccupation with oneself, one's powers, one's rights and one's wrongs. The patient lives in a world of his own, created by his individual fancy. In the thought and view of Paul, to mistake one's true relation to the world involves a misapprehension of the nature and the purpose of God. If the mistake and misapprehension goes too far in a certain direction, it takes a form which we now label by the title insanity. I knew of one case in which a lunatic believed himself to be God, and wrote out his edicts in that character and with that signature; and an experienced physician told me that this same delusion was far from being unparalleled in asylums.

In the Corinthian congregation Paul recognised that there existed a certain tendency towards self-complacency, and especially towards an over-estimation of their knowledge. This tendency to self-confidence is deep-seated in the Greek character: it has often led to bold action and success, but far more frequently it is the cause of failure. The Christians in Corinth were very conscious of, and confident in, their knowledge, whereas they had not as yet acquired any true and real knowledge. Paul has in his mind as one of the guiding purposes of the first Corinthian Epistle the desire to put clearly before his readers the difference between the lower and the higher knowledge, and to make them look on towards the higher and never rest content with the lower.

Yet even in the same Epistle where he warns his readers so often and so emphatically of the danger of partial knowledge it is characteristic of Paul that he pictures true and perfect knowledge in the most entrancing fashion. As Dr. Harnack says, "he contemplates it in trembling emotion and in ardent impulse" . . . as " the absolutely best ". He does not warn the Corinthians against knowledge, but only against a danger that is connected with knowledge. He lauds it as " the absolutely best," provided that the true knowledge, perfect and face to face with God, is understood as the object of his panegyric.

According to Dr. Harnack's interpretation, " this perfect knowledge is not to be expected till that which is perfect has come, that is when (through the second appearance of Christ) this temporal life suddenly comes to an end ". Hence he finds that Paul draws an absolute line of separation between the partial knowledge and the perfect knowledge. The " perfect will suddenly appear " through "a future event," *viz.*, " the second appearance of Christ ".[1] The present partial knowledge can never grow into the perfect: "no bridge leads from the partial to the whole ". The imperfect must be cast aside before the perfect knowledge can come.

This interpretation of Paul's doctrine is not in harmony with the view which we take of his attitude towards the problems of life. It regards Paul's doctrine as static and unphilosophic; whereas in our view the world is to Paul always changing, and the purpose of God rules the world towards development or growth. All that we have just quoted from Dr. Harnack is said quite truly; but it states only one side of the truth, and it requires to be completed. There are two sides to the phenomenon of growth; there is always a past and a future, but the present is only an abstraction; the present has no sooner been observed than it has disappeared and become a thing of the past, while a new stage, which was previously in the future, has taken its place, destined in its turn to pass away forthwith.

It is quite true that perfect knowledge is a thing of the future. But Paul can always say the same about all perfecting, all attaining, and all Salvation: they are in the future. Yet he can say equally emphatically (and even more frequently so far as Salvation is concerned) that they are in the present; they are here and now. The whole of life is a process of attaining, of reaching forward to that which is beyond, of constantly apprehending and then of finding that the Divine towards which one strives is still beyond, and that one must strive onwards towards it by a fresh effort. Paul fully recognises that on the one hand Christ is in him, and that his life has been merged in Christ and therefore has been perfected; but on the other hand he equally and even more emphatically recognises that his life

[1] *Expositor*, June, 1912, p. 493.

is a struggle against the evil which constantly besets him; " I myself with the mind serve the law of God, but with the flesh the law of sin "; and therefore he longs and prays to be " delivered out of the body of this death ".[1] He is made perfect, and he is not yet made perfect: he is saved, and yet he is only in process of being saved, and is working out his own salvation with the whole energy of mind and will and effort.

Perfect knowledge, then, is a thing of the future: it lies ever before us; but I cannot persuade myself that Dr. Harnack is wholly right in positing as the Pauline doctrine that this knowledge is irreconcilable with our progress in this life, and is attained only in the final cataclysm by a stroke from without at the second coming of Christ. Are we not (according to Paul) attaining towards it in this life? Is not the knowledge of God something towards which we are growing? Is it not implied in Salvation? Can man be saved except through knowing God? Is not the whole of life either on the one hand a process of losing right conception of God, and passing through stage after stage of idolatry and falsehood towards utter separation from Him and ignorance of Him, or on the other hand a process of learning to know God as He is? Paul prays " that the God of our Lord Jesus Christ, the Father of glory, may give unto you a spirit of wisdom and revelation in the knowledge of Him; having the eyes of your heart enlightened that ye may know " the hope, the will and the power of God.[2] In these words the Apostle evidently is picturing a process of gradual enlightenment, i.e. of partial knowledge growing towards perfect knowledge. This partial knowledge does not require to be cast aside before the perfect can come: it is antiquated and set aside through growing into the perfect.

---

[1] Rom. vii. 25, 24.   [2] Eph. i. 18 f.

Reversing the words of Dr. Harnack, we believe that "a bridge leads from the partial to the whole".

It is true that this quotation is from Ephesians, which some hesitate to accept as fully Pauline;[1] but to the judgment of the present writer it expresses plainly and characteristically the law of right life as a development towards wisdom through revelation, the end of the development being the perfect knowledge of God, attained finally only in the coming of Christ, but yet in process of being acquired in every step of right knowing. In 1 Corinthians ii. 9 f. the same truth is expressed emphatically, for it lies at the basis of Paul's thought: "Whatsoever things God prepared for them that love Him : unto us God revealed them through the Spirit: for the Spirit searcheth all things, yea, the deep things of God . . . we received, not the spirit of the world, but the spirit which is of God ; that we might know the things which are freely given us of God ". Paul here speaks in the first person ; but what he says is fully applicable to all the saints. The life of the saint is a gradual process of attaining, through the continuous steps of revelation, unto the knowledge of God and the deep things of God.

It is true that Paul might differ from some modern opinion, perhaps from modern views generally, as to what knowledge is worth attaining, and what knowledge leads on towards a right conception of God. The purely verbal and worthless speculation to which the age was given seemed to him, beyond doubt, to be empty, useless, false and bad, because it did not clarify men's minds about God. But was he wrong in that? He condemned, as one cannot doubt, all the science of the time ; but that pseudo-science was false in method and devoid of results. It only spread

---

[1] Dr. Harnack was doubtful when he wrote *Chronologie der altchr. Litt.*, i. p. 239. I think that he feels now less hesitation.

idle fancies through the "educated" world of that time: the more men learned about nature from the popular teaching of the time, the less they knew. No condemnation could be too strong for the current methods of substituting knowledge of words for the study of things. In this judgment Paul was not wrong.

It would, of course, be absurd to say that Paul would have distinguished between right and false scientific method in the study of nature, if the question had been put to him. He knew and condemned the false: he did not know or dream about the true. He would save his own people from empty and foolish speculation. It was not his province, nor did it lie within his power, to teach true method in science. He would turn men from idle talk to study the nature of God in the love of God: he knew nothing else worthy of attention in the world.

It would, however, be equally absurd to argue that, because Paul condemned all the scientific speculation of his time, and because he did not make any exception in favour of the right study of nature, about which he knew nothing, therefore he condemned all that he did not know. There can be little doubt that Paul accepted the principle that he who learns to know the works of God, is learning to know partially the nature of God;[1] but, for himself, he had never come into contact with any formal scientific study conceived in the spirit of truth; and probably he may have disbelieved in the possibility of right method in such study. We must not, however, transform a negative into a positive prohibition, when we try to state fairly and understand

[1] That is implied in repeated statements of his: God has in His works shown His nature and His goodness. Through them the pagan world had the opportunity of learning something about Him in the simple contemplation of His good gifts to men; and some pagans had made good use of this opportunity.

rightly the teaching of Paul. In our modern application of the teaching of Paul we have to ask whether or not any modern institution is in accordance with the essential spirit of his thought, and not whether he condemned a contemporary makeshift which was lacking in all the quality that makes the modern institution worth having.

Paul had a right conception of the growth of knowledge. He did not think that it consisted in adding part to part, and unit to unit. It was, in his view, not a process of simple addition, but a process of creation. The whole is more than the collocation of the parts : there is something vital and spiritual imparted to it beyond the sum of the parts, which makes it a new creature. At every step in the path of knowledge, one eliminates and does away the old, and remakes one's vision of the world : one learns and knows that the old vision was inadequate and therefore false : one sees facts in a new correlation : something of what had been dark in the world around becomes illuminated and clear. This is not a mere addition of a new part : it is the introduction of a transforming element. In Pauline language it comes, not in word, but in power ; and "out of three sounds he frames, not a fourth sound, but a star".

This principle Paul applied only to moral and religious growth in knowledge, for there was in the world of contemporary thought no other department in which it could be applied.[1] In the progress of thought the same principle is now employed far more widely than Paul dreamed of; but such wider application of Pauline principle is not un-Pauline ; it was simply outside of his range and his interest.

But an objection may be brought against the view which

[1] An exception should perhaps in some degree be made in regard to medicine, which, however, though growing, was largely empirical and not scientific in its method.

we have stated : is it not an essential condition of the perfect knowledge that it comes through revelation? Does
not this make an impassable division between the perfect
and the partial? The perfect knowledge is the intuition
of God: the partial knowledge is a study of details in
nature.

One may define revelation too narrowly. Revelation is
proportioned and suited to the character of different men.
God speaks in many voices. The act whereby the human
mind, after combining detail with detail, adds to the parts
that indescribable element which vitalises the whole into
a new creation and a new stage in knowledge, is essentially
creative and spiritual. Does it come wholly from within
the man? Is it not the result of the firm grasp of the Divine
unity and plan in the world, and therefore in a sense given
by a power without, which seizes and holds the mind of the
discoverer? It may be said that the process and growth of
the partial knowledge is essentially different from the gift
of the perfect knowledge, which is recognised intuitively
by the Divine spirit within the man. But does not the
Divine plan of the universe, as comprehended to some degree
in the process of partial knowledge, place some knowledge
of God within the mind? It is true that some have refused
to see this, and have denied the existence of God, while they
study nature. They deny they know not what.

It may be said, also, that the process of acquiring partial
knowledge is different, not in degree, but in kind from the
process of perfect knowledge. But one may well be doubtful about the distinction. We know too little to justify us
in distinguishing degree from kind in such process; and it
is always uncertain whether difference of degree may not
be intensified until it becomes difference in kind. This all
hangs on the meaning and nature of development.

One thing seems certain, that it was impossible at that time to apprehend the scientific spirit in knowledge. The world of the Mediterranean lands had entered on a period of deterioration in the realm of thought. The great age of Greek progress had passed away, and centuries had to elapse before a new time of progessive thought was to begin. In a time of such deterioration, the spirit of progress seemed to have almost wholly disappeared. This spirit is hostile to the selfishness and the arrogant conceit which Paul dreaded so much in the nature of men. In the ardour of discovery all thought of self perishes; and there remains only the eagerness of the search for the truth. The happiness of discovery contains an element of the Divine quality: in its highest manifestation it is unselfish and wholly directed to the unseen, the eternal, and the law of the universe: it does not conduce to self-glorification and self-congratulation, but rather to the recognition of the infinite external power that moves through the processes of nature: it strengthens the love of truth and the zeal for truth within its own range: it makes the discoverer of knowledge set truth above self: it raises man above the sordid glories of international strife and the vulgar struggles of political contention, and places him in the serener atmosphere of eternal truth and the laws of nature.

We cannot for a moment suppose that Paul was aware of this side of knowledge; but we do maintain that he stated principles which are applicable forthwith to this and every other new aspect of a life wider than that which he knew. The development of modern study has widened our knowledge of the works of God, and shown sides of the Divine action and purpose which formerly were not dreamed of. Yet the principles laid down by Paul, when rightly understood, remain as true about the new methods as they were about the old.

XLIII. The Rights of Man

The glorious and happy lot which in the purpose of God has been set before man as the end of his being has not been attained. Paul lays the whole blame upon man, who has deliberately gone wrong, preferred self to God, and as far as possible wrecked for himself and those who came under his influence the Divine plan and intention. Man could not wholly ruin the purpose and thwart the will of God; but he has often done what he could to attain this result; and even his endeavours to do right are usually mistaken and injurious.[1]

In one respect the Apostle runs contrary to the general course of European thought and feeling and history. The development of European history is almost always explained by philosophic historians as the result of a struggle for rights or of a passionate revolt on the part of the oppressed against injustice and wrongs. Paul would reply that man has no rights except the right of helping to realise the purpose of God: he would assert that no one can honestly dare to ask for justice, because man has deserved even less than he has got, and that men are deceiving themselves when they speak about their wrongs. He would maintain with Dante in his treatise *De Monarchia* that justice should not be regarded as the getting of one's rights from others, but as the giving of their rights to others. He would probably not regard the revolt against Charles I. or any other

[1] As Juvenal says, often the gods have ruined households by granting the masters' prayers.

of the violent actions through which the "freedom" of modern Britain has been attained, as specially honourable episodes in the history of the country, or as even consistent with true Christianity; and he would doubtless declare that the price for all this error had to be paid by the children and children's children of the original actors in those great scenes, since they were responsible for beginning, or for fomenting, a spirit of violence and wrong, and turning the people to a mischievous method.

The kind of resistance to oppression which was commended both by Paul and by John was endurance; and the victory over tyranny and compulsion was gained through death. But in Paul there appears little or no sympathy with the tendency to resist the minor injustices and inequalities of an unfair social organisation, and to devote to the task of protesting and to the meaner business of political conflict the time and energy which ought to be spent in seeking the true object of life.

Even in the case of slavery the Apostle has been sharply criticised by many for acquiescing in it as a social institution. That he did think the slave wrong who ran away from his master, that he did think the right conduct for a slave was to perform as well as possible the work that was imposed on him by the custom of society and of the law, that he directed the runaway slave to return to a Christian master—all that is quite true. Whether he would have directed the Christian slave to return to a master who had announced that he would not permit his slaves to practise the duties of the Christian religion is perhaps doubtful; but it seems to be in keeping with his doctrine that he would have bidden the runaway slave go back and endure bonds (1 Cor. vii. 21). Whether he would have directed the slave to return to a master that constrained his slaves to minister to vice and to give up their children to vice—all which was sanctioned by common custom and by law—remains more doubtful. The evidence does not prove it; the case did not present itself; nor do we know anything that can fairly be construed as evidence of Paul's judgment in regard to such a case. We do know that, if a master had ordered his slave to offer sacrifice to the gods and to curse Christ, Paul would not have permitted the slave to obey the command. There was a point at which, in Paul's judgment, the right of the master to command was forfeited and the duty of the slave to obey ceased.

The attitude of Paul towards slavery is a difficult subject for us in modern times; and yet the principle on which it rests is simple and clear. His expressed opinions seem ,almost to mediate between two different tendencies, or to be a mean between two extremes. On the one hand, there shall be in the perfect Church no distinction of slave and free; all are free, all are on an equal footing in the religion of Christ. " There can be no distinction of nationality nor of sex : there can be neither bond nor free; for ye are all one in Christ Jesus." [1] On the other hand, the established social system must not be hastily altered. After all, such a matter as employment of slaves in the household and even (what in practice was much worse) in labour on great estates belonged to an evanescent stage, and must pass away, like the Empire itself, when the time was fulfilled.

The slave according to Paul can live a life as truly Christian as the freeman; he can attain the one great aim of man; and it is infinitely more important for him to live his own life well than to seek for emancipation in the present world. Paul's whole teaching on the subject is an expansion of the Saviour's principle: " Seek first the Kingdom of God and

[1] Gal. iii. 28; Col. iii. 11.

His righteousness, and all these things shall be added unto you " (Matt. vi. 33).

The development of the Church, the conquest of the world for Christ : that was the present and instant duty. For that every Christian must work : having wrought out his own salvation, he must work out the salvation of others. To seek to revolutionise the existing system of Roman society could not conduce to that end, but might on the contrary seriously imperil it, and indefinitely postpone it.

Moreover, for a slave to make emancipation and freedom his first aim was a false system of action. To seek to get one's rights is not so important as to learn and to perform one's duties : the former is a narrower and a more selfish aim : the latter is as wide as the universe. The world in which the Christian has to live is bad : his life must always be encompassed with evils : it is of little importance merely to diminish those evils by one. Let him seek the Kingdom of God, and the evils will be eliminated as that Kingdom is realised on earth. He that loses his life shall gain it : he that sacrifices his freedom for the moment shall gain it in the long run.

Hence the tone of Paul's counsel both in the earlier letters and to Timothy. Not a word is said about the wrongs of slavery, or the right of man to be free. The omission is undoubtedly disappointing at first sight to our modern taste ; and the advice given is apt to appear rather temporising, as if Paul were making terms with evil. Yet, when one takes a dispassionate view of the whole situation, one recognises that the spread of Christianity produced gradually a higher atmosphere of thought, in which slavery cannot live. The more fully Christianity is realised in any society, the more thoroughly will slavery be destroyed. It is not yet destroyed anywhere in all its forms ; but its worst forms have been eradicated in most Christian lands, and lessened over the whole world. The duty of seeking to establish equality of opportunities and rights is more generally recognised and admitted than it was in former ages. " 'Tis something : nay, 'tis much." Above all, it is now fully recognised that the Church should be the champion of freedom ; and it is expected that teachers in the Church should preach freedom and discountenance slavery in every form. The plane on which human society moves and thinks is now higher and nobler.

One difficulty lies in this. Paul emphatically advises Timothy [1] to teach that in ordinary life the Christian slave of a pagan master should honour, obey and respect his master. Apart from the infinitely higher and more compelling reasons which have just been stated,[2] it would bring discredit on the Church, and cause ill-feeling against the Church in the society of the Roman Empire, if Christian slaves were found to be discontented or disobedient. The slave must cheerfully sacrifice his freedom, reconcile himself to his lot, and do the work that is ordered ; the Name and the Teaching will thus be saved from discredit and vilification.

The next part of the advice causes even more difficulty to our modern view. Timothy is not directed to preach that a Christian master should wholly discountenance slavery in his own household, or even that he should set free a slave who is a Christian. One may at first be disposed to think that Mohammed's teaching was better, because Mohammed laid down the principle that a slave who embraces Islam gains his freedom from a Moslem

[1] 1 Timothy iii.

[2] In writing to Timothy Paul has in view the practical possibilities of Timothy's situation as a working minister and teacher amid a pagan society and Empire.

master.   But Paul only advises that the Christian slave of
a Christian master should serve all the more gladly, because
he is doing service and giving help to a Christian ; and
strongly discourages the slave from showing any insolence,
or presuming on the fact that master and slave meet together in the same assembly for common worship.   It is
an opinion too widely spread to be altogether without
justification, that mission training of converts in modern
times has often tended to produce this temper in subject
classes (objectionable in the higher point of view as the
very idea of subject classes is) ; and the impression has
been prejudicial to missions as showing bad method.

We must, however, bear in mind that, practically, Mohammed gave to the slavery of non-Moslems a religious
sanction by enacting that slaves were only set free if they
adopted the religion of Islam.   Mohammedanism has been
a power that strengthened the hold of slavery on society
by formally limiting the right of freedom.   The Christian
teaching always emphasises the duties, and discourages the
seeking after rights.   Cheerful service, renunciation, self-
sacrifice, form the lesson that it drives home into the minds
of men.   All else is secondary.   That is primary, for it
realises the kingdom of God.   The Christian must trust to
the future.

There is, of course, no question as to any discrepancy between the teaching of the earlier and the later Epistles about
slavery.   The passages quoted from Colossians and Galatians express the consummation of the perfect Church.
But in Ephesians vi. 5-9 the same practical advice as in 1
Timothy is given in even more emphatic terms.   Again, in
Philemon Paul sends a fugitive slave home to his master
with an apology for his misconduct.   He does indeed hint
very delicately that the slave might gracefully be set free,

but he does not suggest that freedom is his right, or that Philemon should set Onesimus free as a matter of duty. Rather, he puts as a personal favour to himself his hope that Philemon will receive the runaway kindly. The "rights of man" are not a Pauline idea; he urges only the duties of man.

One thing we can say with confidence as we look back over nearly nineteen centuries of history. Let us suppose that Christian teaching had made it a prime object to redress, either by active refusal or by passive resistance, the superficial evils and even the graver social injustices of Roman law and rule: let us suppose that it had made the Kingdom of God its secondary and merely ultimate aim, and had begun by insisting on the right of every man to be free, as if this were the primary condition for establishing the Kingdom of God: what would have been the result? Assuredly the issue would have been that Christianity would long ago have passed away or sunk to the level of the dead religions that still cumber the world, while slavery would remain the universal rule. It was by disregarding all merely superficial and less important facts in society and by concentrating the efforts of all on the great and real things of life, that the Christian faith succeeded in keeping its place above the level of common life, as a power and an inextinguishable torch to quicken the minds and fire the best emotions of men.

Paul did not approve of the Roman social system and government (p. 59). It was evil, and it must pass away. But it had its purpose in the Divine plan. It was granted a time in which to work. The Christians must temporarily accept it and acquiesce in it, and must obey its laws in so far as these did not order them to curse God or actively to do evil to man. Passively they might have to look on, while the law ordered evil: in the lapse of time, with the elevation of public opinion, the law would be raised to the higher standard. The raising of public opinion is an object to work for; that is the Kingdom of God; but public opinion can only be degraded and deteriorated, as a rule, by war. There are some cases, which Paul had no occasion to treat, in which national existence and ideas may call for defence by war; but these are rare and exceptional.

Not merely was such an aim as the abolition of slavery in the Empire impossible of realisation at the time; not merely would the striving after it have sacrificed purposes that were even more noble and more immediately pressing: it could not have been brought about without fighting; and the Christian teaching is against the pursuit of any object which is attainable only through war, especially civil war.

The European idea, that the man who rebels against what he considers to be the unfairness of established society ought to be praised and admired as a hero, has not yet justified itself by its results. That the world is better than it was, and that progress has been achieved, is true; but no proof has yet been furnished that the tendency to rebellion against injustice in the existing social and political system (wrong and unfair as it always is), and the habit of claiming so-called rights by violent means, have played a beneficial part in forwarding this progress; and the teaching of Paul even in this respect has not been disproved.

On the contrary, it might reasonably be argued that the lesson of history has demonstrated the mischief and false-ness of violent methods. Europe is now engaged in an orgy of insane preparation for war; it is (as might almost be said) parcelled out into a series of great standing armies and permanent camps with entire populations as soldiers in one army or another: the countries are wasting their substance and their opportunities in making engines to kill one another; and there is no end to war and to civil strife. This situation is the logical issue and the *reductio ad absurdum* of the principle that one is justified in seeking to attain by violence the ends which one believes to be right. That is the principle of the Mohammedan "Holy War": it is diametrically opposed to the teaching of Paul and of Jesus. Europe has gone on a false course when it has carried out so completely the method of violence, and is now finding itself in a *cul de sac:* he who admits the method for himself, cannot condemn it when others practise it. There is no way out, except to retrace the path backwards, and find a new course in the teaching of Christianity.

Paul taught in great principles, and does not descend to legislation about details. Even the veiling of women he attempts to enforce on grounds as wide as the universe and as high as the angels; but in this perhaps for once he may have condescended to legislation about a detail.[1]

His guiding principle, however, always is that man must seek first the Kingdom of God and His righteousness; and all the details will gradually be moulded into conformity with that Kingdom. What we call the growth of true education and the raising of public opinion and social judgment to a higher level are simply the slow, gradual approach of the Kingdom of Heaven, which, as it approaches, re-makes human life. But the attempt to re-make human life except through the Kingdom of God must fail. The violence, the vulgarity and the pretentiousness of much that has masqueraded under the show of resistance to wrongs and demand for justice did not raise the social standard, or promote the Kingdom of Heaven; and it is a false judgment that sees in things like this the cause of human improvement.

[1] See Section XXXVI.

The true cause lay deeper, and was sometimes concealed and impeded by the noise and the ostentation of those who stood prominent in the public eye.

Man has the right to save his own soul; and in saving himself he will save society. The rest will be added, if he seeks after this until he has attained it.

XLIV. Did Paul Teach a Selfish End?

The individual shall seek salvation and the Kingdom of God. Against this teaching the charge has been made that it is selfish. We hear this accusation repeated in various forms, and we read denunciations of the narrow and unsympathetic and egoistic teaching that one should seek to save one's own soul. "Am I simply to mind my own wretched little soul?" So I have heard some ardent spirit declare with strong emphasis; "Am I to give only the dregs and the poor remainder of my work and my thought to others, to the world, to the progress of the world, to the improvement of society, to the poor and neglected? I would rather let my own soul perish, while I do something to help others, than save my own soul, while I let others perish."

In this complaint and accusation there is much that savours of the true Christ-nature, along with utter ignorance. Morally and emotionally the feeling it expresses is noble and devoted, and such as Paul would approve and Jesus would accept. Intellectually, however, it shows a singular misunderstanding of the nature of salvation, and of the Gospel of Christ. As has been said in Section III., Christianity makes a high demand on the intellect; and the persons who bring this charge against the teaching of Paul are not showing themselves equal to the demand made on them, and are allowing emotion to speak where some exertion of the intellect is required. The work whereby man saves his own soul lies in perfect unselfishness and in giving all, even life itself, for others.   It is the most perfect expression in conduct of pure love for God and mankind.

It will aid our judgment on this subject, if we can trace in modern literature any expression of a principle that presents some analogy to the Pauline doctrine.   No mere exposition of Paulinism, no conscious and intentional interpretation of the Christian principle to the modern world, will serve our purpose at this moment.   We look for the message of some great modern writer, who has no thought about Paulinism, who is unconscious that the teaching which he enunciates has any resemblance, or owes anything, to the teaching of Paul.   We look for some teacher and thinker, who has his own message springing fresh from his own nature, who spoke to his own time in the words which the time and the situation demand.   For this purpose we take Thomas Carlyle and quote his message in his own words.   Whether or not he could ever have found his message except through the moulding influence of generations that had studied the Gospels and Paul, is not the question.   It is enough that Carlyle spoke his own message in his own way to his own contemporaries, and that he had no intention of expressing the teaching either of Jesus or of Paul.   Perhaps he thought it was a non-Christian message that he had to deliver ; and certainly from one point of view it is non-Christian, below the standard of the Christian teaching and spirit.

He says in his *Signs of the Times :* "to reform a world, to reform a nation, no wise man will undertake ; and all but foolish men know, that the only solid, though a far slower reformation, is what each begins and perfects on himself ".

This is a message rather of despair than of hope.   It is narrower, emptier, and more barren than the message of

Paul; yet it is all that the intellect of a great man could gather from the experience of his own life and the inherited experience of ancestry and nationality. It is exposed, not wholly unjustly, perhaps, to the charge of selfishness. It is exposed, far more justly, to the charge of barrenness. The charge applies to the form of the message : only the fool will try any wider scheme of reformation that reaches beyond himself. Yet every such wider reformation is unsolid, empty, and resultless in the long run ; for the apparent results may be quickly and easily reached, but do no good, and only cheat the reformer and his dupes. He can modify a law, or place on the statute-book, amid the applause of a nation, a new law that promises much ; but the result is naught, if the individual is not reformed, and the nation is not remade. The " reform " turns out to be dust and ashes, mere Dead Sea fruit, unless the individuals composing the nation are recreated and set on a higher platform of thought and character and emotion and morality. The individual, therefore, must seek to reform himself; and this is a far slower and more difficult process than to pass a law.

It were well to reform a world or a nation, and he who succeeds in this will deserve salvation, as Carlyle would have admitted. But can he succeed? It is so impossible to succeed in this way, so futile to attempt it, that only the fool will try. The method is false, topsy-turvy, absurd, foredoomed to failure. You must reform the individual, and you must begin with yourself. There is no other way. The ambitious reformer, who is going to start the nation or the world on a new course and a happier era, can only fail. Such is the message of Carlyle. Paul is in full agreement to a certain point :[1] the reformer who starts off with his great and noble and generous schemes must end in disaster.

[1] Sections XXXII., XXXIII., XXXV.

And yet—and yet—surely it is good to reform the world, and to reform the nation. Such a noble desire must be right. It is good even to wish to reform them, and to try to reform them, although one may fail or die in the attempt. Such was the platform on which Paul stood in the opening years of his public career, as a Pharisee. He aimed at the good: and he tells the result. "The law is holy, and the commandment holy, and righteous, and good. Did then that which is good become death (i.e. sin) unto me? God forbid. . . . For that which I do I know not; for not what I would, that do I practise; but what I hate that I do. . . . For I know that in me . . . dwelleth no good thing; for to will is present with me, but to do that which is good is not. For the good which I would I do not; but the evil which I would not, that I practise. . . . But if what I would not, that I do, it is no more I that do it, but sin which dwelleth in me. I find then the law, that, to me who would do good, evil is present. For I delight in the law of God after the inward man: but I see a different law in my physical frame warring against the law of my mind and bringing me into captivity under the law of sin." [1]

Paul knew in his own case how all the great resolutions of his youth—to live the divine life and to work for the coming of the Messiah, who should realise the Promise and make the God of Israel supreme in the respect and belief of the nations—had resulted only in ruin; and how he had found himself fighting with all his might against the Messiah. In his own intentions, through his own great schemes, man cannot be saved. Another power is necessary, and another way must be followed. Section XXXII.

Carlyle, from another side, has come to the same con-

[1] Romans vii. 12 ff.

clusion ; mere desire to work for the good of the world is
resultless and empty. But he could go no farther. He had
nothing positive to offer. The wise man, he says, will seek
to reform himself: that is the only real reformation. But
how? What wisdom will furnish the effective power to
move the " wise man " in the path of self-reformation? He
must not seek to work for others, and, if he works on himself, he works in a vacuum. A gospel of negation and
narrowest limitation! It is useless to aim at anything outside of self!

This theory of Carlyle is put into action in the life that
Dickens portrays. Dickens probably was not conscious
of the theory and the philosophy that underlay his picture
of human life; but he painted what he could see. The
philanthropist, the man that seeks to achieve anything for
the world's good, the man who seeks to benefit others, is
in Dickens's novels always an impostor and a fraud. For
the phrase of Carlyle, " no wise man," he substitutes " no
honest man ". The knavish man who cheats others, and
the thoughtless empty woman who cheats herself with
cheap philanthropy and thinks that she is deluding others
into a belief in her goodness,—these are the people that
seek in the pages of Dickens to reform the world. They
begin with imposture and end in exposure, as a rule; but
yet they have their dupes and achieve some sham success.

Both Carlyle and Dickens express the same lesson that
Paul taught, so far as it was a negation. That way is
hopeless: it leads only to delusion, to cheating and to ruin.
Paul saw that negative lesson written in every page of
history and on every human effort, but he was not content
with a negative. He had his fundamental axiom to guide
him. " God is good, and His Promise must be fulfilled."
Paul saw the purpose of God in the plan of the world.

There is a cure. There is a way for man to follow. That way is the way of Faith. In Faith we have the force that lifts man above himself and enables him in saving himself to work for others, and in reforming others to save himself.

If the perfecting of the individual nature by the growth of boundless love for others, by living and working for others, by the most absolute passion to attain unto God through the sacrifice of self,—if this is a selfish end, then and only then can the way of salvation that Paul taught be called selfish.

XLV. The Family in the Teaching of Paul

Paul's conception of social life and the importance of the family in the Church has been often judged too exclusively from what he says in his first letter to the Corinthians, and especially from chapter vii. of that letter. From this letter, taken by itself, we should readily gather too narrow a view. At the moment when he was writing chapter vii., Paul was championing the freedom of the individual man or woman; and the same tone runs through the next chapter.[1] The individual must be free to work out his own salvation in his own life. He must not be in bondage to others, not even to a wife or a husband. " Ye were called for freedom . . . for freedom did Christ set you free . . . where the Spirit is, there is freedom." [2] Yet the individual does not stand alone. He was called for social life. He was called for family life. He must sacrifice even his freedom for others, and in the sacrifice find the higher freedom. There is this double call on the individual. The two calls may conflict, or seem to conflict, in human life. How shall they be reconciled?

We must not draw our conclusion from the narrower field of the first Corinthian letter alone, and especially not from one single chapter of that letter. Such a line of reasoning would, as I think, be wrong, for it ignores the peculiar character and purpose of the letter; yet, undoubtedly, it

---

[1] This tone was suggested by the letter of the Corinthians, and intended to correct them.

[2] Galatians v. 1-13; 2 Corinthians iii. 17.

would be easy and natural to infer, by arguing from that letter alone, that in Paul's estimation marriage is the poorer fashion of life and merely the second best, on which a man or a woman falls back because he or she is too weak to be capable of the true life of man, the life wholly devoted to God. The duty of a man or a woman in marriage conflicts with the full and complete devotion to the things of God. He who will devote himself wholly to the latter must not give himself to the former. That seems to be the view stated in chapter vii. ; but chapter vii. must not be taken by itself alone.

If we now turn to the Ephesian letter we see that in v. 22-33 Paul compares the relation of husband and wife to the union of soul and body, and to the union between Christ and the Church, the most intimate and perfect relationships that can be conceived by the human mind. Such comparisons imply that, in Paul's judgment, marriage is in the highest sense the divine life and the perfect harmony of human nature. Christ's existence in the world is consummated through the Church. The Church is the body to which Christ is the soul. Soul does not attain its full existence without body. Each is the necessary complement of the other. The Church is the inheritance of Christ and the completion of the purpose of God. So also marriage is the perfection of the life of mankind. The one member of the pair, is not complete alone. The two form a unit. Marriage is part of the purpose of God. Such is the teaching of the Ephesian letter.

It follows from this that the true unit in the constitution of the congregation is the married pair, and not the individual. The Church is made up of families, and the family forms the basis for the organisation of the Church. " This mystery is great," as Paul says to the Ephesians, for the individual has his own rights and must save his own soul. In the unified pair the two are one ; but yet each member of the pair is a complete unit, the evolution of the Divine purpose and the expression of the Divine power. Each is complete in himself or in herself ; and yet each finds completion in the other. The congregation is based on individual members ; and yet the congregation is based on families.

Here we have another of those apparent contradictions in the expression of Paulinism, which present only an apparent inconsistency. Both facts are true. They are reconciled in the higher truth of growth, evolution, continuity. On the double truth we must build up our conception of human nature and its relation to God.

Paul, in his first Corinthian letter, shows himself quite aware of this double truth. We must not read chapter vii. alone ; or, if we do so, we must bear in mind the breadth of Paul's outlook, and add his own personality as we read. He expresses the other side in xi. 11 : "nevertheless, neither is the woman without the man, nor the man without the woman, *in the Lord*" : the evolution of the Divine purpose requires both, and requires them in the higher unity. The Church is constituted of families, and not of individuals in isolation.

Paul is never unconscious of what we may call the " pastoral" idea. He gives fullest expression to this in his letters to Timothy and Titus ; but it appears elsewhere. A good deal of both Thessalonians and First Corinthians is "pastoral," and the same element is always latent even in his most exalted and mystic moods.[1] He must work

---

[1] The failure to see this is the cause of much error about Paul, and especially of the opinion that the Pastoral Epistles are not his work. Those Epistles, on the contrary, are necessary to the complete understanding of Paul.

with men and women as they are; and he must lead them towards the future ideal. The concrete and perfect truth is made up of the past, the present, and the future, and of the law that runs through the process from the past to the future. He must keep the ideal clear in their minds and before their eyes; and yet they are after all weak, erring, timorous, sinful creatures, who cannot do what they would, and who sometimes would not what they can. The ideal cannot be attained by them, and yet it must be attained; and it is attained in so far as they move towards and desire it and believe in it. Their belief is counted to them for righteousness. They are saved by their faith.

There is equality in the perfect Church of the ideal. There is equality in the Church of the present, and yet there is inequality. Every Christian, male and female, is and must be a teacher: it is part of their duty, and a necessity of their profession. Yet a woman shall not teach in the congregation, says this same Paul. Every one must teach in the way that is practically most useful: there are diversities of endowment, and some are set apart by their heredity and their opportunities for one path of teaching, some for another. A teacher must have pupils; and in the existing state of Roman and Greek and Jewish society, people were not ready to accept women in the office of public teaching; nor had women in that society the education that was needed for such teaching.

Unanimity of will, and not domination of one, is the ideal of marriage. Both should will the right, and thus attain unanimity. But that is the ideal, towards which we strive, yet which man cannot attain. When there is difference of will, Paul seems to say, the husband's will must overcome; and the wife should obey. That was inevitable in the constitution of society at that time. There is, however, a higher law, that the right should be done, and that both should unite in this. That is a far harder law. Can it be attained? Can it be followed? Is it not too hard for human nature? Should we not acquiesce in a lower, but more easily realised aim?

The Christian law aims at the highest and the perfect, and will be satisfied with nothing less. Just because it is most difficult, and remains above human nature, this unanimity of will in the right is the only Christian law. It demands much: it exacts too much from mere human beings. Yet it is the ideal which draws us on towards it through error and failure, and which will conquer us and rule us in the end, if we believe in it. See p. 18 f.

The hardest experience in life is when diverging conceptions of duty, or difference in judgment about what is right, cause separation between friends and allies, as for example between Paul and Barnabas at the beginning of the second missionary journey. Each did what he believed to be right; and, after years of united work and achievement, they parted, and never met again. Each thought that the Spirit was with him, and each went on his own course. Luke, who tells the story, simply states the facts, and expresses no judgment which of the two was right; but the Spirit decided in future history. Barnabas drifted into a backwater. Paul was in the central current of affairs, by which the world was moved.

As we look back now over past history, we see which was moving with the Spirit; but how should the friends and companions of the two decide at the time? At the moment it was not necessary for every one to decide, perhaps not for any one. Paul lays down about a year or two later a rule that might apply.[1] Respect every ex-

---

[1] 1 Thessalonians v. 21 f.

pression by any individual of the will of God, as the individual sees it, or thinks he sees it, in the Spirit. Encourage these expressions; yet test them. They are not always right. They are sometimes discordant. Brethren in the Spirit forbade Paul to go to Jerusalem; but he knew that it was right to go, and the Spirit decided so in the evolution of history. The criterion is to hold fast the standard of moral excellence: nothing that conflicts with the fundamental principles of moral rectitude can come from the Spirit: you must not do evil that good may result from it, even although some individual, speaking apparently in the Spirit, bids you do so.

Paul had to face this great trial; and there are occasions when any one may have to do the same.

XLVI. Conclusion

Starting from the human side, the highest generalisation which science can reach, working by the method of partial knowledge,[1] and rising step by step, is that there is an order in nature, i.e. that the Universe is a rational system, that true scientific knowledge is the comprehension of this system, and that the aim of life is to come into harmony with the order of nature. There is nothing in this which Paul, as we think, would not fully and gladly accept, so far as it goes; but he requires you to go much farther.[2] He insists on the personality of the power that makes, and expresses itself through, this order.[3] To apprehend the personality which thus declares itself is beyond the range of scientific, i.e. (in Pauline phrase[4]) partial or piecemeal knowledge. It belongs to what we may call in modern phrase direct intuition; we must see for ourselves and grasp through the power of Faith the ultimate truth that "God is—the real and personal God".

There is, according to Paul, no inherent and final contrariety between this impersonal generalisation of science, and the personal axiom of direct and complete knowledge from which he starts, that "God is".[5] The former is imperfect and incomplete, but it can naturally and simply be exalted into perfect and complete knowledge by coalescing with the direct perception of God, which is the heritage of man. God has not left Himself without witness, "in that

[1] See Section XLII.　　[2] See Section XIX.
[3] Acts xiv. 15 f., xvii. 24 f.　[4] 1 Corinthians xiii. 12.　[5] See Section XIX.

269

he did good to [man]"[1] and gave order to society and nature.[2]

If we attempt to put this in modern terms, scientific knowledge is abstract; it is not real and concrete. It deals with artificial and arbitrary products, as, for example, to take a simple case, a mathematical investigation into some problem of the external world isolates certain of the conditions and studies the effects of these, without attempting to cope with the infinite complexity of the problem in nature. Hence the so-called "laws of nature" always break down in the progress of discovery; because in that progress we rise to the power of embracing in our calculations a larger, and ever larger number of the conditions in nature, and thus we gradually approximate towards the complexity of the world around us. These "laws" then are merely steps in the process of knowledge: they are not truth, but stages in the progress towards truth. The statements of scientific laws which were customary in the schools forty-five years ago, when the present writer was beginning to study at college, are long ago almost completely antiquated, i.e., they are now stated in a way so different and with such different implication that the old may be said to be abrogated by the new. The new seems almost to be different in kind from the old; but it is not really different; it is reached by continuous growth and by uniform application of the same method of "piecemeal knowledge".

It does not reach truth; and yet it is true, because it is a process towards truth. You have always the same apparent contradiction in every "Paulinistic" expression of thought. Try to think like Paul, and you always find yourself involved in the same double and contradictory pair of statements: "it is" and "it is not": "I have attained" and "I have

[1] Acts xiv. 17.   [2] Acts xvii. 25 f.

not attained ": "You are justified" and yet "work out your own salvation with fear and trembling ".[1]

The solution of the apparent contradiction, as we have already seen, lies in the idea of growth and evolution. A thing is what it is in process of growing to be : it has attained what it must attain to. The apparent contradiction actually disappears when the word "yet" is introduced into the negative proposition, "I have attained" is not really contradicted, but only completed, by saying "I have not yet attained," [2] which implies "I am in process of attaining, but have not yet completed the process ".

The law of process states the truth. In the development of the scientific statement of "laws of nature," there is a movement towards spirit and away from matter. Science now is expressed in a far less material form, and in a form that is, so to say, more "ethereal" and in the line of progress towards the spiritual. It has not reached the spiritual in the perfect sense, but it is approximating towards it. It recognises far more emphatically and explicitly that "matter" is only the expression of our ignorance, that science is the process of analysing and resolving matter, and therefore that we cannot reach truth until we reach spirit. The ultimate spiritual expression is personal, and God does not lie, or does not yet lie, within the domain of scientific statement. Yet the explicit recognition that scientific statement, being abstract, does not give us the concrete world of reality, is not so very far removed from the spiritual expression. The chasm that divides them is narrow ; it can be bridged over ; and the bridge is formed by the natural power which is inherent in every man of recognising the fundamental

---

[1] See Sections XIV., XVI., XLVI.

[2] This has led to the insertion of the word "yet" in Phil. iii. (as is pointed out in Section XVI., p. 99).

truth of the spirit, the truth that God is, that in God is the only reality, that anything else which seems to exist is mere illusion, mere pretence, or mere ignorance.

Moreover, at every step in the growth of this partial knowledge there must occur, as has been already stated,[1] something akin to and not easily to be distinguished from the intuitive perception of the ultimate spiritual truth. Each step is consummated in a flash of revelation; there is added to the process of study and combination "that indescribable element which vitalises the whole into a new creation". This creation is the operation of the Divine element in man grasping the Divine unity and plan that rules in the world.[2]

Now we see more clearly than before the nature of progress, which is the intention of God, and the law of nature, but which has in fact not been so common or so wide-spread in the world as degeneration and degradation.[3] Progress is normal, and yet it has been rare and unusual. There is a condition of progress, both for the individual and for the nation : the condition is that it listens to the Divine voice.

Moral progress of the race is in a certain way analogous to the progress in knowledge which marks the career of the investigator in science. Each takes places, not in a continuous insensible progress, but in a series of steps separated by intervals almost of stagnation, which on the religious side especially tend easily and commonly to pass into degeneration. These steps depend mainly or almost entirely on the outstanding individuals who have a larger spark of the creative force in the sense in which it has just been defined. Every science grows infinitely more through the creative impulse communicated by the genius of individuals than through the slow accretion of details made by the labour of the many. Yet even in these small additions,

---

[1] Section XLII.   [2] *Ibid.*   [3] *Ibid,*

where there is any real growth, there is necessarily involved a spark of the creative fire and the sympathy with the ordered universe of nature.

The moral progress of the race depends largely on a series of revelations to individuals, to whom has been granted the power of sympathetic insight into the will and nature and purpose of God. According as the race is influenced in a series of steps by such powerful individuals, is its moral progress. There is usually traceable an individual force behind every moral or religious movement, a rousing of the many through the one man. This is especially clear in the history of the Hebrew race. The Promise was fulfilled in the succession of the great prophets and seers, whose progressive revelation of truth was not merely the blessing of their own people, but the inheritance of the whole world : " In thy seed shall all nations of the earth be blessed ".

This is progress, and every step in it involves the hearing of the voice of nature, i.e. of God.

All really creative progress in knowledge, then, has in it that element of absolute certainty which is, and marks, the Divine. " I have seen and I know." As Paul or the Apostles thought in their department, so thinks the true scientific discoverer in his. *He knows.* Nothing can take this from him except a higher step in knowledge. It is his absolute possession. He cannot doubt or hesitate about it.

The fundamental and ultimate truth then, the first and the last, is that this process of growth is the real expression of the Divine life and the Divine power, both within man and outside of man ; and man is, or is intended to be, moving towards God, moving from the situation of being separated from God towards the union, i.e. the re-union, with God. If there is to be motion, there must be a force to produce the motion. What, then, is the force that drives man along the way towards God, a difficult way, requiring (as Paul repeatedly declares) the utmost exertion of the whole nature of the individual?

This force Paul calls Faith. We end, as we began, in Section IX., with this force and prime motive power, Faith. This is the one thing needed, without which there can come about nothing else in man : it is the compelling force of life : without Faith there can be no life and no movement towards truth and God. It is " an intense and burning enthusiasm, inspired through overpowering belief in, and realisation of, the nature of Jesus—an enthusiasm which drives on the man in whose soul it reigns to live the life of Jesus ". It exists potentially in all men. It is the Divine element in man, recognising, longing for, and striving to attain to, the Divine nature around man.

PART III. SUBSIDIARY QUESTIONS

XLVII. Paul's Address to the Court of Areopagus at Athens

This speech requires, and will reward, a more minute examination of certain details than was suitable to the plan of Part II. (see Section XIX.). I assume from *St. Paul the Traveller* that Paul was addressing the high Court called Areopagus.

The method of the speech was too remote from the ordinary man's way of thinking, too generalised and abstract. It could not conquer the world. The common man is not convinced by a statement of general principles ; he must be won by the concrete picture of living reality. And so Paul says that, from the very beginning of his missionary career, he " placarded Jesus Christ before the eyes " of the Galatians.[1] He did not require to go to Athens to discover that the abstract method was ineffective. He knew this from the first, and he used the other method from the beginning right on to the end in his work. But where the audience was suited to be approached first of all by the other method, he used that other way.

Moreover, that other way gave him a beginning. He took the pagan idea of a God, where his audience was simple, or of Divine power and Divine nature, where his audience was more educated ; and this he proceeded to raise to a higher level and to fill with a richer meaning. We do not know how he addressed the proconsul Sergius

[1] Galatians iii. 1.   This refers to public and open advertisement intended to be clear to all.

Paullus at Paphos; but I imagine that it was in a style similar to his Athenian address. This was the style suited to the hearer. Even with the pagan rustics of Lystra in the province Galatia he found a starting-point in their simple conception of a God who gives good things. He did not begin by criticising their conception of God, and telling them that it was wrong and poor and barren. He took what was right in it—that God did good to them: later he would go on to " placard Jesus Christ before their eyes ".

What he did certainly find in Athens was that highly educated and philosophic hearers were more difficult to affect than a less sophisticated audience. A group of professors in a University, philosophic lecturers used to give displays of their own powers in moral discourse, was the hardest of all audiences to touch and to move. That is always the case. It lies in human nature.

Professor Rendel Harris has greatly advanced our knowledge of and insight into this Athenian speech.[1] He has shown that Paul took his text from the Greek poets to a much greater extent than was supposed. Epimenides had said, " In Thee we live and move and have our being ".

> A tomb for thee, O Holy and High, have fashioned
> The Cretans, liars always, evil beasts, idle bellies;
> But thou diest not; ever thou livest and standest firm;
> For in thee we live and move and have our being.

Paul knew the passage of the poem " Minos," and quotes another line from it in the letter to Titus i. 12.

Epimenides had taught the Athenians to cure a plague by erecting altars " to the deity concerned " at every place where one of a flock of sheep that he had turned loose lay down. The inscription on the altar, which Paul quotes as the starting-point of his address, brought to his mind the

[1] Syriac version, *Expositor*, October 1906, April 1907, October 1912.

Cretan Epimenides, and recalled that passage in his poem
"Minos," in which occurs the line describing the relation of
man to God. The words of Epimenides are in Paul's mind
throughout the opening of his speech. He reminds his
hearers of the doctrine taught by the famous Cretan prophet
and philosopher, and of the equally beautiful and true
thought which the philosophic poets Aratus and Cleanthes [1]
had enshrined in noble verse.

Such are the principles which he assumes to be accepted
by his audience. They know the fundamental truths—
that God exists, and that we are His offspring, and live and
move in Him ; but yet they are in other respects ignorant of
the nature of this God whose existence they accept. They
begin with the right conception ; and Paul's purpose is to
enlarge and complete their knowledge.

In Luke's brief summary of an address that was evidently
rather long, the opening has been exposed to a mistranslation, which some few modern scholars favour. Luke
uses a word of doubtful sense, *deisidaimonia*, which is capable
of meaning both "superstition" and "religion" ; but Luke
calculated that the context would show the true significance ;
and the great majority of commentators in ancient and in
modern time have rightly caught the intention. Some, on the
contrary, argue that, since in most cases *deisidaimonia* means
"superstition" and was despised as a bad characteristic,
therefore Paul must have used it in the bad sense, and that
he begins his address by accusing his philosophic hearers of
"superstition"—a quality which philosophers contemned.
But the real purport of his address is to praise their
instinctive religious feeling, and to say that the very same
deity whom with this right instinct they worship, though
unknown, is the God whom he declares to them.

[1] Both were Stoics, and were revered by some of Paul's opponents.

It is an untrustworthy line of argument to maintain that a word which, by its plain and evident form and by occasional use, is capable of a good sense, but which is far more frequently used in a disparaging and contemptuous sense, must necessarily bear this bad sense in any given passage. If the word is used by a good authority in any one place clearly in a good sense, it may be used in that good sense in another place: that is a canon of interpretation. Words have a wide range of meaning, and are not always used in one single narrow connotation. But it may be said that Paul starts with this word; and its bad sense, being much more common, would naturally be caught by the audience who were unprepared by the context to catch the good significance. This, however, is an untrustworthy line of reasoning. In the first place, it ignores the effect of tone and gesture, which are so important in conveying the intention of the spoken word: the whole difference would lie in the orator's tone. In the second place, it would be unsafe to assume that, because the context, which to the readers of a brief summary determines the good intention of the word, comes after it in the written report, therefore the much longer oration began with the same abrupt declaration. It may be regarded as almost certain that there was a more formal introduction, which along with tone and gesture, made it clear to the audience that the orator was beginning in the usual complimentary fashion and was commending their natural religious feeling.

The fact that Paul uses two lines [1] out of the short passage, only four lines, preserved from the " Minos " of Epimenides, proves that he was familiar with the entire context, and that he quoted intentionally words which referred to the

---

[1] I assume that Paul wrote to Titus. The double quotation is strong evidence of authorship.

pagan deity Zeus and which were written to rebuke the
false and debased view held about Zeus and his supposed
death and Cretan tomb by the Cretans, "always liars, evil
beasts, slow bellies". At Athens therefore he was not
merely using a tag familiar to the vulgar.

Again, it has been contended by several modern authorities
that he would never have quoted from Aratus, if he had
known that Aratus was speaking of the false deity Zeus,
and that therefore Paul had never read Aratus, but merely
caught up a few words which had become current in
half-educated society.

On the contrary, Paul quotes with deliberate intention
words that describe all mankind as the offspring of Zeus,
"in whom we live and move". These words express the
truth. Zeus is God, an ignorant conception of God, but
yet not devoid of truth ; and this philosophic conception of
Zeus may be elevated to become the true idea of the one
living God. But image-worship in every form is debased,
and inseparably connected with moral degradation and in-
numerable abuses.

I regret to differ absolutely from Professor Deissmann on
this point. I presume he did not know about Professor Rendel Harris's discovery, for he would surely not maintain that
Paul's two quotations out of four lines of Epimenides are
both merely "lines that lived in the mouth of the people".
This would be far too marvellous a coincidence. Paul's
starting-point is an altar whose inscription recalled Epimenides to him ; and this is a clear proof that he knew the
whole circumstances of the poem and the history. He had
read, and he could quote aptly from his reading.

We notice also, in passing, that Luke marks his report
as being only a brief account of a speech, for he implies in
v. 32 that the listeners caught the word "Anastasis" on

Paul's lips, misunderstood it, and mocked at it as the name of a strange deity.   Now the word does not occur in Luke's report, but only a cognate verb in inflected form.   The actual noun must have been used in the address as it was spoken, so that hearers heard "Anastasis," and thought this was the name of a god;[1] and Luke here leaves a proof that he is giving his own summary of a longer address.   That the address was long may also be inferred from the wish of the audience that it should be cut short, though the wish was expressed politely in the form that "we will hear thee concerning this yet again".

[1] The noun in v. 32 clearly refers back to the participle in 31, and implies that the listeners heard and mocked at the name.

XLVIII. The Relation of St. Paul to the Greek Mysteries [1]

An attempt has been made in the preceding pages to describe the character and extent of the influence which Greek thought exercised on Paul. Now the opinion has been put forward by recent scholars that the most impressive side of Greek religion, *viz.* the Mysteries, had a powerful, even a transforming effect on his teaching. No reference has been made in the preceding chapters to this opinion, because the writer considers it erroneous ; but it seems right not to conclude without making some reference to it.

This opinion bears on the recent development of Pauline study, in which the questions that were formerly central have ceased to be so. Stress is no longer laid on the question whether the Apostle wrote the letters that bear his name. It is only among rather old-fashioned theologians that those elaborate discussions about authenticity and the minutiæ of style are still maintained. There will, doubtless, always be some who, unable to comprehend the wide sweep of thought and the extraordinary variety of topic and tone in the few short letters of Paul, condemn one or another as spurious, or fly to the quaint resort that some of the extant letters are elaborated by accretions which have been worked up with original scraps of Pauline writings ; but their questionings are no longer central in scholarship, though the curious will always recur to them, and will learn something from them.

[1] Enlarged from the *Contemporary Review*, August, 1913, by permission.

Yet we cannot get away from Paul. He holds the thought of thinking men as much as ever ; and discussion still rages round him. The question that has of late been most prominent is as to the implication and teaching of his letters. We no longer ask, " What did he write ? " Still less do we inquire, " Who wrote the Pauline Epistles ? " Scholars are now debating, " What is it, after all, that Paul taught ? "— and that old question now meets with a new answer. The view has been maintained that what he did teach was not the religion of Jesus, whatever that may have been and whoever He may have been, but a syncretistic philosophy expressed in ritual, which Paul substituted for that religion.

The modern world has awakened to the complexity and the intensity of the religious questionings that were then burning in the pagan world. Paul, in presenting the religion of Christ to that world, had to put it in forms that could be understood by the men of his time. He had to show them that this religion answered the questions which they were asking. He had to know those questions, and to comprehend and use the language that was employed in pagan religious thought. " The divine nature which you unintelligently worship I declare to you in its real character," as he says to the Athenian audience thronged in the Court of Areopagus ; and (like the lawyers and orators of that time, as known to and depicted by Pliny a few years later) Paul was addressing, not so much the Court, as the *corona* or circle of listeners, idle, curious, full of a certain intellectual interest, ever seeking after some new thing, who thronged the hall of Areopagus.

All men in that age throughout the Eastern Roman Provinces were seeking for " Salvation," and asking how to reach it. Lecturers were expounding philosophic theories and rules of life to classes of disciples. Records of prayer and vow for "Salvation" are found in many hundreds of villages of Asia Minor. St. Paul may have caught the Greek word from the lips of thousands of pagans. It is the same word that became specially characteristic of Christian teaching. Yet it would be a serious error to argue that, because pagans and Christians alike longed and prayed for "Salvation," therefore the thing that they sought was the same. To the pagan and the Christian the same Greek word bore totally different meanings. To the former it was vague; and, where it approached definiteness, it was material. To Paul it was spiritual. There also was a close resemblance in the words which both parties used to describe the way of attaining "Salvation": purification, the new life, seeking after God, and so on, were common terms, but their sense was changed to Paul. The meaning which Jesus had imparted to them was unintelligible to the pagans without a new education of intellect as well as of heart: this is often forgotten by modern scholars, and the demands which Christianity made on the understanding are ignored.[1]

I do not propose, by a comparative examination of the Pauline teaching and thought, to show that it stands on a totally different plane from the methods and the answers of contemporary religious minds in the Graeco-Roman world. I take only one detail of the general problem. The religious ideas of the Graeco-Roman paganism were focussed in the Mysteries. The general character of the Mysteries was certainly known to the Tarsian citizen. What did he think of them? In what relation did he stand to them? I hope to answer these questions by showing that Paul refers to the Mysteries, and states his own opinion about them very clearly.

According to some recent speculations, Paul was not much

[1] See Section III.

more than a borrower from the Mysteries. The tendency is now to regard him as powerfully influenced by the teaching conveyed through those impressive rites. In these speculations the outstanding name is that of Dieterich (whose death we have had to mourn). Loisy and others have crystallised the drift of this theorising into the epigrammatic saying that "the mystery of Paul's conversion is his conversion to the Mysteries": from this source he derived all the ideas with which he overlaid the teaching of Jesus, transforming it into "a religion of Mystery," which promised salvation as a reward for the performance of ritual and sacrament.

Even in this narrower form I shall not try to test the theory by comparing it with the spirit and general tone of the Pauline teaching. That has been done by Professor H. A. A. Kennedy in a series of articles (which we hope soon to see as a book) in the *Expositor*, 1911, 1912, much better than the present writer could do. I shall restrict this investigation to one passage, *viz.* to Colossians ii. 8-24, and especially to verse 18, which presents very serious difficulties. Not merely is there divergence in the MSS. on a matter so serious as whether the word "not" should be added in one part of the sentence: modern scholars regard the text as hopeless and resort to conjectural alterations. It cannot be denied that the word ἐμβατεύων in this verse, if we take it in its simple and natural sense, "setting foot on," or in any derivative sense that is well attested, has an awkward effect. It does not seem to suit the context, but is inharmonious with its surroundings.

Taking some fresh discoveries as to the ceremonial of the Mysteries, I hope to show that Paul knew enough about their rites to employ in this verse of Colossians a technical Mystic term in such a way that the force of his reference can be best given by putting the word within inverted commas. That is the reason of the apparent awkwardness of the term in this context: it seems incongruous and unsuitable, like a fish out of water. But, if we read the words of Paul in this new way, we see that the paragraphs which he devotes to the subject express uncompromising condemnation of the Mysteries and of all attempt to adulterate Christ's gospel by intermingling with it ideas, or forms, or rites derived from the Mysteries.

The discoveries which throw new light on the nature and words of the Mysteries as they were celebrated in Asia Minor must first be described briefly.

The excavations conducted by the Asia Minor Exploration Fund at Pisidian Antioch in 1912 have illuminated Roman affairs in the East and the religion of Phrygia. We cleared completely both the central Sanctuary and a large building near, but outside it. This building, which is oriented so as to lie symmetrically with the south-western wall of the Sanctuary at a distance of about 30 feet from it, was apparently used as a hall for initiation and the celebration of the Mysteries. It was constructed for that purpose, and, in spite of dilapidation, it yields some valuable information. It was destroyed as thoroughly as the principal religious centre, and doubtless along with it, towards A.D. 400 (about which time various pagan temples were sacked by the Christians with the permission of the Imperial Government).

Further, the excavations conducted for the Turkish Imperial Museum by Makridi Bey at Notion (which I should call the Roman Colophon) have been most fruitful ; and one discovery, which alone I shall mention, bears on our subject. This year on January 16th, while waiting in a friend's rooms at Christ Church for his return, I chanced to take up the last number of the Vienna *Jahreshefte*, and to read the article published there by Makridi Bey. Among a series of very interesting inscriptions from the Sanctuary of Apollo of Klaros was one which instantly arrested attention : it contained the verb " entered " (ἐνεβάτευσεν), describing the performance of some act or rite in the mystic ritual. This word is the same that has caused so much difficulty in Colossians ii. 18. A few days later, in the *Athenæum* of January 25th, p. 106 f., I published a short article on the " Ancient Mysteries and their Relation to St. Paul," stating briefly the bearing of this discovery.

The Clarian inscriptions, as a rule, are records of visits paid by delegates from foreign cities and countries to Apollo's oracle. These delegates were one or, generally, more in number ; and they were frequently accompanied by a chorus, which sang a hymn in honour of the god. Laodiceia on the Lycus, the Laodiceia of St. Paul (Colossians iv. 16), happens to have sent several such delegations ; and in one case it was the " prophet " of Pythian Apollo at Laodiceia who represented his city at Klaros.

The delegations came to seek an oracle ; they were " questioners of the god " (*theopropoi*) ; and when they returned home, the oracle was recorded in a public dedication.[1] At Klaros, also, inscriptions recorded the names of the delegates and the chorus of hymn-singers (*hymnodoi*, both youths and maidens, *koroi* and *korai*, or *êitheoi* and *parthenoi*), and stated what they had done at the sanctuary. In several cases the delegate or delegates received initiation in the Mysteries ; and these are the cases which interest us at present.

The record of the initiation varies. Sometimes the delegate "performed also the mystic ritual (in addition to

[1] Of these we possess several: one at Troketta in Lydia (best in Keil and Premerstein, *Reise in Lydien*, p. 8) ; one in North Phrygia (see my *Studies in the Eastern Roman Provinces*, p. 128).

consulting the god)". From such a record we learn nothing regarding the rites. Two cases, however, are more instructive. In one it is stated that two inquirers, "having been initiated, entered" (μυηθέντες ἐνεβάτευσαν). The other case is specially interesting: an inquirer "having received the *mysteria*, entered" (παραλαβὼν τὰ μυστήρια ἐνεβάτευσεν). The general term in the one case, "being initiated," is defined in the other case more particularly, "receiving the mystic things (from the hierophant, the officiating priest)". The correlative term, *viz.*, that "(the hierophant) handed over the mystic things," is also a technical expression. The two terms both indicate the initiation ritual as a whole (as M. Ch. Lecrivain[1] points out): both terms include the showing of the mystic objects, the performance of the mystic actions, and the utterance of the mystic words (δεικνύμενα, δρώμενα, λεγόμενα). Accordingly, the "tradition" or the "reception of the *mysteria*" includes the whole ceremony, all that is given or received, words, enlightenment, etc.

The word "entered," or "set foot on," was evidently also technical for some act in the ritual. This act was not part of the initiation; it followed after the initiatory rites were completed: "having been initiated, they set foot on ——". An examination of the evidence (such as is given in the *Annual of Brit. School at Athens*, 1913, p. 46 f.) would show that the thought of stepping into a "New Life" was natural and familiar in Asia Minor. It would be quite in accordance with the philosophic thought which (as I think) underlay the Mysteries, that the same idea should find symbolic expression in them. The term as used in both the Clarian inscriptions, evidently indicates the climax or

[1] See the art. "Mysteria" in Darmberg and Saglio, *Dict. des Antiquités*, iii., p. 2142 A, note 6.

final act in the mystic ceremonial; "being initiated," or "receiving the mystic things and words," they performed the act called ἐμβατένων, symbolising that they had entered on a new life, and intended to continue therein.

The nature of this act is not defined. What did they set foot on? The want of definition shows that the term was familiar and technical, and therefore there was no need to define what it was that they entered into. An act of entering, or setting foot on, took place as a climax or result of the initiation. Now the idea expressed by this verb is that of beginning, not conclusion. The climax of initiation, therefore, is an act of entrance or beginning. The initiated person, as the conclusion of his initiation, "makes entrance," or "sets foot on —— ".

In the ritual, of course, the action was performed in some apparent fashion, and this performance of the action was the prelude to another stage of the ritual. In Asia Minor, therefore, as at Eleusis, there must have been two stages, a lower and a higher, in the initiation. The lower stage was the initiation proper (μύησις): after it the mystês entered on the higher stage (called at Eleusis the Epoptika). The act of entrance on this higher stage at Klaros was called "entering"; and evidently the same term, ἐμβατεύειν, was used to designate the entire higher stage in those two Clarian inscriptions, which attest a common popular usage.

Now the arrangements in the hall of initiation at the Antiochian sanctuary have been destroyed so thoroughly that at first they presented an almost hopeless problem. From the first, however, we could not doubt that there is in the centre of the hall a shallow quadrangular pool, or *lacus*, like the *impluvium* in a Roman atrium, and that some sort of baptismal or purificatory rite must have taken place there, in which the ministering priest stood on a stone.

This rite was performed in the presence of the god, whose marble throne (with a late dedicatory inscription about A.D. 300) stands overlooking the pool.

This throne of the god is a feature of primitive Anatolian religion: many such archaic thrones are known, the most impressive being a tall pinnacle of the Kara Dagh carved into the semblance of a throne, and covered with inscriptions in Hittite hieroglyphics.[1] The importance of such thrones in Anatolian religion was first pointed out by Dr. Reichel in an interesting article, which, however, contained some inferences that seem incorrect. His premature death took place before he had been gladdened by the discovery of many such "thrones," whose religious purpose is unmistakable, proving the essential truth of his theory (which was very severely criticised at the time in Germany (see Professor Von Fritsche, *Rheinisches Museum*, 1900).

Away in the extreme corner of the hall on the god's right hand as he looked over the *lacus* is a set of stone foundations, one part of which is labelled "Bed" in the plan which I made at the time in my notebook. This title, given as a mere distinguishing description, is probably true to the original intention.

The key to the interpretation of these arrangements is furnished by the Clarian inscriptions. The mystês, who came into the initiation hall by the only door on the south, found on his left a series of arrangements; these belong to the initiation proper ($\mu\dot{\upsilon}\eta\sigma\iota\varsigma$).[2] To his right are the central *lacus* and the throne of the god, and away beyond them

---

[1] This throne, about fifty miles south-east from Konia, is published in *The Thousand and One Churches* by Miss Gertrude Bell and the present writer, p. 507 f., and Figs. 371 A and B, 372, 374 f.

[2] A full description with plans and photographs is published in the *Annual of the British School at Athens*, 1913.

the stone foundations above mentioned. These form a group distinguished from those on the left, and are evidently intended to serve for the second stage of the Mysteries. The remarkable feature is that the second stage takes place in the presence of the god, whereas the first stage of initiation was evidently separate and apart. The first stage, which is still obscure, does not here concern us: the second stage is in part clear.

After the initiation of the first stage (which took place on the left, i.e. west, side of the hall), the mystês was brought towards the centre of the hall, where he passed through a second series of rites (his progress, as before, was in the direction south to north).[1] Before him was a door or entrance-way between two upright slabs of stone, 3 ft. high and 4 ft. 6 in. long: some cutting on the front edge of the slabs imparted a slightly architectual look to the entrance-way, which is 2 ft. 8 in. broad and 4 ft. 6 in. long. Outside the entrance on the left side, there stands close to the slab a very large, thick, shallow bowl of stone. The mystês would pass the bowl, as he came forward towards the end of the entrance-way after finishing the first stage of the rites: possibly it may have held water for lustration.

The entrance-way leads up to the central pool, and ends 1 ft. 4 in. from the pool. It must have been originally higher than the present 3-foot blocks: for the colour of their upper surface shows that other blocks formerly rested on them.[2] When the mystês "set foot on" the entrance-way, the act constituted the *embateuein;* and he emerged from the entrance-way into the presence of the god on his throne. The mortal, fresh from the initiation, had thus

---

[1] Strictly speaking, the wall which I call south, faces a little east of south: the west wall south of west.

[2] Hangings or screens were used in some parts of the ritual.

entered on a new life, which he now was to live in the divine company.

Whether the throne was empty to the eye and only filled by the unseen god, or was occupied by the priest as representative of the god on earth, is uncertain ; but the latter alternative is probable. In the next rite, the active part was played by a subordinate priest ; and the chief priest (who certainly was present) could have no more suitable place than the throne of the god, whose place he filled, and whose part he played on earth in this ritual. The promise to the mystês was : " Happy and blessed, thou shalt be god instead of mortal ". Identification with the deity was the goal of human life, a goal attained at blissful death (as many Phrygian epitaphs [1] show), or as the result of initiation. In the ceremony which makes the initiated equal to the god, the only suitable place for the chief priest was the god's throne.

In the central pool took place the rite described by Demosthenes in his oration *On the Crown.* Æschines, against whom that speech was delivered, was the son of a strolling priestess—one of those persons, despised by the educated but revered by the superstitious, who carried the ritual of Phrygian Cybele through Attica in the fourth century B.C.— and he had acted as his mother's assistant in performing the ceremonies of the cult. Demosthenes paints in sarcastic and contemptuous invective the humiliating character of the life and acts of such a ministering subordinate. Regarding this part of the ceremonial, he says : " When you grew to man's estate, you assisted your mother as she performed the ritual : you recited from the books the words of the formulæ, and assisted her in the rest of the foolery. At night you used to put the fawnskin on, and pour water from the crater over, and perform the purification for, those whom she was

---

[1] See my *Studies in the Eastern Provinces*, p. 273 f.

initiating ; and you used to scrub them with mud and bran, and make them stand up [1] after the cleansing, and bid them say, ' I have escaped the evil : I have found the better ' (ἔφυγον κακόν · εὗρον ἄμεινον)."

This scene took place in the darkness of night, as Demosthenes says. The illumination seems to have been by a very large torch. Reliefs found near Antioch show the torch-bearing priest, the Dadouchos ; and an inscription speaks of the equipping of a cave or closed chamber and of " the torch " (as a familiar object).[2]

From the purification the mystês was led on, perhaps through several stages, to the perfect scene of human life, the representation of that fundamental fact in society, the Holy Marriage of the god and goddess. The divine life is the model and guarantee of human action. The gods teach men what to do in their relation to each other and to the gods, in society and in cult. Religious reliefs show the god doing in heaven what his worshipper does on earth beneath.[3] Hence the marriage of the divine pair is the type and symbol for the imitation of men. The priest and priestess played the part of the divine pair, probably ; and the Christian writers rebuke the impropriety of this scene, which was enacted within the holy *Pastos*, or nuptial chamber. In the Athenian marriage rite the same formula was spoken that has just been quoted from the Mystic ritual. " I have escaped the evil : I have found the better." The Athenian rite, therefore, is derived from the mystic rite ; the marriage was apparently a performance of the Holy Marriage with the

---

[1] In this scene the mystês crouched on his heels, until at the word of the ministrant, he stood up, pure and qualified to go on to the next stage.

[2] These are described in the *Annual of the British School at Athens*, 1913, pp. 40, 70, 73 ; *Journal of Hellenic Studies*, 1912, p. 163. Mr. Anderson and I confirmed this difficult text in 1912.

[3] An example is figured in my *Letters to the Seven Churches*, p. 63.

bride and bridegroom playing the part of the god and goddess; and the priestess taught them (as is recorded). It is
stated by an ancient authority that "the marriage pair
celebrate the sacred marriage in honour of Zeus and Hera".[1]
I have shown elsewhere that the rite in Asia Minor was
similar in character to the Athenian.[2]

Dieterich maintains that the marriage scene in the Mysteries was the marriage of the god to the mystês (regarded
always as female). It is in accordance with the spirit of the
Mysteries that the mystês should be regarded as united to
the deity; but the mystic ritual was the religion of the
Mother-goddess, not of the god (who was originally a subsidiary and secondary figure), and Dieterich's conception
can only belong to a late form of the cult, in which the
deity is conceived as distinctively male, while the Mother
recedes into the background. That was so at Antioch,
where Mên was pre-eminent, and the goddess had only a
small chapel in a corner of his sanctuary and a small temple
outside; yet all that we have as yet been able to learn or
guess about the Antiochian religion suggests that the old
forms were carefully preserved. Drinking from the holy
vessel formed part of the mystic ritual and of the marriage
rite. But this origin of a religious marriage in the Phrygian
religion is a large subject.

The Anatolian religion imposed on devout women a
service at the sanctuary, antipathetic to marriage; and the
character of some scenes in the Mysteries suggests that
human life was presented to the mystæ as a progress from
savagery to civilisation under divine guidance. The union

---

[1] *Lex Rhetor.*, p. 670 Porson, p. 345 Nauck: see Usener, *Ital. Mythen* in
Rh. Mus., xxx. p. 227, who says that the quotation refers to the Athenian
rite (which may be regarded as certain).

[2] *Histor. Commentary on Galatians*, pp. 88-91.

of the sexes was depicted at first as an act of violence, and the Holy Marriage then came in as the new and higher law given of God, and taught by the god and goddess to men. The servants of the goddess had to pass through the same fortunes and the same stages as the goddess herself, and thus gradually learn the higher rule of marriage. On this hypothesis the testimony of ancient authorities about the purifying and elevating influence of the Mysteries becomes intelligible, while the testimony of Christian foes about the hideous nature of certain parts which they select out of the ritual must equally be regarded as true to fact, though incomplete as a picture, and untrue to the general effect of the Mysteries.

At the corner of the Antiochian hall, on the right hand of the god on his throne, are a series of flat supporting stones, on which, as I suppose, rested the Pastos ; and inside it are the marks of three of the four feet on which rested the holy bed. The formula is quoted by Clement : "I have eaten from the tympanon : I have drunk from the cymbal : I have carried the kernos : I have gone into the Pastos". The divine acts were imitated by the mystai ; but this imitation does not imply that Dieterich's theory is correct. They see what the gods do, and learn to do likewise.

Probably the word "enter," or "set foot on," while strictly denoting the first step in the higher ritual, was commonly used to indicate the whole of the advanced stage. When the Clarian inscription stated that an inquirer, after being initiated, "set foot on ——," this implies that he performed the entire series of the rites. One who "entered" did not stop, but continued to the end. The act of *embateuein* implied the whole epoptika ; such is the force of the Clarian formula : the delegates, "having been initiated, performed the higher stage of the ritual".

No *crux* in the letters of Paul has been more frequently discussed than that in Colossians ii. 18, and none seemed more desperate : μηδεὶς ὑμᾶς καταβραβευέτω θέλων ἐν ταπει- νοφροσύνῃ καὶ θρησκείᾳ τῶν ἀγγέλων, ἃ ἑώρακεν ἐμβατεύων, εἰκῇ φυσιούμενος ὑπὸ τοῦ νοὸς τῆς σαρκὸς αὐτοῦ, καὶ οὐ κρατῶν τὴν κεφαλήν κτλ. The varieties of text in the MSS. may be neglected : the omission of ἐν is unim- portant : the insertion of μή or οὐκ; before ἑώρακεν, has found hardly any defenders,[1] and the new evidence shows clearly that the insertion is merely an alteration arising from misunderstanding of the true text.

The Colossians are warned by Paul against some one, probably a known individual, who is cheating them of the prize of Christian life. Such a one could not be an outward enemy, misleading or harassing them. He is evidently a person that endangers the success of their Christian life by spreading false teaching among them as one of their own number; he had a wrong conception of the nature of the Christianity which he professed, being swayed by his older religious ideas and philosophic theories; and his influence was leading astray the minds of others. Whether there was any individual who acted as leader in this movement is of no consequence. My point would be equally telling if the movement was a general one, without a single definite leader. I assume, however, that there was one guiding spirit.

The force of verse 18 is conditioned by its relation to 8 and 16. The whole passage, 8-19, consists of three con- nected and parallel warnings : 8, "See that there shall be no one who takes you captive by philosophy and empty illusion after the tradition of men, after the elemental powers or

---

[1] Rev. Dr. Maclellan has defended μή in the *Expositor*, May, 1910, p. 393 f. His arguments do not convince me. See also Dr. Burgon on the Revised Version, p. 355.

rulers of the world, and not after Christ . . .". [Here follows a statement of the triumphant supremacy of Christ, the Head, over those elemental powers.] 16, "Let no one, then, make himself a judge [or critic] of you in meat and drink, or in respect of festival days :[1] which are a shadow of things future, but the body *that casts the shadow* is Christ's". 18, "Let no one cozen you of the prize of your life-race, finding satisfaction in self-humiliation and worshipping of angels, 'taking his stand on' what he has seen (in the Mysteries), vainly puffed up by his unspiritual mind, and not keeping firm hold on [Christ] the Head".

In verse 8 the life of the Christian is metaphorically regarded as a battle, and in 18 as an athletic contest : both metaphors are frequent in Paul's letters. The use in 16 of "judge" in respect of the relation between one member of the Church and the others is so frequent in Paul and so characteristic of him that one would almost be surprised if it had been absent from this passage, and would have looked for some explanation of the absence (as, for example, one does in the Pastoral Epistles, where it never[2] occurs). Everything points to a member of the Church misleading his fellows : first, by his false philosophy he takes them captive ; secondly, by finding fault with their omission he induces them to observe an order of ritual (largely Jewish) ; thirdly, by teaching them to practise a ceremonial of humiliation, and to pay homage to angels or powers intermediate between God and man, he defrauds them of the prize offered to the true Christians, as he "takes his stand

---

[1] No one should make your action in respect of meat, etc., a ground for judging or criticising you : such matters should be left to the individual conscience and judgment, as in 1 Cor. viii. 1-8. It is only in respect of the really fundamental things that mutual criticism is allowable.

[2] In 2 Timothy iv. it has another sense, equally Pauline. In Titus iii. 12 it means " I have decided " (resolved).

upon " ("entering on") the (non-spiritual) things that he has seen, leading his followers away with him out of the true course.

In 18 the force of "entering on" is got only when we regard it as a quoted word. It is a sarcastic reference to a solemn act, by which once on a time the leader of the movement had symbolically expressed his deliberate choice (θέλων) of a "New Life". This "New Life," however, was not spiritual, but was hedged within a world of sensuous and external actions, and rites, and things. The word was familiar to the Colossians; they knew it in the Mysteries; they had probably heard it used by this teacher, who spoke of the entrance which they should make on a new life, as a higher course of asceticism, and self-denial, and humiliation. As it stands, the word causes a certain awkwardness which every one feels; but when we take it as quoted and put it within inverted commas, we understand that it is like an alien brick imbedded in the living wall of Paul's words.

The movement in the Colossian Church[1] was made under the impulse of a certain teaching in which elements of the popular religion of Phrygia were mingled. Phrygia was "the home of some of the most extraordinary forms of heathen superstition, and the people seemed imbued with the taste for excitement and mystery, which was partly the outcome of temperament and partly of centuries of association". (Rev. G. Currie Martin.) This is so evident as to be almost universally accepted; and Dr. Moffatt speaks of "elements rife within the popular religion of Phrygia" as indubitably present in that "local phase of some syncretistic

---

[1] A movement of similar general type was, apparently, widespread in the province of Asia, where the contact of Greek philosophic thought on its religious side with Jewish thought in a popular superstitious form favoured it (Acts xix. 13). The "philosophy and vain deceit" of Colossians ii. 8 is the "knowledge (*gnôsis*) which is falsely so called" of 1 Timothy vi. 20.

theosophy" against which Paul wrote in this letter. These quotations are given as fairly stating the general views of scholars.

The term, "setting foot on," is a striking word in itself. It is of the sensuous, not the spiritual world; and is in accordance with the fault which Paul finds in the teaching of this unsafe Colossian guide. The great Cambridge school of divines in the nineteenth century proposed to eliminate the word and to replace it conjecturally by an even more markedly sensuous term, which is not religious and does not occur in Greek (though a cognate and more correct form is found); but conjecture has now no place here.

The word which Paul used was technical; and he used it because it was technical. His effect depends on the fact that it was a religious term familiar to his Phrygian readers. They caught the sarcastic innuendo that the person who is alluded to had formerly "entered" (ἐνε-βάτευσεν). A leader in the congregation, prominent in teaching a certain new theosophic and mystic form of Christianity, was introducing ideas which he had brought over from his old belief in the Mysteries. I have elsewhere [1] tried to show that Ignatius had been initiated into some type of Mysteries, and to explain from this early experience some of the remarkable and almost startling passages in his letters.

These popular Mysteries were in the Roman period to a large degree assimilated by contamination throughout the Eastern Roman provinces, so that each took over new elements from others and approximated to a common type. The original character of the Mysteries was probably not essentially different in different places, and therefore the common type was easily produced. Probably what are

[1] *Letters to the Seven Churches*, p. 165.

called the Phrygian Mysteries give the best means of studying the others. While considerable modifications took
place in the Mysteries during the Roman period, the change
probably was almost always in the way of addition. The
original ritual remained as the nucleus of an elaborated and
lengthened ceremonial. In the later third century, perhaps
even earlier, the additions sometimes were modelled on
Christian rites, with the idea of showing that the old religion could do those things and meet the devotees' needs
much better than the new teaching.

Since "emendations" to eliminate ἐμβατεύων are done
away with, along with it ἃ ἑώρακεν must stand safe in the
text. This theosophist has disturbed the Church at Colossai
by introducing the fleshly, non-spiritual ideas, the things (and
words) of the Mysteries ; i.e., what he has seen (and handled,
receiving them from the Hierophant). And so Paul hurls
forth his warning, " handle not, nor taste, nor touch (all
which things are to perish with the using) after the precepts
and doctrines of men. Which things, through their asceticism
in voluntary ritual and humility, have indeed a show of
wisdom, but are not of any real value against the indulgence
of the flesh." Every word here is specially telling and appropriate, if a converted *mystês* is the teacher whom Paul
opposes. On the " humility," self-imposed and voluntary,
of the *mystai*, one may consult Foucart's vivid account,
based on Demosthenes and Clement, in his *Associations
Réligieuses chez les Grecs*, pp. 68-84, and elsewhere.

The language of Paul throughout the whole passage shows
not only disapproval and condemnation of this mystic theosophy, but also a certain tone of scorn, or at least of lofty
and absolute superiority. The man who could think and
write in this strain moves on a plane of thought infinitely
above the level of that philosophy, or (perhaps one should

rather say) pseudo-philosophy. Both taught the Way of Salvation, or simply "the Way" (Acts xix. 9, 23, etc.); but in the Mysteries the Way was a literal path marked by a white poplar tree and other signs, which the soul learned through the esoteric and mystic lore, whereas in the Gospel it was an idea, making itself into a driving force in the conduct of life: it was the intense, overpowering belief in a spiritual fact. Both in Paulinism and in the Mystery-religion there was taught the means of escaping out of servitude to the seven dæmonic rulers (Archontes), who preside over the seven planets and control the fate of men. The belief in this influence has its early stages (we should not say its roots, for we cannot penetrate historically to the roots) in old Egyptian and Chaldæan or Babylonian doctrines. The influence is evil, crushing the individual development under a hard and dreadful servitude; and it was organised in a sort of hierarchy of bad powers, "angels and principalities and powers" (Romans viii. 38) under "the ruler (Archon) of the power of the air" (Ephesians ii. 2). To escape from this slavery man must be enabled to enter into communion and fellowship with still higher powers. This was "the Way," as taught in the Mystery-religion: prayers, rites, incantations, magic arts, purifications, were called in to aid the struggling soul; but these were all earthly, fleshly, sensuous, and non-spiritual. These elemental powers of the air and the heavens, "angels" intermediate between God and man, were real powers according to the general belief: in Paul's opinion they were "the weak and beggarly elements" which he mentions with so much contempt in Galatians iv. 9. Paul's means of escape from this enslavement of the human spirit was spiritual, and not ritual. The Gnosis which he denounced was a knowledge of fleshly means.

At the same time, his tone is not that of thorough denunciation and abhorrence, such as appears in his attitude to the base and vulgar forms of idolatry. As Lightfoot, in his note on Colossians ii. 8, justly says, " Clement (*Strom.*, vi. 8, p. 771) had a right to contend that Paul does not here condemn ' philosophy ' absolutely ". Philosophy is here disparaged as erroneous groping after truth, somewhat in the style of Acts xvii. 22 ff. This philosophy is deception without any real meaning or content, κένη ἀπάτη, purely verbal and external, never penetrating below the surface to the hidden nature of God, taking shadow for truth, and putting the material in place of the spiritual; but it is, after all, an effort, well-intentioned but misdirected, in search of truth and good and God.

The passage, Colossians ii. 8-19, as thus interpreted of the Mysteries, is a profoundly significant piece of evidence. In the first place, it shows Paul was no absolute enemy of philosophy, though he easily lost patience with the philosophers as he knew them.[1] In the second place, it proves that he regarded the Mysteries and their ritual as having a certain philosophical side, and appealing to a certain religious feeling in mankind : this justifies by unprejudiced contemporary authority a general tendency among modern students to regard the Mysteries as a veiling of philosophic thought in outward ceremonial.[2] In the third place, and most important of all, it shows that Paul in the last resort was an uncompromising enemy of the religious ideas and thoughts embodied in the Mysteries. While making allowance for good intention, he has to condemn them finally as absolutely wrong in their methods and views. The importance of this

---

[1] 1 Cor. i. 19 f.; Acts xvii. 23.

[2] There was no doctrine expounded in the Mysteries, there were only acts and some brief cryptic verbal formulæ.

is in reference to the above-mentioned recent speculations about the influence exercised on his views by the Mysteries. We now have his clear, explicit, and thorough condemnation of the attempt to introduce into the teaching of Christianity any element, or idea, or rite, or method that was characteristic of those pagan Mysteries, and a convincing statement of his reason for condemning them : the religion of Jesus is spiritual, the ritual of the Mysteries is external and non-spiritual.

To understand this statement of Paul's, to understand the difference between his doctrine and the "Way" of the Mysteries, one must be able to comprehend the difference between prescribed ritual and the really spiritual ; and it is painfully evident in the writings of the school whose views we are discussing, that they are so habituated to consider ritual the only way, as to miss the essential character of the Pauline "Way".

He that has understood Paul can understand the pitying contempt which the Jew of Tarsus felt. He that has sympathy with the spirit of Hellenism can understand the indignant contempt with which Demosthenes describes the perpetration of such antics in Athens. Yet this does not exhaust the situation. There were minds which could see a deeper meaning in these rites ; and "it is easy to imagine the answer that the neo-Platonic philosophers who admired the Mysteries would make to their assailants. Religion places men face to face with the actual facts of life : when the mind is exalted and ennobled by intense religious enthusiasm it is able to look with pure insight at phenomena of life in which the vulgar unpurified mind sees nothing but gross materialism. The language of religion is plainer and more direct than the language of common (modern) life. Symbolism can be looked at with gross eyes or with idealised eyes." The Aphrodite of Praxiteles was refined from a rude Asiatic prototype.

That is a totally different, and absolutely non-Pauline and anti-Pauline view, which must not be ignored; and I state it in these words, which I used as the conclusion of the article on Mysteries in the Ninth Edition of the *Encyclopædia Britannica.*[1]

[1] That article was written in Asia Minor, relying largely on notes and memory. For the later edition I suggested that it should be cancelled, and the subject entrusted to a younger scholar, who has made a special study of the literature.

XLIX. The Theory that Paul was an Epileptic

One other preliminary question still demands our consideration. It affects the very foundations on which rests our right to accept as in any degree valuable Paul's belief in the truth and power of his own personal experiences.

The question whether Paul was afflicted with epilepsy is not a matter of mere pathological curiosity. An affirmative reply opens the way to very grave inferences which are drawn by many, who know what an epileptic condition means. "Epileptic insanity" is the explanation of Paul's visions given confidently by numerous modern scholars and physicians. The same explanation for the visions of Ezekiel was stated to me with full assurance by an experimental pathologist of great distinction whom I knew well.[1] As he declared, he could produce any number of similar examples to the visions of Paul and of Ezekiel from any asylum for epileptic lunatics, and they were all on the same level of rationality.

Elsewhere[2] I have stated the reasons which made me reject any such hypothesis, and maintain that Paul was not an epileptic degenerate, and that the illness from which he suffered was a different ailment. Since I am not a physician, however, and since my first statement of opinion on the subject was set aside as on that ground unworthy of

[1] Another medical friend, also an extremely able pathologist, was equally confident that the visions of Ezekiel were the dreams of an eater of hashish.

[2] The opinion is quoted in my *Historical Commentary on Galatians*, p. 423 ff.

consideration by a much-respected scholar who had probably even less medical knowledge of the special disease than I had, I will give to the present section the form of a review of a small dissertation on the subject by Professor Adolf Seeligmüller, of Halle,[1] who has long been a specialist in cases of epilepsy and brain disease, and can therefore speak with authority. I shall simply re-state his opinions in the rougher and less scientific language of the ordinary man. In some respects my statement must fail to reach the standard of scientific accuracy which a trained medical man would desire. Such a physician will find the scientific statement in Dr. Seeligmüller's work.

Dr. Seeligmüller in several places takes occasion to point out how much this question has suffered from being treated by persons who possess no medical training or experience, and in particular by persons who have not had special experience in nerve-diseases, and who have a quite incorrect conception of what epilepsy is. He mentions in the outset that the identification of the "thorn in the flesh" with epilepsy had for many years seemed to him to be medically unsound and impossible; and he had gradually been drawn on, first to discuss the subject with friends, then to give a public lecture in 1902,[2] and finally to embody in a formal treatise the arguments over which he had so long meditated.

The suggestion that Paul was afflicted with epilepsy was, so far as the German professor is aware, first made by Ziegler at Göttingen in 1804; but Krenkel in 1890[3] is

[1] Geh. Medizinalrat and Professor of Nerve Diseases in the University of Halle; the pamphlet was published in 1910 (Leipzig, Hinrichs) under the title of *War Paulus Epileptiker ?*

[2] Already in 1895 he had begun to work on this lecture.

[3] *Beiträge z. Aufhellung der Gesch. u. der Briefe des Ap. Paulus* (diss. iv.), 2nd edition, 1905.

reckoned responsible for the prevalence of the epileptic theory in theological circles. Professor Seeligmüller has restricted his attention to German circles. The late Bishop Lightfoot advocated at great length the same theory in his edition of the *Epistle to the Galatians* before 1875 ; but it may be correct to say that Krenkel had the biggest share in spreading that belief, which according to Dr. Seeligmüller has now come to be regarded among the German theologians almost as an established fact. I hope that he is mistaken in thinking that they accept so unanimously theory for fact.

It need hardly be said that Lightfoot did not accept, or even think of, the inferences that physicians must inevitably draw from his own theory. Ask any medical man what degree of foundation or reality belongs to the visions and fancies of an epileptic. Those who accept that theory must be prepared to sacrifice the visions as mere delusions.

It is too often the case that we regard such epileptic attacks as mere episodes interrupting the usual course of life of an ordinary man. Even a medical man,[1] discussing the subject many years ago, put his opinion to me in the form that "when the brain and nervous system is strained to the highest pitch of exertion, it is nearest the breaking point," and the breaking point is an attack of the evil. But he did not add, as the German Professor does, that after the breaking point has been reached, the system does not resume its former power of activity and endurance. It begins anew on a lower level than before. This is the fundamental idea in Dr. Seeligmüller's treatise, if I take him aright; and the following paragraphs are merely a statement of the outward aspect of this fundamental fact.

The first step is to clear the non-medical mind of the false

[1] Not, however, an expert in nervous diseases.

idea that convulsive fits and epilepsy are equivalent terms, or that fainting fits furnish proof of epilepsy.

To do so the reader is conducted through the epileptic division of a great lunatic asylum at Nietleben, near Halle. Examples are pointed out and described fully of the two kinds of epileptic fits, the severe and the mild (which are called in Germany apparently by the French terms *grand mal* and *petit mal*).

As to the former the physician gives a typical example of the *grand mal*. He tells how with a piercing shriek a tall powerful man suddenly falls down senseless, and his head as it strikes the ground causes a loud crash. The sufferer is wholly unconscious. The physical effects are horrible; but the epileptic remembers nothing of them afterwards. He has for the time ceased to be a part of the world of men.[1] In another place we are informed that the disease is not to be counted as a painful one, except in so far as accidents, such as a blow sustained in falling, produce injuries which are still felt painful after consciousness returns. The return to life is slow. The sufferer often lies for hours in a deep sleep. He comes back to the world of human existence with clouded and dulled brain, and is in a surly excitable frame of mind: he feels extremely weak and faint, and this sense of extreme fatigue continues often for days. In many cases several or even many fits occur in quick succession one after another, before the attack ceases for the time.

Such attacks are preceded by certain premonitory symptoms, technically called *aura*.

It has been common to class as epileptic all diseases in which fits, whether accompanied or not by unconsciousness, are a symptom. But such fits are only a symptom, and are

---

[1] Except that the extremities of the body quiver, and certain other physical effects are observed; but the sufferer knows and remembers nothing of them.

induced by other diseases besides epilepsy. Epilepsy is a disease of the brain, as yet utterly obscure ; and it is of two kinds, partial (due to injury of the head affecting the brain, or to abscesses or other evils on the brain surface, the seat of which can usually be determined accurately), and idiopathic or true epilepsy, whose cause lies in the brain, though not even autopsy has yet been able to determine any precise cause or locality. The latter class is far the more numerous.

Owing to the insufficiency of earlier diagnosis, the statements even of physicians previous to about 1860, when neurological investigations took new life, have to be received with great caution. The distinction between hysteria and epilepsy is often difficult, and requires the most careful observation both during attacks and in the interparoxysmal periods. Of difficulties like these Krenkel evidently had not the faintest conception, says Dr. Seeligmüller (p. 10).

It is laid down in this treatise as a canon in diagnosis that no skilled neurologist would venture to infer epilepsy from one attack of convulsions and unconsciousness, however closely the symptoms might resemble those of an epileptic fit of the severest kind. There must be repeated attacks before epilepsy can be diagnosed or even safely spoken of. Among the external symptoms there is hardly any which, judging from one attack, might not be attributed to other causes. Of the internal cause, as it lies in the brain, one can as yet gather nothing, except to some degree in the case of " partial epilepsy," as already described.

The milder class of attacks (*petit mal*) are much less terrible, taking the form of a short unconsciousness (*absentia mentis*) or even of mere melancholia and confusion of mind,[1] after which the sufferer resumes his ordinary action.

[1] " *Epileptische Schwindel*," explained as *Benommensein und Wirrwerden*, p. 6.

This class, though sometimes continuing at intervals for many years, chiefly in the case of young persons, passes sooner or later into the severer type.[1] The ultimate result is the same.

It is the terrible issue of epileptic fits on which Dr. Seeligmüller insists: "if only epilepsy, as so many persons ignorant of medicine assume, meant nothing more than occasional fits with passing loss of consciousness!" (p. 7). Epilepsy turns through loss of intellectual and moral power and activity into insanity; and epileptic madness is the most dangerous to the friends of the sufferer.

One of the points on which Dr. Seeligmüller most strongly insists is that the *petit mal* furnishes no sort of explanation of St. Paul's visions and experiences, especially the "thorn in the flesh". The *petit mal* is not recognised or dreamed of by any but physicians as a milder stage of epilepsy. It has no resemblance even in the faintest degree to what Paul and Luke mention. When a person falls to the earth as by a sudden stroke,[2] it is either the *grand mal*, or it is an affliction different from epilepsy. Not even Dr. Krenkel or Bishop Lightfoot would have thought of *petit mal* either as epilepsy or as explaining the case of Paul. The *petit mal* may therefore be left out of consideration. We are dealing with the disease which in the ordinary world is called epilepsy, and which is regarded by many as covering the phenomena before us.

The connexion between epilepsy and what may roughly and unscientifically be called insanity is very close. One who suffers from epileptic fits may at any moment be overtaken by insanity; and in more than 75 per cent. of epileptic

---

[1] *Schwere Störungen der Intelligenz, welche bei längerem Bestehen der epileptischen Krankheit sich fast regelmässig einstellen*, p. 8.

[2] Acts ix., etc.

cases there follows insanity through " *epileptische Degenera-tion* " (p. 10). Apart from pronounced insanity the earlier (which in a few cases are the only) consequences of this general and slighter character are sufficiently awful, and they are described in some detail as follows :—

(1) The intelligence suffers : the epileptic begins to fail in mental grasp, he becomes slow of wit, he cannot easily understand a question, he loses power of language and may even repeat meaninglessly words or syllables : common symptoms are obstinate conceit, opinionativeness, etc. : his feeling of his own importance is exaggerated : even the aspect of the face alters (pp. 11-13).

(2) The character deteriorates : the epileptic becomes excitable and irritable, he feels keenly that he is harshly or unjustly treated in comparison with others, and that his merits have not been fairly recognised :[1] sometimes he is affected by fits of passion accompanied by shrieking or growling or purposeless acts of destruction, which may even take the form of injury to the person or attempted suicide, and the recollection of acts done at such times is faint or sometimes entirely lost.

(3) The energy to act and the power of action deteriorate in the epileptic. It is very rare to find that the sufferer can maintain himself in a position equal to that of his family and origin. He often sinks into gravest misconduct ; and at last there remains nothing for his parents except to keep him at home, where he is either an idler or a nuisance of whom every one stands in dread : and if he has no family to

---

[1] Many of the symptoms are, of course, merely external, and the same symptoms often result from other causes. In my own experience there is no calamity so great for a young man as to begin to feel himself unjustly treated, whether his feeling be right or wrong : this feeling tends towards permanent deterioration of character and moral power.

look after him and keep him within bounds, he becomes a criminal and a vagabond (pp. 17-19).

Such are the milder consequences which result from epilepsy; and Dr. Seeligmüller says expressly that his whole description is taken from his own experience and private practice as a physician.

There are certain conditions (*Dämmerzustände*) which usually happen in the intervals between fits (*grand mal*), or appear as "epileptic equivalents," i.e. take the place of fits. In such states the sufferer is in a condition not unlike sleepwalking : he seems conscious, does his business, goes about, and then suddenly, after hours or days, recovers his proper consciousness, having forgotten entirely what happened during the intervening period. Not seldom journeys are made in such a condition (*Poriomania*) ; Dr. Seeligmüller mentions among others a business man, who recovered to find himself on a ship in Bombay harbour instead of in Paris; but it is characteristic of these attacks that the travels are wholly purposeless and detrimental to the proper work of the sufferer. All the conditions called *Dämmerzustände* either are completely forgotten after the attack is ended, or are remembered only in a vague, imperfect and confused fashion.

The conditions called *Dämmerzustände* are found in 60 per cent. of cases treated in an asylum. They usually begin only after epileptic attacks have continued for a long time.

It is needless to go into further detail. What has been already stated is enough to give a fair idea of the situation, as a professor of this and allied diseases in Halle describes it.

If I do not err in briefly summarising his argument, it is as follows.

(1) Paul's attacks of illness, the "thorn in the flesh," and

his visions, must be identified either with the phenomena of the *grand mal*, or with the pathological phenomena of the intervening periods (*Dämmerzustände*) and of the *aura* preliminary to an attack of the *grand mal*. Neither the illness nor the visions can be identified with the former, because these are always accompanied by complete unconsciousness and leave no memory of themselves. Luke's account, twice given in a summary of Paul's own words, once as his own narrative, is that during the great experience of his conversion Paul retained consciousness and was able immediately afterwards to continue his journey to Damascus, though he had lost his eyesight.[1] Paul himself describes his visions as if he were fully conscious of them and remembered them afterwards.

Moreover the visions, apart from the Conversion, have no resemblance to attacks of the *grand mal*, but must on the epileptic theory be identified with phenomena either of the intervening periods or of the *aura*. Now such phenomena are either utterly purposeless acts done in a state of changed consciousness (so to say, his changed personality), and forgotten when the sufferer returns to his ordinary consciousness and personality, or they are evidence of growing moral and mental deterioration, which cannot be mistaken or regarded as interludes in the life of a man of exceptional and extraordinary powers and activity.[2] Paul was certainly much given to travelling ; but the purposefulness and method and premeditation of his journeying forms a most marked

---

[1] Dr. Seeligmüller does not mention blindness as one of the symptoms supervening on the *grand mal*. Rather it recalls the temporary blindness that afflicted Barjesus after the encounter with Paul at Paphos ; but no one could suppose that the magician had an attack of epilepsy.

[2] Paul was as purposeful and resourceful, quite as great a writer and thinker, after attacks continuing over thirty years. This alone is a complete proof to the Professor that the disease was not epilepsy.

feature of his career. Some might perhaps adduce the journey of Acts xvi. 7 f. as an example of Poriomania, because it involved change of plan, and led him into a new sphere of activity, but his choice of Bithynia and his turning towards Troas were chosen by him as a *pis aller* (unless we suppose that a wholly unpremeditated North Galatian mission should be interpolated), and in any case he did not regard these changes as interferences with his work, but as conducive to it.

With this exception Paul's journeying was a marvel of constructive purpose; and even this exception is more difficult to understand only because of its having long been encumbered with misconceptions. The exception was merely a stage in his gradual formation of a plan as wide as the Roman Empire: he did not start with a preconceived plan; he worked out a plan by tentatives; and this exception was one of the tentatives, turned to good purpose in the country where it led him.

(2) The theorists leave out of sight the most grave aspect of epilepsy, as a disease of the brain which is steadily progressive and produces deterioration of mind and usually of character. Nothing in the career of Paul suggests the slightest tendency to degeneration. His spirit only grows more elevated as time passes.

Dr. Seeligmüller's method of exhibiting his proof is, in the first place, to take the description of Paul's character and achievements and activity as stated by Krenkel, to compare this description with Krenkel's epilepsy theory, and to show the inconsistency of the two. No neurological expert, as he says, could for a moment think of regarding a character like Krenkel's Paul as afflicted with epilepsy in any degree.

Every reader has formed for himself his own conception

of Paul's boundless and inexhaustible energy, his vast intellectual power, his marvellous command of the resources of the Greek language, and his lofty moral character growing more lofty and noble as time passed : this he can compare with Dr. Seeligmüller's picture of the epileptic. The two are obviously irreconcilable. Either the German Professor's picture is coloured and untrustworthy, or Paul was not afflicted with epilepsy. Whether he was afflicted by some other disease, which would reduce his visions to mere delusions, is another question, on which we need not here enter. There will be something more to say about it later.

In the second place, the Halle Professor takes up in detail Krenkel's positive arguments. He shows that certain facts recorded by or about Paul have no value as indications of an epileptic condition, as for example Krenkel mentions that the sensation which Paul experienced of suffering blows on the head points to epilepsy[1] (p. 46). No expert in neurology would consider such sensations as pathologically indicative or helpful in diagnosis. Moreover, this argument depends on a doubtful interpretation of 2 Corinthians xii. 7.

Wendland,[2] who supports Krenkel, quotes Ilberg on the *Strafrechtliche Bedeutung der Epilepsie*[3] to the effect that recollection is not necessarily destroyed in the case of the milder phenomena occurring during intervening periods (i.e. *Dämmerzustände*) between severer attacks of *grand mal*.

---

[1] Presumably Krenkel's argument is founded on the fact that the epileptic, falling in a fit (*grand mal*), strikes his head hard on the ground. He suffers no pain from the blow, however, and remembers nothing about it, although the blow might produce effects which would remain and be felt after consciousness returns.

[2] *Hellenisch-römische Kultur*, p. 125 ff. I have not read either Wendland or Krenkel: I started to read the latter's *Beiträge*, but found very soon that there was nothing to gain from it.

[3] *Zft. f. d. gesammte Strafrechtswissenschaft*, xxi., 1901, p. 45.

Dr. Seeligmüller replies that this assertion rests largely on the common tendency to mistake automatic continuance of the interrupted action for real recollection of what occurred during the unconscious moment (*absentia mentis*): in different parts of his treatise he gives various examples of this resumption of the interrupted action, which is a quite well-known phenomenon. The same mistake is often made in the case of *petit mal*. Recollection of *Dämmerzustände* is at best faint and confused, and often fails entirely. There is nothing in it like Paul's vivid and powerful memory of his vision.

Further, nothing but the *grand mal* could for a moment be thought of as explaining Paul's conversion with its strongly marked phenomena.

The occasional expressions of self-glorification that occur in Paul's writings—what he himself calls "boasting" or "glorying"—might perhaps be regarded by some persons as examples of the egotistic and self-centred view that characterises the epileptic in the process of degeneration. But, first, these expressions are forced from Paul in self-defence, and he generally apologises for them: secondly, we must set against them the general tone of extreme humility that characterises his writings, for he regards himself as nought and worthless and criminal, saved from moral death by external power: thirdly, his whole life of self-sacrifice and his extraordinary power of understanding others and sympathising with them, contradict the idea that those occasional expressions indicate a self-centred view or show satisfaction with himself. Krenkel rightly does not even mention this argument, but passes it by as not worthy of consideration.

No evidence results from Krenkel's use of the description of Paul's personal appearance, as given in the *Acta of*

Paul and Thekla. This description contains nothing that possesses even the smallest value in diagnosis. Epileptic sufferers are quite frequently tall, well-proportioned, and handsome. Paul's plainness, or even ugliness, his small stature, his bowed legs, his meeting-eyebrows, might have a thousand other causes than epilepsy, and are in no way indicative of epilepsy. The one detail in that description that is of value is the eyes, which expressed the fire and spirit of an angel. Through the eyes the mind speaks most directly; and the mind that spoke through Paul's eyes was not that of an epileptic.

One of Krenkel's arguments is founded on Paul's depreciation of his own powers as a preacher in 1 Corinthians ii. 1-3. He omitted to study ii. 4-7; and he was evidently unable to perceive the irony of 1 Corinthians i.-iv., that masterpiece in all literature of graceful and delightful irony. It is not uncharacteristic of Krenkel's work that he shows himself so insensitive to the finer qualities of literature.

The person who, like Krenkel, finds in Paul's shaving of his head at Cenchreae (Acts xviii. 18) a proof of epilepsy, could easily find such proof in every act of Paul's life, if he only set himself resolutely to do so, and in every act of every man's life.

The truth is that the epileptic theory in Paul's case (where not due to the straining after originality) arises largely from the desire to eliminate the visions and other apparently marvellous phenomena as untrustworthy. We have the strongest evidence for them in Paul's own words. We cannot get rid of that evidence without getting rid of Paul (as Manen did). Krenkel and others, however, try at once to keep their Paul and throw him overboard: when he talked of visions, etc., he was an epileptic in a developed stage of degeneration : in all other respects he was the sanest, the ablest, the most vigorous of men. The nerve-physician can only reply that this is impossible : you cannot have an epileptic like that. There was only one Paul, not two. The theory is merely a proof of ignorance. "Kren-kel's knowledge of epilepsy must be called very scanty and defective, and often fundamentally false ; and he is quite unable even to distinguish the phenomena of the *grand mal* from those which occur during the intervening periods" (p. 42).

Krenkel, however, has already attempted to meet this counter-argument : Paul's ability to do so much, although he was an epileptic, is a proof of his marvellous genius and lofty character—or shall we say, of the Divine power and inspiration which worked through him and in him ? Then we are landed in a more marvellóus theory than the plain and simple one. To avoid accepting a "miracle," Krenkel proposes to accept a greater "miracle". There is nothing to say except that the whole theory is "*grundfalsch*".

The theory of epilepsy, as our author thinks, could never have been started, except by persons who knew nothing about neurology. It has been unwarily taken up by a few medical men without carefully studying the evidence, simply because it suggested a medical cause for certain remarkable and obscure phenomena in the career of Paul.[1] However these phenomena ought to be explained, epilepsy furnishes no explanation. There is, of course, a marked tendency in the last thirty or forty years to explain all unusual mental phenomena, from the visions of Paul to the character of the confirmed criminal, as due to pathological causes. The tendency to explain genius as a form of insanity has also been strong in recent times, and since

[1] Lombroso is dismissed in the sharpest word of criticism that Dr. Seeligmüller uses as " already quite antiquated ".

Dryden (or a much earlier time) people have pleased themselves with the empty idea that "great wits to madness are allied". This alliance, however, is due not to the greatness of the wit, but to the want of balance in the moral character.

This leads on to another question and another subject of discussion. It is maintained that many of the greatest men in history have been epileptics. If they were epileptic, why should not Paul also have been epileptic, and yet have retained for so many years his marvellous powers of mind? Julius Caesar, Charles V., Napoleon I., Mohammed, Cambyses, etc.,[1] are all enumerated among those who were victims of epilepsy.

Dr. Seeligmüller meets this argument with a flat negative, almost with contempt. It was in the infancy of medicine, even before neurological science had been born, that this idea arose. He asks who records the evidence, what is the authority of these writers, what the credibility of the assertion. He regards all the cases mentioned with the utmost suspicion. As for Cambyses the sole evidence is one single sentence in Herodotus to the effect that on account of the severe bodily pains that he endured through the "sacred sickness" which afflicted him from birth, his mind suffered along with his body, and he used to act in the style of a madman towards his relatives. Dr. Seeligmüller wastes not one word in refutation (p. 63). He has previously pointed out that epilepsy cannot be called a painful disease in itself; and just before, as bearing on this subject generally, he quotes a paragraph from Kussmaul's article *Ueber Epilepsie.*[2] No historical

---

[1] Cromwell is, I think, given by others as an example of an epileptic.

[2] *Deutsche Revue,* Oct.-Dec., 1902. The following sentences are a loose and abbreviated translation of Kussmaul's paragraph.

person, even if his general character corresponds to the
description of an epileptic, can be taken as proved to have
been an epileptic, except on the ground that typical attacks
of epilepsy are recorded of him : the diagnosis will be more
or less probable according as attacks of the less developed
kind, like *absentia mentis*, preliminary symptoms (*aura*), and
Dämmerzustände, have been proved. Even these only
warrant a conjecture of epilepsy. On the other hand, it is
not justifiable to explain striking personalities in history
as epileptics, merely because they gave free play to their
passions and inclinations, and showed themselves changeable, and because their motives for action are not clear.

In the case of Mohammed one should prefer to the theory
of epilepsy almost any conceivable form of illness which is
accompanied by ecstatic conditions. Both Sprenger and
Pelman reject expressly the epilepsy theory about him ;
but Dr. Seeligmüller, not being an Orientalist, refrains from
detailed discussion of this case.

It is recorded that Julius Caesar suffered from epileptic
fits. The Professor at Halle does not investigate this case ;
but the tone of his treatise leaves little doubt what his
answer would be. We have no trustworthy evidence that
those fainting fits were really epileptic. We are not informed whether they became worse as time passed ; and
everything that is known about Caesar negatives conclusively
the idea that he was afflicted with the brain-disease called
epilepsy.

The case of Napoleon is one to which Dr. Seeligmüller
has given considerable attention. Krenkel's proof of
Napoleon's epilepsy is completed within eight lines of text
and two footnotes. That distinct traces of moral degeneration, such as is characteristic of epileptics, can be seen in
the career of Napoleon is true ; but is every person that

degenerates morally an epileptic? As has been stated above, all such symptoms occur equally distinctly in non-epileptic persons. As to Napoleon's fits, those who call them epileptic are learned men and great historians, but they are not nerve experts. Krenkel quotes from a nerve expert, Wildermuth, a sentence to which every expert will assent, that in pronounced cases of degeneracy the epileptic shows the ugly picture of the typical scoundrel; but the expert does not say either that Napoleon and Paul were epileptics, or that every scoundrel is an epileptic.

The learned Professor quotes the case of a boy four years old, strong, full-blooded, spoilt by parents who thought that the fits of passion, to which he abandoned himself with increasing frequency as he found that they procured him his desires, were epileptic attacks. The cure which was prescribed was a tumbler of cold water dashed in his face and a good sound thrashing thereafter. This boy's type of mind seems to the expert to be as like Napoleon's as one hair is to another; and the Professor proceeds to sketch, on the authority of Lombroso, the almost inevitable effect produced on such a nature by his early training and surroundings.[1] On Taine, Napoleon makes the impression of a great bandit; the laws of morals and propriety did not exist for him; at school he was a master of lies; the lives of two million of men were nought in his eyes compared with the attainment of his aims; but his vast powers of mind and energy enabled him to comprehend that his world-wide purposes, selfish as

---

[1] In a character which possesses little natural strength of will and purpose, but only irrational obstinacy in trifling matters, the effect of such training is in some cases to produce (so far as my experience in the East goes) a state of mind like demoniac possession, in which an originally ill-balanced mind is given over wholly to the dictates of evil passion without any counter-balancing influence. The only possible cure is "conversion" and a growing sense of religion and duty.

they were, could be realised only through the imposing of law, order and discipline on the subject world.

As to Napoleon's attacks of sleepiness and his nerve-fits (which he experienced already at school), the Halle Professor of nerve-diseases regards them as wholly lacking the true character of epilepsy. Taking one typical case of a so-called epileptic fit, described by an eye-witness, Talleyrand, he quotes the whole account, and shows that in numerous respects it either lacks certain characteristics of an epileptic seizure, or presents positive characteristics that are inconsistent with epilepsy. He regards it as a nervous attack due to extreme excitation, great fatigue from overwork, and above all to the sufferer's habit of eating hurriedly and ravenously: it occurred a few minutes after dinner, probably an indigestible dinner, at Strasburg. The two attacks of sleep during battles recorded (but not well described in detail) he considers to have been simply the result of over-fatigue, in which nature at last overpowered even the energy and endurance of Napoleon.

These symptoms show nothing but the most superficial resemblance to true epilepsy. Binswanger [1] has been far from careful in his diagnosis of the evidence regarding Napoleon, Mohammed, etc. Dr. Seeligmüller mentions cases from his own practice, and describes in some detail a case of fainting with almost all the external appearances of epilepsy, which occurred to a young man of good family, exposed during his year of military service to the cruelty and injustice of a vulgar non-commissioned officer: the fit was due to extreme fatigue caused by long-continued marching at the double in great heat, and to suppressed anger at the injustice of this punishment, which was inflicted from mere personal spite. This fit proved to have

Die Epilepsie, Vienna, 1899, p. 314.

no real epileptic character, as the sequel showed; for the youth grew into a strong and mentally gifted man.

The dictum of Lombroso, a writer whose work is pronounced to be "already quite antiquated"—that "Epilepsy is possibly the foundation of genius, and the occasion of genius is a degenerative psychosis of the epileptoid species"—is one which Dr. Seeligmüller cannot accept. The idea that Paul was an epileptic is an instance of the attempt to apply this dictum to a special case, and is as false as the dictum itself.

There are some places in which the Halle Professor's arguments may at first sight disappoint readers, because they are founded on lack of evidence that certain phenomena can be proved in the case of Paul. This kind of reasoning approximates to, or is identical with, the argument *a silentio*, which is in most respects false and worse than useless. But, in this case, it is employed because the general principle has been laid down by high medical authority[1] that in all cases where the individual cannot be subjected to direct personal examination, epilepsy must not be presumed, unless typical attacks of epilepsy are recorded. This is not a rule devised for the case of Paul, but is a universal principle. Even where the positive indications demanded by the principle can be established, only a presumption and conjecture as to the existence of epilepsy follows. Without the proof of such positive indications, there is not even a presumption. How necessary then is it to demand some positive evidence of *aura* and *Dämmerzustände* before saying point-blank that Paul and other great men were epileptics.

Still it must be remembered in the case of Paul that the last thing Luke would have been likely to think of, and the thing most completely discordant with his design as historian of the Church, was to record such phenomena. He

[1] From Kussmaul.

was not, and never intended to be, a biographer of Paul; and all studies or criticisms of the Acts, which proceed on the supposition that Luke desired to give an account of the life either of Paul or of Peter, or of the history and achievements of any or all of the Apostles, deserve forthwith to be set aside as valueless.

Such record as the Professor demands could not be expected; and the argument that there is no such record, though conclusive to the mind of a judge trying a case in court, suffers in the estimation of ordinary historical students. After all, ancient history must often be reduced to a balancing of probabilities; and in the case of Paul we could not venture to dismiss a theory in this matter because it is not positively proved. We have rather to disprove it by positive reasons, and Dr. Seeligmüller succeeds in doing that without having to trust to the mere lack of evidence in support of the epilepsy theory.

From the medical point of view, what was the disease from which Paul suffered? The Professor (p. 70 ff.), rejects without a word such suggestions as temptations of the flesh, the sting of conscience for his sins in the past, and opponents or difficulties that hindered his work. Headaches of a bad kind, especially the so-called *Migräne*, present some of the features of the "thorn in the flesh"; but lack the supremely necessary feature. Headache, however extreme, cannot be supposed to have prostrated so utterly a man of Paul's energy: in the Professor's practice they have never proved sufficient to make a man of high energy and determination abandon his work. Only in the form of *Augen-migräne* might this explanation be admitted as possible, because such attacks are accompanied by loss of consciousness, delirium, and a condition resembling a fit (p. 73).

On the other hand, the theory of ophthalmia or any other

disease of the eyes cannot be brought into accordance with modern medical knowledge. Equally unworthy of serious consideration are toothache, stones, hæmorrhoids, hypochondriac attacks of fits of melancholia, leprosy, neurasthenia. The last is suggested by the Professor's esteemed medical friend, Professor Herzog of Munich, who was presumably interested from childhood in Pauline topics, owing to his upbringing in the house of his father, the famous Encyclopædist. The phenomena of neurasthenia, though to some degree worthy of consideration, do not produce in the nerve-expert such an impression as suits the case of Paul.[1]

The theory of malaria, according to Dr. Seeligmüller, stands in quite a different category. Malarial fever is marked by periodic or intermittent attacks, which temporarily incapacitate the sufferer. It induces a chronic liability to attack, which is lasting, and often life-long.[2] It produces as its consequents or "equivalents" sharp neuralgic attacks of an obstinate and temporarily debilitating character, and these present the same general phenomena that give on the first view some plausibility to the theory of headaches or of neurasthenia. As an incidental proof of the connection between malaria and neuralgia, Dr. Seeligmüller mentions that neuralgia in the head has been for centuries familiar to physicians as *malaria larvata*. Malaria was a disease common in the country, and therefore one to which Paul was readily exposed.

Between these two possibilities — *Augen-migräne* and

---

[1] Herzog, though a respected and valued medical colleague, is not (says the Halle Professor) a specialist in nervous diseases. The Munich Professor agrees in rejecting epilepsy, because it induces in greater or less degree a progressive weakening of the mental powers, which is irreconcilable with the character of Paul.

[2] Medical friends of my acquaintance maintain that it is never completely eradicated.

malaria—Dr. Seeligmüller for the present cannot decide. He is not aware of any other sufficient medical cause ; but he leaves the case open as regards these two.

One consideration must be added to the learned Professor's argument. There is no proof that *Augen-migräne* was considered in that country and at that time to be the result of Divine anger,[1] except in so far as the popular mind may have looked on it as simply a kind of malaria-fever (which was to the non-medical mind very natural, since the phenomena of *Augen-migräne* present much similarity to certain effects of chronic malaria). It is, however, now well established by many imprecations, inscribed in ancient times on stones or leaden tablets which have been found in Asia Minor and published in recent years, that in that country fever was believed to be caused by a special visitation of Divine anger, and that the gods were entreated by the composers of such curses to afflict with fever the person or persons against whom the curse was directed.[2] Thus malaria fulfils the conditions in a way that *Augen-migräne* does not do. In some of those curses the eyes are mentioned merely as a part of the human body, on which any and every disease or mutilation is invoked. The imprecator would be quite satisfied with any other disease, but the one that he specially prays for is the unseen fire of fever which burns up the bodily strength without any external affection through the direct destroying power of the god.

I may be allowed to add that, from the time when I began to study the biography of Paul minutely, chronic attacks of malarial fever appeared to me to be clearly and

---

[1] That Paul's disease was considered to be so is implied in Paul's own words (Gal. iv. 13 ff.) ; and this is universally admitted.

[2] See references and examples in the present writer's *Hist. Comm. on Galatians*, p. 423.

inexorably indicated by the words which Paul himself uses in describing the attacks from which he suffered. Every one who lived in Asiatic Turkey before the cause of that disease, and the way of averting it, were known, had abundant opportunity of observing its symptoms and external character in his friends, and of experimenting in them with his own person. Paul, like the moderns until the pathological character of the illness was discovered a few years ago, could only state external character and symptoms; and hence his words were full of meaning to one who had seen and felt that kind of fever, which formerly no one in the country[1] escaped. Every one who had lived long in the country, and was not totally devoid of medical sense and aptitude, must learn to treat it, to watch it, and to observe every symptom.

Note.—In respect of the general theory that genius is a form of epileptic degeneration, I may refer to the first chapter of William James's *Varieties of Religious Experience*, where that opinion is criticised and dismissed as valueless. I owe the reference to Dr. Ormonde, formerly of Princeton, now President of Grove City College.

[1] That no one escaped, and that every one, however invulnerable he at first appeared to be, succumbed in the long run, was the opinion expressed to me more than thirty years ago by many residents in Western Asia Minor.

L. THE HYMN OF HEAVENLY LOVE
(I CORINTHIANS XIII)[1]

Section XLII. has the form of a survey of part of his Excellency Dr. Harnack's remarkable and suggestive study of the thirteenth chapter of First Corinthians, the "Hymn of Heavenly Love".[2] It is therefore suitable to add here a survey of certain other points in this notable article, which bear on our subject.

Beginning after the thoroughgoing and methodical German fashion from a minute study of text and words, it moves onward to a broad and lofty survey of religious thought ; and in the discussion of the words used by the Apostle it sometimes throws a brilliant light on his thought and on his outlook over the world and man and God. One hardly ventures to praise a writer who stands so high as Dr. Harnack. We learn from him, and are thankful to him ; but he stands as a classic, above the level of mere laudation. One learns method and nobility of thought from studying him, even when differing from some detail in his interpretation ; and the result is to strengthen our conviction that Paul is, in one way, the greatest among those who interpreted to men the religion of Jesus, and that we never understand the Apostle rightly until we take him

---

[1] This name is applied to the chapter in the writer's *Pictures of the Apostolic Church*, 1910, p. 232 (published 1909 in the *Sunday School Times*) : it is taken from Spenser's "Hymn of Heavenly Love".

[2] It appears in an authorised translation from the Berlin Academy's *Sitzungsberichte*, published in the *Expositor*, May and June, 1912.

on the highest moral plane to which human nature is capable
of rising.[1]

The title " Hymn " is naturally applied by every sympathetic reader to this chapter ; *das hohe Lied von der Liebe*
is the name that Dr. Harnack uses. The chapter is not
written in plain prose: it has the measured stately movement and rhythm of a hymn.[2] We notice that when Paul's
religious emotion rises to the highest pitch, it has a certain
note of enthusiasm—in the literal sense of the Greek word,
viz., possession by the Divine power—which tends to
impart to the verbal expression a rhythmic flow. This Dr.
Harnack brings out by printing the Greek text and his own
German rendering in shorter verses and in three longer
measures or stanzas.

---

[1] *Pauline and Other Studies*, p. 38.

[2] It is not the rhythm of the rhetorical schools, as taught in Paul's time :
in that we must agree with Deissmann against Blass. Yet there moves through
the " Hymn " a natural rhythm, perfectly spontaneous and untaught, accommodating itself to the thought, which Dr. Harnack has rightly recognised
and well described in this study. Dr. Deissmann rather scorns the idea that
there is any rhythm in Paul. Because the artificial rhythm of the rhetoricians
can only be discovered through the too violent process applied by Blass,
therefore Deissmann holds that there is no rhythm. The defect lies in
the ear and the sense of the modern scholar. Blass had the ear for the
rhythm, but being accustomed to think of the Greek rhetorical style, he tried
to prove that Paul's rhythm is identical with that of the schools. It is
an equally great error to miss the natural perfection of the Pauline rhythm
and to deny its existence. The defect of Dr. Deissmann's work is that,
having got the true idea that Paul wrote letters in the language of the time,
he concludes that this is almost purely the language of the uneducated,
that Paul was uneducated, non-literary, "unknown" in the fullest sense
(see his *St. Paul*, p. 77 and elsewhere). He cannot feel the delicate irony
of Paul's language in 1 Cor. i.-iv. To Deissmann Paul's expression, being
intended for the uneducated, is couched in their own words : because Paul's
work takes the form of letters, therefore it is not literature, but rude, unpolished,
non-literary. On the contrary the letters are for the most part in the highest
class of literature. I appeal from Blass to Wilamowitz, who knows (if any
man does) what Greek literature is.

It is especially when he speaks of the unspeakable and illimitable kindness of God or His love to men that Paul's expression casts itself in a lyric form. Hence the renewed study of I Corinthians xiii. only deepens our conviction that the lyrical tone of I Timothy iii. 16, or of some verses in Ephesians, springs out of the heart of the writer, and is not due to their being quoted from a contemporary hymn.[1] Amid marked diversity on the surface the deep-lying psychological resemblance in nature between the Epistles to Timothy and the earlier letters of Paul is the most powerful argument that they are all the work of one mind and heart.[2]

The Hymn, as Dr. Harnack says, stands in close relation to the needs and defects of the Corinthian character; and yet rises far above any individual and personal reference to a perfectly universal expression of the nature of God and His relation to men. The quality of which the Hymn sings "embraces the most comprehensive and the strongest kind of good-will to all men, a deep and burning desire to seek after the progress of the race and the benefit of every individual with whom we are brought into relations; it develops the side of our nature in which we can approximate nearest to the Divine nature, because it is the human counterpart of the feeling that God entertains to man".[3]

That is the invariable character of Paul's letters. He never applied superficial remedies to mere external symptoms. He treated the failing or evil in a congregation as the outward effect of a deep-seated want or misapprehension to which all human nature is exposed; and he tried to raise the Church to a higher view of life by purifying and

---

[1] If there was such a hymn, which is a quite possible and even probable supposition, it is more likely to have been founded on Paul than quoted by him.

[2] *Expositor*, April, 1912, p. 359.

[3] *Pictures of the Apostolic Church*, p. 230.

elevating their conception of the Divine nature. The only way in which a merely individual and external treatment comes into play is when penalty and punishment must be applied : this is apportioned according to the individual action and the circumstances of the particular case.[1]   Otherwise he treats errors by moral and religious principles, which are universal in their application.

I may be permitted, in gratitude for what I have learned from Dr. Harnack's study of this *Hohe Lied*, to add some remarks on three points.   In the first, I am obliged to differ from him, not I think in a contrary direction, but rather through proceeding further in the same direction and thus appreciating more highly the perfect harmony and beauty of Paul's tone.   In the other two points, where Dr. Harnack compels perfect assent, my aim is to proceed to certain arguments about the authorship of the Pastoral Epistles. Amid the differences which divide those Epistles from the earlier letters of Paul, there reigns a psychological unity and a real identity of originating heart, which prove the authorship; and Dr. Harnack's exposition of the Hymn recalls to my mind analogous phenomena in the Pastorals.

I. Dr. Harnack is fully justified in laying much stress on the transition by which Paul passes from the general exposition to this lyric and emotional Hymn, and in studying closely the manner in which this transition is effected in the last verse of chapter xii.   A strong light is thus thrown on Paul's character, and on the tact and delicacy of his dealing with the Corinthians.

As to one point, however, in Dr. Harnack's interpretation of the verse of the transition, xii. 31, I regret to be unconvinced by his reasoning : a view diverse from his seems to place Paul's thought and tone and method on a higher level.

[1] See Section XXXI.

In respect of the construction of this sentence, it may be added that Westcott and Hort differ from him in placing the paragraph division in the middle of xii. 31, and incorporating the second clause of that verse in the Hymn of chapter xiii. ; whereas he (like most scholars) connects closely the two clauses of xii. 31 (in which he seems to me to be right).

According to the interpretation of xii. 31, for which Dr. Harnack contends, Paul places his own "super-excellent way" in marked contrast with the Corinthian way. The Corinthians admire spiritual "gifts," and eagerly desire them as the crown of the Christian career; but Paul, on the contrary, advises these young converts rather to admire and strive after the Christian virtues, and indicates this to them as a more excellent way than theirs of leading the Christian life. They should seek the Christian virtues and not the gifts. Dr. Harnack takes the word χαρίσματα in xii. 31 to mean "Christian virtues," whereas in the rest of the passage χαρίσματα, according to its usual sense, denotes "gifts". This is violent and awkward; and (as I think) it misses the beauty of the thought.

Such a pointed and strong contrast between the Corinthian and the Pauline way seems, moreover, not to be in harmony with Paul's tone in this part of his letter. He here studiously suppresses his own individuality, makes light of his own merits, and avoids everything that could seem like pressing his way on the Corinthians or depreciating theirs. Anything of that kind is out of keeping with the tone of chapter xiii. The delicate and gracious courtesy which lights up this part of the letter is quite remarkable. By a skilful use of the first and the third person he avoids suggesting either that the Corinthians are lacking in love (though their want of it prompts the praise of its excellence and necessity) or that he himself possesses love. All hint of fault is put in the first person singular: "if I have every merit and good action, but have not love, I am value-less". On the other hand, where he in positive terms praises the quality of love, he avoids the first person singular, lest this should seem like a claim to the possession of it.[1] There is no trace in chapter xiii. of the irony, subtle and polished and gentle as it is, that rules in chapters i.-iv. The time for that has passed, or perhaps one should rather say the Apostle's mood has changed.[2]

Paul sees what is lacking in the Corinthians' spirit and conduct; but he does not, as yet, criticise or find fault with their way. He merely praises what is good in it, while he gradually leads them up to a higher level of judging and acting.

There is in xii. 31 no comparison, no direct contrast be-tween Paul's way and theirs. The adverbial expression, $\kappa\alpha\theta'$ $\dot{\upsilon}\pi\epsilon\rho\beta o\lambda\dot{\eta}\nu$, which at first sight appears rather awkward as attached to a noun, is carefully chosen to avoid any suggestion of contrast. The connection is made by "and" not by "but"; only the word "still," $\ddot{\epsilon}\tau\iota$, imparts to the "and" a touch of hesitation and pondering: "and still,

---

[1] *Pictures of the Apostolic Church*, p. 232 f.

[2] That the longer Epistles of Paul were written, not at a single effort, but in parts with some interval between, seems to me to be the explanation of many of the phenomena in both First and Second Corinthians. A dictated Epistle, which treats of such varied topics in a tone so lofty and legislative and philosophic, was thought out in sections. This was stated in my *His-torical Commentary on Corinthians*, §§ xxxix.-xliv. (*Expositor*, March, 1901, pp. 220 ff.). It might be illustrated from Spenser's first letter to Gabriel Harvey; Gregory Smith in his edition recognises that the end of the letter is written a week earlier than the beginning; but my friend Mr. J. C. Smith points out to me that the end of the letter had been written earlier and sent as a separate letter, but was lost on the way, so that Spenser repeats it at the end of his new letter, after explaining the circumstances. The dates are 16 and 5 Oct. 1579.

along with the excellence of your conduct in desiring eagerly the gifts, you should always remember that there is a way, a super-excellent way," *viz.* the way of love, which is then described in the Hymn.

Like the introduction of the Hymn, so is the conclusion, xiv. 1, with which Paul resumes his didactic exposition in plain prose. "Pursue love; hunt it as a hunter seeks his prey, determined to get it; but strive after the spiritual gifts, and especially the gift of prophecy." Here, again, the two ways are mentioned side by side: both are worthy of eager desire: neither is recommended exclusively or even preferentially (unless διώκειν can be interpreted as a markedly stronger term [1] than ζηλοῦν). The parallel between xii. 31 and xiv. 1 is perfect, though the order must of course be reversed: in the introduction the way of love has to be mentioned last, in the conclusion it is necessarily placed first.

Hence Paul does not use in xii. 31 the comparative degree of an adjective; he does not say "I will show you a more excellent way," for that would suggest a comparison of his own way with the Corinthian way. He does not even employ the definite article, for that form would suggest that he is showing "the super-excellent way," the one true and supreme way. So perfectly chosen is the language here, that even the addition of that little word "the" would spoil it. Dr. Harnack's interpretation of "the better gifts" as "the Christian virtues" misses this! Hence he feels the want of the article to be rather awkward: he is a little surprised at the omission of "the," and even points out that occasionally in Paul the article is omitted carelessly.

On the contrary, the language in xii. 31 is so perfectly

---

[1] Such an interpretation can hardly be justified; both are strong and emphatic terms.

chosen that the smallest change would weaken the delicate effect.

We might attempt to express in rough modern words the run of the expression in the end of chapter xii. thus : " all the gifts of the spirit are good and desirable, each in its own way : they are, however, diverse, and they vary in dignity, and men cannot possess them all : all cannot be prophets, or teach, or speak with tongues. But strive ye after the gifts in proportion to their worth. They are good. They are excellent. Be eager to attain them. And yet—and still—there is a super-excellent way, and this I show you in the Hymn."

The term "gifts" must therefore be understood in the same sense throughout chapters xii.-xiv. It would be an obscurity very unlike Paul's style to pass in the middle suddenly to a different sense for the word, and then return to the former sense. The difficulty of his style arises from other causes : his reasoning moves with rapid and long steps which are not easily followed ; often he sees intuitively rather than reasons, giving an argument that seems to us arbitrary or far-fetched to justify his intuition ; but he does not commonly operate with terms whose meaning he consciously changes back and forwards in the sequence of his expression.

Still, if the supposition of such rapid change gave a better flow to the passage, we should have to accept it. We find, however, that it lacks the perfect sympathy with the spirit and harmony of Paul's thought.

Against the uniformity for which we contend in the meaning of the term "gifts" throughout this passage, Dr. Harnack brings the objection that the Apostle, who has recently described the "gifts" as imparted by God according to His free will and choice, could hardly advise the Corinthians to "strive after" those same gifts. There is, however, no real inconsistency, but only an apparent difference, which is felt when one contemplates the situation with too narrowly logical a view. It is truly and perfectly consistent with the Pauline and the Christian philosophy to strive earnestly after the gifts of God: they are the free gift of God, imparted at His own will, and yet men may and should eagerly desire them and strive after them.[1] Such is the nature of the Divine gifts and graces: such is the true relation of the Christian man to his God.

The common interpretation of xii. 31, which Dr. Harnack mentions, is rightly rejected by him: it is indefensible from every point of view, and fails to catch the gracious and lovely current of Paul's thought. As he says (and I assume that he is right in this: I have not read carefully their exegesis), almost all the commentators understand that, in the first clause of xii. 31, Paul advises the Corinthians to strive by preference after those spiritual gifts which serve best for edification, i.e. to prefer prophecy or teaching to *glossolalia*.

This is to be rejected for two reasons. In the first place, it disregards the order and natural connection of words: $\zeta\eta\lambda o\hat{v}\tau\epsilon$ $\tau\grave{a}$ $\chi a\rho\acute{\iota}\sigma\mu a\tau a$ suggests forthwith, "strive after the gifts"; then the addition of $\tau\grave{a}$ $\mu\epsilon\acute{\iota}\zeta o\nu a$ $(\kappa\rho\epsilon\acute{\iota}\tau\tau o\nu a)$[2] gives an almost predicative sense, "according to their degree of excellence". The force of this sentence is not to be interpreted as if the words were equivalent to $\tau\grave{a}$ $\mu\epsilon\acute{\iota}\zeta o\nu a$ $\chi a\rho\acute{\iota}\sigma\mu a\tau a$ or $\tau\grave{a}$ $\mu\epsilon\acute{\iota}\zeta o\nu a$ $\tau\hat{\omega}\nu$ $\chi a\rho\iota\sigma\mu\acute{a}\tau\omega\nu$.

[1] We have found abundant occasion to remark the tendency of Pauline thought to express itself in two apparently, yet only apparently, contradictory statements: see Section XLVI. and elsewhere from IX. onwards.

[2] It is difficult to determine whether $\mu\epsilon\acute{\iota}\zeta o\nu a$ of some MSS., or $\kappa\rho\epsilon\acute{\iota}\tau\tau o\nu a$ of others, is the true text. We refer to Dr. Harnack's discussion: he prefers $\kappa\rho\epsilon\acute{\iota}\tau\tau o\nu a$.

In the second place, it is not the Apostle's purpose here to draw hard and fast distinctions, or to insist that the Corinthians should make *glossolalia* a secondary matter: what he means is that all gifts are good, and should be sought after in proportion to their goodness. By his form of expression he leaves open for the moment the possibility that some may be better than others; that topic will come later. Yet even when in xiv. 1-4 he gives the preference to prophecy over speaking with tongues, he immediately adds in xiv. 5, "I wish you all to speak with tongues, but still more that you should prophesy". This is just a re-emphasising of xii. 31a and xiv. 1; but now, after the distinction has been drawn in xiv. 2-4, the statement of the thought becomes more definite and precise: "All gifts, however, are good: *glossolalia* is good: my wish is that you should all have that gift, but still more that you should have the power of prophecy as a higher and greater gift".

This gradual movement towards definiteness about these gifts is evident, when xii. 31a is correctly interpreted. The movement continues throughout the following passage from xiv. 12, "since ye are eager strivers after spiritual gifts, seek that you may be rich unto the edifying of the church," to xiv. 39, "strive after the power of prophecy, and forbid not to speak with tongues". In this last verse prophecy alone is prescribed as the object which one should strive after; and *glossolalia* is merely "not forbidden". This is the climax.

The whole passage, xii.-xiv., is concerned with the gifts of the spirit; with infinite courtesy and tenderness Paul tries to raise the Corinthians' minds to a higher outlook and a nobler aspiration. In the middle of this passage it is not allowable to interpret "the gifts" once in a totally different sense as if it meant the fundamental Christian virtues.

All that I have said regarding the delicacy of Paul's atti-tude towards the Corinthians' way would be falsified, if Weiss's view were correct that already in xii. 29 f. Paul "has reproved and found fault with the Corinthians' habit of ambitiously striving after the higher gifts".[1]   This mean-ing I cannot gather from Paul's words.   Weiss forces pre-maturely into xii. the depreciation of one gift (not of all gifts), which is expressed very tenderly and very lovingly in xiv.; and he transforms Paul's gentle, delicate deprecia-tion into a harsh and brusque condemnation, which has no resemblance to, and no justification in, the kindly, yet emotional, words of the letter.

Weiss's words would be justifiable if he were expressing his own opinion about the Corinthians in the language that best suited the strength of his personal feeling; but he is here giving a *résumé* of Paul's words.   One feels obliged to say that the exegesis of Paul which expresses in such strong, sledge-hammer style the courteous and gracious language of the Apostle is dooming itself beforehand to misunder-stand Paul's attitude.

II. Dr. Harnack's defence (which, in the present writer's opinion, is perfectly successful and conclusive)[2] of the read-ing καυχήσωμαι in verse 3, is one of the most delightful and illuminative things that I have ever read about the character of Paul.   It shows us the great Apostle in his relation to the Pharisaic and Judaic view of life; it illustrates the influence which the strictly Pharisaic way of thinking exercised on his mind, and his invariable custom of taking that thought on the highest level of which it is capable; and, finally, it lets us trace his triumphant emergence from the Pharisaic view to a higher level.

---

[1] *Nachdem er soeben das ehrgeizige Streben nach höheren Gaben zurück-gewiesen und gemahnt hat . . .* (v. 29 f.).

[2] See note p. 343.   It is rejected by Dr. Deissmann in *St. Paul, a Study*.

This gradual victory over Pharisaism—in other words, the whole life of Paul in his relation to the Pharisaic mode of thinking—might be illustrated at greater length; the path which Dr. Harnack has here indicated might be followed throughout a wide range of ideas; but I here refer to it only in order to draw an inference from it. Without intending it, Dr. Harnack's exposition makes it easy to see why an idea like this, which is in Paul's letters so frequently expressed by the verbs καυχάομαι, ἐγκαυχάομαι, and the nouns καύχησις, καύχημα, never occurs in the Pastoral Epistles.

Those Epistles differ as regards vocabulary from the other letters, not merely in using many words not found in the letters, but also to some extent in making little employment of certain ideas and words which are much more frequently used in the earlier letters. None of those four Greek words, which occur fifty-five times in Paul's earliest eight letters, are found in the three Pastorals.

Now, to quote Dr. Harnack's own words, "the Pharisaic fashion of thinking was fundamentally amended by Paul, until he at last did away with it entirely". It is true that this group of words is absent from the Pastorals; but also it is the case that none of them occur in Colossians, and there is only a single occurrence in Ephesians.

The Apostle was naturally most prone to use this form of expression where he was most on the defensive, and where he was recommending and fortifying against attack his own conception of the Gospel: therefore the words are most frequent in Second Corinthians. The same way of contemplating his own life was exemplified in the opening words of his *Apologia* before the Sanhedrin—an *Apologia* which was never completed—see Acts xxiii. 1, where there is the expression of a strong and self-confident, almost thoroughly Pharisaic καύχημα, though the word itself is not used. If his action were attacked he would defend it, and with good reason glory in the purity of his motives and conduct. Yet, as he grew older, he rose above this way of defence, and used it and the words which express it less and less.

These words are almost wholly confined to Paul in the New Testament. Besides him James thrice uses them, once in the Pharisaic good sense (i. 9), and twice in the bad sense (iv. 6): James too had something of the markedly Judaic character. In Hebrews also the noun καύχημα is once used ; but only as a synonym and completion of παρρησία, which precedes, limits and defends it.[1]

This word παρρησία, denoting freedom in expression and thought, is the Christian term and idea, which is characteristic of the later books in the New Testament. It originates as a Christian term with Paul, being used by him both in the noun and the derived verb παρρησιάζομαι. In 1 Thessalonians ii. 2 the verb is employed in a somewhat hesitating way, conjoined with λαλεῖν, " we used freedom . . . to speak to you the Gospel ". In Ephesians vi. 20 the verb is used more freely " to speak boldly (as I ought to speak) " ; and Luke in the Acts uses the verb frequently[2] in this sense, catching it from the lips of Paul. The verb is Pauline and Lukan. The noun occurs regularly in the later Pauline letters (Second Corinthians twice, Ephesians twice, Philippians, Philemon, First Timothy). It is also a characteristic word in Luke,[3] and still more in John

---

[1] Hebrews iii. 6, ἐὰν τὴν παρρησίαν καὶ τὸ καύχημα τῆς ἐλπίδος μέχρι τέλους βεβαίαν κατάσχωμεν.

[2] Only in Acts, not in the Gospel, where he was under the iufluence of the earlier tradition : the noun occurs once in Mark viii. 32.

[3] See preceding note.

(both in the Gospel nine times and in the first Epistle four times).   Hebrews is transitional (παρρησία four times, p. 341).

The mere statement of the facts shows how, in harmony with Paul, the language that expressed to the Church the Christian ethics lifted itself above the Pharisaic standpoint. The word παρρησία is entirely free from the unpleasing connotation of καύχησις.   The latter carries with it the suspicion of self-confidence : Paul himself feels this, and apologises for the word and the idea of καύχησις in 2 Corinthians xii. 1 and 5.   It commonly has degenerated in Greek speech and acquired a thoroughly bad sense : in 2 Corinthians x. 13 and Ephesians ii. 9 there is the suggestion that such degeneration is possible,[1] while in 1 Corinthians v. 6 the degeneration is actually exemplified.[2] Regularly, however, the word has in Paul the better sense vindicated for it by Dr. Harnack in the Hymn, verse 3. In James iv. 16 the bad sense of καύχησις is complete.[3]   The word thus comes to connote much the same as ἀλαζονία or κενοδοξία : the latter is purely Pauline[4] (found twice, Phil. and Gal.), the former is found in James, in Romans, in First John, and in Second Timothy (each once).   The development in the use of the word καύχησις καύχημα, therefore, is from the use in a good sense of a term that is readily capable and even suggestive of a bad sense to the full and proper distinction between the good and the bad meaning by the use of two contrasted terms, and the disuse of the doubtful word or the condemnation of it to the bad sense alone.

[1] " We will not glory beyond measure, but according to the measure of the province which God apportioned to us " : and " Not of works : that no man should glory ".

[2] " Your glorying is not good."

[3] " Ye glory in your vauntings : all such glorying is evil."

[4] The noun and the adjective are lumped in the statistics.

The language of the Pastorals stands in this matter on the level of the developed Christian usage. The question is whether there is reason to think that this level was attained in the lifetime of Paul, or not. If not, there would result a probability in favour of the opinion that the Pastorals cannot be the work of Paul; but, on the other hand, if it is probable that Paul himself gradually attained to this level, those Epistles would, so far as this matter is concerned, retain the place which, in our opinion, properly belongs to them as the latest stage in the expression of his thought.

The statistics already quoted place the answer beyond question. The middle Epistles show progress towards this level, whereas the earlier are remote from it. Dr. Harnack's argument that Paul was gradually emancipating himself from the Pharisaic point of view, until he triumphed over it completely, is perfectly correct. Take the Epistles of the Captivity. Philippians is least advanced, while the three closely connected Asian Epistles are more so, as there is only one occurrence in them of these words; but even in them the thought still lingers that καύχησις before the judgment of God is justifiable.

This process, then, is completed in the Pastorals; but the steps are clearly marked in the preceding Epistles and nearly completed in the latest of them. In this as in so many other matters we need the Pastorals to justify Paul, and to complete and consummate our picture of him.[1]

III. In the Hymn we find that verses 4-7 are a good

---

[1] It should not be omitted that the argument of the great German scholar regarding this reading is a complete vindication of the skill and judgment applied by Westcott and Hort in the formation of their text. Alone among modern scholars (with the partial exception of Lachmann) they preferred καυχήσωμαι and placed it in the text, relegating καυθήσωμαι to the Appendix as " Western and Syrian ",

example of Paul's way of heaping together a long series of characteristics and modes of action in order to express the real nature of the topic which he is discussing. In doing so he employs a rich vocabulary, and exhibits great carefulness in regard to delicate shades of significance. Any one of these enumerations of a series of words shows the mind of the philosophically educated man. Only a person who has been accustomed to think much and to philosophise can practise such refinement in language. In such a list Paul's tendency also was to employ strange and rare words, or even to invent new words. It is a Pauline characteristic to be an innovator in language in proportion to the great advance that he made in philosophic thought. Such a characteristic is the mark of a great thinker and great writer, whose thought forges its own lofty expression.

χρηστεύομαι is found only here in the New Testament, and in later Christian writers is probably taken from Paul. Dr. Harnack suggests that Paul derived it from a recension of Q,[1] which was used and quoted by Clemens Alexandrinus.

πepπepeύoμαι is found only here in the New Testament: it is rare in Greek, as is the noun πepπepeία.

φυσιόω is never used in the New Testament except by Paul, who has it six times in First Corinthians, and once in Colossians.

ἀσχημονεῖν is never used in the New Testament except twice in First Corinthians. In this place Dr. Harnack, following Clement of Alexandria, rejects the sense "behave unseemly," which suits better the other occurrence of the word (vii. 36).

---

[1] Q indicates, according to the usual convention, that early document, separate and distinct from Mark's Gospel, which was freely and abundantly used by both Luke and Matthew. As I believe and have argued in *Luke the Physician and Other Studies*, p. 71 ff., it was written while Jesus was still living.

παροξύνομαι occurs only twice in the New Testament. The other instance is in Acts xvii. 16, where Luke uses it about Paul's indignation at the idolatry practised in Athens, probably catching it from the Apostle's own lips. The word was therefore probably a characteristic Pauline word, but it is only once found in his writings. Occasion to use it positively would naturally be rare in Paul's letters, because the idea occurs rarely in them. Here there is a need to use it negatively.

στέγειν, used four times by Paul (twice in First Corinthians) and not elsewhere in the New Testament, has its sense doubtful here: yet it is evidently a characteristic Pauline word like the three preceding.

In such a list Paul tends to refinement in language, he seeks out rare words, some of which remain peculiar to himself in the New Testament; and of these some are characteristic of him at one stage of his life and in one letter.

Now, if one turns to the Pastorals one finds many such lists of qualities and characteristics. The subject lends itself to them. There also many of the words are rare, and found only once in the New Testament, or found only in one Epistle, or confined to that stage of Paul's life when he was writing the Pastorals. It was a Pauline characteristic to be an innovator and experimenter in a certain class of philosophic moral terms. This philosophy he was expounding to the world in terms that would be generally intelligible. The fact that the author of the Pastorals is an innovator and experimenter in language is no proof that he was not Paul, but rather affords psychologically a presumption that he was Paul, because he shares with Paul a certain deep-seated quality of mind.

The Pastoral Epistles cannot be omitted from our estimate of Paul without sacrificing much of the many-sided character of the great Apostle.

LI. The Imprisonment and Supposed Trial of Paul in Rome   (Acts XXVIII.)[1]

It has sometimes been made a charge against the method of investigation which is employed in my study of Luke, that I have pressed too closely the words of the *Acts*, that I have sought to read too much in (or into) the terms employed, and have laid too much stress on the more delicate features and on the principles of method which can be observed in the book as a whole and which must be applied in reading the individual parts and scenes of the narrative.

After many years of study, however, I have on the contrary learned that I did not carry my method far enough, and that the words and terms of the *Acts* are far more vivid and full of meaning than I had ventured to suppose. It is not easy to press Luke's words too closely; and at least I have not done so. With better understanding of the authorities and increased knowledge of the country, I now find the history recorded in the *Acts* much more informative than I previously did; and it seems as if I had barely begun in my older writings to appreciate the true value of Luke's narrative.

The whole work of the past has to be done over again. The previous results, on the whole, stand;[2] but they require much addition and receive confirmation from further study and wider knowledge.

[1] Sections LI. f. affect our views about the range and the development of Paul's teaching.

The chief change is in respect of the date of Galatians, Section LII.

The attempt to carry out this deeper and minuter study in respect of Acts xxviii., and the so-called "first trial" of Paul, is a matter of great importance for the later career of the Apostle. What are the facts which Luke had in mind, and which lie behind and beneath the narrative describing the fortunes, the imprisonment, and the supposed trial of Paul in Rome? The historian does not say anything overt regarding many facts which he must have known, the character and issue of the trial, the conduct of the Jews, and so on. Yet those facts are to us of the most absorbing interest.

There are two questions to be answered: first, what were the main facts? Secondly, why does not Luke mention them or say anything clear and explicit about them, i.e. why does he content himself with stating how the Gospel of Paul came to Rome, and for what length of time it was preached there by him, while he says nothing regarding Paul's personal fortunes in the trial?

Now, first, as to the facts. Was Paul tried in Rome during his residence? If so, before whom was he tried, and what was the result? Was he condemned on the capital charge, and his career brought to an end? Or was he acquitted, and allowed (as must have been implied in acquittal) to continue his missionary and confirmatory work?

In the latter case, the "first trial," in which the circumstances described in the *Acts* culminated, must be distinguished from a "second trial" with fatal issue. That a trial of Paul ending in condemnation must have occurred at some time in Rome is proved by tradition and by Clement of Rome, and is clearly implied in Second Timothy. If, however, the supposed "first trial" ended in condemnation after its two or more stages (2 Tim. iv. 16), then there was no "second trial," and the Apostle's life ended in 61 or 62

A.D. The proof that Gallio was governing Achaia during A.D. 52, which is now furnished by epigraphic evidence, makes it certain that Paul's arrival in Rome cannot be placed later than spring A.D. 61 at the very latest,[1] and was in all probability earlier.

If he was acquitted at first, did he carry out his intention of going on into Spain (Rom. xv. 28)? Or did he return to the East, as is implied in the Pastoral Epistles? Or did he do both?

Further, a most important question is about the conduct of the Jews of Jerusalem. The action and attitude of the Jews towards Paul in almost every city that he visited is a subject to which Luke gives much space and attention. Not merely in Jerusalem, but also in Damascus, Antioch the Pisidian, Iconium, Lystra, Thessalonica, Corinth, the Jews (apart from a minority in his favour) were his determined opponents, and used all their influence with the Gentile magistrates and leaders against him. In the cities of Cyprus, in Antioch the Syrian, in Athens, in Beroea, the Jews were on the whole favourable to him: as to Antioch and Beroea we know from his narrative (and from Paul himself as regards Antioch) that the Jews were generally with him, and trouble there was caused by strange Jews. In Derbe there were probably no Jews: nothing is said about their action to Paul or his conduct towards them. As regards Derbe, we notice that no person gave any evidence about Timothy, as people in Iconium and Lystra did: he was unknown to them, whereas the Iconian people, having a considerable Jewish element in their number, were

---

[1] I hope to treat this date elsewhere. Dr. Deissmann's treatment of it in his *St. Paul, a Study*, 1912, pp. 240-260, seems to me far from satisfactory. The statement that he quotes from Professor H. Dessau is fundamental; but all that he builds on that foundation involves misconceptions, and his dating seems to me impossible.

interested in him as a half-Jew by race. Gentiles were not naturally interested in the son of a Greek, whose wife chanced to be Jewish, though she had not treated her son after the Jewish fashion in infancy. In Philippi Jewish associations were on the side of Paul, although no Jews are mentioned. All this Luke carefully tells.

It is plain that the relations of the Jews to Paul were considered by Luke to be a very important feature in his narrative. He devotes a considerable part of his history to this subject.

In Rome the Jews were numerous, as is known from many sources. Luke tells that Paul's first action when he came to Rome was to enter into communication with them ; and twelve verses are devoted to this subject while only three are given to Paul's circumstances otherwise in Rome. The Jews came in large numbers to hear him, after the leaders had intimated their neutral and non-committal attitude : some of them believed and others did not accept his teaching. Not a word, however, is said about any overt action of the Roman Jews against him.

Now, it is laid down by almost every scholar and commentator that Jewish influence was the one great factor in deciding Paul's trial. It was a case of Paul against the Jews. There was no accuser except the Jews. The whole tendency of the Romans who were concerned in the case was in favour of Paul, as Luke tells us in chapter after chapter. The one chance for the Jewish accusers lay in exercising private influence with great personages and notably with the Empress Poppaea, who is supposed to have been inclined towards Jewish associations.

The question then is this. Are we to suppose that Luke, who elsewhere records so carefully every act of hostility on the part of the Jews to Paul, and who assuredly has a certain anti-Jewish bias,—are we to suppose that Luke leaves out this opportunity of completing his account of Jewish opposition by telling that the Jews in Rome turned against him? There was no possibility that the Palestinian Jews could bring influence privately to bear against Paul except through their compatriots in Rome. It was to the Jews of Rome that Poppaea would be inclined to listen, more than to strangers from Palestine unsupported by the Roman Jews with whom she was acquainted. Either the Jewish leaders in Rome must have acted against Paul, or this supposed powerful private influence could not have been brought to bear against him effectively.

According to Luke the Jews in Rome preserved from the first an attitude of neutrality. It was, of course, easy for the unbelieving Jews to take part against him, as they did at Iconium; but it is in Luke's manner to say so, if they did. It is indeed natural that this section of the Jews should take part against him; and, if Luke does not record their action, must not the reason be that there was not in the sequel any opportunity for them to do so? Hence the picture remains, the Jews of Rome were neutral, and took no action against Paul. That is asserted positively by Luke. Those who say that they did act against Paul in the end ought to show why Luke leaves a wrong impression on this point, abandoning his usual attitude and bias.

There is, however, a third alternative. Neither was Paul formally tried and acquitted at this time, nor was he tried and condemned. He spent two full years in Rome, as Luke says: and then the Roman residence came to an end without any formal trial.

It is characteristic of all Lukan research that, as soon as one enters on any investigation, one is involved in some difficult questions of law and procedure; and these often require much minute study. This, incidentally, affords a complete proof that the subject is thoroughly historical. Invented, or distorted, or misunderstood incidents wander far from the paths of real life. It is because Luke states each point in such intimate relation to reality, and with such vivid surroundings of actual life, that he compels the reader to grasp the facts of law and custom which are involved in the narrative before he can gauge its full significance.

To understand the position of Paul during the two years of his Roman captivity, therefore, we have to enter on obscure questions of Roman law and procedure during the first century. Obviously, one cannot adequately understand Luke's allusive and suggestive account of the circumstances in which a defendant awaiting trial under custody was situated, unless the principles and practice of the law are known. Now, as it happens, legal points are involved which have never been properly investigated, and which seem never to have occurred to the commentators whom I have consulted.

It is, accordingly, necessary to go into some difficult and minute points of legal and historical detail, which may prove tedious to the reader. It may therefore be well to state first of all in succinct terms the conclusion which results from this investigation, and afterwards to show the steps of the reasoning.

Paul was detained at Rome until his prosecutors should appear. The trial could not begin until there was an accuser to state the ground of complaint against him. Palestinian Jews, however, did not appear. They knew that their case was too weak to bear statement in a Roman court, as they had learned from the conduct and words of two successive Roman governors of Palestine and from the plain

language of King Agrippa (Acts xxiv. 24 f., xxvi. 30-32) :[1]
and that they would have to depend largely on private influence with important persons in Rome.   In those circumstances they considered that the best course for them was
to delay the case and keep Paul shut up as long as possible ;
and the most effective way was to refrain from appearing
in court.   After a certain lapse of time, perhaps eighteen
months,[2] the accused party was presumed to be innocent, in
accordance with a rule laid down some years before by the
deceased Emperor Claudius.   Thus Paul was set at liberty
after two years.   This space of " two years " (Acts xxviii.
30) is equivalent to the legal term eighteen months, together with some additional time required for the formalities
of release.   There was therefore no proper " first trial," but
only an acquittal in default.   Paul was henceforth free to
preach and to travel, until some years later he was arrested
during the Neronian persecution, probably in 65 A.D.

Such is the general purport of this Section.   Now for the
details of the reasoning.

The situation in which Paul found himself on his arrival in Rome (Acts xxviii. 16) requires careful consideration.   He had come up on his own appeal for trial before
the supreme tribunal of the Empire.   In order that the trial
should proceed, there must be some accuser : the Crown did

---

[1] Acts xxvi. 31, " This man doeth nothing worthy of death or of imprisonment ".

[2] The term cannot be proved, but seems probable.   According to the
usual ancient custom, eighteen months is loosely called two years : see the
present writer's article in Hastings' *Dict. Bib.*, vol. v., p. 464 ff.   In this case
Paul was detained in prison two full years : this should be understood as the
whole of A.D. 61 and 62.   Paul had reached Rome probably in February 61
A.D. : a release in the latter part of 62 would quite satisfy Luke's expression.
After the eighteen months was at an end, there were formal proceedings and
the final hearing and dismissal by the Emperor.   " Two full years " does
not necessarily imply in Luke twenty-four complete and exact months.

not prosecute, but left such cases to private initiative. When he reached Rome, fully seven to eight months, if not more, must have elapsed since the appeal had been allowed[1] by Festus, the Procurator of Palestine, and the case had been remitted to Rome. Abundance of time had therefore passed for the accusers to travel to Rome and to be there before Paul making their preparations to push the case actively.

Such were the possibilities of the situation. What is it that had actually occurred?

When he arrived, no accuser was present in Rome. No official representative of the nation, and no letter or message from the national leaders in Jerusalem, had come to " those that were the chief of the Jews " in Rome. The latter had no authoritative information about the case. Their statement in verse 21 must be understood in this way : as officials they had received no documents bearing on the case, nor had any of their Palestinian brethren arrived who were authorised to make accusation or charge against Paul.

It is not uncommon for commentators and moralists to enlarge on the duplicity of the Jewish leaders in Rome, who certainly knew a good deal in an unofficial way. In fact, they by implication in their concluding words acknowledge to Paul that they have heard bad reports concerning him and his hostility to his own nation : those must have been talked about in all Jewish circles throughout the empire. But they were not bound in any way to take official notice of private tales and gossip. They are speaking as officers of their people ; and their reply is a complete proof that no

---

[1] That the appeal had to be allowed by the Governor of the Province is now well known : see Mommsen's article reprinted in vol. iii., p. 386, of his collected legal papers from the *Savigny Zeitschrift für Rechtsgeschichte*, 1890. Galba, when he was Governor of Spain, refused to permit an appeal to go forward to the Emperor (Suetonius, *Galb.*, 9).

person properly authorised, and no letter intimating the coming of any such person, to act as accuser of Paul, had reached Rome. It would be the natural and obligatory course that any national representative should report on arrival to the heads of the nation there. As to the tales, they say that they are ready to hear dispassionately Paul's side and plea.

It is difficult to see why these words of the rulers should be blamed for duplicity or cunning. Their silence about charges against Paul, except in this slight reference to current talk, amounts simply to a refusal to regard gossip and vague reports as any ground for action or ill-feeling against him. They treat him as a Jew, entitled to the rights and privileges which all Jews could expect from their own nation in a strange city. Their reply to his question is dignified, courteous, and apparently fair. It commits them to nothing; but that is not a ground for blaming them. They profess neutrality and a wish to learn more, as they may have to be, in a sense, judges hereafter in the case.

The blame thrown on them for duplicity is founded on the fixed prepossession in the minds of modern scholars that the Roman Jews actively persecuted Paul. Luke, however, never says or hints or suggests this.

Evidently the leaders of the Jews in Palestine were not pressing the case very actively. If they had had any confidence in the success of their cause they would probably have ere this been in Rome employing all the arts of skilful solicitors to push their case and secure conviction. Much for them depended on the favourable reception of their first plea; and it was believed that they were able to use strong indirect influence through the partiality of the powerful Poppaea.

They had, however, no good ground for feeling such confidence. All appearances pointed to a verdict in Paul's favour. Festus and his assessors evidently thought there was not even a *prima facie* case against him (Acts xxvi. 30 ff.), though the Governor had gladly used the loophole of Paul's appeal to the supreme court as an excuse, in order to avoid the responsibility of deciding : he shrank from putting a slight on the national leaders at the beginning of his relations with them, and getting involved in a quarrel, which would certainly be the result if he dismissed their charges as unjustifiable.

The expenses involved in carrying this prosecution before the Roman tribunal were considerable ; and the Jewish leaders probably thought that it was not worth while to incur them in a case where success was so unlikely. They had got rid of Paul, and made it difficult for him to return to Jerusalem ; and they felt that the wiser course was to content themselves with this. After acquittal Paul would be more dangerous to them and more secure against them than if the case were left unfinished. So long as the scandal remained that he was a practically unacquitted defendant, released owing to the accusers having failed to appear so far away from Jerusalem, there would always attach some stigma to Paul in the Jewish estimation.

The Jews had probably been using their influence to protract the case in Palestine (see Acts xxiv. 26 f.) ; and certainly the leaders in Palestine had allowed the matter to lie for several months after Paul's departure, without taking any steps to appear in Rome.

Now is there any apparent probability that they would revive the case after that interval ? In the first place, Luke's narrative gives no ground to think that envoys arrived to conduct the case in Rome during the two years of Paul's residence and detention there. And, in the second place, it is not *a priori* natural or probable that the national leaders in Jerusalem should resume Paul's case and send envoys later, after they had neglected it for a good many months. They had many more important and pressing matters to keep them occupied. In the immediate irritation caused by the presence of Paul in Jerusalem and the troubles that arose out of it, they had been impelled to take steps against him; and thus succeeded, not in gaining their case, but only in keeping him shut up in the quiet of a prison. Paul's action in claiming the privileges of a Roman citizen resulted in his case being carried before the Roman governor at Caesareia. The plea against him proved to be poor and thin, when it had to be put in legal form and specific acts proved in open court.

On the part of the accusers the case rested on the Roman desire to maintain order. They could calculate that Felix was far more anxious to keep the peace and to avoid disturbance than to aim at justice. They knew, and he knew, that the ability of an official was gauged in Rome mainly by his success in preserving peace and quiet in his province, and that some injustice done to the rights of one individual in the interest of public order would probably escape notice, or if noticed would be pardoned as conducing to the general peace of the province.

The speech of the Jewish advocate Tertullus (Acts xxiv. 2 f.) was pitched on this key. He praised the success of Felix in maintaining peace and order. He rested his whole case on the plea that the national leaders would not come before the Governor except for the reason that they had found the prisoner to be a cause of disorder over all the world, since wherever Paul appeared disturbance ensued. Tertullus produced no witnesses, and made no specific charge against Paul, except that of *trying* to profane the Temple. The plea was simply that, if Felix got rid of Paul, peace would reign ; but so long as Paul lived, disorder would abound.

This line of argument shows a cynical disregard for justice, except in the fashion that it is expedient for one man to be sacrificed to secure the peace of the nation ; but it was one that had force under Roman rule.

The only positive charge made against Paul was that he had attempted to profane the Temple. This attempt, however, had been frustrated by the riot. The riot was the weak point in the Jewish position, and it was disguised and palliated by the charge of intended profanation ; the riot had been provoked (as they said) by Paul's supposed intention to profane the Temple. Roman law treated leniently a disturbance arising from profanation of the Temple, and would take little cognisance of it, if peace was restored as soon as the immediate occasion was past.

This form of accusation was, probably, the most effective attack that was possible in the circumstances. In no other way could the Jewish authorities make up a case. They had no good ground to stand upon, because they themselves were the real breakers of the Roman law, as being in a sense responsible for the riot ; but, as they knew, the weak point in most Roman governors was their eagerness to avoid disturbance and so gain credit for having kept their province free from serious disorder.

If the Jews' case was weak, it must be admitted that their hand had been forced. The riot had not apparently been planned, but was sudden and unpremeditated (Acts xxi. 27 f.). Doubtless, the leaders had found on inquiry that they could not base a charge on any act of Paul's. Certainly, they failed to make any such charge. They only maintained that he had *intended* to profane the Temple. The very form of the accusation shows that the attempt had been unsuccessful. There was no accomplished act of profanation for them to found upon. Hence they could not bring witnesses to prove any misconduct. The crowd had thought that Paul was bringing Gentiles into the Temple, and had effectually prevented this supposed intention from being executed.

If the Jewish leaders had been free to choose their own time they would doubtless have waited for a better opportunity, but the lawless conduct of the crowd compelled them to act. They had now to explain away the riot, and they did so by attacking the sufferer, and declaring that he was in fault, not only then, but frequently on previous occasions: he wilfully and intentionally outraged the Jewish feelings and violated the religious Law.

The weak point of Paul's case was that disturbance among the Jews dogged his steps, and broke out wherever he was. The Jewish leaders seized on this. "Eliminate Paul," was their plea to Felix, "and then you will find the Jews quiet and peaceable: believe us that this will be so: you can take this on the faith of us, who are responsible for preserving order."

Intention to profane could not be proved by witnesses, hence none were offered. The accusation rests on the credibility of the accusers. They, as responsible for order and peaceful conduct in their own nation, declared that Paul's intentions were suspicious, and that they could not preserve order among their people where Paul came. That seemed legally weak to a governor of the province at the time. It was a case that could hardly be brought forward years afterwards in the Imperial court except as a mere cloak for a concealed attack.

Felix, evidently, felt no doubt about the weakness of the Jewish arguments in the case. He was, however, anxious to keep the leaders of that troublesome nation in good humour, and he had an eye to possible bribes from Paul (who must have appeared to be a man of substance).[1] Accordingly, he remanded the prisoner, kept him in custody for two years, and did not even release him on departing.

The successor of Felix had equally little doubt regarding the case. He saw that there was no real accusation in the Roman sense against Paul, and he said so quite frankly: it was a matter of Jewish religion and procedure (Acts xxv. 18 f.), and he would gladly have rid himself of it by sending it to Jerusalem for trial before the Sanhedrin according to the national law (Acts xxv. 9, 20).[2] Paul, however, refused to go before this prejudiced court, where his accusers would practically be his judges, and appealed from the provincial to the Imperial tribunal.

Festus evidently shrank as much as Felix had done from offending the Jewish authorities. His proposal to send the case back to the Sanhedrin was manifestly unjust; it was merely a device to please the Jews, and showed stronger leaning to their side than ever Felix had shown. He now seized on this way which Paul's appeal opened to him of treating the case. If he sent Paul to the Supreme Court he avoided all responsibility and escaped giving offence to the Jews. He therefore, after considering the matter with his *consilium* or board of assessors, according to the proper

---

[1] Felix was wealthy and lived with a queen: he would not look for a small bribe, such as a man of humble rank could give.

[2] It is true that, according to Josephus, *Bell. Jud.*, vi. 2, as Professor J. S. Reid points out, even a Roman could be brought before the Sanhedrin for trial on the charge of profaning the Temple. But Paul had been prevented from committing the sacrilege which he was charged with attempting; and accusation based on frustrated intention was weak.

form, allowed the appeal and sent it up to the higher tribunal in Rome.

At the same time Festus indicated in an extra-judicial way his own opinion on the case. The private conversation between him and Agrippa, in which they agreed that Paul was innocent, became a subject of general talk.

The truth is that Festus was not a strong enough man to pronounce a judicial judgment in favour of Paul, and so to alienate Jewish feeling and provoke the enmity of the national leaders. If he had had the moral courage to do so, it was still quite within his power. He was not bound to wash his hands of the case as soon as the appeal was made ; but he eagerly seized the chance of shuffling off responsibility.

It is necessary here to refer to an opinion which has been suggested as possible by my friend Professor Vernon Bartlet in his edition of the Acts [1] regarding these words of Agrippa, " This man might have been set free, if he had not appealed to Cæsar " : perhaps there lies in them a reference to the approaching doom of Paul : Paul might have escaped, if he had not appealed to Cæsar.

This opinion, which Professor Bartlet gives only as an alternative, seems to me more ingenious than sound. Festus, when he could do so without annoying the Jews, stated his opinion to the king, who sat with him on the tribunal, and the king emphasised it. Although the opinion was private, rather than formal, yet it was on hearsay recorded by Luke as showing the mind of a Roman governor in respect of Paul's innocence : the prisoner was guiltless so far as Roman law and official opinion were concerned. This, however, does not and could not carry any implication that the Supreme Court would decide differently, for the gover-

[1] In the *Century Bible.*

nor and the king were thinking only of the present situation and the verdict. Moreover, Luke takes every opportunity of bringing out that the Roman administration decided in favour of the Christian right to preach and teach freely. He tells facts, and does not employ innuendo of this kind.

Luke too had in mind a certain analogy between the case of Paul and the trial of Jesus. In both instances the Roman judge thought that the accused party was innocent. In each case the judge's opinion, though expressed in court, was stated in an extra-judicial way and did not influence the result. The judge was weak, and yielded to the influence of the Jews. Pilate thrice declared that Jesus was innocent.[1] Felix practically, and Festus explicitly, regarded Paul as innocent.

If we are justified in speculating as to a deeper intention which led Luke to quote Agrippa's statement, the opinion suggests itself that there was during these proceedings a third Roman judicial decision in Paul's favour. Agrippa was a friend of Rome and a client-king. Felix, Festus and Agrippa pronounced Paul innocent.

All the circumstances which are stated by Luke were equally well known to the Jewish national leaders. Therefore, either Luke's account is prejudiced and partial, exaggerating the Roman judgment of Paul's innocence and concealing circumstances which gave reason to look for an adverse decision, or the Jews must have gathered that they had a weak case against Paul and little prospect of success. The best that they could do for their cause was to lengthen out the proceedings, to postpone the final stage of the trial, and to keep Paul as long as possible in custody. His seclusion was a gain to the Jews, whereas to bring on the trial would probably mean the speedy release of the prisoner.

Now in Rome there was one very effective way to keep

[1] *St. Paul the Traveller and the Roman Citizen*, p. 307.

Paul secluded. If no prosecutor appeared there, the law presumed for a long time that the absence was only temporary, and detained the defendant in expectation of the complainant's arrival.

The Jews therefore played a waiting game. This procedure was clever : it meant success to a certain degree : it was economical for the Jews, and expensive for Paul. That was the line of conduct that imposed itself, and all that Luke records points to that way of action. For the space of two years Paul had to maintain himself and his guards and personal attendants, to hire a house, and to defray the other expenses of living. The custody, however, was of the mildest type. He had not been tried. His trial was not even imminent, for no prosecutors were in Rome. He could see all that chose to visit him, and speak with perfect freedom. Thus there was great opportunity for him to teach and preach.

By Luke's custom,[1] two years must be taken as the whole time of the Roman residence, not as a part followed by a period during which the trial was proceeding.

It is evident and certain that during this period of two years no trial occurred. Such freedom of action as Paul enjoyed is inconsistent with the procedure of a trial on a capital charge. Especially is it totally and absolutely inconsistent with a trial such as is implied in Second Timothy, a trial which evidently was accompanied by confinement in a prison, by almost complete solitude, by depression and even fear in Paul's heart.[2] On the contrary, Acts xxviii. implies success, joy, and hope ; this is also the spirit of Colossians, Philemon, Philippians and Ephesians.

---

[1] This custom is pointed out at various places in the writer's *St. Paul the Traveller and the Roman Citizen.*

[2] 2 Tim. iv. 6-8, 9, 11, 16-18.

The second letter to Timothy, therefore, cannot be placed during this period of two years. The circumstances are irreconcilable.

It must, of course, be understood that the detention was always of the nature of mild captivity.[1] Paul was a prisoner in Rome, just as he had been on the ship. Soldiers were in charge of him, and were answerable with their life for his safe custody. He was bound with a chain, so that his movements were not free. He was confined to the house and his friends had to come in to see and hear him. He was not out of danger[2] so long as there was a chance that the accusers might appear and the trial proceed. It was always possible that Jewish accusers, by their private influence and by their weight as representing the nation, might carry even a weak case to success.

Hence the letters composed during this detention vary in tone. Paul writes as a prisoner in bonds; he is in affliction and suffering; and yet he is fairly confident that he will be set free and be able shortly to visit Philippi and Colossae.[3] On the whole their spirit is one of quiet confidence, and even of marked joyfulness, especially Philippians iii., iv.

The only words in these Epistles that perhaps conflicts with the foregoing interpretation is *prætorium* in Philippians i. 13. The meaning of this term is obscure and disputed. In my *St. Paul the Traveller*, p. 357, I have followed Mommsen's explanation that the word denotes " the whole body of persons connected with the sitting in judgment ". This, however, now seems to me unjustifiable. The trial was only a possibility of the future when the letter was written. Lightfoot's explanation seems preferable, that, as Paul's guards were always changing, the prisoner after a time

---

[1] *Libera custodia* is the term.   [2] Phil. ii. 17.
[3] Phil. ii. 24 ; Philem. 22.

became known in the whole prætorium, i.e. among all the prætorian soldiers;[1] and it is entirely consistent with our view of the situation.

Luke's account leaves no opening for the idea that after two years the trial came on, and passed through its stages amid strict detention, anxiety and solitude, to its issue in condemnation and death.

Now what was the rule and procedure of the Roman law, when a case came up on appeal from a province and the prosecution did not put in an appearance? The Crown did not prosecute. The Crown waited the action of the private prosecutors. Until the Jewish representatives appeared nothing could take place, except that the defendant was detained in view of future trial; and the case of Paul may serve as proof that ordinarily the detention of such defendants was of the mildest type.

How long would this continue? Was the defendant kept in custody, even of a mild kind, far from home and friends, for as long time as the prosecutors chose to delay? Evidently there must have been some term, for indefinite detention of a Roman citizen at the instance of despised foreigners who never appeared to push their case is inconceivable and inadmissible. Was the term fixed by formal law, or was it left to the defendant to claim release after a certain delay?

We are imperfectly informed on this subject, but yet the evidence is sufficient to justify a confident statement. In this matter I am indebted to Professor J. S. Reid, of Cambridge, for kindly placing his great learning and long study of the subject at my disposal.

---

[1] Mommsen objects that *Prætorium* does not mean the body of prætorian soldiers; but the use of the Latin term does not govern Greek usage. There is often a difference between Latin and Greek in the use of a word.

In the third century the procedure had been already settled by custom or enactment; and definite rules existed about the time within which a prosecutor in a case transferred to Rome must carry out the prosecution: for non-capital charges six months were allowed if the appeal was from Italy, nine months if from the provinces: for capital charges the times were twelve and eighteen months respectively. The longest term would apply in a case like Paul's.

How long had these rules been in existence? and is there any reason to think that these or some such principles had been formulated, and the same or other limits fixed, in the time of Paul?

There can be no doubt that some limitation of the period allowed for prosecutors to appear became necessary as soon as cases began to occur in which no prosecutor appeared. A presumption arose that in such circumstances they had no good ground to stand on, and after a certain time probably this presumption would have almost the force of an acquittal. As Professor Reid says, "one would suppose that some rules of the kind must have been laid down very soon after the right of appeal to Rome began to be allowed".

Some term, therefore, was necessary to prevent flagrant injustice. The Romans were skilful in using the forms of law in order to harass an opponent. Philo supplies a case in point, where he tells that a certain Lampon of Alexandria had been accused of disrespect to the Emperor Tiberius, and the proceedings were protracted for two years by Flaccus, the Prefect of Egypt, in order to keep Lampon in terror of death.[1] A defendant could not be allowed to

[1] This case has a certain superficial resemblance to that of Paul; but there is no true parallel. There was no want of a prosecutor in Lampon's case; and the delay in the proceedings is attributed to the intentional malignity of the Prefect who acted as judge.

remain for ever at the mercy of a wily prosecutor, who delayed to appear in Rome.

That cases of such failure to appear had become numerous before Paul's imprisonment is attested by Suetonius and Dion Cassius.[1] The Emperor Claudius took steps to bring these cases to an end by condemning the absent party, i.e. by presuming the innocence of the defendant. According to the usual fashion of dynastic history in the first century, Claudius's action is described by Suetonius in such a way as to make it unreasonable and erratic;[2] but Dion Cassius places it in a fair and proper light. Claudius checked and ended what had become a scandal in Roman law, by acquitting all defendants in these long-standing cases.

The action of Claudius constituted a precedent, which would be acted upon in later cases. He must have presumed some term of limitation. The principle, on which he acted, when it had been once recognised, became a feature in Roman law for the future; and the term which his action fixed would become a rule guiding the constructive spirit of Roman law, until a different term was settled by some subsequent formal enactment. It is not at all improbable that the limits which were observed in the third century were those fixed by Claudius. We hear of no change;[3] and it would be quite characteristic of Roman law that the term, when once established, should continue.

It would appear from the two accounts of Claudius's proceedings that his action was an innovation. Suetonius

---

[1] Suetonius, *Claud.*, 15; Dion., lx. 28, 6.

[2] Suetonius says that Claudius condemned the absent party whether his absence was avoidable or unavoidable. But there could be no real excuse for absence extending over two years.

[3] It is, however, true that our information is very incomplete. The apparent incompleteness, however, may be due partly to the fact that there was nothing to record.

speaks of it as if it were strange and unprecedented, and makes this a charge against the Emperor. We see, however, that an action and a principle were urgently required.

Be that as it may, the principle and the term were fixed by Imperial action before Paul entered Rome. At the expiry of a certain period the case against him fell, and he was set free. For the third time in this case the Roman law determined in his favour.

From this conclusion I can see no escape. It is inexorably determined by the historical facts and by the established principles of the Roman law.

Why, then, does not Luke say this in so many words? To this I would answer that the issue is implicit in the narrative: the final chapter, and the whole story of the trial, point to this solution. Just as the narrative is overcast with gloom and bad omen during the final journey to Jerusalem, and the reader is filled with the thought of evil, so from the time that Paul leaves Palestine the narrative becomes brighter and happier. Even in Jerusalem the prospect of escape lay in the thought of Rome: see xxiii. 11, "As thou hast testified at Jerusalem, so must thou bear witness also at Rome". Riot and plots of assassination, imprisonment and guards, surrounded him at Jerusalem. But on the voyage, as soon as it began, the officer who commanded the convoy showed marked kindness to his prisoner, allowing him to go on shore to recruit after a rough passage;[1] and asking or permitting him to offer advice in council regarding the future voyage. In the crisis of the voyage, when all others were in despair, Paul comforted the crew and passengers, took command, issued orders, and saved the lives of all. The voyage was dangerous, but the narrative is

[1] xxvii. 3. The west wind keeps that Syrian sea always tossing uneasily, so that a coasting voyage in a small ship is trying to landsmen.

never gloomy or despairing : there is always the assurance that the danger will be surmounted. In Malta Paul was honoured and complimented and regarded as almost divine. And so he came to Rome,[1] encouraged by meeting friends and brethren along the way ; and in Rome he was courteously received by the leaders of the nation, and invited to explain his views. During two years he enjoyed great freedom to receive all visitors, and to teach in the most outspoken way.

Only in one detail has an omen of trial been found. As Paul says on shipboard (xxvii. 24), a messenger of God not only promised him the lives of all his shipmates, but also said, " Thou must stand before Cæsar ". This has been re-garded as foreboding misfortune and condemnation ; but there is no warrant for this interpretation of the words. It is here mentioned by Paul as an encouragement to his hearers. He knew already that he must bear witness in Rome to the Gospel. The " appearing before Cæsar " is not a terror, but an omen of good. To stand before kings is the expression, not of misfortune, but of honour.

But does this not forbode a trial as the issue of the journey ? Certainly it does. The procedure of Claudius ruled the case as a precedent. As no accuser appeared, the trial ended in a verdict of acquittal, not in a mere dismissal of the accused. In ordinary appeals it cannot be supposed that the Emperor had time to preside in person at the trial ; but it is not improbable that, where the issue was assured and the verdict certain without a trial and without loss of time, the Emperor may have himself pronounced judgment. The historians' account of Claudius's procedure in such cases

---

[1] The double statement of the coming to Rome has caused needless difficulty to commentators, who miss the sense. It is pointed out in the writer's *St. Paul the Traveller* that the company reached first the bounds of the great city, then Forum of Appius, and then the inhabited city.

suggests that he during his reign intervened personally; and his successor may have followed the precedent: to pardon was easy, and likely to be popular.[1]   Thus the words of the divine messenger (xxvii. 25) were literally fulfilled. Paul stood before Cæsar.   If a tedious trial, with speeches of the prosecution and the defence, had been required, it is probable that the case would have been heard by the usual delegates: the Emperor, burdened with the care of all the provinces and of Italy and of Rome, could not spend time in hearing the case of a Tarsian citizen and his Jewish accusers.

Why, then, does not Luke clinch his case by recording the acquittal more definitely?   We must understand that the real climax, as it seemed to Luke, is recorded.   The free and bold preaching in Rome is the consummation of the narrative of Book II., though not the consummation of the work as a whole.   The personal fortunes of even Paul are a secondary matter in comparison with the bringing of the Pauline Gospel into the capital of the Empire.

But, further, as I have always maintained from the time when I began to understand Luke's method, the history is not ended.   The story of the working of the Spirit in the Church and in the world was not confined to one book, the second of the whole work, but was continuing according to the plan of this great history.   No third book was ever written.   The second, perhaps, had not received the final touches from the author's hand.   If the second book had been intended to be the last it would have concluded with some expression indicative of the future that lay before the Church outside the limits of this history.   As it is, it ends with a forward reference: it stops abruptly in the middle of

---

[1] Claudius loved to sit in judgment: see Hirschfeld, *Röm. Verwaltungsbeamten*, p. 329.

an action: it shows that the narrative is to go on. It points on to Book III. as clearly as Book I. points on to Book II. by its abrupt ending, and as Book II. points back to Book I. by repeating and completing the account of the last action in that Book, *viz.* the Ascension.

The last action described in Book II. is to be resumed and completed in Book III. When the legal term was reached the trial was formally ended, and a new period ensued in the career of the Apostle and of the Church: missionary work had gone through a series of legal proceedings extending over four years, and had emerged triumphant from the ordeal, while its enemies had failed.

At the beginning of Book II., in the very first words, τὸν μὲν πρῶτον, Luke points forward to a succeeding book. As has been pointed out,[1] the expression "first book" implies at least three books: in this emphatic position the fullest stress must be laid on the word "first". The Authorised and Revised Versions [2] both recognise the emphasis which falls on the word in this prominent place, and their recognition leads to the mistranslation, "former," instead of "first". The most striking analogy is "the first enrolment which took place when Quirinius was governing Syria" (Luke ii. 2): the importance which attaches to the word "first" there has been explained elsewhere.[3]

The ending of Book II. can be rightly understood only with reference to a coming Book III. That Book III. was never written, and that Book II. was not finally completed by the author's latest revision, appears in some small details, one of which will form the subject of our next

---

[1] *St. Paul the Traveller and the Roman Citizen*, pp. 27 f.

[2] "Former" in both; but the Revised Version gives "first" in the margin.

[3] *Expositor*, Nov. 1912, p. 393 f.; *St. Paul the Traveller*, p. 28; *Christ Born in Bethlehem*, p. 124 f.

Section. It is possible that varieties due to the incompleteness of the author's work in Book II. may be the ultimate cause of some of the divergences of the Western Text from the Standard Text; but this I should be disposed to apply only with great hesitation. As a rule, those divergences arise from early modifications in difficult passages, and are non-Lukan, though often significant and indicative of the true text, which has been subjected to modification.

The preceding paragraphs have not exhausted, but only opened up, this subject. Much depends on a correct decision; and it is useful to have the arguments against my view presented clearly and concisely, in order that the reasons on both sides may be weighed by the reader. My friend Professor Vernon Bartlet, in the *Expositor*, May, 1913, has fully stated the arguments by which he tries to establish the date to which he assigns the Pastoral Epistles, *viz.* during the imprisonment of Paul in Rome, i.e. the time described in Acts xxviii. 17 ff.

Now we are agreed that the method of settling the relative date of Paul's letters by tracing in them a development of doctrine from the earliest to the latest is unsound; and that the teaching in the letters is graduated according to the position and knowledge of the people addressed, and is not determined by the growth in Paul's thought.[1] When, however, Professor Bartlet asks us to accept the theory that Paul at Rome could write First Timothy to the Asian Christians [2] a very short time before he despatched to them the letters which we call Ephesians (not to add Colossians [3]),

---

[1] This is more fully stated in Section I.

[2] He lays much stress (perhaps even too much) on the view that this letter was intended as much for the Asian Christians as for Timothy himself.

[3] A letter like Colossians was intended, not merely for the people of Colossae, but for others, as Paul says in iv. 16. See p. 428.

I cannot but ask how his conception of the needs of the Asians could change so radically in the course of a few weeks or at the most months.

Except in respect of date, I am in sympathy with almost all that Professor Bartlet says in his series of articles on the Pastoral Epistles;[1] but I think he has not yet explained this difficulty. I suspect that there may be an explanation in a different line from that which he takes; but meanwhile he bases his theory upon a system of chronology which seems to me to pervert the story of Paul's life and the meaning of Luke's history.

Let us take the arguments one by one: we may fairly assume that Professor Bartlet, with his characteristic sureness, has marshalled every consideration that can be brought to bear. He puts his argument in six positions. I put them, as far as brevity permits, in his own words :—

(1) "If Luke had meant this to be understood" (*viz.* that "the case simply went in Paul's favour by default at the end of the two years"), then "it would have been easy for him to say so".

That form of reasoning is devoid of strength. One might with equally cogency reply that, if Luke had meant it to be understood that Paul was tried and executed at the end of the two years, it would have been easy for him to say so.

The historian writes the concluding part of his narrative in a tone of gladness and confidence which contrasts strongly with the gloom and despondency of the preceding chapters (down to the beginning of the voyage). No person used to judging literary method would naturally understand that the joyous spirit of the end of Acts heralded the condemnation and execution of Paul. It is true that a martyrdom was a victory; but still the prelude to martyrdom was a severe

---

[1] *Expositor*, January, etc., 1913.

strain on the martyr and on the Church, and the tone of such a narrative is grave and sombre.

Moreover, that way of reasoning is always bad. Luke was not writing to clear up our minds, and to save us from making historical errors. He might in numerous places have saved us from mistakes and from interminable discussion —sometimes from controversies in which tempers have been lost and reason has been flouted—if he had told us in a word or two that such and such a thing happened. If he had put one or two more notes of time in his history, what thousands of pages about the chronology of the Gospel and the Acts would have been avoided. But he had no eye to the difficulties created by the modern commentator. His object was unconcerned with our wandering ignorance. He was concerned only with his own audience and his own subject, which was the action of the Divine Spirit in the growing Church. He assumes knowledge of surroundings which we do not possess.

(2) " The analogy between the case of Paul and the trial of Jesus" tends, as my friend says, to prove that Paul, like Jesus, was put to death. If one were to argue from analogy after that fashion, it would follow that Paul was put to death in Jerusalem by crucifixion. There are analogies in certain points between the one case and the other, and these Luke mentions; but no progress can be made if we argue that the analogy is complete in respect of some other point which Luke does not mention.

(3) Professor Bartlet has now become quite confident about the innuendo in Agrippa's comment (xxvi. 32): " This man might have been set at liberty, if he had not appealed to Cæsar". Formerly he stated merely as a possible alternative that this might be taken to imply, " but Paul had appealed, and the reigning Cæsar was Nero ! "

Now he says positively that "the very fullness with which Acts records the preliminary hearings in Palestine and the favourable verdicts, points to the condemnation by an 'abnormal monster' like Nero".

Professor Bartlet here argues as if the point in question were whether Paul was or was not condemned under Nero; but it is a matter of history that Paul was condemned by Nero. The question is not whether the Emperor condemned Paul, but only when and in what circumstances the condemnation took place. Tacitus says in clear and explicit terms that the Christians began to be persecuted by Nero in the autumn of the year 64. What has to be proved by Professor Bartlet is that Paul was condemned more than two years earlier. That proof he does not enter upon through this line of argument, even if it were valid in itself.

He adds, too, that in Luke's history the condemnation of Paul "is naturally passed over in silence as well known, and dangerous to refer to explicitly from the Christian standpoint". This last statement is one which he can hardly support on longer consideration. Did Luke not dare to mention in his history that Paul was condemned, because it was "dangerous to refer to" this fact?[1]

From what point of view can Professor Bartlet count it dangerous, or think that Luke would shrink from at any rate briefly mentioning it, even supposing it had been dangerous? He holds that the book of the Acts was written between 72 and 75 A.D. under Vespasian. Nero was then a proscribed and condemned Emperor. There could be no danger, so far as politics and the Roman State were concerned, in saying that a man, even though innocent, was executed by order of Nero. Nero was then

---

[1] Was it dangerous to record that Jesus, or Peter, or James was condemned?

officially treated as an "abnormal monster". His very name was expunged, so far as possible, from history; and his acts were declared invalid. To have been condemned by Nero was at that time rather a proof of good character. Why should Luke on any view think it dangerous to say so, or shrink from saying so?

For my own part, I hold that Vespasian originated the Imperial condemnation of Christianity; but, if Luke had shrunk from defending Christianity in spite of the official condemnation, he would not have written at all. His book is from beginning to end a defence of Christianity, and a protest against the Imperial condemnation. As to recording that Nero condemned Paul, such a record could in no way have been dangerous to the Christians or to the man who wrote the words.[1] The only danger under the Flavian Emperors lay in speaking well about Nero. To cast blame on Nero was politic, if Luke had ever wished to be politic.

As to Paul's "foreboding at Ephesus that he would never again see the Ephesian elders," on which Professor Bartlet lays such stress, I have pointed out elsewhere that there is no foreboding in the speech. Paul had no time to waste in forebodings at that time: he stated plans: he did not know, or forecast, the future: he never pretended to forecast future events: perhaps he would have thought it wrong to do so except by revelation. His plans were now formed, and he stated them to the Ephesian bishops —doubtless at greater length and in more detail than in

[1] My view that Vespasian originated the anti-Christian policy, and that Nero's persecution was personal to himself and did not commit the government permanently—inasmuch as Nero's acts were abrogated and his memory condemned—has not yet been accepted by historians. The prevailing view regards Vespasian as good-naturedly indifferent to Christianity (and of course also as absolutely hostile to Nero). That is still more fatal to Professor Bartlet's argument.

the *résumé* which Luke gives. His face was now set to-wards wider plans in the centre and the west of the Empire, as soon as the final act in his mission to the Four Provinces was concluded, *viz.*, the delivery in Jerusalem of the charities of all his congregations. In the pursuance of those plans he did not intend to be in Ephesus again, but to go from Syria direct to Rome, and thereafter to devote himself to Western work, leaving the East to others as his representatives.

If my friend would start afresh on this new line, I think he would have a better road to success in proving his case. He might reasonably argue that First Timothy and Titus were written in pursuance of the plan which Paul had intimated to the Ephesian elders (and generally to his friends). Timothy was to carry on his work in Asia, Titus in the new Crete; and they required a certain charge. Then, in the development of events, Paul found that more was needed in Asia: first came the needed Epistles, and finally the return implied in Second Timothy.

This involves a long interval between First and Second Timothy. Professor Bartlet makes a distinct gap, both in thought and circumstances, between them. A longer gap in time is quite in consonance with the real meaning of his theory.[1]

(4) In his argument under this fourth head Professor Bartlet is singularly indifferent to the facts and methods of Roman legal procedure. Admitting that, as I have proved, there was a period fixed within which the prosecutors in an appeal must appear, and that eighteen months was probably the period, he suggests "that the Jews had at least given

[1] I may add that the arguments which I formerly stated against Professor Bartlet's placing of First Timothy on the voyage from Ephesus to Jerusalem do not apply to his latest view, that it was written in Rome, soon after Paul's arrival there.

notice within the legal limit that they would press their case as soon as the winter of 61-62 was over and their witnesses could arrive ". But it made no difference what notice they might give ; the practice had been instituted by the preceding Emperor that the prosecutors must appear to begin proceedings and not merely give notice that at some future and remoter time they would come forward to take practical action. Their time for acting and for appearing to press their case with witnesses and evidence, assuming that witnesses were required and permitted, was limited.[1]

Professor Bartlet argues respecting the difference between Luke's "two full years" and "eighteen months". But the force of Luke's phrase is not to be pressed to the exact limit of twenty-four months. A study of usage does not suggest anything more than that Luke is guarding against the quite possible understanding that "two years" might mean only a year and a bit. He means the substantial part of 60 and 61 (the Roman years, beginning 1st January) ; and a term ending in autumn 61 would fully explain his expression. Luke is always loose in definitions of time : e.g., when in chapters xx., xxi., he gives so many numerical statements of days, he leaves it open to dispute and diverse opinion whether or not Paul actually reached Jerusalem before Pentecost, as he so eagerly desired.[2] After the lapse of eighteen months, there followed necessarily (as I have pointed out) various legal proceedings and forms, which took some time. The limit did not open the door

---

[1] I assume that witnesses were brought forward, as my friend makes a point of this. But in appeals to the Privy Council in Great Britain now, no witnesses are allowed to be called : lawyers state the case on both sides, but new evidence is not admitted.

[2] Personally I entertain no doubt that Paul arrived in time, and that Luke in his own way intimates this ; but many commentators argue on the opposite side. A careful study of Luke's usage seems to me to eliminate all doubt.

and unlock the chain of the prisoner automatically. It merely started the new series of forms, culminating (as I have argued from the action of Claudius) in a formal acquittal by the law (in which sometimes the Emperor personally appeared). Claudius loved to appear personally ; and, if we are to judge from Acts xxvii. 24, Nero appeared personally in the case of Paul, and " Paul stood before him " (a favourable augury). The words of the vision imply success and inspire hope.

On the other hand, in the case of a tedious trial, in which an obscure Roman[1] from Tarsus was concerned and witnesses from many provinces and cities (as Professor Bartlet urges) had to testify, the idea that the Emperor would take part personally in the proceedings is in the last degree improbable—especially an idle and careless Emperor like Nero. From Acts xxvii. 24 alone it seems highly probable that the condemnation did not occur at this time. Some years later of course the trial did occur ; but Luke's words seem to point on to the success of Paul at this stage and the failure of the Jews.

It was only later, in the degeneration of tyranny, that the condemnation occurred, when Roman government was admittedly all going wrong. A sort of prepossession seems to affect the minds of many writers on this subject. There was a condemnation under Nero : Luke mentions an accusation under Nero : therefore the two must be placed together. Tacitus with his absolute negative is set aside, or perhaps not even thought of.

Professor Bartlet even quotes " the analogy of the case of Lampon ". As I have just pointed out above, there is no

---

[1] Obscure among the hundred of thousands of *cives Romani*, but actually a member of a great aristocracy of birth and influence in his own surroundings in the Eastern province.

analogy : a governor with autocratic authority in Egypt kept a case hanging over Lampon there for two years : there was no time limit,[1] because this was not an appeal : the governor could do as he chose, and might have kept the case impending for ten years if his tenure of power lasted so long. It is really not right to harp on this old quotation, which merely proves that those who quote it as an analogy are disregarding facts and law. The one analogy is that "two years" occurs both in Philo and in Luke ; but the term is a very wide one ; in Philo it might perhaps mean only fourteen months, but in Luke it certainly means fully twenty-one or twenty-two months. The end was fixed by legal considerations in the one case, and by the governor's caprice or convenience or fears in the other.

(5) "The nature of the references to his prospects made by Paul in Philemon and Philippians respectively is against the theory that the Jews did not support their case at Rome. For if so we should expect the tone of Philippians, as nearer the end of the time-limit for such action, to be *more confident* than that used in the earlier Philemon ; whereas the opposite is the case." So Professor Bartlet writes.

This is a reason of rather flimsy character. It is quite obvious, as I have pointed out, that in that long imprisonment, Paul, with his weak health, was exposed to alternations of confidence and apprehension ; and the situation itself changed. Moreover, the date of Philippians is after all not accepted as certain. Lightfoot puts it earlier than Philemon. Like Professor Bartlet I have argued that it is later ;[2] but my mind then was largely influenced by the

---

[1] The time limit under consideration operated only in case of appeals from the provinces to the Emperor. Lampon was a provincial, charged with treasonable words or acts ; and the governor of the province had full authority to protract or to decide the case.

[2] *St. Paul the Traveller and Roman Citizen*, p. 358.

same prepossession which dominates Professor Bartlet's mind, that the trial for life came towards the end of the " two full years ". Just as he does, so I formerly read everything under the colouring influence of that fixed idea. Things appear different when one looks through a colourless atmosphere. In any case, as has just been stated, the argument has no bearing on the case and no value in either direction. As I fancy, Professor Bartlet would incline to place Colossians and Philemon and Philippians early in the imprisonment and Second Timothy at some interval after them.

Moreover, my friend himself only a month before saw no great variation in Paul's tone when he refers in those two Epistles to the prospect of his release. I have just quoted what he printed in May, 1913 ; but in April, 1913, in the same magazine, p. 327, he says : " Somewhat confident forecasts of relief and consequent journeying were to be found in the so-called ' Imprisonment Group,' *viz.* Philemon 22 and Philippians i. 25 f., ii. 23 f.". The difference that may exist between two fairly confident anticipations of release forms a very slight and unstable foundation on which to build an argument of this kind.

(6) Professor Bartlet now brings up his final and, as he thinks, conclusive argument. " This new view is excluded by the joint witness of 1 Peter and 1 Clement, which (as I have pointed out in the article ' Paul ' in the *Encycl. Britannica*) do not permit of Paul's having survived the Neronian persecution of 64, in which Peter also suffered. For Clement says (c. 6) that the Neronian victims of 64 were 'gathered together' unto those two Apostles just referred to."

Unfortunately the argument from Clement is based on a double misinterpretation. The first misinterpretation is that Peter and Paul died first, and then the Roman martyrs were "gathered together" to them. This results from an incautious application of such a translation as that by Lightfoot: "unto these men of holy lives was gathered together a vast multitude of the elect". Lightfoot was guided by the right desire to keep close to the order of the Greek;[1] but, so far as I remember,[2] he never used this argument from his own expression which Professor Bartlet employs. The dative case at the beginning cannot bear the sense which the argument requires: the dative is determined by the sense of the verb—not "was gathered unto," but "was gathered along with"—and the proper suggestion is "along with these men of holy lives there was gathered together a great multitude of the elect". There is no suggestion of sequence: the other elect do not follow, they go along with, Paul and Peter.

In the second place, the other elect are not simply the martyrs of the Neronian persecution. They are the whole band of martyrs that have suffered in Rome, and perhaps universally. Considerations of time play no part in the mind of Clement: all the band of martyrs down to his own day are associated in the great "cloud of witnesses" with Peter and Paul.

The argument is based, from first to last, on a wrong prepossession, and involves a wrong view. As long as one looks simply at the Greek, and keeps all prepossessions far from one's mind, no such inference as Professor Bartlet draws can possibly suggest itself. The weakness of his arguments is due to the prepossession that holds his mind: ordinarily he reasons in a far freer and more convincing way.

---

[1] τούτοις τοῖς ἀνδράσιν ὁσίως πολιτευσαμένοις συνηθροίσθη πολὺ πλῆθος ἐκλεκτῶν.

[2] I write far from books.

His argument based on First Peter touches such a big issue and involves so many preliminary steps, each of which is a subject of grave controversies, that I may be permitted here to set it aside. One cannot go into it on the necessary scale. I would only say that, while I (like very few others) am very much in agreement with him in almost all the steps of the complicated train of reasoning which he assumes as the preliminary to his inference, I draw from these steps a widely different conclusion.

With regard to Professor Bartlet's reason (3) we may add that the method of drawing auguries in a totally different sense from words which were spoken with a clear and definite meaning, is not a sound one. In Acts xxvi. 32 Agrippa spoke a definite acquittal. He had no thought of contrasting his judgment with the Emperor's: he simply stated that the case might have ended at this point if Paul had not by his appeal removed it from the authority of the present court. Now the Roman pagan system of augury laid much stress on the unconscious innuendo conveyed in words intended to have a quite different meaning. Personally, I am satisfied always to take the historian's words in the sense in which each speaker intended them, and to trace no innuendo as to the light in which future developments might place them to later observers; and the other method as Professor Bartlet employs it seems to me a dangerous one. When he was writing as a commentator, with no case to prove, he regarded Acts xxvi. 32 in a fair and unprejudiced way, and he stated only the plain meaning (which I take) as being really "of the greatest significance," while the innuendo was to him a matter on which " opinions may differ "; but now he founds an argument on this innuendo as if it were a matter of certainty.

LII. The Date of the Galatian Letter

Much depends on the answer to the question regarding the date when, and the place where, the letter of Paul to the Galatians was written. Several able writers have recently contended that the letter must be assigned to a very early date. One of the first to do so was Professor Valentin Weber of Würzburg in a series of books and papers. Quite a number of English and Scottish writers have taken the same view: they are too many to enumerate, as I might probably omit some, and I should regret to leave out the names of any to whose courtesy and historical acumen I am so much indebted.

For my own part I have long been in a state of uncertainty and dissatisfaction, and hoping for the opportunity of reaching a decided opinion. After one has argued in favour of a date and place, it is not easy to contemplate the whole question from a quite unbiassed point of view; and I waited for leisure and a quiet mind, which are conditions not easily attained.

The theory of early origin was maintained, if I recollect rightly, by Calvin. It frequently came up in my mind, but was always set aside. Now it has established itself in the form that the letter was written at an early stage in the controversy which is described in Acts xv. 1 ff. Emissaries from Palestine, acting with a general commission from James, though not with instructions on this special matter (which had never yet been brought up as one pressing for definite decision), had come to Antioch, and some also into the Galatian churches. In the latter, which were quite newly formed (Gal. i. 5),[1] and in which there was at the moment no authoritative and experienced teacher, these emissaries, being of old standing in the Church, exercised (as was natural) very great influence. They were able to quote words or acts of Paul as implying that he agreed with them: Paul himself, as they declared, was a "preacher of circumcision".

The acts or words are admitted by Paul.[2] He disputes only the interpretation placed upon them : for the sake of peace and harmony he was willing to make great concessions, but these were only concessions to Jewish weakness and must not be regarded as doctrinal and obligatory.

The Galatians, of course, knew that Paul had never ordered them to accept circumcision ; but the emissaries evidently maintained that this rite was the completion of their Christian profession : they had begun well, and now the perfect stage of full communion with the original Church awaited them. If (as seems to me probable) the emissaries quoted on their side an act of fullest concession by Paul, this would be an extraordinarily effective argument. However that may be, it lies in the nature of the case that the familiar idea of a progressive instruction, i.e. of stages in knowledge, was employed. Paul himself had used words of this kind,[3] which quite naturally and reasonably sug-

---

[1] As has been generally recognised, the words here used, coming in the forefront of the letters, the first after the address, must be meant quite emphatically. Formerly I erred in not laying sufficient stress on this.

[2] Gal. v. 11, i. 8-10.

[3] Such teaching was evidently characteristic with Paul, and may be assumed as imparted by him to the Galatians. 1 Corinthians ii. 6, iii. 1 f., ii. 15, if read in this order, imply the idea of steps in knowledge, and of teaching withheld from beginners as not intelligible to them, but communicated to advanced Christians.

gested the idea of successive stages in Christian knowledge and life. Beginners heard less, and learned less, and were called on to do less, than Christians of tried experience, who were more fully endowed with the Spirit of God.

This conception of progress or growth is involved in the very idea of Paulinism. Increasing knowledge is increasing strength, and this increase inevitably brings about greater demands and increasing responsibilities. That is human life ; and that is the divine life. As faith grows stronger, it acts itself out in a more vigorous course of work. A faith which does not produce ever more and more exertion is not growing. Such was everywhere the teaching of Paul.

Without this conception of stages in knowledge the action of the Galatians, and the Epistle to the Galatians, cannot be understood, as is maintained in my *Historical Commentary*, § xxvii. p. 324. The Galatians thought that they were progressing to a more perfect stage of spiritual knowledge. Paul points out to them that really they are changing to a different form of Gospel, fleshly and not spiritual ; but he acknowledges that they think they are progressing : " After beginning through the Spirit, are you now perfecting yourselves through the flesh ? " [1]

Even the Apostolic Decree, while it is in word so remarkably complimentary to Paul and Barnabas, yet lends itself without difficulty to a similar interpretation. The concessions regarding meat, etc., are laid down as obligatory, but are called " burdens " : it is an easy thing to go on from this thought, and to say that burdens are proportioned to the strength of the bearer, and that more perfect Christians can and should bear more than the minimum imposed as necessary on weaklings and beginners. This conception of de-

[1] Gal. iii. 3. The Galatians, an Anatolian people, had natural affinity for Hebraism, and they misinterpreted Paul's doctrine of τελείωσις in the sense of progress in Hebrew observance.

grees lies at the basis of the whole Galatian trouble. Paul
had to remove it by convincing the Galatians that they were
running contrary to the spirit of his teaching, and that what
they thought progress was really retrogression.

It has been argued that the question of Acts xv. 1 might
have become acute in Antioch long ago. That, however,
did not take place. So Luke and Paul both say. In Antioch
Jewish and Gentile Christians had for years been dwelling
side by side, and the conditions of amity must have been
settled by agreement, either tacit or formal : the general
body of Jewish Christians in Antioch were in full fellowship publicly and privately with the Gentiles of the Church.
They all ate together and lived together harmoniously.
Luke and Paul are in full agreement on this point.[1]   Dis-
cord arose only when the Christian Jews from Palestine, who
were far more strict and narrow than those of Antioch and
of the Diaspora in general, found themselves confronted
with the question whether they were to sit and eat with
the uncircumcised.

This question Peter answered at Antioch forthwith in
the affirmative (Galatians ii. 11), just as previously he had
eaten with Cornelius and other Gentiles (Acts xi. 3). But apparently he did so impulsively and naturally and without
full consideration : he looked only to the fact that these also
were Christians, that all nations were admitted to the
Church,[2] that Cornelius and his friends and the Antiochian
Church in general had received the Spirit ; and he acted on
impulse accordingly.

Afterwards, when the protest of the Jewish Christians
from Jerusalem made him realise all that was involved in
his action, he withdrew from full communion with the
uncircumcised Gentiles in Antioch. In Acts xi. 5-17 it is

---

[1] Gal. ii. 11 f. ; Acts xv. 1 f.   [2] Acts x. 34.

noteworthy that he does not reply to this part of the charge against him. He speaks in general terms : he had had Cornelius and his friends baptised,[1] and vaguely he adds, "Who was I that I could withstand God?" That he ate with them, he does not expressly acknowledge, and he does not deny.

The charge in this respect, however, was allowed to drop at that time : it was not urgent, and it was not pressed even at Jerusalem. In Antioch among the freer Jews full intercourse became the rule ; and, when Peter went there, he followed the rule.

Until the emissaries from Judaea came to Antioch, therefore, there had been no trouble regarding intercourse among the converts, Jews and Greeks. Such a case as that of Titus in Galatians ii. 3 f. could not have arisen at an earlier date.

Nor can the case of Titus be placed during the controversy after the emissaries arrived in Antioch, for the controversy was a universal one and not about the treatment of an individual. Moreover, the circumstances in which the case of Titus came up are of quite different character from what existed in Antioch. The emissaries found there a general rule of common life and intercourse, public and manifest ; but the case of Titus was brought forward by some persons, called in strong terms "sham brethren," who spied secretly and found that Titus was eating along with certain Jews. In Antioch this could be seen every day by all men. Hence I cannot entertain the suggestion (which has been made by some) that the case of Titus occurred at Antioch.

There seems therefore to be no doubt that the case of Titus must be placed at Jerusalem. Nothing in it suits

---

[1] It is noteworthy that he did not baptise them himself (x. 48) : he had with him one or more ministers for such work. Compare the rareness of Paul's personal action in baptising at Corinth.

Antioch.   Everything in it points to Jerusalem.   In Jerusalem there were doubtless many Jews that, without being fully Christian, were in a certain degree sympathetic with the new Faith.   These might be called "pseudo-Christians"; and some of these, looking askance at Titus as a Greek, and watching carefully though in a covert way the private life of the Antiochian delegates, observed that he ate with the Jewish colleagues.   This is just what would naturally occur in Jerusalem; and doubtless it took place within the first day or two of their arrival.   At once there was an explosion similar to that in Acts xi. 2 f., but ending as quickly as in that case, through the prudence and sympathetic action of Titus (as we shall see).

Some of the writers who argue in favour of an early date for *Galatians* seem to lay most stress on the difficulties which accompany the theory (as yet the dominant and generally accepted theory—but after all only a theory) of a late date for the Epistle.   Personally I attach great weight in all such problems to positive arguments of one particular class: which date makes the Epistle most illuminative of Christian history and of Paul's mind and character?   As to difficulties, it is often the case that the solution of a seeming difficulty opens the gateway of advance in knowledge; and I do not feel any serious dread of difficulties as such, even although my ignorance may at the moment prove unable to dispose of them. The only real difficulty is the impossibility; and it is not always easy to distinguish between what is only difficult and what is impossible.

Approaching the question on a different line, I am glad to feel that I have reached the same conclusion as Professor V. Weber and the rest, even though it has involved abandoning my former view.   I find, however, that the change of view is not so great as might appear. The place of origin remains the same, and this involves the important question who it was that joined with Paul in issuing the letter. Who were the persons that added their authority to his in making the weighty decision pronounced in this letter? As has been already maintained in my *Historical Commentary*, § ii. p. 238 ff., Syrian Antioch, and no other Church but Antioch, could be in the position to join with Paul in authorising this letter. With the earlier date, there can be no possible place of origin except Antioch (or the road thence to Jerusalem).[1]

As has been stated in the book named, there was the most complete difference between the class of persons who might be mentioned in the end of a letter as joining in sending salutation to Paul's correspondents, and the class of persons who could be admitted as joint-authorities in issuing the letter. Paul took no humble view of his own relation to his correspondents. He composed his letter as one having authority, like an Emperor using a rescript; and few could be associated in composing the rescript.

Generally his authority was Divine inspiration and knowledge of the mind of Jesus; but even where he "has no commandment of the Lord," and gives his own personal opinion (as in 1 Cor. vii. 25), he still regards his judgment as carrying weight to his own spiritual children. He did not admit as joint authors of his letters any except persons who occupied a position of authority in respect of the correspondents addressed in the special letter.[2] Timothy,

---

[1] The latter view, which is that of Professor Lake, arises apparently through the idea that the phrase "all those who are with me" implies travelling companions. It puts *Gal.* some weeks or months later.

[2] The proof of this has been given in detail already: see *Histor. Comm. Gal.* § II.

for example, could co-operate in the first letter to Corinth, or in that to Colossae, but not in the circular letter to the Asian Churches which was written at the same time. He had authority in Corinth and in Colossae,[1] but not until later in the Asian cities generally. The person who is associated as an authority was present with Paul, and approved the doctrine and judgment delivered in the letter.

Antioch was the one church that could and did possess special authority in respect of the Galatian congregations.[2] Antioch had sent forth Paul to them, and had received him back to give an account of all that had occurred to him in that mission, and of the new step that he had taken in the course of it (Acts xiv. 27).

If, however, that was so, why did not Paul mention the name of the Church which lent its authority to his letter? Why did he veil it under the vague phrase "all the brethren who are with me"? This question did not occur to me formerly. Now I would suggest that the Church in Antioch was not itself unanimous; and that Paul could only claim the authority of "all those who are with me".

Though there can be no doubt that the overwhelming majority of opinion in the Antiochian Church was with Paul, yet there can also be no doubt that the emissaries who came from Jerusalem had their supporters. Paul, in Galatians ii. 12, tells the story: in the Church of Antioch, the Christian Jews, including even Barnabas, deferred to the emissaries and ceased to maintain social intercourse with the uncircumcised Christians. Hence Paul claims to speak with the authority only of "all those who are with me," and

---

[1] On Colossae, *St. Paul the Traveller*, p. 274.

[2] Even Jerusalem could not well be considered. It would indeed have generally the authority of prestige and seniority, but not in this case, where its authority is treated rather slightingly.

not of the Church as a whole. He will not claim support from any man that is not in full agreement.

What light does the early date throw on the difficult sentence in Galatians ii. 3 f.? "Not even Titus who was with me, who was a Greek, was compelled to be circumcised : but by reason of the pretended brethren. . . ." The sentence was never completed. Paul breaks off, being carried away by the tide of his thought; and he never resumes the interrupted thought—perhaps avoiding, in the hurry and rush of his ideas, the repetition of a matter which was doubtless known in a general way to the Galatians. Paul completes their knowledge by adding some less known details; but does not repeat the public and familiar facts.

Perhaps the right clue is furnished by Acts xvi. 3 : "because of the Jews that were in those parts". In *St. Paul the Traveller*, p. 158 f., the close parallelism between Acts xv. 1 f. and Galatians ii. 12 f. is pointed out, and the parallelism is used to date the incident described in those two passages. That date now stands fast on the earlier dating of the letter ; but the parallelism with the language of the Acts extends further. There is a certain analogy between the case of Titus in Galatians ii. 3 f. and of Timothy in Acts xvi. 3. Each was an uncircumcised Hellene ; and each had to be treated in some way "because of the Jews in those parts". διὰ τοὺς Ἰουδαίους is exactly parallel to διὰ τοὺς ψευδαδέλφους. Two possibilities seem to be open as regards the case of Titus.

(1) Not even Titus was *compelled* to be circumcised ; but, because of the sham brothers who came about to spy upon our actions, he voluntarily accepted the rite, though we (*viz.* Barnabas and I) did not for a moment yield by deferring to their demands and requiring him to comply : his conduct was purely voluntary, and arose through his desire to avoid

anything that might wound their feelings and produce enmity or strife. In that case Titus, by his unselfish devotion, served as a model for the case of Timothy; and Paul, by accepting his devotion, might be said by enemies to have become a preacher of circumcision. That this was actually said in Galatia by his enemies is fully admitted by himself;[1] and it is of course clear that their account was founded on some acts or words of Paul's, even though the acts or words were, according to him, misrepresented.

This theory has some advantages. It well explains the words of v. 11 and i. 8-10 (which otherwise constitute rather a difficulty as we shall see below, when the early date of Galatians is accepted).[2] It puts Paul's conduct on a uniform plane throughout; he acted towards Timothy as he had consented to Titus's voluntary action some years before: he was always willing to go a very long way practically in concession to Jewish prejudices and customs. It has one very great advantage in respect of Galatians v. 2 f. : " I, Paul, say unto you that, if ye receive circumcision, Christ will profit you nothing. Yea, I testify again to every man that receiveth circumcision, that he is a debtor to do the whole Law. Ye are severed from Christ, ye who would be justified by the Law; ye are fallen away from grace." This passage would have a strange and almost an ugly look, if it were taken *au pied de la lettre ;* but, if it was written to correspondents into whose ears the case of Titus, as now interpreted by the theory we are considering, had been dinned by the insistence of Paul's emissaries, there was no danger of their taking it in the extremest sense, and no

---

[1] Gal. v. 11; compare i. 8-10.

[2] When the later date of *Gal.* is accepted, these passages are naturally understood as a reference to the case of Timothy; and to my mind that has always constituted the strongest argument in support of the later dating.

question of Paul's intending it in that sense. They would know at once that Paul was not condemning Titus, whose conduct he has just been explaining and justifying. They would catch Paul's real meaning, that, if you get yourselves circumcised as a rite necessary for salvation and incumbent on every Christian who desires to be in the fullest sense a Christian, then you are asking that the Law, not Christ, should be your means of justification ; but if you accept the rite as a concession to the feeling of others, this is an act of love and sympathy.

The objection to this way of supplying the suppressed thought is that it requires such strong emphasis to be laid on the verb " was compelled ". It has, however, been maintained by a number of exegetes, and must be admitted, that this strong emphasis is quite possible grammatically, and is not inconsistent with the force of the Greek language.

Considerable difficulty was experienced from early time with this passage and with the facts of the case. *Οὐδέ* in Galatians ii. 5 is omitted in the Western text and by many Fathers, though the difference among the Fathers on this matter does not determine or depend upon their opinion whether Titus was actually circumcised : some careful authorities have maintained that he was, and yet read *οὐδέ*.

(2) Not even Titus was forced to be circumcised ; but, because of the sham brethren, he retired from Jerusalem, in order to avoid outraging their scruples, and to facilitate the success of our mission—though we personally did not for a moment yield to their demand that Titus should be circumcised. The advantage of this interpretation is that it explains the statement of Acts xi. 30, xii. 25, in which Titus is not mentioned as a delegate ; and thus it produces perfect harmony between the two accounts of this second visit ; but it makes the verb " was compelled " rather feeble :

one asks why, on that interpretation, Paul did not say περιετ-μήθη in place of ἠναγκάσθη·περιτμηθῆναι.

On this interpretation we cannot determine, except by pure conjecture, what part of Paul's teaching and conduct it was that had been construed by his opponents as imply-ing the concession and admission that Gentiles should be circumcised ; no word or act previous to the case of Timothy is recorded on the part of Paul, from which the teaching of circumcision by him could by any twisting be elicited. But, of course, conciliatory teaching in general on Paul's part may be assumed as having always been his way.

Further, the strong words of Galatians v. 2-4 would be more liable to be interpreted by Galatian readers in the extreme and most literal way. There would not remain any case, so far as we know, in which Paul had practically demonstrated his opinion that a converted pagan might voluntarily and justifiably, in courteous and sympathetic consideration for Jewish custom and feelings, accept the rite as a concession to them. We should then have to explain both v. 2-4 and v. 11, i. 8-10, by the same supposition, that in his early Galatian teaching Paul had laid great stress on the duty of making concession to Jewish feeling—which is of course quite probable in itself, though not actually recorded—and had said that for this conciliatory purpose any Christian might justifiably accept the Jewish rite.

(3) It cannot be admitted that there is any third alterna-tive. Either Titus retired from Jerusalem and relieved the delegation of the difficulty caused by his presence, and thus the question was shelved for the time ; or Titus sub-mitted voluntarily in deference to Jewish prejudices. It cannot for a moment be regarded as possible either that the straitlaced Jews of Jerusalem submitted quietly to the con-

tinued presence of the unclean Gentile at the same table with Jews in their midst, or that Paul and Barnabas consented to dissimulate their relations with Titus and their feelings towards him. If Titus stayed on in Jerusalem uncircumcised, the whole question must have been raised. "They of the circumcision" could not possibly have tolerated the daily presence among them of an uncircumcised Hellene in intimate intercourse with Jews.

If Titus retired from the city, the problem might have been quietly postponed, since neither side cared to force it to the front, and both probably thought that time might bring about a solution. The question had threatened to emerge in the case of Cornelius; but as Cornelius was far away, it did not become active, and was left undecided (Acts xi. 1 ff.). Not until some of the strictest class of Jewish Christians, "they of the circumcision," found themselves daily confronted by this question in Acts xv. 1, Galatians ii. 11, did a final and authoritative decision become necessary. So Luke clearly intimates, and nothing that Paul says is discrepant.

It is not easy to choose between the two open alternatives. The arguments which occur to me are now stated; and they tend to favour the former alternative, that Titus accepted the rite. This seems to make history more harmonious; and it explains well the text of Galatians ii. 5 and the remarkable variation there.

The reading of οὐδέ in Galatians ii. 5 is preferable in history as well as in authority and in sense. The omission of the negative is an early error, which disappeared again comparatively early. It arose in the time when the memory still survived that Titus had submitted to be circumcised; and the apparent contradiction—not really a contradiction—was solved by eliminating the negative word.

Considering what immense importance in this controversy attached to the willingness of Gentiles to make concessions to Jewish feelings, one is surprised to find that in the Apostolic Decree, which decided the question, there is, according to the generally accepted text, no recognition of what after all was the most powerful force and motive to action in this problem. The Decree is almost harshly anti-Hebrew in this Text. It has not a word except condemnation of the old-fashioned Hebrews. It makes little allowance for their point of view. The concessions which it commands as necessary are slight ; and they are called burdens, not concessions. Since that is so, one fails to understand why the Decree does not say anything about the point which to Paul always seemed the most important in this question—the duty of sympathy and voluntary wider concession.

In the Western Text, on the other hand, the supreme duty not to do to another what you would not wish to be done to yourself is emphasised. This, beyond all doubt, is a strong point in that Text : it relieves us of a difficulty in the Decree. Those who reject the Western Text, however, can always find an explanation in the accompanying verbal message, which is expressly referred to in the Decree, and which (as may fairly be urged) must be regarded as needed to complete the Decree. Judas and Silas were to convey the Decree, and to complete and explain its terms. They were to show the power and the need of love and brotherly feeling and mutual concession in the give-and-take of ordinary life. Hence Paul, when treating this subject in 1 Corinthians x., and in Romans xii., lays almost the whole stress on love and concession. He was completing the Decree, as the Council had expected that the messengers should complete it. He does not quote the Decree, which was so completely in his favour : he assumes it as familiar : it is in the minds of all his correspondents like the Ten Commandments : its meaning is what his readers are seeking for, and this he expounds.

Therefore, Paul never quotes the Decree to Corinthians and Romans : he only adds to it the savour and the grace of love. In the letter to the Galatians, on the contrary, he does not add love to it : he rather intensifies the sternness and the bareness of its rebuke to the extremists on the Jewish side.

This is why, on mature consideration, I find myself forced to put the letter before the Decree. The letter was written in the stress of conflict. It states the Pauline side in the strongest form. Though it mentions[1] the duty of love, and condemns quarrels and strife, yet it does not apply love to this question of conduct, and it is open to the criticism of suggesting that the cause of quarrel and strife lay always on the side opposed to his view. It was not written after the victory was gained and the Decree issued ; for the Decree requires that those who carry and deliver it should add what Judas and Silas were commissioned to add orally. Paul acts accordingly in Rom. xii., 1 Cor. x.

When the Galatian letter is placed early, the result is that the stages in early Christian development are more clearly marked in history, and the conduct of Paul is always seen to be actuated by the same spirit ; he is from first to last full of sympathy and ready to make concession in his attitude to the Jews, so far as practical conduct is concerned, but from first to last he is resolute and uncompromising in his teaching of principles. In this he never hesitated : it is always wrong to make any external act or any bodily mutilation a condition of entry into the fullest

---

[1] See Gal. v. 22 f.

rights of the Christian Church.   Salvation is a spiritual fact, in the spirit and through the spirit.   To abandon that essential principle is to be severed from Christ, and to be fallen away from grace.   In practical conduct, however, one should be ready to go very far in self-denial, and even to submit to privation and suffering, in the way of accommodating one's deserved liberty to the scruples and prejudices of a weaker brother.

From this point of view the accepted form of the text of the Apostolic Decree is found justified; and the Western reading would be an early error, arising so early that it reaches back to the time when the real facts were still in the memory of the Church and the text was accommodated to them.   As in Galatians ii. 3, so it is in Acts xv. 29.

I can quite imagine that many, when the case is clearly before them, will refuse to believe that the Apostles' Decree could wholly omit a reference to the duty of being conciliatory and sympathetic, and could leave this to be added orally by messengers.   All such must be driven to prefer the Western Text of the Decree, not necessarily as exact, but as proving that there has occurred dislocation and mutilation of the original form.   For my own part, however, I must regard the accepted Text as true, though difficult.

However this may ultimately be determined, the Decree is not a good specimen of legislation for the Universal Church.   The Council had not attained to easy mastery of its own powers.   The mere fact that the Decree is not subsequently quoted in the early history shows that it was not found in practice to be sufficient.   The congregations could not neglect the duty of being conciliatory to Jewish feelings, yet this duty is either omitted or put in a very vague way, according as the " Eastern " or the " Western " text is selected as nearest the true form.   In all probability the Corinthians, when they consulted Paul and were answered in his First Epistle, had in mind the Decree, perhaps quoting it explicitly ; and in his reply Paul was expounding what he conceived to be the spirit which actuated the Apostles in framing it.

It seems, then, clear that, during the visit to Jerusalem described in Galatians ii. 1-10 and Acts xi., xii., the question regarding the circumcision of Gentile converts did not reach an acute form, and was not discussed publicly. Nor was it discussed even in the private meeting of Paul and Barnabas with the three leading Apostles (ii. 2). The latter heard the two future missionaries describe their action and attitude in Syrian Antioch. Perhaps this private conversation took place on the eve of Paul's departure, immediately after he had received the command described in Acts xxii. 17-21, to go right away into the Gentile world ; and at any rate it is clear that Barnabas and Saul indicated their plans for future mission work. The three fully approved of the division of work : Paul and Barnabas were commissioned to the Gentiles, and they themselves to the circumcision. But in Paul's statement there is nothing to suggest that the conditions of future social intercourse between Christian Jews and converted Gentiles were considered.

Every difficulty was met when it emerged in the early history of the Church. It was met always[1] in the same way by reliance on the guidance of the Spirit. The Apostles, as a rule, did not go out to meet future difficulties or discuss ways of solving questions that had not yet presented themselves in practice.

Personally, I find myself strongly influenced by the argument which the Rev. J. Ironside Still briefly states in a private letter, and which I restate in my own fashion, as

---

[1] *Pictures of the Apostolic Church*, § xiii.

well as I can. In the Galatian letter the tone of i. 16 f.,
ii. 6-9, seems a little ungracious towards the older Apostles,
and hardly justifiable as a complete statement of fact, if
Paul, while he wrote, was carrying with him the Decree in
which they speak so cordially and generously of him, and
in which they decide a difficult case on his appeal to them.

Could he so emphatically assert his complete independence of them? Could he say, as if this were complete
and final, without introducing some qualification and restriction, "I conferred not with flesh and blood, neither
went I up to Jerusalem to them that were Apostles before
me," after he had actually gone up to Jerusalem, and had
referred to their decision a controversy that had arisen in
Antioch? Those words would be correct for the moment
referred to, but they had at that later date ceased to be a
sufficient statement of the case, and it was urgently necessary that the modification needed after the meeting of the
Council should be mentioned. Contrast the tone of Galatians ii. 6 with the words of the Apostles about Paul, Acts
xv. 25 f. It is, of course, true that at a later time Paul's
statement of his relation to the older Apostles is very strong,
but yet it is qualified: 2 Corinthians xi. 5, xii. 11, "I
reckon that I am not a whit behind the very chiefest
Apostles, though I am nothing"; 1 Corinthians xv. 9,
"I am the least of the Apostles".

Such statements of equality are, however, essentially different from the assertions in Galatians i. 16, "I conferred not
with flesh and blood," and in ii. 6, "they imparted nothing
to me". Paul could always assert emphatically his equality
in authority. His sphere of action and his co-ordinate
authority under divine guidance had been recognised by the
older Apostles frankly and generously and fully. But after
the Council and the Decree he could not say with the gracious-

ness and courtesy that characterised all his relations towards the older Apostles and breathed through their words regarding him (Acts xv. 25 f.)—he could hardly even with truth say—" they imparted nothing to me ". And, further, after he had publicly conferred with them and discussed the whole question in the Council, he could not be held justified in asserting to the Galatians that he had only privately and not publicly discussed plans of action with them. Such a statement would be disingenuous, to use the mildest possible term. It has even been explained by some modern scholars as an instance of the lower standard of truth that prevailed in Paul's time. To me it seems essentially un-Pauline.

If the Galatian letter was written early, this would fully confirm the confidence expressed in Section I., that Paul had thought out his Gospel completely before he went to the Gentiles; and that there is no development in his own religious position and doctrine from letter to letter. There is indeed development in his missionary methods. He learned much in that respect through experience. There is also some development in his way of presenting his Gospel to his audience. But, on the whole, the difference between his letters is mainly due to the varying character and needs of his correspondents. In writing to the Thessalonians he was addressing an audience of pagan hearers, from whom he had been torn after a very few weeks of preaching, and who were in their infancy as converts. Their needs and their difficulties were quite different from those of a community where Paul had taught for months or years, and where he had instituted a body of officials charged with oversight of the congregation.[1]

The Galatian letter is the earliest, yet it is perfectly mature in its teaching, and in that respect it naturally goes

[1] See also Section I.

with the Roman and Corinthian letters.   The resemblance, however, forms no proof of date; although it has been classed with them on that account by most scholars, and assigned to the same period.   Paul was addressing congregations of maturer character.   He had been a considerable time in Antioch, Iconium, and Lystra[1] (we know little about Derbe, which was less important in Pauline time and throughout Christian history): he returned to those cities and spent some time there, organising them, appointing presbyters and (as we may say with confidence) giving some training to these officials in their congregational duties.

On these two visits he had formed bodies of not merely enthusiastic, but also in some degree matured, converts; and it was to such people that his letter was addressed. Their very error, which he is correcting in his letter, was a sign of thought and of anxious painstaking search for truth, though they had not understood his religious position.   It is, however, quite clear that some word or act of Paul's had been misconstrued, and his explanations and recurrence to the topic show that the misunderstanding was easy and not unnatural.

Those Galatian converts still needed much further training; but the training was that which was suited for a more mature class than the Thessalonians; and this training was conveyed to them both in the letter and in two subsequent visits (Acts xvi. 1-6, xviii. 23).

The desire to avoid pressing too far the South Galatian theory long influenced me, and made me shrink from disturbing the general consensus that *Galatians* should go with *Romans* and *Corinthians*.   I could not trust myself

---

[1] I adhere to the views expressed about times and seasons in my first books on the subject: the first journey lasted from spring 47 A.D. to autumn 49, or 46 to 48.   Mr. Turner would cut the time shorter by a year.

completely in this matter. I feel, however, that the early date brings out better the conduct of Paul as eagerly seeking after unity from first to last. Only in the very beginning of the controversy, when he was contending, as it appeared, for the very existence of a Gentile Church, he seems in some small touches to claim too complete independence. But quickly he recognised that such complete independence was inconsistent with the unity of the Church, and he accepted (probably, as I think, he suggested) the reference of the controversy bearing on this matter to the senior Apostles and the whole governing body in Jerusalem for an authoritative decision. This was a sacrifice of complete independence, and is therefore subsequent to the Galatian letter, which claims absolute independence.

One may briefly mention a circumstance which has been emphasised by Calvin and which evidently determined his opinion : *Gal.* is the letter of a younger man than the other great letters. It has the temper of youth. It is not a work of such ripe judgment and experience as *Cor.* and *Rom.*, and may fairly be called one-sided in comparison. Such a statement as v. 2 has to be explained by the addition of unexpressed circumstances before it can be admitted as true (see p. 392). It was not true in a bare and absolute sense that, if a Galatian accepted the Jewish law, Christ would profit him nothing, and Paul did not subsequently endorse this dictum. The sarcastic temper of Gal. ii. 4-5 is like Phil. iii. 2, but Gal. v. 2 and 12 are unique. Some things that have been said about Paul are true only of this early letter ; and the growth of his character is not rightly understood until we take it so.[1]

[1] Reasons against the early date stated by Mr. M. Jones, *Expositor*, Sept., 1913, show how little can be said against the early date. He makes seriously inaccurate statements about my chronological views on p. 199, and my views on Roman antiquities and facts on p. 208.

LIII. THE USE OF THE WORD "MYSTERY" IN THE LETTERS

There are no two words which are more peculiarly characteristic of the Greek spirit than "grace" (χάρις) and "mystery" (μυστήριον),[1] one in the sphere of art and philosophy, the other in the sphere of religion.

The very essence of that delicate product which we call Hellenism lies in χάρις. The spirit of Greece breathes in the word. Without χάρις there is no Hellenism. With this Hellenic noun there is associated the adjective καλός, a word which cannot be rendered by any single English word, and which is difficult to express even in a long description : it means what in virtue of being beautiful is good and excellent, and in virtue of its delicate excellence is lovely and honourable.

The only spark of real religious fire and life that remained burning in Greece at this period was contained in the Mysteries. The rest of the old national cults in the Hellenic cities were at this time mere survivals of dead forms, retained mainly as brilliant patriotic ceremonial, on which much money was spent, and to which national art and individual ambition or ostentation imparted splendour. It was only at a much later time that those old cults were galvanised into life again through an alliance with the Imperial power and the

---

[1] Our English word "grace" is a very inadequate rendering of χάρις : it wants much of the connotation of χάρις, and it adds an element that is not found in the Greek word. If we combine it with "graciousness" and "charm," we get a little more of the force of χάρις.

popular philosophy in the great final struggle against the new Faith; but that does not belong to the Pauline age. The educated Hellenism of Paul's time either despised any real and fervent religious belief as " superstition," or received it under philosophic protection[1] and national recognition as the worship of "a god unknown" or "gods unknown". A certain exceptional position was accorded to the " Mysteries," and great philosophers or poets like Plato, and men of high personal character like Cicero,[2] speak with profound respect of the Mysteries of Eleusis. In those rites they were ready to believe that philosophic views were dimly shadowed forth in ceremonies and obscure words.

Both words, χάρις and μυστήριον, are specially characteristic of Paul in the New Testament. It is quite impossible to suppose that he was ignorant of, or disregarded, the point of view from which his Greek readers would naturally contemplate them, as they read his letters. He spoke to Greeks in the language that they knew, and he would not write of " grace " merely as if it were a part of the Greek translation of the Old Testament, carrying only the meaning that it has there, but also would bear in mind its significance in the popular language of the Graeco-Asiatic world. A study of Paul's use of χάρις and καλός from this point of view would be instructive, but would carry us too far at present.[3]

In an even greater degree this remark about significance to Greek readers must be applied to the word " Mystery ". A knowledge which had been previously the appanage of the few select, but was now declared through Jesus to all men, was an idea which is fundamental in the teaching of

---

[1] This movement began before there was much formulated and regular philosophy ; but a philosophic outlook on life is characteristic of Hellenism from the beginning. See p. 280 f.

[2] Cicero speaks the opinion of Greek philosophers.

[3] Elsewhere I have had something to say about Paul's use of χάρις.

Paul. This knowledge is both the knowledge which God possesses, and the knowledge of God which man may come to possess. It is the Divine power of God and in God.[1] It is a knowledge which is in process of being revealed to each individual man, in so far as he wishes and desires to receive it, yet it is a knowledge which is revealed once for all to the world in Jesus. It is the Promise of God, and it is the Salvation of all mankind. "Brethren, both Jew and Greek, to us is the news of this Salvation sent," says Paul to the first Galatian audience at Antioch in Acts xiii. 26 ; and, as he goes on to say, " Be it known to you, brethren, that through this man . . . every one that believeth is justified ".

A similar statement was equally true in another way in Greece : the knowledge of a God unknown was now set forth by Paul. The mystic promise, "thou shalt be God, instead of mortal," which had been restricted by esoteric ritual, was now being declared to all : " He is not far from each one of us ".[2] If Paul, as we have seen in Section XLVIII., was acquainted even with the popular term used to designate the advanced stage of knowledge and ritual in the Mysteries, he must have known what a wealth of meaning the word " Mystery " carried to the Greek world ; and he could not use the word without some thought of this meaning. Since he could quote from the poets such words regarding the deity Zeus, as " in Him we live and move and are," and "we are His offspring," with a view to making intelligible to a pagan audience his teaching about the nature of the true and living God, so it must be in his use of the word " Mystery ". He had regard to the significance which the word carried for his audience and his readers.

We must therefore cordially agree with Professor H. A. A. Kennedy's words in the *Expositor*, October, 1912, p. 312,

---

[1] See Sections XXXVIII. to XLII.   [2] Acts xvii. 27.

that while Paul's "use of the term 'knowledge' is affected by the . . . Old Testament . . . it seems equally certain that . . . he presupposed his hearers' acquaintance with these through the medium of the Mystery-religions, and to some extent at least identified himself with the current usage".[1] Knowledge and revelation are closely related to one another, as we have shown above,[2] and as Professor Kennedy there expressly recognises. Every step in the growth of knowledge is a revelation of the will of God and the order of nature.

That there is a certain analogy in all this to the "*paradosis* of the *mysteria*"[3] is as certain as the infinite inferiority of the latter idea to the teaching of Paul. Now, just as he writes to the Colossians rebuking them for the way in which they were allowing the material and unspiritual ideas of ritual which they got from the pagan Mysteries to colour and degrade their ideas of the "knowledge of God," so we must interpret certain other places in which he writes to the Asian Christians.

In no letter does he speak so clearly and strongly about the glorious lot of the Christian and the close relation in which the whole body of Christians stand to God and Christ, as in Ephesians. He wishes to show the Asians whom he was addressing that the Promise, which he is interpreting to them in his Gospel, is immeasurably superior to the promises made in the pagan Mysteries. The rewards promised to the initiated in the Mysteries, both in knowledge and in happiness, were great ; but the Saints have far greater things to expect. It is not merely happiness that

---

[1] He adds in a footnote a reference to the "admirable excursus" on 1 Cor. xii. 10, by J. Weiss (in the ninth edition of Meyer) and Lietzmann's Note on 1 Cor. viii. 3.

[2] See Sections XLIV. and XXXII.

[3] See Section XLVIII.

is promised them—after all for the *mystai* a too material conception of happiness. The Saints are actually the inheritance of the Lord Jesus Christ, they are the consummation of the purpose and will of God which He has had in mind in the creation of the universe, they are the crown of His plans, they are necessary to Him.[1] There is in this nothing that is not in perfect accordance with his earlier letters : " ye are a letter of Christ, written not with ink, but with the Spirit of the living God . . . we are not as Moses, who put a veil upon his face . . . but we all with unveiled face beholding as in a mirror[2] the glory of the Lord are transformed into the same image through stage after stage of glory ".[3] The same truth is all there ; but the expression is different and less emphatic ; the Corinthians see after all " as in a mirror darkly," although they gaze unveiled, yet they only behold a reflection troubled and dimmed[4] of the glory of God : the direct vision is reserved for the future revelation. In Ephesians the Saints are encouraged with the confident anticipation of this direct and complete revelation.

We can hardly doubt that it was through Paul that the word "mystery" came into the Christian vocabulary, and was used rarely in the three Synoptic Gospels[5] and rather more frequently in the Revelation. The influence of the earliest Christian writers on one another is a subject that we can only obscurely guess at : we see it "as in a glass darkly". In Section XXXVI. an example of the influence of older Christian language on Paul is pointed out. The

[1] Eph. i. 9, 18 : see Section XXXVII.
[2] Yet still only " as in a mirror in obscure fashion," 1 Cor. xiii. 12.
[3] 2 Cor. iii. 3-18, where the reference to 1 Cor. xiii. 12 is unmistakable.
[4] Dim as in the poor bronze mirrors used by the ancients.
[5] Mark iv. 11 is a good example. The word is used to translate in Greek a saying of Jesus expressed originally in Aramaic.

language of Christian philosophical and religious thought was being elaborated step by step in the first century, largely, but not exclusively, by Paul.

The word "mystery" is specially characteristic of Ephesians and Colossians, but is found sporadically through Romans, First Corinthians, and First Timothy. In Thessalonians it is once used of the evil thing, "the mystery of iniquity": the Christian religious use seems not to begin until later than the first year of Paul's residence in Corinth. We have here a development from evil towards good : the word " mystery " begins to be used in reprobation, and is adapted to the highest good. In the verb " boast " (καυχάομαι), we have a development in the opposite direction : the Christian ethics, as Harnack points out, revolted from the use of that term in a favourable sense, and substituted another word for it.[1]

If we are right in inferring from the contrasted use of the word "mystery" in 2 Thessalonians ii. 7 and 1 Corinthians ii. 1, that Paul began by using this pagan religious term as an expression of disapproval, and afterwards developed the better side of its connotation, and that this development took place after the earlier months of his stay in Corinth, we should have a confirmation of the view which we have taken[2] that in that city Paul by no means repented of, or determined to abandon for ever, the tone which he had employed at Athens. On the contrary, we find that he continued the same tone where it was suitable. A pagan religious thought seemed to him quite proper for Christian use, where it offered the best means of making a Christian idea plain to the pagan mind. In Corinth, it is true, he had no intention of knowing anything except Jesus the Messiah and His death on the cross ;[3] but this message

[1] See Section XLIX.   [2] See Section XLVI.   [3] 1 Cor. ii. 2.

required to be made intelligible to the pagans : they had to be educated morally and intellectually to the level of understanding this conception, and the best way of doing so was to take the germ of higher thought that lay in their word "mystery," and employ this as an instrument for his purpose. Hence, even in Corinth or immediately after his residence there, he was using the same method as at Athens : he was taking a thoroughly and characteristically pagan term, and developing it to a higher standard of thought.

Again, from the beginning of his Christian career he was using the characteristically pagan term " Salvation " for his purpose : the new sense for the term he found already in Christian use, and merely continued.

The truth is that either a new language had to be created to express the new truth, or the existing language had to be turned to the new purposes, and the customary pagan terms for religious ideas filled with a new content, wherever they were capable of receiving it. One word, at least, "love," ἀγάπη, was substituted for the common pagan term ἔρως. The latter was condemned as unsuitable : it had been too much corrupted by "evil communications". The new term was very rarely, if ever, used by the pagans, though some isolated example of it may yet be found, as it is etymologically a correct word.

The growth of a Christian vocabulary in the first century is an interesting and important subject ; but one that has to be treated with great judgment and care. Deissmann, Moulton and Milligan have substituted a new method for the old in the treatment of New Testament words ; but more of the creative fire and a deeper sympathy with the spirit of that age is needed than is applied in the latest work of the distinguished Berlin Professor.[1] We must, on

[1] See Preface, and also p. 4 and next Section.

the one hand, not judge under false prepossessions about
the use of words in the New Testament,—and Deissmann
has played a prominent part in doing away with antiquated prepossessions: on the other hand, we must look
more deeply through the word to the thought that it conveys,
and we must remember always that a word exists only in
relation to the idea that lies behind it. He who fills up the
content of a word, and enriches its connotation, is as much
a creative artist in language as he who introduces a new
word. Paul was in both senses a great innovator and a
master of language.

I agree with what is said by Mr. Ed. Bevan in the
Quarterly Review, July, 1910, p. 219, and by Wilamowitz,
whom he there quotes (under the mistaken idea that the
Berlin Hellenist is dead). "The preachers of the New
Life, in breaking through the traditional literary conventions, . . . were not sinking to a lower level, even from a
literary point of view, but rising to a higher." Then he
quotes Wilamowitz: "That this Greek of his has no connexion with any school or with any model, that it streams
as best it may from the heart in an impetuous torrent, and
yet is real Greek, . . . makes him a classic of Hellenism.
Now at last, one can again hear in Greek the utterance
of an inner experience, fresh and living." Then he proceeds: "it is only judging by very false and artificial
standards that Paul can appear, as Bossuet represented
him, a speaker destitute of power and charm, effective
only by a transcendent miracle. Simply as eloquence or
literature, 1 Corinthians xiii. is superior to anything in
Dio Chrysostom."

LIV. Dr. Deissmann on the Letters of Paul as Literature

According to the opinion expressed by many theologians, a chapter bearing the above title might be completed in one sentence, *viz.*, there is no literary character in the letters. This is most sharply put by Professor Deissmann of Berlin in his recent book, *St. Paul, a Study in Social and Religious History*, 1912 (translated from the German). He speaks repeatedly of "the non-literary character" of the letters: see e.g. pp. 12, 14, 78. He says that "they are not the products of literary art, but of actual life" (p. 12); and from this he draws the inference which he elaborates through many pages, that the letters have no literary quality or power, and that they are produced by an uneducated person, a horny-handed son of toil, whose handwriting was "the clumsy, awkward writing of a workman's hand deformed by" labour, and who dictated by preference because writing was so difficult for him.[1]

This opinion carries with it many inferences diametrically opposite to the views which we have always advocated; and, if it were correct, I should have to reconsider my whole attitude in judging the nature of Paul's teaching. It is therefore necessary to say something in criticism of a theory which, if our view be right, involves a wholly erroneous estimate of the position and aims, the work and nature of the great Apostle. The opinion of Dr. Deissmann

[1] *St. Paul, a Study*, p. 51 f.

is not new; it is merely a harsher statement of the view most prevalent in ordinary circles, and my opinion was formed with full knowledge of it.

In the present section I shall set before the reader for his judgment a part of one letter as a specimen of literary art. Then I shall examine Dr. Deissmann's statement that Paul in each letter addressed one single individual or church without any thought of a wider public. Finally, I shall mention some causes which may perhaps have contributed to lead the distinguished Berlin professor to an opinion which seems to me so erroneous.

One need hardly say a word about the antithesis which Professor Deissmann states between literature and actual life. He thinks that literature and life are mutually exclusive. He sees, as every one sees, that Paul's letters spring out of actual life; but his inference therefrom that they have no rank or quality as literature is worse than meaningless: it suggests an erroneous view regarding the letters, and it leads to a misconception of the Apostle's whole life and method.

There is no opposition between literature and actual life. The highest literature springs from life, and deals with real life. But Dr. Deissmann compares the details of Egyptian letters of the period with the letters of Paul, and because the arrangement as regards address and thanksgiving to God at the beginning and some other matters is the same in both classes and is evidently customary, therefore "the non-literary character of the Pauline texts" is "clearly shown". Let any one who possesses literary feeling compare the exordium in such a letter as First Corinthians or Ephesians with the stereotyped and commonplace forms in the Egyptian letters to which Dr. Deissmann compares them, and he will see what grandeur and elevation Paul could impart to

the customary forms of epistolary communication.   The differences are world-wide, just as great as between the mastery
of speech which characterises Paul's letters and the difficulty
in expression along with the superficiality of the thought,
that mark most of those papyri (so far as I have read
them).   In Paul the thought is natural and deep, in those
Egyptian letters it is natural and shallow.

If one be required to select any one passage calculated to
serve as a specimen and proof of Paul's power in pure
literature, it would probably be well to offer the first four
chapters of First Corinthians.   These four chapters form a
special section of the whole letter ; they were written (or
dictated) in all probability at one effort and are clearly
divided from the next section, which was apparently written
after an interval.   I should take this passage, not as one of
the most famous or the most exquisite pieces in his letters ;
it has not the continuous and lofty dignity and beauty of
chapter xiii., or of chapter xv. 12-49, or of Ephesians i.-iv. ;
but it is eminent in respect of the great variety of feeling
and effect which it exhibits.   Most of the devices for attaining literary effect are here brought into play, not with any
purpose of ostentation, but simply because the alternations
of feeling dictate and demand them.   The dominant emotion changes rapidly back and forward between thankfulness,
hope, protective love, disappointment, and the keenest irony,
or even sarcasm.   The tone is sometimes one of affection,
sometimes of congratulation, sometimes of sharp rebuke,
sometimes of deep thankfulness.   At one moment Paul
writes in the elevated and remote spirit of the mystic, at
others in the anxious spirit of the careful pastor.

In these chapters we should direct special attention to
the marvellous dexterity with which Paul plays on the

famous Stoic doctrine, a saying which often lies in his mind and guides his expression,[1] that the philosopher, the truly wise man, is always superior to circumstances, master of his fate, rich, contented, in short, a king. This paradox was familiar then to almost every one except the lowest and the absolutely illiterate, who rejected all care for literature;[2] and it is not Paul's knowledge of the paradox,[3] but the use which he makes of it, that demonstrates his education. He could calculate that his Corinthian audience knew it. They were not of the lowest class. Although not, as a rule, trained in the schools, they had some philosophic interest and pretensions; they were quite eager to reform others; and in their letter, to which Paul replies in First Corinthians, they had stated some ideas for reforming the world, and some thoughts about the rights and duties of men; and they had displayed a marked spirit of self-confidence and satisfaction with their knowledge of things divine and human. Paul saw that this spirit was not good, and his letter is designed to show them a better way.[4] The intention of the whole letter is disclosed fully in chapter xiii.; but the thought and spirit of that chapter are latent in his mind from the first, and occasionally reveal themselves for a moment, as for example in viii. 1-3.

He begins by expressing his thankfulness that he has a Corinthian Church, so rich in knowledge and in power of expressing its knowledge. Here there is not the faintest

---

[1] Some examples are given in Section XXVIII.

[2] It is doubtful whether any such class existed among the Greeks. Even at the present day the poorest, rudest, and most uneducated Greek has an inborn respect for education and a belief in the absorbing interest of historical study and literature.

[3] For the moment let us grant that he might, as his Corinthian readers mostly did, learn it as a popular saying.

[4] See 1 Cor. xii. 31 and Section L.

touch of irony:[1] Paul is profoundly thankful that he
has children in Corinth, and that they are interested in
higher thoughts and schemes for the good of the world and
the church, and are in the brotherhood and fellowship o
Christ.   This " is something ; nay 'tis much ".

This complimentary exordium is not merely demanded
by custom and courtesy : it springs from the writer's heart.
These children of his are, in a sense, rich and wise and
enlightened: they have the grace ($\chi\acute{\alpha}\rho\iota\varsigma$): " I thank my
God always concerning you, for the grace . . . which was
given you . . . that in everything ye were enriched in Him
in all utterance and all knowledge . . . so that ye fall short
in no gift . . . waiting for the revelation of our Lord Jesus
. . . through whom ye were called into the fellowship ".

After gently rebuking their tendency, a truly Greek tendency, to split into factions and parties (the cause of which
was largely emulation and competition in quick success),[2]
Paul begins to show the ironical turn which is working in
his mind.   Generally in his letters he contrasts false and
true knowledge as verbal and real, in word and in power ;
but here he ironically contrasts them as wisdom and foolishness.[3]   There is in his mind the idea that the beginning
of true philosophic thought is to strip off all assumed and
conventional knowledge and to penetrate to some deep
and certain first principle.   So Descartes began his *Method
of Using the Reason Aright* by getting down to the initial

---

[1] The opening words after the address are purely thankful, and devoid
absolutely of irony ; but the irony soon after begins, very faintly at first, but
gradually increasing, though the increase is in successive waves, and not
continuous.

[2] 1 Cor. i. 10-13 : this fault is alluded to subsequently from time to time,
and the rebuke is thus suggested as an inference which they shall draw from
the line of argument : see iii. 4 ff. 22 ; iv. 6.

[3] i. 18 ff.

and simple truth, which came to him not through convention or dogmatic assumption, but through direct perception :
" I think, therefore I am ". All assumed and second-hand
knowledge is to Paul mere verbal quibbling, as he calls it to
Timothy (wisdom, he ironically calls it here). The true knowledge with power is God's knowledge, and the way to reach
it is through Jesus and His Cross, as a compelling idea that
takes possession of the mind and guides the will. In
calling this simplicity "foolishness," and in contrasting it
with the pretentious " knowledge " of the Corinthians, lies
the irony of the situation.

He is gradually leading up to the point that the knowledge on which the Corinthians pride themselves is false,
assumed, and not really their own ; but to this his train of
thought has not yet conducted him. It is, after all, through
the preaching of Jesus that they had learned their knowledge, such as it is. There are among them few that possess
philosophic education, or official position and authority, or
nobility of birth ;[1] and therein lies his hope of them. God
has chosen to reveal His knowledge in them, who are the
uneducated and the humble and who lack formal training
and official dignity and high birth. The way which had
been shown them was the way of Jesus. This way was
never put before them in learned language, or by finely-
chosen rhetoric, or through authoritative announcement,
but in the simple placarding before their eyes of Christ and
His death on the cross.[2]

The plain fact was that the Corinthian Church in the
main was drawn from the artisan and industrial class, and
that its members were rarely educated in the teaching of

[1] i. 26 : it is however implied that there are some who belong to these
higher classes in society.

[2] i. 27 - ii. 4.

the schools; and Paul puts this very delicately in i. 26 - ii. 5, so as to make it a compliment to them, while he expresses it almost as a disparagement of himself.[1]　They, the uneducated, learned through one who spoke simply and humbly the Spirit and power of God.

Yet Paul would not be quite true to himself and his Gospel if he conveyed the impression that this was all that should be said.　It is his part also to preach a true wisdom among those who are advanced and perfected in training; but the wisdom that he teaches is not the wisdom (i.e. the philosophy) of this world or of the demonic powers of this world, who are in process of being done away.[2]　This wisdom is the deep truth of the plan which God has had in view from the creation for working out the glory of mankind. It is the mind of Christ that Paul interprets.　The deepest and the highest truth of the world is what he claims to deliver.[3]　In this claim for himself Paul intermingles skilful and exquisitely courteous recognition of the real advance in knowledge that the Corinthians have made,[4] toning this with the reminder of the great future that remains before them as a hope.[5]

This is no humble claim.　These are not the words of the unlettered, untrained, illiterate man.　The Greek in which the claim is expressed is so direct, so perfect, so comprehensive, and so simple, that one can only wonder how Dr. Deissmann can compare it with the stumbling, halting, dull, unselected words of those letters in Egyptian papyri, which for the most part express in rudest Greek the superficial ideas of the really illiterate peasant or workman.

---

[1] This is the spirit of the whole letter: where Paul speaks of defect he puts it in the first person usually (xiii. 1-3, 11-12), where he speaks of excellence he uses the third person (xiii. 4-8, 13).

　　ii. 6, 8.　　　[3] ii. 6 - iii. 17.　　　[4] iii. 6, 9 f.　　　[5] iii. 6, 16 ff.

In the paragraph beginning iii. 18, Paul writes in the lofty spirit of the true mystic. The wisdom of this world is foolishness with God; and you should voluntarily strip off your affectation of wisdom and philosophy, and acknowledge your "foolishness," in order to begin afresh with God and in God. Then comes the Stoic paradox set in the words of the Christian mystic: "All things are yours; whether Paul, or Apollos, or Cephas, or the world, or life, or death, or things present, or things to come; all are yours; and ye are Christ's; and Christ is God's". Dr. Deissmann can rightly appreciate that this is the exquisite greatness of religion, but he does not understand that this Greek is the exquisite and natural greatness of literature.

And now Paul's tone gradually changes to something like impatience with these children of his, who cannot see what is before their eyes, blazoned and placarded,—who are blind to the glory and the beauty and the riches that are theirs, if they will only stretch out their hands to grasp and strain their eyes to see and their minds to know—who are competing with one another as to which has learned most and chosen the better teacher, forgetful that what they have learned and what they have attained is nothing in comparison with the splendour of the knowledge that lies before them. They are proud of what they have, as if it were gained by themselves, and not received as a gift.[1]

As he thinks of this, Paul's tone changes to keen irony and even sarcasm, and he contrasts in iv. 8 ff. these men, so wise and so rich in their own esteem, with the Apostles and himself, who had projected and carried out the task of preaching the Gospel to them: "Already are ye filled to satiety; already ye are become rich; without help from us ye have become kings. And indeed I would ye were kings,

[1] iv. 6 f.

that we too might be kings along with you." You are the successful ones: you are the blessed and favoured of God; and we Apostles who know our unworthiness, would fain be helped along to heaven by you. "For, I think, God hath exhibited us the Apostles last in the race, as men doomed to death; for we are made a spectacle to the world and to angels and to men. We are fools for Christ's sake, but ye are wise in Christ; we are weak, but ye are strong; you have glory, but we have dishonour." [1] He continues in a marvellous picture of the Apostles "as the filth of the world," wandering forlorn, ill-treated, in sore need, working to earn their bread, answering curses with blessings.

Then follows a word of apology for the vehemence into which he feels himself to have been betrayed.[2] The irony had hardened almost into sarcasm, and in the sarcasm he might seem to be holding the Corinthians up to ridicule: "Yet I write not these things to shame you, but to admonish you as my beloved children". The spirit that moves in this letter is a spirit of love, of allowance for the weakness of others, of eager desire to benefit, never to chastise or punish. It is the spirit that is fully expressed in chapter xiii.

Much has been made of the fact that in writing to the Corinthians, Paul calls himself "a layman in speech," [3] contrasting their confident assumption of "wisdom," i.e. philosophical knowledge, with his own "foolishness," and the cleverness in speech on which they plume themselves with his own simplicity and want of wit. But this interpretation misses the irony that lies in the words.

What does the term "layman in speech" mean? A "layman in speech" is one who does not practise the rhe-

---

[1] Paul uses few rhetorical devices in this passage; but the chiasmus is here noteworthy.

[2] iv. 14.   [3] ἰδιώτης τῷ λόγῳ, 2 Cor. xi. 6.

torical devices of the schools, who does not seek effect by the arts and verbal tricks of rhetoric, who speaks about a plain topic in simple words such as all may understand, and does not employ artificial or learned technical terms, which are intelligible only to the few.

Now there are two reasons why a speaker chooses simple language and does not employ learned terms or elaborate devices of rhetoric. One reason is that he is himself not educated enough to use them. The other is that he rejects them, because they are unsuitable to his purpose and his subject. Without any consideration, Dr. Deissmann assumes that Paul employs simple language and an un-adorned style, because he is an uneducated man, who has never learned the tricks of the schools, and is conscious of his inferiority in this respect.

The uneducated man does not know what he has missed ; he has only a vague feeling that those other better educated speakers possess some resource or some power which is wanting to him ; but he cannot tell exactly what it is that he lacks. Now that is not the case with Paul. On the contrary, he knows well what he is doing and what it is that he refrains from using, and he states clearly that he has deliberately resolved to use a plain style suitable to a single and simple topic : " I came not with excellence in oratory or in philosophy, proclaiming to you the testimony of God ; for I determined not[1] to know anything among you, save Jesus Christ and Him crucified . . . and my talk and my preaching were not expressed in persuasive philosophic terms, but in open exhibition of the Spirit and of power, with the intention that your conversion should not be founded on human philosophy but on God's power ".[2]

---

[1] οὐ must be taken closely with τι, as in the Authorised and the Revised English and American editions. Some doubt this.

[2] 1 Cor. ii. 1, 2, 4.

Nothing can be clearer than this. Paul's style and method were deliberately chosen, and he had a good reason and purpose in his choice. The subject did not suit human verbal skill; and the result which he desired, even if attained by the devices of human education, would be unstable and liable to be overthrown by similar devices, whereas if it were attained by the simple manifestation of God's power, unaided by alluring tricks of style, it could not be affected by any skilful rhetoric hereafter. Also Paul knows quite well what it is that he refrains from using. The few contemptuous words in which he hits off the character of those rhetorical tricks show that he understood their nature. Finally Paul goes on to say that he possesses the philosophic knowledge though he has not spoken it to the Corinthians: "We speak philosophy, however, among the mature; but our philosophy is the philosophy of God, got through direct intuition and revelation of the highest divine truths; and this philosophy we set forth, not in skilful elaborate rhetoric, but in the words that the subject, i.e. the Spirit of God, prescribes".[1]

In that paragraph, from which I have quoted a few words, Paul expresses with the sure hand of a master in thought and an artist of the highest order in the use of words, his purpose, his subject, and his choice of a style, *viz.*, the style which the subject imperatively demanded. The subject expressed itself through his mouth: it clothed itself in its own words. "It was not I that spoke, but the Spirit spoke through me:" such might almost be given as the fair statement of Paul's meaning.

I have spoken only of the movement of the thought, and of that general quality which can be gathered through a translation; and have refrained from taking the Greek text

[1] 1 Cor. ii. 6, 7, 10, 13.

phrase by phrase. To do so would need too much space, but it can be done by others better than by me. Every one can appreciate the simple directness of the Greek, and the skill with which everything is expressed in the language of contemporary society. There is no need to look for rare and to coin new words to express delicate shades of meaning, as in chapter xiii. The common words are the best for this purpose. All this every one can appreciate for himself, provided that he knows Greek as a speech, an instrument for communicating thought, and not as a lexicon of words.

Paul never sought after literary style. In him the thought makes the style. He never aimed at rhythmical effect after the rules taught in the schools of rhetoric. The late Professor Blass felt that there is a rhythm in his expression; and, being familiar with the studied rhythm of the rhetoricians, he tried to show that Paul observed the rules. Deissmann was right in maintaining against Blass that Paul had no thought of rhythmic effect, but wrote as the spirit and the subject moved him, freely, simply, and naturally. When, however, he proceeds to infer that there is no rhythm in Paul's sentences and no flow in his paragraphs, he shows defective sense for the finest effects of rhythm.

In reading the letters of Paul, one is not readily struck with the excellence of the literary style. That is not because there is no style, as Dr. Deissmann maintains, but because the style suits so perfectly with the subject as to be entirely natural. The words are so unstudied and so harmonious with the thought that they are by the reader readily taken for granted as inevitable, as if the writer could not help using them. There are no others that he could use when he had such thoughts to express. Hence we forget the art in the perfection of the art, for the art has lost itself in the thought.

Where the skill of a writer obtrudes itself on the reader, where the reader finds himself called on to admire the perfection of the art, the variety of literary devices employed and the skill with which words are harmonised and selected for the effect that is desired, there the work is after all only of the second class, and not of the supreme quality. The last thing that a reader should notice is the art with which a great thing is said : the first thing he should notice is the thing itself. If the style strikes the reader forthwith as specially delicate and effective and careful, or as possessing any other marked quality, the writer may be a great stylist, but he cannot be ranked among the supreme artists in literature.

Now, inasmuch as the literary style of Paul is never obtruded, but seems to be the natural and inevitable dress for the thought to wear, therefore it has been inferred by many modern theological scholars that there is no style at all in his writings.[1] Such an error is not made by a scholar like Harnack, who in his remarkable paper on Paul's "Hymn of Heavenly Love,"[2] devotes special attention to the linguistic devices through which the marvellous dignity and harmony and literary quality are attained. Such an error is far from the trained and delicate Greek sense of Wilamowitz, who, in words which have been quoted above,[3] speaks of

[1] " St. Paul does not write literary Greek," says Dr. Deissmann, *St. Paul*, p. 53. He quotes Nägeli, whose work is useful, though his opinions and conclusions are antiquated. He concedes, however, that in spite of the clear predominance of the colloquial tone, Paul's Greek " is not really vulgar to the degree that finds expression in many of the contemporary papyri " (*ibid*. p. 53). This concession means little, for those papyri which he means are the letters of uneducated persons and children.

[2] The paper was published in the *Expositor*, May and June, 1912, in an authorised translation from the original German of the *Sitzungsberichte* of the Berlin Academy.

[3] See p. 411.

the relief which it gives, after the wearisome artificialities of the Hellenistic period, to come once more on the true and natural Greek expression of Paul, a great master of Hellenism.

Again, Professor Deissmann draws a quite arbitrary distinction between "literary art" and "actual life," as if life were set over against and irreconcilable with literature.[1] He is betrayed into this by his perception, correct in itself, that Paul was careless of the formal rules prescribed for the artificial Greek literature of the later Hellenistic and the Roman age; and he presses this truth to the fatally false conclusion that what was written in contempt of such artificiality was not and could not be literature. He reasons with terms to which he gives artificial meanings. Literature to him means something quite different from what it means to us in the English-speaking world; and I doubt whether the German-speaking world would accept such cast-iron distinctions. Thus, for example, he puts the dilemma that the letter to Philemon must be either a letter or "a tractate on the attitude of Christianity towards slavery".[2] If it were a tractate, he seems to imply it would be literature; but, inasmuch as it is a true and beautiful and natural letter, " a delightful document," therefore it cannot be literature. "The doctrinaire and literary theory," as he says, "fails completely in this case."

I do not with certainty know what "the doctrinaire

[1] *St. Paul: a Study*, p. 12.

[2] The English of the translation is often bad: words are used in a sense which they do not possess in our language: I have substituted "attitude" for "position" in the text. It is unpleasant to criticise a book without having the German before me. In some cases I doubt whether the English fairly represents the German; but as the translation is authorised and revised by Dr. Deissmann, and as I write at a distance of 4000 miles from Germany, I must take the translation as it stands.

theory" is; but I doubt if even the dullest and stupidest of commentators ever described this letter simply and solely as "a tractate on the attitude of Christianity towards slavery". Some commentator might use those words to bring out one point of view from which we may contemplate the letter. It is, in fact, possible, as we shall show, to find in the letter a statement of universal principles that ought to guide the judgment and action of the contemporary Church in the difficult problem of slavery; but that is only one single aspect of a many-sided composition.

First and foremost, this composition is a letter, written from heart to heart, from Paul to Philemon, on a particular occasion, for the special situation at that moment. Dr. Deissmann sees this correctly and clearly, and he sees nothing else than this. The letter is and remains for him a letter. Like the primrose to Peter Bell, the letter was a letter, "and it was nothing more". But this letter is far more than a letter; and the above-quoted commentator, who could find in it something further that made him call it, in rather ill-chosen phrase, "a tractate," saw something that is really there. That "delightful document" is written on the basis of, and penetrated with, the consciousness of certain wide principles, fully and carefully thought out, regarding slavery and the attitude which the Church should take towards slavery. It does not state those principles as such, but it decides the special case on general conceptions, and in so doing it reveals what those principles are.

Further, I am not concerned to controvert Dr. Deissmann's *dictum:* "St. Paul cannot have intended that these confidential letters should be still extant after centuries, nor did it ever occur to him that they would be".[1] No one who thinks rationally would fancy that Paul wrote in-

---

[1] *St. Paul: a Study,* p. 12.

tending his letters to be in use after the lapse of centuries. He thought of the present and in the present. But when Dr. Deissmann proceeds to treat this dictum as implying that Paul's letters were sent for the use of one single congregation in a single copy on a special occasion without any thought of Christendom as a whole, he is taking a narrow and, as I venture to think, hasty view. Those early Christian letters were true letters, written for a special occasion; but they stated profound and world-wide principles with full deliberation, in a way that applied to the whole contemporary Church.

We know from Paul himself that he intended his Colossian letter to be read aloud in the congregation of the Laodiceans.[1] He was conscious that he was stating principles for the whole Church of God. He wrote, as he spoke, with authority, i.e. universal authority. He is in the position of an Emperor issuing a rescript (if I may compare that smaller fact with the great religious document): the Emperor replied in his rescript to a question of detail on which an official or a city had consulted him, but his reply stated or implied general principles, and became an embodiment of law and procedure to guide and regulate future progress.[2]

Further, I do not hesitate to affirm that Paul was not writing only for a single correspondent like Titus, Philemon, or Timothy, or for a single Church like Corinth or Thessalonica. Dr. Deissmann, when he contends that the Apostle wrote solely with an eye to the single correspondent, is wholly mistaking the spirit of Paul, who was fully

---

[1] Col. iv. 16: the Laodicean letter was intended likewise for Colossae (and for the Christian world).

[2] Something of this is demonstrated in my *Letters to the Seven Churches*, in an opening chapter, where this subject is touched.

conscious of the true nature of his letters, and thought of a wider public than a single Church or a single man. He had in mind all who were in like difficulties. He thought of Christendom as a whole, or at least of all his Churches, and not of one. He was writing to the individual, and yet he was writing universal principles for the whole world.

Take the first Corinthian letter.[1] It is sent (i. 2) to "the Church of God, which is at Corinth . . . with all that call upon the name of our Lord Jesus Christ in every place". When it ends with a double benediction, xvi. 23 and 24, I should be inclined to understand that 23 may be for the Corinthians primarily and especially: "The grace of the Lord Jesus Christ be with you"; but 24 is addressed to the wider audience of i. 2, the whole of Christendom: "My love be with you all in Christ Jesus. Amen."

Exactly the same remark applies to Second Timothy. In iv. 22 the first part is for Timothy: "The Lord be with thy spirit"; the second part is for the whole of Christendom (or for a smaller audience associated with Timothy, as some scholars would maintain): "Grace be with you" (plural).

The same applies to Titus. In iii. 15 the first part is for Titus: "All that are with me salute thee"; the second part is for the world of Christ: "Grace be with you all".[2]

---

[1] In what follows I follow the text of Westcott and Hort simply, and pay no attention to diversities of reading among the manuscripts. The reader can readily add the diversities of MS. authority, which are not important, except in one case.

[2] Like many others, Professor Vernon Bartlet in the *Expositor*, February, 1913, p. 162, quotes the last words in First Timothy and Titus as proof that each of them was an "open letter; fit for quotation so far as might seem needful in order to silence challenge of Timothy's authority and win over local public opinion". He contrasts this with "the more intimate and personal second epistle to Timothy," where he rejects the ending (which Westcott and Hort accept). As is shown below, all Paul's letters, however

First Timothy is, of course, intended primarily for one individual, and the charge which forms the main message of the letter is expressed in the singular, "thee" and "thou"; but the plural is used in the final salutation, vi. 22, "Grace be with you".

A similar width of intention animates Philemon, the very letter which Dr. Deissmann selects as most specially and markedly a letter from one man to another.

In this he is altogether right. It is a private letter on a private matter. Yet, when this is said, the case is not exhausted. There is more to say, for there is more than this in the letter.

In the first place, the writer has in view a wider audience than Philemon in his private house. The last sentence but one conveys greetings from Paul's companions to Philemon individually: they "greet thee". The last sentence, however, is expressed in the plural: "the grace of the Lord Jesus Christ be with your spirit": the benediction is to many readers, not to one.

There are therefore but two alternatives. Either the letter is intended to be read also by the Colossian Christians generally, or the thought of all Christians, "all who call upon the name of our Lord," lies in Paul's mind (just as he utters that thought in 1 Corinthians i. 2). In either case the exclusively private character of the letter is done away. It concerns Philemon primarily, but others in the second place. So it is with First Corinthians. That letter is as thoroughly personal to one individual Church as Philemon is to one individual person; but in the former by express address and in the latter (as I think) by implication, the whole body of Christians in the world is included.

personal, were also in a sense almost as much "open letters" as First Timothy and Titus.

In the second place, it is not permissible to cut away the last sentence as a gloss attached in later ages to the letter. Such a farewell sentence is customary and could not be omitted. Moreover, the plural is used in the body of the letter in an instructive way. The letter is formally addressed to Philemon and Apphia (probably his wife) and Archippus (some relative or friend) and to the Church which assembles in Philemon's house. All these are included in the opening address, as in the conclusion all are meant. Moreover, although the business which occasions the letter is certainly a quite private and personal matter; and the main body of the letter is expressed in the singular, "thou" and "thee"; and although the Epistle was certainly intended first of all to be meditated over by Philemon privately, and to move his individual conscience: "Having confidence in thine obedience I write unto thee, knowing that thou wilt do even beyond what I say: but withal do thou prepare me also a lodging: for I hope that through your prayers [plural] I shall be granted unto you" [plural]; yet Paul was not writing for Philemon alone. It was not even the prayers of the Colossian Church alone that he knew to be working for him and with him. He was here thinking of the prayers of the whole body of Christians: the same was the case when Peter was in prison: [1] all who knew were praying for his release.

This observation gives the clue to the right and full comprehension of 2 Corinthians i. 11: "Ye also helping together on our behalf by your supplication". This letter is formally addressed, not merely to the Church in Corinth, but to "all the saints that are in the whole of (the province) Achaia". In i. 11, however, I feel no doubt that Paul for

---

[1] Acts xii. 5.

the moment was thinking not of Achaia simply, but of the whole Christian world.

It would be easy to pick out passages throughout the letters where Paul for a short time forgets the person or the Church to which his letter is addressed, and feels himself writing for the whole of Christendom ; but this would seem speculative and fanciful to those who have no insight into the nature of Paul, and I confine myself to the cases where the reference is plainly marked as wider than the nominal addressee.

In Philippians the instruction in iv. 21, " Salute every saint in Christ Jesus," is not restricted to Philippi : Paul has before him in a secondary view the entire Christian world. There are in this letter three concentric circles over which his view extends. The narrowest contains one man alone, Paul's " true yoke-fellow " (iv. 3). A wider circle embraces the whole Philippian Church, and the address is sometimes expressly restricted to them, as in the initial words and in iv. 15. The widest circle extends to include " every saint in Christ Jesus ". Chapter iii. in general is addressed to the widest circle. There were hardly any Jews in Philippi : there was no synagogue there ; hence it was unnecessary to warn the Philippians alone against the Jews. That warning is for all the saints, and is suggested by extra-Philippian events more than by anything that was happening in Philippi.[1] In iii. 1 the words, " Rejoice in the Lord," are universal. Professor Deissmann, surely, cannot doubt the wide reference in this instance.

In Ephesians vi. 24 the reference is explicitly universal : " Grace be with all them that love our Lord Jesus Christ "

---

[1] The argument (and a right argument) is that a letter is suggested by the special circumstances of the Church addressed ; but this chapter is suggested by events outside of Philippi.

The man who wrote like this was not restricting his counsel to the Ephesians, nor to the Asian cities: he knew and meant it to be universal. In passing, we note that there need be no difficulty regarding the address of this letter. It is to Ephesus and it is to all Asia, just as is the case with Second Corinthians.[1] There is no necessity to call Ephesians a "circular letter," any more than Second Corinthians. Both letters include the whole province: in Asia, Ephesus was the commercial capital, and Pergamum the religious capital, and both cities (like Smyrna) claimed (and had legal justification in claiming) the title "First (city) of Asia": in Achaia, Corinth was the administrative and commercial capital, while Athens was the educational capital of the whole civilised world. There is less reference to occasional matters in Ephesians than in Second Corinthians, but there is some such reference even in Ephesians, as was shown formerly by Professor Rendel Harris;[2] and the presence or absence of such individual concern is not really so important as it might seem. Both epistles are letters at once to a capital city and to a whole province, even though the name of the province is formally mentioned only in one of the two.[3] In Byzantine lists of equivalent names Ephesus is mentioned as equivalent to (the province) Asia.

The Epistle to the Romans was not suggested by any circumstances that had arisen in Rome and were known to the writer, for he had never been there and had not been brought into direct relation with the Roman Church. It consists mainly (apart from the initial address and the concluding chapters, xv. 14 to the end) in a statement of

---

[1] 2 Cor. i. 1.

[2] He published an ingenious and penetrating article on this subject in the *Expositor* about ten years ago.

[3] We need not repeat the familiar facts about the reading ἐν Ἐφέσῳ in the address. The bearing is obvious.

universal principles, applicable not to any particular situation
and occasion whether at Rome or elsewhere, but expressed
in the widest terms as general truths of religious thought
and of practical administration.[1] This has been generally
recognised; and I take the latest theory as expressed by
the Rev. J. Ironside Still. It is to the effect that,[2] when
we deduct i. 1-17 and xv. 14 - xvi. 27, there is left "a document which, without the alteration of a single word, could
be sent to any or all of the churches of the Gentiles" (with
Jews in small numbers mingled in each congregation).
This "treatise (for it is a treatise)" is intended to "set
forth the way of salvation by faith in Jesus Christ, from
the points of view of both the Jew and the Gentile,
showing the historical, doctrinal, and practical bearings of
this teaching," together with certain "general rules for the
settlements of such questions of conduct as had already
arisen, e.g., obedience to civil government, eating certain
meats, and fellowship between Jew and Gentile in the
Church".

I do not commit myself to Mr. Still's view; but the
mere fact that a scholar can suggest it, and that it must
be regarded as deserving very careful consideration and
study, shows how narrow and inadequate Dr. Deissmann's
statement about Romans is.[3]

He says: "That also is a real letter, not an 'Epistle';
there are parts in it, certainly, that might find a place in an
'Epistle,' and it might here and there be called an epistolary
letter; but all the same it is a letter . . . he addresses him-

---

[1] The rules of practical administration are all put at the end together,
xiii. 1-xv. 13.

[2] *The Early Gentile Christian Church*, 1913, p. 113.

[3] It is almost identical with his earlier statement in his *Bibelstudien*,
1895, p. 241.

self to a handful of people resident in the more modest quarters of Rome, of whose existence the public knew practically nothing ".

We ask what sentence or phrase or word marks the correspondents as persons specially unknown or as " resident in the more modest quarters of Rome "? Rome is specified in i. 6 ; but I see nothing that points to "the more modest quarters" of the city, or to the rank of the readers. In xiii. 1, " Let every soul be in subjection to the higher powers," does not imply humble rank : "all men must obey the magistrates and the law " is a free paraphrase of the thought. Statius gives a different expression of the same truth in a fine passage of the *Silvae*, where he says that obedience is a rule of universal application, that each must serve the power above him, that even the Emperor is a servant, and that sun and stars obey a higher law.[1] There is here no suggestion of humble station in those addressed, but only the statement of universal principle in the conduct of the whole Church: " Render unto Cæsar what is Cæsar's."

Dr. Deissmann's touch about the " handful of people in the more modest quarters " is a purely theoretic and subjective and wholly unauthorised addition, justified by nothing in the letter, and founded only on his own views (which, of course, are largely right) : he inserts this touch almost unconsciously, because he is trying to impart to the letter an individual character, which it does not in itself possess.

He maintains that Paul sent this letter " only to Rome," and did not " send copies to the gatherings of Christians at Ephesus, Antioch and Jerusalem ". In this contention he

---

[1] The germ of Statius' words is found, concisely but far less finely expressed, in Horace : *Regum timendorum in proprios greges : reges in ipsos imperium est Iovis.*

pointedly contradicts a view expressed by others, and most fully worked out by Rev. J. Ironside Still in the little book quoted above. In the form which the latter has given it, the body of the letter was general. A copy sent to Rome had the address i. 6 prefixed, and the conclusion xv. 14-33 appended: these are personal to the Roman congregation. Another copy with appropriate address and with the conclusion xvi. 1-20 was sent to Ephesus or to the whole province of Asia.[1] A third copy was sent to Macedonia with the conclusion xvi. 21-24. As to xvi. 25-27, Mr. Still considers that this " Doxology, an unusual ending for a letter of Paul's," may be the conclusion of the treatise proper, i. 18 - xv. 13, placed after the special conclusions to individual copies of the letter.

Dr. Deissmann carries his advocacy so far as to maintain that "the decreased prominence of personal detail is no evidence that the letter to the Romans is epistolary and literary in character; it is the natural consequence of the letter-like and non-literary situation underlying it". Everything is pressed by Dr. Deissmann into subservience to his purpose. First Thessalonians is " thoroughly letter-like," because it " is full of personal reminiscences " ; Romans is equally letter-like, because it contains hardly any " personal detail ".

He began with an observation which is entirely correct and instructive, *viz.*, that true letters differ in quality and character from literary Epistles, which are written with an eye to the public; but this observation he carries out with a relentless and one-sided thoroughness that can see nothing except these two classes. There is much in the world of letters besides these two classes. Only for a moment is he

---

[1] Mr. Still is disposed to conjecture that xvi. 17-20 may belong, not to the Ephesian copy, but to a Corinthian copy.

disturbed, when he speaks of Romans as in parts " an epistolary letter " ; but even here, in place of recognising a third
category, he sees only a chance blend of the initial two,
and he does not clearly explain what " an epistolary letter "
is.   In " an epistolary letter " had Paul in his mind any
thought of a public? If not, why is the letter " epistolary " ?
If he had such thought, it cannot be right to assert so positively that the letter was written only to a single small and
humble Roman audience, and was not intended to be known
to Ephesian or other readers.

If we are to judge from the positive indications which
Paul gives of his outlook towards a larger audience than the
single Church or individual whom he addresses, we must
allow that he was usually conscious that his letters applied
to the whole of Christendom.   I would make an exception
in the case of the letter to the Galatians, which seems to
have poured forth from his mind in one effort, like a flood
of lava from a volcano.   That however was his first letter,
and it was partly from it that he learned how powerful an
instrument the letter was, and what important effect it might
exercise in the consolidation of the Church as a whole.

It is in this last respect that the great fault of Dr. Deissmann's theory lies.   It hides from him the perception of
Paul's constructive power, which he minimises in an un-
illuminative fashion.[1]   He concedes that Paul made " the
modest beginnings of an external organisation " ; but maintains that he " cannot be called the father of the constitutional church ".   His reason seems to be only that these
" modest beginnings were fairly obviously suggested by the
needs themselves, but could also be adopted from the various
models of associations that existed in antiquity, especially

[1] *St. Paul*, p. 186 ff.

from the religious unions of the pagan world and the synagogues among the Jews of the Dispersion ".

He does not, however, see how much is implied in the fact that these "modest beginnings" are *beginnings*. From the first Paul saw that something was required, and he furnished it. The fact that these " modest beginnings were suggested by the needs " does not prove (as Dr. Deissmann infers) that they were not the first steps in organisation : it is because they were imperatively demanded by the needs of the case that they became the germ of a great constitutional system. As Dr. Deissmann truly says, they could be adopted from existing models. Paul took what was vital and germinative in the existing associations and unions ; but it was this adaptation to the time which made his institutions fit to grow. It was, as Deissmann rightly says, "the personality behind them all," that quickened them into a living organism ; but they did not die with the maker ; they developed into a vast system, which became a power in the world (not always a power for good, as every one must grant, but still a great power, and generally a beneficent power).[1]

Dr. Deissmann maintains that Paul had no " conception of the church," a phrase that he quotes from some authority : "his churches were all assemblies summoned by God ". He gives no reason for holding, but simply assumes, that the "church" in Paul's letters is not the germ " of the constitutional church ". I do not know if any scholar has ever gone quite so far as this in ignoring the constructive ability and purpose of Paul.

As to the term "church" (or " assembly " as Deissmann restricts it), Paul began in his first letters by speaking of

---

[1] We may acknowledge and regret the faults of the constitutional Church in all its branches, and yet recognise its essentially good quality and its apostolic origin.

" the churches of Galatia," and "the church of the Thessalonians," where "assembly" would probably quite fairly cover
the thought.   In Philippians, Colossians and Ephesians, the
term is avoided in the address, which speaks of "the saints
that are at Philippi," etc.   In Romans the phrase is "all
that are at Rome".   The word might be, perhaps, quite
adequately expressed by "assembly" or "congregation" in
such passages as Romans xvi. 5, Colossians iv. 15, Philemon
2, I Timothy v. 16, and many others.   The unity of the
universal Church, however, was a thought that Paul already
had in his mind; and this unity was necessarily an organisation consisting of many members with diverse functions,
co-ordinated into a single body, which he describes with
remarkable emphasis in Colossians ii. 19 and Ephesians iv.
11-16, ii. 20.   This unified and universal and single Church,
the body, of which Christ forms the head, is clearly meant in
Ephesians i. 22, iii. 10, v. 23, 24, 25, 27, 29, 32, Colossians
i. 18, 24, Romans xvi. 23, etc.; and the other passages
quoted above from those letters and Philemon would be
better interpreted as implying the "portion of the universal
church, which is at Colossae," etc.

 This unity of the whole Church was certainly in Paul's mind
in I Corinthians x. 17; and I should interpret generally the
word "church" in the two Corinthian letters conformably
to this conception,[1] although it is quite feasible, and in some
cases preferable, to take it in the sense of "assembly," as
Dr. Deissmann takes it.

 It is clear from this brief enumeration that in his letters
Paul moved towards, and reached, the full conception of the
unified and organised Church of God in the whole world.
I do not see how this conception can be distinguished from

---

[1] This sense is compulsory in I Cor. xii. 28.

a "constitutional church," though I do not profess to determine whether or not Paul's conception "would satisfy a lawyer," as Dr. Deissmann requires. There are, however, many "constitutions" that, as people say, would not satisfy that condition; and perhaps it is not the highest quality of a constitutional Church that it should fulfil the rigid requirements of the pure lawyer.

What is clear is that from the beginning of his missionary work as described in Acts xiii., and in his early Thessalonian letter,[1] Paul had the idea before his mind that the foundation of a church was not completed by the conversion of a certain number of individuals, who might come together in an "assembly". Zahn rightly distinguishes between the mere conversion of many individuals and the formation of a church. A simple missionary progress through a country was not enough. When Paul was suddenly expelled from Pisidian Antioch, Iconium, and Lystra, he had to return and complete his work by appointing presbyters, whose function, as we know from the Pastoral Epistles and from other sources, included both teaching and business management in the congregation. Each congregation needed persons to discharge various functions; the fundamental requirement always was the *charisma*, the revelation through the grace of God of His will and counsel. All had not the *charisma*, but every example of it should be encouraged and should also be tested whether it was true. All had not the same power in teaching, but all ought to bear this purpose in mind. All were not equally good in managing the common business and duties. To each his proper function; and the co-ordination of all in a unified life made the constitutional church in a city; and the co-ordination of all the

---

[1] The Galatian letter is inconclusive; and from its character it furnishes no evidence.

scattered churches was the universal and single Church, the body whose head was Christ.[1]

There was no such deep chasm dividing a charismatic from a constitutional Church, as Dr. Deissmann thinks..[2] In the earliest church there was *charisma* and there was also teaching, and there were regular instructors and managers of business. The collection and storing of the weekly contributions for Jerusalem, which continued for months, and probably for years,[3] was a financial affair of some magnitude. Enterprises like that are business; and some business ability is needed to plan and to manage them. The early Pauline Church was charismatic, and it was also constitutional.

One of the great difficulties in the unification of the Church was to overcome the obstacle of distance. The only way to solve this problem, as has been emphasised in all my earlier books, lay in frequent inter-communication by visit and by letter. Paul and the whole Church fully recognised this from a very early time. The letter became the true and the most characteristic expression of the Church unity. Paul's letters were felt by him to be individual, and yet universal. This is the great and vital truth which Dr. Deissmann has cast away.

His error seems to be due to a tendency towards hasty geographical generalisations. True, he rather prides himself on being no "layman in geography". Travel in the Pauline cities is the "new teacher," to whom he owes so much. He has, "with some small exceptions, visited

[1] See an article, " What were the Churches of Galatia ? " in the *Expository Times*, 1912-13, § 1.

[2] *St. Paul : a Study*, p. 186, where he dates " this *charismatic* age before the days of the church ".

[3] This was, as I doubt not, planned from the inception of the third journey, and was ordered in Galatia (Acts xviii. 23).

all the places of importance in the primitive history of Christianity," and expresses in his Preface a gentle compassion for those who have not had this advantage.

He does not enable us to judge what are the exceptions to his knowledge. He speaks in general of seeing Galatia and Lycaonia. Doubtless this implies more than Iconium and Ancyra, and the line of the railways. He cannot have omitted Lystra, which is only eighteen miles from a station, and Pisidian Antioch, which is about twenty by horse-road, and Derbe; or Pessinus, and the other churches of North Galatia (as he holds), and Philippi, which are all within easy reach of railway stations. When he states (p. 36) the height of Pisidian Antioch as 3936 ft., I should be glad to learn what is his authority, and what the figure means. This is a point which deeply interests me, and on which I should be glad to learn from a great geographical authority. Is the elevation taken at the modern town, or the ancient? Is it taken at the lowest or the highest point of the ancient city, if it refers to that? These are questions involving a difference of more than 250 ft. Is the height estimated from his own observation, or taken from some authority? If it is based on some published authority, it probably refers to the modern town. If it depends on his own observation, what instrument did he use? I have only employed an aneroid, and know how far from exact are the results which it gives. All these questions arise, when one tries (as I have tried) to learn from this book. He says that he was at Antioch (p. xi), without specifying whether he means the Syrian or the Pisidian; and naturally one understands that the greater city, the Syrian, is intended. Moreover, as he tells us elsewhere, he visited Syrian Antioch. Are we then to suppose that, when he was making these extensive journeys in Asia Minor, he omitted the places which are not railway stations? Must we conclude that the heights which he states are all borrowed estimates, and that such geographical facts he learned only from books? One can learn them without a journey along the railway.

Is Lystra so much as 4034 ft. above the sea?[1] I should have thought this an over-estimate. The height of Iconium is taken by Kiepert from the railway survey, and is printed on the wall of the station according to the admirable German custom (which I would that other railways imitated).

Dr. Deissmann lays great stress on such points: "these facts," he says, "are at least as interesting to me as the question about the addressees of 'Galatians'" (p. 36); but, if he wishes to make his statements into facts available for reasoning, he must give more information regarding the authority on which they rest.

His experience of the great countries of Bithynia, Phrygia, Galatia and Lycaonia was quickly gained in 1909 : he tells us that he was in a snowstorm on a Phrygian pass in March of that year, and two days later saw peach trees blooming in an orchard. Elsewhere we find some clue to the dates and the facts. He was at Ancyra on 3, and at Konia on 6 March of that year: on 13 March he travelled from Ephesus to Laodicea (both railway stations),[2] and on 15 March back to Ephesus ; and 16-19 March he spent on a steamer, where he learned a great deal "about the modern (and ancient) popular life of the East," observing Russian and other pilgrims on the way to Palestine *via* Mersina (where he stopped to study Cilicia).[3]

---

[1] *St. Paul: a Study*, p. 36.

[2] He did not visit Colossae, twelve miles from the station at Laodicea, and only two from the line of the railway.

[3] Dr. Deissmann gives statistics of days and visits in a sporadic way, just so much as to make a zealous disciple like myself wish for much more.

Formerly I imagined that Dr. Deissmann had travelled by road from Iconium or Cybistra to Tarsus, and that the reference on p. 36 to "a violent snowstorm at the top of a Phrygian pass," pointed to the pass leading from Pisidian Antioch to Ak Sheher, and that the peach gardens which he passed next day at noon might be near Ak Sheher.

The dates, however, imply that, instead of making the land journey through Lycaonia to Tarsus, Dr. Deissmann took the train from Iconium to Smyrna, and then after visiting Ephesus and Laodicea, sailed to Mersina in a Russian Levant liner to study Cilicia. The point interests me. From 1909 I have been quoting his journey as a proof that traffic passes through the Cilician Gates in the middle of March. That still seems the natural inference from his words on p. 31 : "if you come from the interior of Asia Minor and from the west coast and enter the Cilician plain in March". One does not at first comprehend that this is an imaginative way of describing a voyage in a Russian steamer from Smyrna to Mersina.

Taking the dates, which he gives on pp. 29, 18 f., 36, one can reconstruct his journey in outline : it was spent largely in trains and steamer. I conjecture that he left Constantinople [1] on—

1 March :	train to Dorylaion.	
2 ,,	train to Angora (half day).	
3 ,,	exploring Ancyra and Galatia.	
4 ,,	train to Dorylaion (half day).	
5 ,,	train to Konia (15 hours 20 mins.).	
6 ,,	exploring Konia.	
7, 8 ,,	exploring Phrygia and Lycaonia.	
9 ,,	train to Kara-Hissar (9 hours).	
10 ,,	train to Ushak (half day).	
11 ,,	train to Smyrna.	
12 ,,	train to Ephesus : exploring Ephesus.	

[1] Perhaps he started 2 March, leaving two half days for Ancyra and Galatia.

13 March : train to Laodicea.
14   ,,   exploring Laodicea, Hierapolis, Lycus valley.
15   ,,   train to Ephesus (and Smyrna).
16   ,,   embark for Cilicia.
17, 18 ,,   on board Russian steamer.
19   ,,   land at Mersina.
20, 21 ,,   train to Tarsus and back each day.
22, 23 ,,   at Pompeiopolis and Cilicia generally.
24   ,,   voyage to Alexandretta.
25   ,,   to Antioch of Syria.

The train journeys are not short ; most of them take the whole day : shorter journeys of six hours are marked as half days. One journey is uncertain : of old the train took two days from Konia to Ushak : now it does the whole distance in one long day. I am not certain whether the new system had begun in March, 1909 : if it had, this would leave a third day for exploration of Lycaonia and Phrygia. At the best we have in twenty-six days only ten free from trains and steamers. The most hurried American tourist, doing the country with his Baedeker, is leisurely when compared with Dr. Deissmann studying the Eastern world.

If one wishes to know why Dr. Deissmann misunderstands "the World of St. Paul," one has only to read his opening note to the chapter to which he gave that title, p. 29 : "On the pilgrims' ships . . . you learn ten times more about the modern (and ancient) popular life of the East than you do on the big Levant steamers". In these surroundings for two days Dr. Deissmann studied the "life of the East"; and the result inevitably is inability to comprehend Paul, and perfect satisfaction with false knowledge.

The idea that one can study the popular life of the East in the sordid and degrading surroundings of a crowded Russian steamer deck shows an erroneous point of view. I have travelled in a Turkish steamer crowded with pilgrims for Mecca, and know that the wise man would not go there to learn about "the popular life of the East". You see in such a steamer quaint and strange incidents; but you do not see the natural East; you see the East struggling to adopt itself to unfamiliar Western circumstances; it is the East mean and denaturalised.

Equally extraordinary is it that Dr. Deissmann should fancy he was studying the life of Asia, when he watched the "Russian and Siberian peasants" on a Russian steamer. He saw much that was strange to him; but was it the ancient popular life of the East that he beheld? Why, too, should Turks and Arabs travel in a Russian "pilgrims' ship"? Probably it was not specially a pilgrim-steamer after all, but one of the ordinary Russian Levant service, less frequented by tourists because Russian ships are dreaded as dirty and uncomfortable: in March the Easter pilgrims were travelling.

He says that "the zone of the olive-tree, if we leave out Tunis, Algiers, and Morocco, coincides almost exactly with the map of St. Paul's missionary work" (p. 41). We must leave out a great deal more: we must leave out Spain,[1] France, the southern Alpine slopes, all the islands of the western Mediterranean, and many other districts where Paul never penetrated. On the other hand, we must remember that there were no olives in Lycaonia and in North Galatia (where Dr. Deissmann places Pauline churches). What is the use or value of a generalisation which requires so much restriction on one side, and so much widening on another? It would be as true to say that Paul's mission work does not coincide with the olive zone, because it embraces much where olives are unknown and leaves out many large Mediterranean countries where olives are cultivated.

---

[1] Perhaps Dr. Deissmann holds that Paul was not condemned on the so-called "first trial" in Rome, in which I should gladly find him as an associate, and that the journey to Spain was actually performed, which is doubtful.

The truth is that early Christianity coincided largely with a certain phase of Mediterranean civilisation ; and the relation to the olive-tree is accidental.

It is no wonder that an ardent and devoted scholar like Dr. Deissmann grows enthusiastic about the olive-tree, "the tree of civilisation" (as I have called it in one of my studies on the subject). But in scientific statement greater exactitude is needed.[1] He is too apt to take book results for certainties. Fischer's map of the olive zone he assumes to be complete, forgetting that Strabo speaks of the olive-planted plain of Synnada, high among the Phrygian mountains.[2] If Strabo is right, Fischer's restrictions are far too narrow.

Dr. Deissmann quotes from Philippson a contrast between the "scarcity of rain" on the plateau of Asia Minor and the "ample winter rainfall" of the west coast. So far as my experience goes, there is a very large fall of moisture, both rain and snow, on those parts of the plateau which I know best. Pisidian Antioch and Afiom-Kara-Hissar enjoy an abundant rainfall. What is wanted on the plateau for agriculture is not so much a greater rainfall, as means of storing the moisture.

When he finds no difficulty in supposing that Paul visited Angora, is he reasoning on the same principle as on p. 18, where he estimates the time of a runaway from Colossae to Ephesus by his own railway journey between Laodicea and Ephesus? He could leave Ancyra one day, sleep in the German inn at Dorylaion, and reach Iconium the next day. Nothing can be easier, when the train runs.

---

[1] *Pauline and Other Studies*, p. 219 ff.

[2] I formerly proposed to read ἀμπελόφυτον for ἐλαιόφυτον (*Journal of Hellenic Studies*, 1887, on Synnada): recently I have been disposed to withdraw this conjecture. If it is right, all the earliest Pauline churches are outside the olive country.

From these hasty and unstudied geographical generalisations springs much of the error into which, as I believe, Dr. Deissmann has fallen. But I am glad to agree with him that geography is so important in Pauline study; and I congratulate him on his good fortune as a tourist in seeing the storks arrive—a wonderful sight—on the Cilician plain, though perhaps this does not give so much power to comprehend Paul as he thinks (see his remarks on pp. xi and 32 f.).

INDEX

I

449

INDEX

II